State and Civil Society in Northern Europe

EUROPEAN CIVIL SOCIETY
Editors: **Dieter Gosewinkel** and **Jürgen Kocka**

Civil society represents one of the most ambitious projects and influential concepts relating to the study of modern societies. It encapsulates their structures and their gradual restructuring as well as their changing polities and cultures. Scholars working in this field aim to secure greater equality of opportunity, democratic participation, individual freedom, and societal self-organization against both the overbearing and overburdening powers of the modern state as well as the social deficits of globalizing neo-liberalism. This series deals with the multiple languages, different layers, and diverse practices of existing and emerging civil societies in Europe. Its leitmotif is to analyse whether and how far the renewed interest in the concept can contribute to the gradual evolution of a larger European civil society.

Volume 1
The Languages of Civil Society
Peter Wagner

Volume 2
Civil Society: Berlin Perspectives
John Keane

Volume 3
State and Civil Society in Northern Europe:
The Swedish Model Reconsidered
Edited by Lars Trägårdh

STATE AND CIVIL SOCIETY IN NORTHERN EUROPE

THE SWEDISH MODEL RECONSIDERED

Edited by
Lars Trägårdh

Berghahn Books
New York • Oxford

First published in 2007 by

Berghahn Books

www.berghahnbooks.com

© 2007 Lars Trägårdh

Library of Congress Cataloging-in-Publication Data

State and civil society in Northern Europe : the Swedish model reconsidered /
edited by Lars Trägårdh.
    p. cm. — (European civil society ; 3)
    Includes bibliographical references and index.
    ISBN-10: 1-84545-187-2 (hbk.) -- ISBN-13: 978-1-84545-187-5 (hbk.)
    ISBN-10: 1-84545-232-1 (pbk.) -- ISBN-13: 978-1-84545-232-2 (pbk.)
    1. Civil society—Sweden. 2. Democracy—Sweden. 3. Social capital (So-
ciology)—Sweden. I. Trägårdh, Lars. II. Series: European civil society ; v. 3.

JN7945.S72 2006
300.948--dc22
                                                                    2006044452

British Library Cataloguing in Publication Data

A catalogue record for this book is available from
the British Library.

Printed in the United States on acid-free paper

ISBN-10: 1-84545-187-2   ISBN-13: 978-1-84545-187-5   hardback
ISBN-10: 1-84545-232-1   ISBN-13: 978-1-84545-232-2   paperback

CONTENTS

LIST OF TABLES AND FIGURES

Tables

Figures

CONTRIBUTORS

Erik Amnå is Associate Professor and Senior Lecturer at Örebro University, Sweden.

Douglas Baer is Professor and former Chair of the Department of Sociology at the University of Victoria in Victoria, British Columbia, Canada.

Jean Cohen is Professor of Political Science, Columbia University.

Eva Jeppsson Grassman is Professor at the National Institute for the Study of Ageing and Later Life (NISAL) at the University of Linköping in Sweden.

Bo Rothstein is the August Röhss Professor of Political Science at the University of Göteborg, Sweden.

Per Selle is Professor of Comparative Politics at the University of Bergen, Norway. He also serves as a Senior Researcher at the Rokkan Centre for Social Studies in Bergen.

Lars Svedberg is Professor of Social Work and Director of the Research Institute at Ersta Sköndal University College in Stockholm, Sweden.

Tommy Tranvik is a Researcher at the Rokkan Centre for Social Studies in Bergen, Norway

Lars Trägårdh is the Co-Director of the Program on Trust at the Research Institute of Ersta Sköndal University College in Stockholm, Sweden.

ACKNOWLEDGEMENTS

This volume was inspired by the conference "Studies of Civil Society and Its Social Implications," organized by Ersta Sköndal University College on 12–13 June 2003 in Stockholm, Sweden. The editor would like to thank the Director of the Research Institute at Ersta Sköndal, Professor Lars Svedberg, for his encouragement and patience. The members of the seminar at the Sköndal Research Institute are also to be thanked for their comments on various drafts of several of the chapters in the book. The completion of the book was made possible by the financial support of The Bank of Sweden Tercentenary Foundation. Finally, the book would not have been completed without the loving attention and critical eye of my wife, Vanessa Barker.

Editors' Preface

Is there a "European Civil Society" which cuts across national borders and spreads, though unevenly, through the continent? Does it help to form a European identity from below? Can it be seen as an answer to the obvious democratic deficit of the European Union?

For two and a half years, more than 40 political scientists, sociologists, historians and other scholars from 15 research institutions in 10 different countries have worked together on the project "Towards a European Civil Society". They were supported within the 5th Framework Programme of the EU. The network was coordinated by the Social Science Research Center Berlin. The results of the project are published in the five to six volumes of this series which include studies by other authors as well as far as they are closely related to the topic of "European civil society" like the present study on "State and Civil Society in Northern Europe".

"Civil society" means many things, the concept varies and oscillates. To give a working definition: "Civil society" refers (a) to the community of associations, initiatives, movements and networks in a social space related to but distinguished from government, business and the private sphere; (b) to a type of social action which takes place in the public sphere and is characterized by non-violence, discourse, self-organisation, recognition of plurality, orientation towards general goals and civility; (c) a project with socially and geographically limited origins and universalistic claims, which changes while it tends to expand, socially and geographically.

Civil Society is a deeply historical concept. For a quarter of a century, the concept of "Civil society" has experienced a remarkable career, in several languages. Having a long tradition of many centuries, it had nearly disappeared during most of the 20th century before being rediscovered and reinforced in the 1970s and 1980s when the concept became attractive again in the fight against dictatorship, particularly against communist rule in East Central Europe. But in non-dictatorial parts of the world the term and its promise responded to widely spread needs, as well. Western Europe can be taken as an example.

Civil Society as a political concept of our time has come to formulate critique of a broad variety of problems in contemporary society. To name three tendencies: First, the concept emphasizes social self-organisation as well as individual responsibilities, reflecting the wide-spread scepticism towards being spoon-fed by the state. Second, "civil society", as demonstrated by the phrase's use by present-day anti-globalization movements, promises an alternative to the unbridled capitalism that has been developing so victoriously across the world. The term thus reflects a new kind of capitalism critique, since the logic of "civil society", as determined by public discourse, conflict and agreement, promises solutions different from those of the logic of the market which is based on competition, exchange and the maximization of individual benefits. Thirdly, civic involvement and efforts to achieve common goals are specific to "civil society", no matter how differently the goals may be defined. In the highly individualized and partly fragmented societies of the present time, "civil society" promises an answer to the pressing question of what holds our societies together at all.

On the basis of broad empirical evidence, the project has analysed a large number of core problems of "civil society", among them the complicated relation between markets and civil society; the impact of a European civil society on a European polity and vice versa; the importance of family and household for the ups and downs of civil society. The project has dealt with resources, dynamics and actors of civil society. It has dealt with questions of gender and other forms of inequality. It has compared developments in different European regions. It has begun to open up the perspective towards the non-European conditions, consequences and correlates of European civil society. It has reconstructed the language of civil society, including different semantic strategies in the context of tradition, ideology and power which explain the multiple uses of the concept for different practical purposes. These are some of the topics dealt with in the volumes of this series. The authors combine a long historical perspective with broad and systematic comparison.

What does it mean to speak of a "European" civil society? It implies a certain common European development, a parallel or even convergent trend towards the emergence of civil society in Europe. Such a development may be based on the activities of civil society groups. From the 18th to the 20th century, civil society circles, associations, networks and institutions largely evolved in local, regional, and national frameworks. Trans-national variants, however, which might contribute to the emergence of trans-national coherence and similarities remained secondary. It is in the second half of the 20th century that the quality of the process changed. In this phase, the development of civil society in Europe increasingly assumed trans-national, 'European' and sometimes global dimensions. This is a basic hypothesis of research in this series of studies. European Civil Society will concentrate on trans-national dimensions of civil society in Europe, by comparing and by reconstructing interrelations.

The evolution of a European civil society in the process of trans-nationalization is based on actors as well as on mobile concepts. The ideas and practices of civil society have evolved in a very uneven way, starting to emerge mainly in Western Europe, where it was initially restricted to a few proponents and to specific circles. In the course of its development, civil society spread to other parts of Europe (and into other parts of the world) and gained support within broader social spheres. As they expanded into widening social and spatial environments, the ideas and realities of civil society changed. Thus, the potential of an approach is explored which takes civil society as a geographically and socially mobile phenomenon with a good deal of travelling potential and with the propensity to become a European-wide concept.

European Civil Society focuses on Europe in a broad, not merely geographical sense. This includes comparing European developments with developments in other parts of the world, as well as analyzing processes of – mutual – transfer and entanglement. Europe in this sense transcends the institutional and spatial realm of the European Union. Yet, studying the emergence and dynamics, the perspectives and problems of civil society in Europe may produce insights into the historical process of European integration, which is underway, but far from complete, and presently in crisis.

"European Civil society" is a common endeavour of European and non-European scholars. It centres around a topic which is both the object of scientific analysis and political efforts. The political success cannot be taken for granted. Scientific analysis, however, may help to work out the conditions under which the utopia of civil society in Europe has a chance of realization.

Dieter Gosewinkel
Jürgen Kocka

Introduction

Lars Trägårdh

The Paradox of Swedish Political Culture: State and Civil Society in Sweden

The Swedish political tradition is marked by a seemingly mysterious paradox. On the one hand, many historians have emphasized the early emergence of a modern, centralized state in the sixteenth century. Indeed, Sweden is at times viewed as one of the first and most fully realized examples of an absolutist state, one that served as a model for Prussian and Russian state builders in the centuries that followed. On the other, Sweden is also often celebrated as an open, democratic society in which citizens enjoy easy access to political leaders and the political process.

The notion that Swedish political culture is particularly statist has shown itself to be an enduring one, not least among critics of Sweden. In his controversial book from 1971—*The New Totalitarians*—Roland Huntford develops this thesis to its extreme conclusion. Viewing Sweden as the incarnation of Huxley's dystopian nightmare, Huntford castigates the Swedes, whom he deemed to be "not quite of the West," for their "worship of the State." To be sure, they possess the trappings of constitutional democracy, "but they do not have democracy in their hearts," according to Huntford. Instead, he goes on, they have "a preference for government by bureaucrat rather than by politician" and like true denizens of a brave new world, they do not even suffer under the rule by central administration; rather, "they love their servitude." (Huntford 1971: 9 and 347–48).

Most serious academics would not go as far as Huntford, but ever since the 1950s, leading Swedish political scientists, from Gunnar Heckscher in the 1950s to Bo Rothstein in the 1990s, have described Sweden as a "corporatist" state, even though they would carefully distinguish Swedish "democratic" corporatism, however statist, from its fascist cousins (Heckscher 1946, Rothstein 1992). The emerging Social Democratic welfare state, known domestically as the "people's home" and abroad as the "Swedish model," with its large public sector, high taxes, and legacy of social engineering, came to inspire passionate attention from both detractors and enthusiasts of radical state intervention. In the era of highly charged cold war dichotomies the Swedish welfare state was viewed by some not only as a shield from the insecurities of the free market, but also as a liberator of the individual—not least women, children and other "dependants"—from the shackles of traditional, hierarchical, and patriarchal institutions such as the family, charities, and churches. Conversely, others who celebrated these very institutions as crucial to a free and autonomous society, saw the growing state as an ominous threat to individual liberty and a form of insidious, creeping state socialism.

In marked contrast to this vision of a state-dominated society, stands another, equally potent and deep-rooted conception, that of Sweden as a quintessential popular democracy. At times, this essentialist narrative about Swedish national identity has rivaled even English and American tales of "exceptionalism" in portraying Sweden as a "chosen land" of democracy and freedom. The Swedish version would emphasize the unique status of the peasantry—which never suffered under feudalism—along with Sweden's long-standing traditions of rule of law, local self-government, and personal freedom. All this built on a tradition that goes back to the father of modern Swedish history, Erik Gustaf Geijer. In the 1930s and 40s it was common to depict an unbroken tradition that linked legendary peasant leaders from the distant past to popular movements of the nineteenth century and the breakthrough of modern democracy in the twentieth (Trägårdh 2002).

From this perspective, what scholars like Heckscher and Rothstein describe as corporatism is instead conceived as a particularly vibrant form of participatory and deliberative democracy, in which the free associations—not least the unions, the cooperative movement, and the employers organizations—co-govern Swedish society in close but free cooperation with the representatives of the state. Another Swedish political scientist, Hilding Johansson, who was a contemporary of Heckscher, calls this "a democracy of popular movements, or *associative* democracy." Rejecting the label "corporatism," Johansson emphasized that: "In Sweden the organizations are free and self-governing. Primarily they pursue their own purposes and seek to safeguard the interests of their members. The cooperation with the state is voluntary" (Johansson 1952: 244).

Looking back at the history of how Sweden has been represented in the Anglo-American world, one can detect a similar tension. It is noteworthy that the earlier accounts from the 1930s and 40s, inspired by Marquis Child's bestseller, *Sweden: The Middle Way* (1936) portrayed Sweden in terms of its democratic system of governance, highlighting the crucial role played by civil society organizations. A good third of Child's book was, for example, focused on the cooperative movement. Only with the onset of the Cold War did the perception of Sweden in the US shift toward a more critical, at times Huntfordian vision of a centralized state dominating society through "socialist" policies. By 1955 one could read reports such as this one from the Massachusetts *Herald News:* "Everything shines in Sweden like polished chromium. And Sweden is a chromium nightmare, sterile and empty and faceless. But people cannot be held in shackles forever, no matter how beautiful the chains are ... Perhaps the Swedes will one day take up the sword against their well meaning but stupid bureaucrats." Such stark visions found their way to the very top of the American political establishment, most famously expressed in Eisenhower's speech at the Republican National Convention of 1960, where Sweden was identified as a "socialist" country characterized by "almost complete paternalism," along with drunkenness, high rates of suicide, and "lack of ambition." On the liberal left, meanwhile, Sweden was held up as an icon of progress and enlightened social policy, a "prototype of modern society," as the sociologist Richard Tomasson put it in a book from 1970 (Tomasson 1970).

Whether one wants to conceive of modern Sweden as a state-dominated society or as an associative democracy in which the state is primarily an arena in which free associations negotiate with each other under the benign and neutral guidance of state representatives, is to a great extent a matter of political ideology. But beyond political rhetoric, the two perspectives are not incompatible. Empirically speaking, both Heckser and Johansson appear to be right. As the data presented in subsequent chapters will show, Sweden scores comparatively very high when it comes to measures of trust, social capital, and membership in voluntary associations. At the same time, there is no doubt that the Swedish State plays a large role in the affairs of the land, or that taxes and public sector spending are very high.

Therefore the case of Sweden appears to challenge the idea that the struggle between state and society is a zero sum game in which a strong state typically undermines popular self-organization and democratic governance, and a large public sector stands in opposition to an autonomous and vibrant civil society. Symptomatically, until very recent times, coinciding with the introduction of the concept of civil society, the words for "state" and "society" were often, if not usually, used as synonyms. The simultaneous presence of an exceptionally large public sector and an unusually vital civil society in Sweden thus poses an interesting and important conceptual and theoretical challenge with serious implications for politics and policy.

Empirical and Theoretical Aims of the Book

The objectives of the book are in this light twofold. On the one hand, several contributors will present and analyze empirical findings pertaining to the vitality of social capital and the state of civil society in Sweden. In some cases data from international, mostly quantitative studies are presented from a comparative perspective. In general these studies indeed suggest that Sweden enjoys comparatively robust levels of social capital. However, viewed more closely the data are by no means clearcut and unambiguous. For this reason, these and other chapters will provide a more nuanced analysis of this body of Swedish empirical data, attempting to disaggregate the findings and to analyze them along different dimensions (social, economic, political; age, gender, class; etc), so as to determine more precisely the areas of relative strength and weakness.

Against the backdrop of the empirical findings, the book's second aim is to engage with the theoretical challenges that the Swedish data pose to current thinking on social capital and state-civil society relations. It is our contention that a reconsideration of the dynamics that inform the so-called Swedish model could provide fresh insights that are highly relevant to social capital and state–civil society theory. Furthermore, reversing the traditional perspective, by focusing not on the state but on the importance of civil society organizations, will allow for a reconsideration of the basic structure and dynamics of the Swedish social contract, providing a different interpretation of the fundamental character of the so-called "Swedish model."

Thus the book is intended to foreground a (civil) societal perspective of Sweden, on the one hand by analyzing civil society per se, on the other by investigating the crucial and complex relationships between the state and civil society. In the former case, the focus is on questions such as the construction of social identity, social exclusion, and the reproduction of class stratification. Against the backdrop of statist policies aimed at standardization and social equality, how do we explain persistent patterns of difference and inequality, not only in terms of income and wealth, but also in terms of ethnic differences and gender? In the other case, we consider the roles played by the civil society organizations in democratic governance, that is, the political institutions and processes through which policy is formulated and laws are made. To what extent are trust and social capital created through these interactions between state and civil society organizations, as opposed to interactions within civil society itself? In engaging with such questions, the ambition is ultimately to inspire the creation of theoretical models and analytical tools that can prove useful not only in analyzing the Swedish data but also in carrying out cross-national comparisons, thus making a contribution to general social capital and state–civil society theory, as well as to our understanding of democratic governance.

The Organization of the Book

In the first chapter, Lars Trägårdh begins with an overview of the fraught history of the concept of civil society in the Swedish political and academic context. This section of the chapter serves to introduce the topic to those readers who are not familiar with Sweden in general or at least not with the peculiar inflection that the "civil society vs. the welfare state" debate took during the 1990s. In the second part of the chapter, he attempts to situate Sweden within the broader comparative framework of the state–civil society theory. Following Margaret Somers (1995a, 1995b), he argues that the concept of civil society, such as it is most commonly used in the academic literature, is firmly embedded in an Anglo-American narrative on citizenship. In this tradition the state is viewed with suspicion as a constant threat to the autonomy of civil society and the freedoms and liberties of the citizens. In Sweden, by contrast, what he calls a "Hegelian" conception of state–civil society relations prevails. Civil society is seen as legitimate and important, but also as the arena of particular and private interest, need, and desire. The state and its civil servants and institutional network, on the other hand, is viewed as a necessary antidote, embodying the universal interest and promoting the common good of the nation.

In the next chapter, Jean Cohen builds on and updates her classic work (with Andrew Arato) on "civil society," placing emphasis on the relationship between state and civil society that lies at the heart of the concept of civil society itself. Her analysis devotes particular attention to the challenges posed to theorists of the concept of civil society now that the nation-state is facing changes associated with "globalization." Given that Sweden is a nation-state par excellence and, as chapter one attempts to show, a country in which the autonomy of civil society is a less salient feature than the profound and symbiotic intertwining of state and civil society, this means that the trends Cohen anlyzes are of particular interest to students of Sweden.

Cohen's theoretical analysis is followed by a series of more empirical chapters. Douglas Baer presents and discusses international comparative empirical research, primarily data from the World Values Surveys, concerning voluntary associations, with special emphasis on the so-called new social movements. He also considers how empirically identified differences between countries can be understood and conceived of theoretically, engaging with a variety of attempts to construct typologies for different regime types in terms of the strength and vitality of the civil society sector. According Baer, the Nordic countries, including Sweden, rival the US when it comes to the aggregate size of the voluntary sector, but differ, on the other hand, when it comes to the composition of the sector.

Next the two Swedish scholars Eva Jeppsson Grassman and Lars Svedberg present results from their own large-scale empirical research concerning the extent and character of Swedish civil society. Based on their survey data, they test and critique theories that have suggested that the large size of the public sector has undermined Swedish civil society, supposedly leading to a shrinking of social capital. Their data indicate that there is no firm empirical basis for such large claims, and they warn against undue alarmism when it comes to the decline of volunteering and social capital in Sweden. However, they also conclude that some changes are occurring and that ones perspective depends on whether one is chiefly concerned with associations that function as "schools for democracy"—which do appear to be declining—or if one takes a broader view that accounts for other forms of engagement, including sports, culture and formal and informal social work—which are not.

Erik Amnå focuses on the relation between social capital and democracy. Based on several major empirical studies, Amnå identifies several troubling trends affecting the structure and character of Swedish civil society from a democratic point of view. He also analyzes changes in the government's policy with respect to the free associations that he considers ominous for the future of democratic governance in Sweden. He pays special attention to recent comparative research on young people's attitudes toward government and their own sense of (dis)empowerment with respect to political influence. He analyzes these findings in the context of the conclusions elaborated by several Scandinavian commissions on empowerment and democracy. While Amnå's analysis is broadly comparative in its reach, he is in particular looking at the Swedish data from a US comparative perspective.

In chapter six Tommy Tranvik and Per Selle scrutinize the relations between the state, local communities, and the voluntary sector from the point of view of democratic governance. They conclude that what they describe and analyze is an erosion of the democratic infrastructure in Norway. This is due to a set of interrelated trends, including changes in the organizational structures in the voluntary sector, new ideas about how the public sector ought to be modernized (New Public Management), and new values among the citizenry that give more emphasis to individual freedom at the expense of older, more collectivist and communitarian ideals. While they work with Norwegian data, their research and the conclusions they reach are highly relevant to the Swedish experience as well.

The following essay takes as its point of departure the empirical data on Sweden in a comparative perspective. Through a historical institutionalist lens, Lars Trägårdh and Bo Rothstein analyze the origins of the cooperative relationship between the Swedish state and the organizations of civil society. This takes them back to the late nineteenth century, when the budding labor movement first sought to gain a hearing from the agents of the Swedish state. Although Sweden at this time was not a full-fledged democracy, the state was still open to challengers, especially at the administrative level. They argue that the particular way in which state–civil society relations were institutionalized at that point created a template for future interactions between the agents of state and the interest organizations with far-reaching and long-lasting consequences for the particular character of Swedish democracy and the relations between the state and civil society.

The book's concluding chapter by Lars Trägårdh continues the analysis of the state–civil society nexus by focusing on the peculiar system of governmental commissions that, Trägårdh argues, should be seen as the linchpin of the Swedish democratic political system. These commissions effectively provide the institutional context in which civil society organizations are able to influence the writing of laws and the making of new policy. This in turn is crucial to creating trust—in the political system as well as among the contending actors in civil society itself. The chapter ends by juxtaposing this legacy with the data presented in several other chapters of the book that suggest a structural transformation in both the way civil society organizations themselves work and how they interact with the institutions of the state.

References

Childs, Marquis. 1936. *Sweden: The Middle Way*. New Haven: Yale University Press.
Heckscher, Gunnar. 1946. *Staten och organisationerna*. Stockholm: KFs bokförlag.
Huntford, Roland. 1972. *The New Totalitarians*. New York. Stein and Day.
Johansson, Hilding. 1952. *Folkrörelserna och det demokratiska statskicket i Sverige*. Karlstad: Gleerups.
Rothstein, Bo. 1992. *Den korporativa staten*. Stockholm: Nordstedts.
Somers, Margaret. 1995a. "What's Political or Cultural about Political Culture and the Public Sphere? Toward a Historical Sociology of Concept Formation." *Sociological Theory* 13, no. 2: 113–144.
——— 1995b. "Narrating and Naturalizing Civil Society and Citizenship Theory: The Place of Political Culture and the Public Sphere." *Sociological Theory* 13, no. 3: 229–274.
Thomasson, Richard. 1970. *Sweden: Prototype of Modern Society*, New York: Random House.

Trägårdh, Lars. 1999. "Det civila samhället som analytiskt begrepp och politisk slogan." In *Civilsamhället*, ed. Erik Amnå. SOU 1999: 84.
———. 2002. "Welfare State Nationalism: Sweden and the Spectre of 'Europe'." In *European Integration and National Identity: The Challenge of the Nordic States*, ed. Lene Hansen and Ole Wæver. London and New York: Routledge.

Chapter 1

THE "CIVIL SOCIETY" DEBATE IN SWEDEN: THE WELFARE STATE CHALLENGED

Lars Trägårdh

This chapter will seek to accomplish two objectives, one essentially narrative and descriptive, the other analytical and theoretical. It will first provide a historical overview of the short but vexed career of the concept of "civil society" in Sweden, as a political slogan and a theoretical concept.[1] Second, it will attempt to situate the intense debate that surrounded the introduction of this concept in Sweden in the context of Swedish political culture viewed from a comparative perspective. In particular, I will address the question of why this concept proved so controversial, in spite of the fact that associations have played a very important role in Sweden—politically, socially, and economically.

The Age of Civil Society

In the fifteen years that have passed since 1990, the concept of "civil society" has established itself in Sweden as a central concept in both political language and academic discourse. This parallels a similar development around the world; indeed, the idea of civil society has become one of the most positively charged buzzwords of the recent past along with related concepts such as "social capital," "empowerment," and "governance," ubiquitous but also contested notions used by politicians on both the left and the right and by academics with varying definitions (and degrees of definitional precision).

The rise of this cluster of concepts is related to a broad set of challenges to national democracy and the welfare state, both from above—"globalization," the EU, neoliberalism—and from below—modern individuals and collectivities less inclined to defer to authorities, experts, and elites. New spaces for politics have opened up, and in them a range of actors from outside the traditional political parties, from within an increasingly complex and chaotic society, have become important players actively engaged (or at least aspiring to engage) in politics. This is a structural transformation that sometimes is described as a move from government to governance, in which state actors must more or less willingly govern in cooperation with other actors, ranging from new social movements, foundations, and voluntary organizations engaged in local charity and social work to national business organizations, multinational companies, and transnational NGOs.

From the outset the idea of civil society contained a strong normative component as challengers sought to carve out a new discursive space in which to project bold and innovative political visions. While some would claim a deep historical pedigree for the concept, for example tracing it back to the liberals and civic republicans of the Scottish enlightenment or to Hegel's formulations in mid nineteenth century Germany, in fact the explosive growth in the use of the concept had more contemporary origins.

One point of origin was the politics of the cold war, or to be more precise its endgame. Dissidents in Eastern Europe deployed civil society as their rallying cry in the struggle against the communist state in countries like Poland and Czechoslovakia. The experience of the oppressive communist states translated into a critique and distrust of the state at large (Vajda 1978) as well as of the corrupt party structure and its leadership, which the Serbian dissident Milovan Djilas called "the new class" (Djilas 1957). So deep was the loss of faith in the state and ordinary party politics that leading dissidents like the playwright Vaclav Havel, a President of the Czech Republic, called for a fresh start that at least rhetorically involved a complete negation of politics as usual, what he referred to as "anti-political politics" (Havel 1988). In this reading civil society was conceived of as the realm of authentic human relationships, while ordinary politics tied to the state, by contrast, was seen as always tending to corrupt natural community and threaten liberty. This is a legacy that still resonates in postcommunist Eastern Europe, where in comparison to the countries of "Old Europe" there is less interest in constructing elaborate welfare states on the Western European model. Instead, their citizens appear more inclined to trust the market's capacity to ensure freedom and prosperity and in civil society to provide community and social security.

On the other side of the Atlantic, a similar analysis was launched by the conservative American sociologist Peter Berger and his co-author Richard John Neuhaus, whose book *To Empower People: The Role of Mediating Structures in Public Policy* (1977) was one of the first and most seminal elaborations of a critique by the welfare state to use the notion of civil society. Berger and Neahaus did not actually use the word "civil society" at first, but instead referred to what they called the "mediating structures" between the state and the citizens. However, when they republished the book in 1996, they also changed the title to the less convoluted and more hard-hitting: *To Empower People: From State to Civil Society.* Berger and Neuhaus argued that the welfare state had undermined the institutions of civil society, by which they meant the family, the neighborhoods, and churches and other faith-based institutions that traditionally had provided both a sense of natural community and social security in times of trouble. They also argued that the growth of the welfare state disempowered already poor and disadvantaged people further by making them dependent on the state.

Here their analysis is similar to another influential conservative critique of the welfare state, that by Charles Murray, whose book *Losing Ground: American Social Policy 1950–1980* (1984) was essential to the politics of welfare reform in the US that started with the Reagan years and reached an apogee in Clinton's campaign to "end welfare as we know it" during the 1990s. Clinton also appropriated the language of "empowerment," which Berger and Neuhaus were among the first to have used, to promote so called Empowerment Zones, a largely failed attempt to revitalize poor urban neighborhoods by stimulating community institutions rather than imposing state power from above (Gittel 2001; Trägårdh 2000).[2]

Berger and Neuhaus were joined by other scholars such as Adam Seligman, who produced a major book on the idea of civil society in 1992 in which he traced the idea back to the early Anglo-American political tradition and then cast its career within the framework of a grand struggle between the champions of freedom and its enemies. Along similar lines Francis Fukuyama, perhaps best known for his book that saw in the end of the cold war the very "end of history" (1992), argued that the vitality of civil society was crucial to the survival of a free and prosperous society, just as an overbearing state was a potentially fatal threat to liberty. These were themes that both Fukuyama and Seligman continued to pursue in their books on "trust" during the latter part of the 1990s (Fukuyama 1995; Seligman 1997).

The emphasis on the crucial role that voluntary associations played for economic prosperity, political vitality, and social community was not limited to conservative critics of the welfare state, however. Operating in the Tocquevillean tradition, many American academics and public intellectuals of a more left-of-center stripe had for some time been focusing on civil society. Sociologist Robert Bellah and his collaborators published their important book *Habits of the Heart* in 1985, it was followed up in 1991 by *The Good Society* by the same group of authors, and around this time other influential works were authored by academics, communitarians, and civic humanists such as Sidney Verba, Christopher Lasch, Paul Piccone, Amitai Etzioni, Alan Wolfe and others (Bellah et al. 1985, 1991; Etzioni 1993; Lasch 1991; Wolfe 1989). What unites these writers is their affinity for the civic humanist, or "Atlantic republican" tradition (Pocock 1975), with its emphasis on the active citizen who, infused with a spirit of civic duty, serves his or her local community.

Directly influenced by Pocock and the communitarian tradition, Robert Putnam (1993, 1995, 2000) emerged in the 1990s as perhaps the most influential proponent of the Tocquevillean idealization of civil society. Via James Coleman (1988, 1990), Putnam added the concept of social capital to the analysis, thus opening up for a more quantitative approach to what had until then been a mostly qualitative project chiefly of concern to political theorists like Pocock or sociologists of religion like Berger, Bellah, and Wolfe. While Putnam's early work on Italy was directly focused on the relationship between associational life and democratic institutions, his later work, *Bowling Alone* (2000), has been more particularly concerned with the specter of a decline in social capital per se. His work was quickly translated into Swedish and as many chapters of this book attest, it has been highly influential if at times also subject to deep criticism.

A third point of origin for the concept of civil society at the international level was the launching, or re-launching, of the concept by politically left-leaning intellectuals in Europe and the US. There existed both a native Swedish and an international tradition of the left that in fact not only came to embrace the idea of civil society in the 1990s but did so well before the communitarian right discovered the concept. A number of influential international scholars (I will return to the Swedish tradition below), such as Jürgen Habermas (1989, 1996), Jean Cohen and Andrew Arato (1992), John Keane (1988), and Michael Walzer (1991), to mention only a few, operated within a neo-Marxist tradition that worried about what Habermas described as the increasing colonization by the state of the "lifeworld" of civil society. They tended to see, in the so-called new social movements, hope for an invigorated civil society capable of revitalizing and strengthening democratic political culture from below.

Cohen and Arato took their departure from and engaged deeply with Hegel's path-breaking nineteenth century analysis of state and civil society. However, they significantly departed from Hegel's model in a key respect. Whereas Hegel distinguished between only two spheres—the state and civil society—Cohen and Arato chose to develop a three-sphere model in which the market too was conceived of as a constituting its own sphere. This was consistent with their Habermasian anxiety that civil society as a "lifeworld" was facing two threats, market forces on the one hand and the colonizing state on the other. However, this was also a move that brought their analysis into measurable harmony with the politically more conservative interpretations coming from Eastern European dissidents and American communitarians.

To be sure, Cohen and Arato were far from promoting the a- or antipolitical visions of civil society that were common among conservatives. Nor did they subscribe to the kind of unbridled antistatism that characterized right-wing interpretations of the idea of civil society. Rather, they envisioned civil society as a sphere of citizen action and grassroots movements, as well as an active Habermasian public sphere. They were not hostile to the universal provision of social rights such as healthcare through the organs of the democratic state.[3] However, purging the sphere of civil society of the troublesome market, which was marked by the morally dubious pursuit of profit and self-interest, left Cohen and Arato's definition of civil society—the family, the voluntary associations, social movements, and public forms of communication—free of the odors of the market society and thus more easily romanticized in terms of community, social movements, and "positive" political and collectivist values. One suspects that the subtraction of the market reflects a lingering hostility to capitalism on the part of leftist intellectuals, post-Marxist though they may be.

In the Hegelian scheme, on the other hand, civil society is the sphere in which private interests, needs, and desires play themselves out. Inspired by his reading of Smithian economic theory, Hegel embraced the market as a legitimate, necessary, and ultimately positive force for enabling the private pursuit of gain, pleasure, and self-expression in addition to its laudatory aggregate effect on societal wealth creation. At the same time, however, he also argued that the internal contradictions of civil society, including poverty, atomistic individualism, and social disorder, could never be resolved by civil society itself. Only the state could promote and safeguard a greater purpose of rationality, by which Hegel meant the "unity and interpenetration of universality and individuality." (Hegel 1991, Wood 1991) Thus, for Hegel the state was not a threat to individual freedom; quite the contrary, it was only through membership in the state and through the superior rationality of the state that the highest form of individual freedom was made possible. In concrete daily life, this merging of individual freedom and the state's universalist rationality, was mediated and realized in what Hegel called the "corporations." These were the various associations that individuals, otherwise isolated as atoms in the market system, joined to pursue common interest. In the very act of joining, the individual began the journey to transcend self-interest, forge a social identity, and begin to contribute to the welfare of society as a whole.

This Hegelian interpretation of the idea of civil society is notably absent from all three of the traditions that I have discussed above. Thus the particular notion of "civil society" that in practice was imported into the Swedish political and discursive context around 1990 is one that is firmly embedded in what Margaret Somers has called "the meta-narrative of Anglo-American citizenship theory" (Somers 1995a, 1995b). This is a conception that understands civil society as an autonomous entity, consisting of self-organizing voluntary societies, free associations, and a free press, bonded through the common law and a carefully circumscribed representative government. Civil society is prior to and distinct from the state, which always represents a threat to the liberty of the citizenry. In this narrative the State is always seen as harboring a potential for domination, intervention, regulation, collectivism, and positive law imposed arbitrarily from above. In so far as there is a state that is acceptable from the perspective of Anglo-American citizenship theory, it is what Somers calls a "de-institutionalized state," a state that remains subject to popular sovereignty and does not usurp powers that belong to the "people" but remains reined in firmly within the confines of contract law, laissez-faire economics, and liberal democratic institutions that protect against concentration of power in the hands of state agents. However, even in this relatively benign form, the state is always "on the brink of being a source of tyranny," as Somers puts it (Somers 1995b: 259).

As we will see below, even though this conception of state-society relations is a normative vision that critics of the welfare state have mobilized with relish, it does not easily harmonize with Swedish political culture and tradition. By contrast, the Hegelian formulation of the ideal social order is one that at least imperfectly "fits" with the actual structure of Swedish society and its political culture, and in many ways constitutes a better theoretical account of the actual ways in which state–civil society relations in Sweden have been configured historically. It is also a conception that implicitly informs the thinking of the defenders of the Swedish social contract and the welfare state.

The Timbro Institute: Civil Society versus the Welfare State

The concept of civil society burst upon the political and academic scene in Sweden in the early 1990s, when writers associated with Swedish business and employers' organizations and the Conservative Party began using it in a pungent critique of Swedish social democracy and the welfare state. Partly in reaction to this, many left-leaning intellectuals and academics who supported the welfare state viewed the new concept with a great deal of suspicion. For them "civil society" was, at least at first, a code word, a discursive innovation that emanated from deep within an aggressive neoliberal ideology. In this reading, the concept amounted at heart to a thinly veiled call to "dismantle" the welfare state (Antman 1993). However, as will be discussed in more detail below, the concept of civil society had ironically enough originally been launched a decade earlier by a different group of left-wing journalists and academics who were critical of what they saw as an increasingly centralist and statist Social Democratic Party. This earlier attempt at introducing the concept, however, enjoyed much less success and failed to mobilize the idea as an integral part of left-wing political language. Nonetheless, once the concept was launched anew by right-wing welfare state critics, these left-wing writers also entered the debate. Their the aim was to extend and deepen citizen participation in democratic self-governance, and they deployed the concept of civil society from this point of view. This set the stage for a sometimes confusing three-way debate between the defenders of social democratic statism and the critics of this statism on both the left and the right.

A key moment in the concept's breakthrough into public discourse was a series of debates that took place in two major Swedish newspapers, *Dagens Nyheter* and *Aftonbladet*, in 1992 and 1993.[4] As noted before, the debates were fueled by the embrace of the new discourse on civil society by figures close to the Conservative Party. The institutional incubator for this project was the Timbro Institute, a conservative think tank that had been founded in 1978 to challenge the hegemonic position that the left had enjoyed for decades when it came to formulating the political agenda in public discourse. Over time the institute came to employ and promote writers and scholars working in a variety of traditions, representing a mixture of neoliberal economic ideas, libertarian political thought, and traditional social conservatism.

The use of the concept of civil society can be traced back to a number of Timbro publications that appeared in 1988 and 1990. In the first one, *Demokratins små plattformar* (1988), PJ Anders Linder made one of the Swedish political right's first attempts to deploy the concept. Linder was directly inspired by Peter Berger and Richard John Neuhaus, whose work is discussed above. Following in their footsteps, Linder combined hostility toward the welfare state with a communitarian ethos that saw in the "natural" institutions of society—the family, the churches, the clubs and associations—both protection from the cold and overbearing state and the locus for self-realization and the experience of true community.

The preface of Linder's book, written by the leading Conservative politician, Gunnar Hökmark, succinctly captured the sentiment that would come to suffuse the right-wing critique of the social democratic welfare state in the idiom of a communitarian and antistatist understanding of civil society. Groping for a label and a concept that was not yet available, he referred vaguely to "that part of society that is not controlled by the state, and which is largely undiscovered in the political debate." It is, he went on, "a remainder," under attack and steadily shrinking, "faced with a political power that recognizes no limit to its own competence and legitimacy" (Linder 1988). The "remainder" (whatever was left after the state was done in its colonizing mission) was what soon would be called civil society.

While Linder's essay is of great interest to the historian, in its own time it was not as important as a book published two years later by Timbro, entitled *Det civila samhället*, meaning "civil society" (Arvidsson and Berntson et al. 1990). In this anthology, two former Marxists, Håkan Arvidsson and Lennart Berntson, reintroduced the concept of civil society, a concept that they had already written a book on ten years previously, that time for the left-wing publisher Zenit (Arvidsson and Berntson 1980). This time they removed the Marxist trappings and instead adopted an understanding closer to that of the Anglo-American readings of Linder and Berger and Neuhaus, and it was this version of the concept that in the following years was at the heart of the public debate.

Swedish critics of the social democratic welfare state obviously found the ideas from the US and Eastern Europe quite useful. While accepting that Sweden was not quite the Soviet Union, they nonetheless drew what they saw as a parallel: a too dominant state that diminished the space for both private actors in the market and the communitarian institutions of civil society. From this point of view, the social democratic welfare state was fundamentally part of the same tradition, if a more benign variation on the theme. It was a system that privileged state-sponsored social engineering and central planning over the "spontaneous order" (Friedrich Hayek) of an "open society" (Karl Popper) based on the twin pillars of the free market and a self-organizing civil society.

However, while Timbro had its share of free marketers—the early 1990s was perhaps the moment when libertarianism and classical liberal thought reached their height of influence (though always limited) in the Swedish public debate—the critique coming from Timbro soon became less neoliberal and more communitarian, especially after the conservative sociologist Hans Zetterberg became the leading force at Timbro. Zetterberg, who helped write the new program of the Conservative Party, "Ideas for our future" (Moderata samlingspartiet 1990), took a position at the City University, a private institution associated with Timbro, as the director of an ambitious research program highly critical of the welfare state (Zetterberg 1992). Called "The Social State," it produced a number of studies probing various aspect of the Social democratic welfare state, including an new book by Arvidsson and Berntson on the topic of civil society, this time with a third author, Lars Dencik (Arvidsson, Berntson and Dencik 1994; see also Zetterberg and Ljungberg 1997 for a final report and summary of individual studies).

Zetterberg, while no enemy of the market economy, nonetheless worried not just that the state would corrode and undermine the institutions of civil society, but that the market, too, posed threats to the ethos, moral logic, and communitarian spirit that he associated with civil society. His critique emanated less from an analysis of the economic costs and high taxes associated with the welfare state than it did from a sociological analysis focused on the social and human consequences of impersonal and institutionalized state care of society's old, young, and disabled.

In emphasizing that the communities of civil society faced threats not simply from the state but also from the liberal market society, Zetterberg showed affinity with American civic humanists and conservative communitarians, thinkers like Lasch, Murray, and Etzioni (Etzioni 1993; Lasch 1991; Murray 1984; Zetterberg 1993, 1995; Zetterberg and Ljungberg 1997). Symptomatically, when Timbro organized their annual conference in the fall of 1994, they chose a communitarian theme and invited Oxford's John Gray, who launched a passionate critique of the neo-liberal onslaught in the formerly communist states of Eastern Europe, suggesting that they had gone from being oppressed by a totalitarian state to suffering under "wild east" capitalism.

Zetterberg, following what by now had become the standard account, based his analysis on a theory of society that involved the three spheres of the state, the market, and civil society. In this scheme civil society included the family, voluntary associations, faith-based institutions, and neighborhood organizations. He noted that it was an arena characterized by a moral logic different from that which pertains in the market or in the world of politics and public administration. Its fundamental principle was that of unconditional love and voluntary, unselfish care, alongside an unabashed privileging of those near and dear. In the market, on the other hand, the moral logic was one of competition and the pursuit of self-interest. And in the public sector, the ideal was fair and neutral treatment of all and an overarching concern with the common good. Thus, what constitutes virtue in one sphere becomes vice in another. An act that in civil society is viewed as an expression of love—naturally privileging one's own family and friends as a matter of honor, for example—is viewed in the public sector as corrupting nepotism.

However, as is discussed above, the three-sphere conception was actually a novel innovation in the theory of civil society, in Sweden and elsewhere.[5] Up to that point a two-sphere theory had prevailed, pitting civil society—including the market—against the state. In Sweden it was only in 1990, in an article written by Nils Karlson, a political scientist working with the Timbro Institute, that the two-sphere conception was expanded (Karlson 1990). Karlson actually retained the two-sphere scheme nominally, but he drew a crucial distinction between "markets" and "communities" within the category of "civil society." A few years later the move to a three-sphere model was fully realized, by Zetterberg as well as by Arvidsson, Berntson, and Dencik. As I have already noted, this was a key development given the more general division among civil society theorists, namely those who follow Hegel's two-sphere theory and those who, like Zetterberg, subscribe to what can be called the Anglo-American, three-sphere theory.

The Swedish Left and the Question of Civil Society

The attack from the right naturally created a counter reaction on the left. While communitarian critics such as Zetterberg in fact differed from those on the free market, neoliberal right, they were united in a common antipathy toward the welfare state, be it for economic reasons or for moral and social ones. However, politicians, writers, and academics who, broadly speaking, sympathized with the Social Democratic Party and the parties to its left did not respond uniformly. This reflected a longstanding division on the left. In one camp there were those who saw the state as the primary mechanism for emancipation of the working class and the realization of a political agenda aimed at full employment, social and gender equality, and the provision of extensive social services and a social safety net. And then there was a smaller but still influential group for whom democracy had to come from below and be grounded in democratic self-organization and empowerment at the local and small-scale levels. This tradition, the "movement" wing of the Social Democratic Party, had always been characterized by its far more suspicious attitude toward centralized power in the hand of the state, and it had historical ties to the cooperative movement and the syndicalist wing of the labor movement. This tendency found new political and intellectual sustenance in the heady atmosphere that prevailed in the late 1960s and 1970s (Salomon 1996, Östberg 2002).

In the statist, camp, the leading figures were influential public intellectuals with close ties to the Social Democratic Party, like the poet and political journalist Göran Greider. Greider and his compatriots, especially Peter Antman and Tomas Lappalainen, fiercely attacked both Zetterberg and Arvidsson, who were associated with Timbro, and those on the left who tried to promote a left-wing interpretation of the civil society ideology. They viewed the celebratory talk about the many virtues of associational participation as dangerously romantic. Such voluntary organizations, they argued, mostly benefit the well-to-do in the middle- and upper classes, while the workers and the poor needed the strong and protecting arm of the state not to loose further ground in a society dominated by the wealthy and the ruthless logic of the market.

According to Antman, a closer analysis of who joins such associations and what they actually do in them quickly reveals that they are strongly elitist and mostly devoted to sports, hobbies, and recreation. The vision of a civil society made up of social movements that mobilize the poor and the weak for common political purposes is "a myth," Antman concluded (Antman 1993). Shifting responsibility for education, daycare, care of the elderly, and healthcare for all to the institutions of civil society, let alone the private for-profit sector, would result, Greider argued, in a "nightmare for the weak" (Antman 1993).

While Greider and his compatriots directed much of their fire against the circle of writers, journalists, and academics associated with Timbro, the internal debate within the left was every bit as bitter and charged. Indeed, this fight had been brewing off and on for many years, with roots going back to the very origins of the socialist movement and renewed since the revolt against the established parties by the "68er" generation. Even within the Social Democratic Party one could identify voices of protest, often younger figures who were associated with SSU (the youth organization of the Social Democratic party).[6] As early as 1974 SSU organized a major campaign that drew a lot of attention in Swedish media—*Tillsammans för en idé* ("Together for an idea")—in which the revitalization of popular movements *(folkrörelserna)* was the central theme (Isling 1978). The campaign drew a lot of attention in the mass media, but the proponents of a larger role for what would later be called civil society organizations also faced a lot of criticism. Foreshadowing the later debates, the defenders of the statist approach worried about the consequences of letting non-state actors take responsibility for key social services like day care, housing, education, or health care. Liberal and conservative critics, on the other hand, viewed enthusiasm for voluntary organizations with suspicion, as a form of hidden corporatism or even socialism on the sly.

Another attempt to introduce a similar set of ideas took place in the 1980s. As I have already noted in passing, Håkan Arvidsson and Lennart Berntson, who later became part of the Timbro circle, at least for a time, published in 1980 the first book to introduce the idea of civil society in Sweden. Picked up in turn by writers and journalists associated with SSU, the book was subsequently written up in the SSU debate magazine *Tvärdrag*, which also featured a sympathetic interview with Arvidsson and Berntson (*Tvärdrag* 1984). This group, in which the writer and journalist Håkan A. Bengtsson was a leading force, had for some time been promoting the notion of *självförvaltning*, which literally means "self-administration." In particular, they supported a greater role for cooperatives and associations that would allow citizens to manage their own affairs and administer on their own the social programs that were at that point run through state bureaucracies. Again, the success was limited in terms of influencing the mainstream leadership of the Social Democratic Party, but these so-called "renewers" would remain active within the party.

By the time of the "civil society" debate in the early 1990s, this faction of the left was, therefore, ready and more than willing to enter the fray. The new leader of SSU, Karl-Petter Thorwaldsson, launched a concept that had been borrowed from the US, *egenmakt*, the Swedish translation for "empowerment." This is another concept with a contested and highly politicized meaning. In Sweden and the US the term "empowerment" has been deployed by both right-wing and left-wing proponents of civil society and community-based mobilization (Trägårdh 2000). In the Swedish case it was a direct continuation of the earlier emphasis on the role of popular movements, cooperatives, and self-administration. Not surprisingly, Håkan A. Bengtsson, Karl-Petter Thorwaldsson and others whose sympathies ran in this direction embraced the concepts of civil society and empowerment and used them to continue criticizing what they saw as a state that had grown too strong at the expense of voluntary associations and cooperatives, institutions that they saw as fundamental to the continued vitality and strength of a popular and decentralized democracy (Antman 1993; Bengtsson 1992; Eneroth and Olsson 1993; Thorwaldsson 1994).

The rhetoric of the left-wing proponents of civil society in some respects echoed that of the critique coming from the Timbro circle. They voiced concern that the "citizen had become a client," and that ordinary people felt disempowered in their relationship with the all-powerful state (Thorwaldsson 1994). According to Jan Olsson and Tomas Eneroth, each of whom had ties to both SSU and the cooperative movement, the solution was to "empower" people, which could only happen through organizations that "take their own initiatives to assert the interests of the citizens," as Olsson put it (Eneroth and Olsson 1993). Foreshadowing a theme that would become common soon thereafter, once Putnam's work on social capital and its decline became widely read in Sweden, they also worried that they were witnessing a sharp drop-off in membership and engagement in associations.

Critics of the welfare state found support for their arguments in a number of studies carried out within the framework of a major parliamentary commission appointed in 1985 by the Swedish Prime Minister Ingvar Carlsson, a Social Democrat. The commission was given the task of broadly investigating the question of power and influence in Swedish society and its ramifications for the future of democracy. The commission, on whose advisory committee several influential American academics served, including Theda Skocpol and Sidney Verba, published a series of reports between 1987 and 1990, the year of its principal and concluding report, entitled "Democracy and Power in Sweden" (Maktutredningen 1990). Taken together these reports painted a less than flattering picture of the Swedish welfare state as paternalistic and unresponsive in relation to the citizens, who, it appeared, were more often treated as clients and supplicants than respected as full citizens (Petersson et al. 1987). One widely read and debated report from 1987 contained a wealth of survey data, suggesting that ordinary citizens often felt disempowered in relation to the state (Petersson et al. 1987). A follow-up report published some ten years later largely reconfirmed this rather bleak picture of a Swedish civil society in a state of decay (Petersson et al. 1998), although its findings have since been challenged (see Jeppsson Grassman in this book; also see Amnå this book and Bear this book for data on Swedish associational life, civil society and social capital).

The sense of crisis that these reports tended to fuel was exacerbated by the deep financial and economic problems that beset Sweden in the early 1990s. The Swedish currency came under attack, interest rates shot up, the deficit grew, economic growth slowed, and unemployment rose dramatically. To be sure, these were trends that had been visible ever since the mid 1970s, but the dire state of the economy became fully clear only in the early 1990s. This naturally lent credence to those critics who sought to effect what was at the time often referred to as a "change of system" in a vague allusion to the dramatic changes that swept through Eastern Europe as communism collapsed during the heady days of 1989 and 1990.

Civil Society as a Theoretical Concept: The Response of the Academic Community

The Swedish academic community at first greeted the concept of civil society with considerable skepticism. Some simply argued that the concept was useless in a scientific context (Lidskog 1995), others questioned it as theoretically incoherent and politically suspect (Dahlkvist 1995), as loaded with incorrect assumptions regarding the state–civil society relation (Rothstein 1995), or fraught with gendered, if not patriarchal, normative values (Sommestad 1995.)

Some fifteen years later the situation has changed completely. The concept of civil society is not only seen as legitimate and useful by many academics, but if anything the study of civil society and social capital has acquired something of a "most fashionable" status. A recent inventory of research in the area of democracy, public administration, and popular movements, published by the Swedish Research Council, holds out the research concerned with civil society as particularly innovative (Vetenskapsrådet 2003: 14). The Swedish government recently voiced agreement with that conclusion, noting that "it is above all research about civil society, for example the nonprofit sector and the voluntary associations, which has distinguished itself as groundbreaking."[7] In response to an increasing number of applications from the academic community for funding to carry out research in this area, the Bank of Sweden Tercentenary Foundation, which (along with the Swedish Research Council) is the largest source of funding for social science research in Sweden, has recently made research in this field a special category earmarked for particular attention.[8]

Back in 1990, by contrast, most of the political scientists and sociologists focused their attention on the state and the public sector. Indeed, some of the funding then (and now) devoted to civil society studies came from the new and amply funded Center for Public Sector Research, founded in 1992. The study of civil society, or more accurately of what in Sweden is and was called "popular movements" (folkrörelser), had largely been left to historians who viewed this history mostly as a prelude to the study of the labor movement, the rise of the Social Democratic Party, and the building of the welfare state. To be sure, almost everyone in Sweden paid homage to this heritage and regarded the associations as "schools for democracy," in particular the labor movement of old, when it was still heroically struggling against both old-fashioned industrialists and a less sympathetic state. (The other associations commonly collected under the rubric of folkrörelser, such as the free churches and the temperance societies, attracted less attention, not fitting as neatly, perhaps, into the teleology of the secular and Social Democratic welfare state.) But there was a whiff of nostalgia to this ritual nod to the "movements": everyone knew that the "real" story was about the state and the fast-growing public sector.[9] As Erik Amnå has pointed out, in the political science textbooks of the 1980s civil society organizations were viewed as "complements" to the political parties and the organs of the state (Amnå 2005, 21).[10]

Symptomatic is a story told by one of the pioneers of the "modern" study of Swedish civil society. According to Erik Blennberger, an academic theologian who played an important role steering the small but influential Sköndal Institute in Stockholm toward the study of voluntary social work in particular and Swedish civil society in general, it was rare to even think and speak about sectors other than the public one as late as 1990. Indeed, the word for "society" in Swedish, samhället, was not used to denote the sphere distinct from the state and the government institutions, but on the contrary referred precisely to the public sector and its agents and institutions. This resulted in an acute conceptual crisis since there literally existed no word to describe the phenomenon that Blennberger and his small band of compatriots wanted to study and analyze. Thus Blennberger describes how at this time, around 1990, one still had to resort to the empty negation "non-public sector" when gesturing vaguely toward what is now called civil society.[11]

Furthermore, this absence of a concept not only suggested a certain poverty of theory but also reflected a lack of empirical research. Indeed, this was one reason why the intense debate during the first few years of the 1990s could become so polemical, overheated, and politically charged. No one had much hard empirical data at hand, the theoretical situation was unclear, and in this vacuum anyone could claim anything. However, while the debate at the time did not resolve any political or theoretical issues, it did make some people in the academic world aware of this relative dearth of empirical research carried out with respect to this sector, whatever it was called. This led over time to an empirical turn in the field of civil society studies, as the acute political debate subsided out of sheer exhaustion.

As it turned out, several efforts were in fact just completed or in progress. One study was the one already mentioned, by the Parliamentary Commission on Democracy and Power, which provided troubling data on the state of Swedish civil society. But it was also clear that, from a more comparative perspective, membership in voluntary associations remained high, even if, as we have just seen, there was concern about who was joining and who was not, and about what members of these societies actually did.

The early 1990s, however, saw the instigation of a few projects that eventually would lead to several ambitious empirical studies; these in turn provided a clearer picture of the size and character of Swedish civil society. In particular, crucial work was carried out by scholars associated with the Sköndal Institute in Stockholm and the Economic Research Institute (EFI) at the Stockholm School of Economics. The genesis of this body of work was the initiative taken by Erik Blennberger at the Sköndal Institute. Blennberger joined forces with Lars Pettersson, who at that time was the national director of the Swedish Red Cross. Pettersson was interested in supporting both empirical research and theory production in a field that he perceived as understudied. With the Red Cross providing funding, the Sköndal Institute hired a number of young scholars who later came to produce seminal empirical research, particularly in the area of voluntary social work. These scholars included Lars Svedberg, Eva Jeppsson Grassman, and Tommy Lundström. By 1993 the Sköndal group had produced an initial overview, including a literature review, a population survey, and a first stab at a conceptual analysis (SOU 1993).

A further link created between Sköndal and Filip Wijkström at EFI, led to a joint participation in the Johns Hopkins Comparative Nonprofit Sector Project, a large-scale, international, comparative study based on massive survey data. From 1993 to 1997 and beyond scholars such as Erik Amnå, Eva Jeppson Grassman, Tommy Lundström, Lars Svedberg, and Filip Wijkström, to mention some of the more prominent, laid the groundwork that enabled further empirical and theoretical work, this volume included (Amnå 1995a, Amnå 1995b, Jeppsson Grassman and Svedberg 1995, Jeppsson Grassman and Svedberg 1999, Lundström and Wijkström 1997, Wijkström and Lundström 2002).

The empirical studies focused on several different but related areas. Some research, particularly associated with the work done at the Sköndal Institute, has focused on the *social* arena, trying to determine to what extent Swedes in fact engage in voluntary social work. Other studies, primarily by the group around Filip Wijkström at EFI, have been concerned with the *economic* dimension, attempting to ascertain how large and how autonomous the sector is in sheer economic terms. Finally, several political scientist, Olof Petersson, Erik Amnå and Bo Rothstein among them, have been chiefly preoccupied with the *political* aspect, asking questions about the relation between civil society, social capital, and democracy, often with an eye to identifying trends that reflect the vitality of civil society and the state of democratic governance.

What this work indicated was that, contrary to the expectations generated by the theory that a strong state and a large public sector would crowd out the civil society organizations, Sweden was characterized by a very large nonprofit or voluntary sector.[12] However, it also became clear that at the theoretical level confusion reigned, as suggested by the large number of labels used by different scholars. Some chose "nonprofit sector," some "voluntary social work," some preferred the old Swedish term *folkrörelser* (popular movements), and others wrote about "new social movements." This rapid acceptance of the idea of civil society in broad terms thus came at the price of diluting the theoretical precision of a concept that, for scholars like Cohen and Arato, was firmly embedded in an elaborate theoretical structure (Cohen and Arato 1992). Take as an example Karin Busch Zetterberg, who was one in a new wave of researchers to take a more empirical approach. She placed emphasis on the collection and analysis of survey data and avoided theoretical debate, instead opting for a pragmatic and almost purely descriptive definition of civil society. The simplest way of distinguishing it was, she wrote, to simply enumerate the institutions and activities that belong to neither the market nor the state: "family life, the neighborhood community, associations, religious groups, and cultural activities" (Busch Zetterberg 1996).

Busch Zetterberg is quite representative of the way in which the concept of civil society is used today. Even though different researchers do in fact use slightly different definitions—for example, some include the family, others do not; some include looser networks of friends and acquaintances, while others focus on formal associations of different types—what most have in common is a relative lack of engagement with theory as such. While such an ad hoc approach has probably served to simplify and speed up the collection of sorely lacking empirical data, it also tends to avoid or postpone equally important theoretical questions. Specifically, it tends to accept as given a certain, readily available reading of the idea of civil society, one that places emphasis on communitarian and/or even antipolitical ideals, instead of engaging with alternative conceptions in which politics, the market, and the judicial system are at the center, along with a focus not just on harmony but also on conflict and power struggles (if in civilized and civilizing forms).

As Lars Svedberg and Eva Jeppsson Grassman have pointed out in an essay from 1999, it may well be that some of the disagreements over the size of the Swedish civil society can be traced back to variations in method and measure, depending on what the focus of the research was. Some studies have been strictly concerned with membership in formally constituted associations, while other have also counted less stable forms of engagement, or even looser networks formed for various purposes (Jeppsson Grassman and Svedberg 1999). In any case, as is indicated by the contrast in this volume between the work of Jeppsson Grassman and Svedberg and that of Erik Amnå, there still exists a tension between those who view the state of Swedish civil society with a considerable degree of concern, and those who argue that such alarm often is overstated, especially from a comparative vantage point.

The past several years have seen yet another shift in focus when it comes to civil society research in Sweden. Above all it is a response to the influence exerted by the work of Robert Putnam, who is a relatively frequent visitor to Sweden. By introducing the concept of social capital, Putnam sharpened the analytical focus and helped move the debate away from the political polemics of the early 1990s and into sync with a mainstream academic concern with counting, labeling, and analyzing. Both *Making Democracy Work* (from 1993) and the later *Bowling Alone* (2000) were translated and widely read. Furthermore, the influential Swedish political scientist Bo Rothstein collaborated with Putnam on a collected volume with a comparativist ambition (Putnam 2002 and Rothstein 2002). Rothstein's encounter with Putnam is of interest not least because it reveals not only the influence of Putnam's work but also the lingering unease that could be detected among many Swedish scholars regarding the collision between Putnam's theoretical assumptions and the facts of the Swedish experience. Specifically, Rothstein resolutely rejected the notion that a large welfare state by necessity would lead to a decline in social capital and an atrophied civil society.

Finally, the story of how the study of civil society in Sweden gained legitimacy and prominence would not be complete without mentioning the large Governmental Commission on Democracy that was led by Erik Amnå under the formal direction of Bengt Göransson, a former Social Democratic minister. Both Amnå and Göransson had long been active promoters of a "movement" and civil society perspective, and under their leadership the commission produced a number of texts, including a major anthology, that generated publicity as well as funding for new research—both empirical, historical, and theoretical (Amnå 1999).

This returns us to the point I made earlier, that much of American thinking and writing about civil society is based on an implicit embrace of what we, following Somers, referred to as the "the meta-narrative of Anglo-American citizenship theory." As was discussed, this involves a conception of a fundamentally antagonistic relationship between the state and civil society, with the latter marked as the positive foundation for a liberal-democratic society and the former viewed with suspicion as a potential threat to liberty. The notion that underpins much of the work on social capital and civil society, more or less explicitly theorized, is that social capital is created through meetings and experiences in the associational life of civil society. Furthermore, it is this production of social capital in civil society that, in Putnam's words, "makes democracy work."

Just as the empirical work by Jeppson Grassman and Svedberg and Lundström and Wijkström has done much to discredit the zero sum thesis with respect to the size of the state vs. civil society, so has Rothstein's writing pushed to the fore a possible reversal at the theoretical level. His analysis suggests that, at least in Sweden, trust creation occurs not in a civil society that is autonomous from or even antagonistic to the state, but rather in the various relations that individuals and organization have with the state. It appears, he has argued, that it is precisely a well-functioning state, by which he means a universalist welfare state with an uncorrupt civil service, that breeds the conditions under which social and political trust can develop. It is this trust that underpins the accumulation of social capital and the vitality of civil society organizations (Rothstein 1995, Rothstein 2002).

The Civil Society Discourse, the Meta-Narrative of Anglo-American Citizenship Theory, and Swedish Political Culture

Rothstein's critical engagement with social capital theory spotlights the question of how well this body of concepts and theories, in turn informed by civic humanism and various strands of American communitarianism, fits with the Swedish experience and helps us analyze it. Given that these political traditions are themselves embedded in Anglo-American citizenship theory, with its peculiar conception of the state–civil society nexus, it is imperative that we now examine the Swedish political tradition more systematically. Having done so, we will be in a better position to understand why it is that the critics on both the left and the right who have attempted to deploy the communitarian discourse on civil society vs. the state have, in fact, not met with great success at the political level, even though the concept of civil society has been integrated in the academic discourse.

To start with, let us return to the early 1990s, a time of fundamental challenges to the Swedish political consensus and the Swedish social contract. While the confrontation that pitted the enthusiasts of "civil society" against the defenders of the welfare state was an important debate, it was actually overshadowed by another political struggle, namely the question of whether or not Sweden would join the EU (Trägårdh 2002). In fact, the two issues were deeply related, and the political playing field saw the same contenders line up in much the same way. The parties to the right—the Conservatives, the Liberal Party, the Christian Democrats—were all in favor of Sweden joining the EU. The left, on the other hand, was split along the same lines as in the civil society debate: hardcore defenders of the Swedish welfare state wanted Sweden to stay out of the EU and retain full national sovereignty, whereas the pro-EU faction were much the same people who also supported a left-wing vision of a less statist Sweden.

How do we explain this EU-negative attitude on the part of the Swedes who otherwise would seem to be well-poised to take advantage of the benefits afforded by EU membership, not least given their longstanding commitment to free trade and their dependence on large, export-oriented companies? And what parallels exist combining this euro-skepticism with reluctance to embrace the idea of a society in which the institutions of civil society play a larger role and the state a lesser one? My argument here is that the idea of European integration, and the idea of shifting from a statist social contract toward one that prioritizes to the institutions of civil society, both pose a deep threat to the way in which many Swedes have come to understand the proper relationship between "state," "society," "nation," and "people." That is, Swedish national identity has come to be tightly linked to the welfare state, understood not simply as a set of institutions but as the realization of *Folkhemmet*, the "people's home," the central organizing slogan of the Social Democrats, the party that has dominated Swedish politics since 1933.

The extraordinary and lasting potency of this concept derives from the seamless way in which the two concepts of "the people"—those of *demos* and *ethnos*—have been fused into one coherent whole. The Swedish concepts of *folk, folklighet,* and *folkhem* are all part and parcel of a national narrative that has cast the Swedes as intrinsically democratic and freedom-loving, as having "democracy in the blood," as Social Democrats put it in the 1920s and 30s. Thus, since to be a Swedish nationalist meant perforce that one embraced democratic values, it was possible in the 1930s for the Social Democrats to successfully harness the power of national feeling, to become "national socialists," and fight off the challenge posed by domestic Nazi wanna-bes.

Furthermore, and just as importantly, the "Swedish Model," as it came to be known, was characterized by a particular form of statism built on a vision of a social contract between a strong and good state, on the one hand,

and emancipated and autonomous individuals, on the other. Through the institutions of the state the individual, so it was thought, was liberated from the institutions of civil society—the family, the neighborhood, the churches, the charity organizations. The inequalities and dependencies associated with these institutions were to be replaced by an egalitarian social order. In this scheme the state and the people were conceived of as intrinsically linked; the people's home was a *folkstat*[13] the state was the homely domain of national community, the context in which the ideal of solidarity could be joined to that of equality. At the same time, this Swedish ideology, with its dual emphasis on social equality and individual autonomy, was understood to be distinctly modern and highly efficient from an economic standpoint; the *welfare* of the welfare state implied not just solidarity and equality but also prosperity and progress.

From this point of view, the left-wing supporters of the nation-statist Swedish welfare state often viewed Europe to the south of Denmark as a backward bastion of patriarchy, hierarchy, corruption, and inequality. Continental notions like federalism, subsidiarity, and civil society were perceived as insidious, neoliberal even "papist" ideas, fundamentally antithetical to the founding principles of the welfare state. Conversely, the political parties to the right have tended to see in Europe the possibility of accomplishing through the back door what they have consistently failed to achieve at the national level: the dismantling of the oppressive welfare state and the revitalization of the atrophied civil society. Liberals came to see the EU as a project promoting the freedom of the market from state regulation, and the freedom of the individual from the narrow confines of Swedish egalitarianism. Social conservatives and Christian Democrats, for their part, imagined the restoration of the "natural" social structures of civil society they felt had been undermined by the unholy alliance between big government and big business.

This statism that links social equality, national solidarity, and individual autonomy to the beneficial power of the state makes Sweden, Swedish democracy, and the Swedish social contract profoundly different from those of most other countries, not least the Anglo-American ones. In England, the story of parliamentary democracy is the story of successful gentry resistance to the Crown in the name of defending and preserving the "ancient English liberties." In France and Germany, "civil society" and the "public sphere," as Reinhart Koselleck and Jürgen Habermas have shown, formed as a response to absolutism, as a free social space for (critical) moral and increasingly political discourse (Habermas 1989; Koselleck 1988). The institutions of bourgeois civil society—at first secret or semi-legal societies, later officially sanctioned, if still feared, by the state—became the locus for social and political utopianism as well as for the production and dissemination of public opinion, and came to serve as a powerful, "fourth estate."

In Sweden, on the other hand, the ethos of modern democracy is informed by the legacy of the unique position of the Swedish peasantry. Because the Swedish peasantry largely escaped feudalism and even retained its rights to be represented as a separate estate in the *Riksdag*, it could play a role unparalleled elsewhere. In particular, it allowed for an enduring alliance between the quasi-absolute monarchy and the peasant estate against their common enemy, the nobility. Thus the Swedish gentlemanly class never came to play the same leading role that it took elsewhere in Western Europe. The consequence was that the Swedish political culture came to be cast in a mold very different from that of other Western democracies. Far from generalizing noble or bourgeois privilege, the organizing principle was that of leveling, of eliminating rather than extending privileges and special rights. Ultimately it was a process of universalizing the egalitarianism of the peasant community, of reducing noble and bourgeois "rights" until there were but "peasants"—"the people"—left. If in the West the ideal type was the honorable gentleman, in Sweden it was the modest peasant (Zaremba 1987).

It was the luck and, some would claim, the political genius of the Swedish Social Democrats to be able to tap into this potent tradition, half-myth, half institutional reality, during the high age of statist nationalism after the First World War. Thus, during the famous "deals" between the peasants' and workers' parties during the early 1930s, the Social Democrats managed to shoulder the mantles of monarchical statism and peasant populism at once by becoming, on the one hand, the party of the state, and on the other, the voice of the people's movements. The time-honored tradition of seeing the king/state as an ally against the upper classes mutated and deepened with the democratization of the political system and the rise to power of the workers' and peasants' parties. Instead of seeing "civil society" as the crucial repository of freedom and protection against the power of the state, the state was seen as having a legitimate and decisive role to play in eradicating inequalities and the remaining privileges of the upper classes.

Swedish political culture can thus be said to be democratic rather than liberal. It is characterized by centralized power and uniformity as well as by an ancient tradition of inclusive, participatory democracy. It offers the peasant communes' broadly defined access to the democratic process even as it places rather narrow limits on the possibility of diverging from the communal consensus. In sharp contrast to Continental Europe, the social contract on which the welfare state was built is one between the individual and the state at the expense of the intermediary institutions of civil society, such as the family, the churches, and private and voluntary charity organizations. The latter are associated not with pluralism and freedom, but with demeaning private charity, unequal patriarchal relations, and informal (ab)uses of power. In Sweden the state is conceived as the liberator of the individual from such ties of dependency, an order of things I have termed "statist individualism" (Berggren and Trägårdh 2006; Trägårdh 1997).

In other words, "freedom" has in Scandinavia come to be extremely "positive" rather than "negative," and it is hardly surprising that a liberal critic like Maciej Zaremba has been able to argue convincingly that Sweden is dramatically lacking in the area of civil and individual rights (Zaremba 1992). The state-individual alliance has allowed for relatively equal positive freedoms—"social rights"—at the expense of individual liberty and free choice. Indeed, if we want to define Swedish political culture in terms of broader intellectual currents, it is Rousseau and the notion of general will, rather than Montesquieu's notion of separate powers, or Locke's liberal suspicion of excessive state power, that proves enlightening. Turning to the *Social Contract* one finds a passage from Rousseau that in many ways could serve as the motto for at least the Swedish welfare state:

> The second relation is that of the members of the body politic among themselves, or of each with the entire body: their relations among themselves should be as limited, and relations with the entire body as extensive, as possible, in order that each citizen shall be at the same time perfectly independent of all his fellow citizens and excessively dependent on the republic—this result is always achieved by the same means, since it is the power of the state alone which makes the freedom of its members (Rousseau 1968: 99).

While this position is one that tends to alarm readers of a more liberal bent, and partly for good reason, it is for many Swedes, as indeed it was for Rousseau, part and parcel of an outlook that holds the informal and unchecked power of families, churches, and charities to be a much greater evil than the formal, distant, and politically controllable power of the state (Trägårdh 1997). As one defender of the Swedish welfare state has noted:

> Few welfare states are as consistently based on the idea of individual autonomy as is the Swedish. Virtually all of our welfare programs are tied to the individual person, not to the family or to the job as is the norm in other Western countries.… the struggle for full employment … follows the principle that each person should have power over his or her own life.… The delivery of welfare services through the public sector rather than within the family has constituted a process of emancipation … the pressure on the family has decreased … The dependency on other family members has diminished as the performance of many, often instrumental tasks have been placed outside the family domain (Antman 1994: 24).

This perspective has prominently informed Social Democratic gender policy in Sweden, where the autonomy of women in relationship to men has been gained largely through the provision of day care, on the one hand, and the encouragement of female participation the labor market, on the other. Thus, in so far as Swedish national identity is tightly linked to the welfare state, the emphasis should be equally on "welfare" and the "state." A decoupling of nation and state would appear to be wholly foreign to the Swedish political tradition; indeed it would be hard even to formulate in intelligible terms. As critics of Swedish "statism" like to point out: in Swedish the terms nation, state and society are virtually synonymous. This must be understood against concepts like subsidiarity and federalism that are so central to the Christian-democratic model for the EU, a model fundamentally based on precisely the separation between the (cultural) nation, the (civil) society, and the (political-economical) state.

Until quite recently, Sweden was missing the kind of critique of the state that has become common among leading leftist thinkers on the continent and in Great Britain who are not only wary of any talk of "healthy" nationalism,[14] but who also tend to view statism, in Habermasian terms, as the "colonization" of civil society by the state. Not so in Sweden, where it has been the "bourgeois" parties on the right along with the conservative-libertarian think tank Timbro who have tried to mobilize the rhetoric of "civil society" in an attempt to associate the Swedish welfare state with the totalitarian regimes to the East and the dangers of excessive state power and Big Government. Conversely, left-wing opposition to the EU is rooted in both worries about there being no egalitarian, democratic tradition of the Scandinavian variety in Europe south of Denmark, and in a concern that harmonization of social policies will spell the end of Swedish-style statist individualism in favor of the dreaded Christian-democratic alternative, returning the individual to the care and capriciousness of civil society.

This is a conception of civil society that does not, however, negate the importance of organizations and associations at large. As we have seen, even those who take a statist position tend to celebrate the tradition of social movements as well as the longstanding practice of inviting and involving organizations in the long process of turning a proposal into a law or policy. However, two concluding points need to be made about both the character of these associations and their relationship to the state. As other chapters in this book make clear, comparative data show that while Swedes are active as association members, they tend to flock to associations of a type different from what is the case in other countries, such as the US. Unions, clubs that cater to sports and leisure, as well as associations that focus on culture tend to attract the largest number of members, whereas religious institutions, charities, and social welfare do not figure as prominently (see chapters by Amnå, Baer, and Jeppson Grassman and Svedberg). Furthermore, the organizations are not seen to occupy an oppositional position in relation to the state, but rather have been viewed as an intrinsic part of a broader democratic structure, exhibiting democratic practices internally and linking up to the national democratic structure externally. This again suggests that the ideal-typical vision of the relationship between state and society is much closer to the Hegelian than the Anglo-American conception of the state–civil society dynamic. The lack of hostility towards the state in Sweden turns on the idea that the state is less a threat than it is a vehicle for emancipation from the point of view of the individual citizen. I will return to this matter in the final chapter of this book, when I discuss the parliamentary commissions and argue that they can be viewed as the linchpin in the system that links the state to the organizations in civil society.

Notes

1. This account builds on previous attempts to sketch this history (Trägårdh 1995, 1999). Also see the recent chapters by Erik Amnå and Lars Svedberg in Amnå (2005).
2. Neuhaus, who began his career as a Lutheran pastor fighting against the Vietnam War, later converted to be become a Catholic priest, in the meantime emerged as a key advisor to President George W. Bush and his top adviser, Karl Rove. In this capacity Neuhaus has advanced the role of religion in public affairs and assisted Bush in promoting what they both call a "culture of life." Bush for his part has stressed the role to be played by "faith-based institutions" when it comes to social services, education, and even foreign aid.
3. Although, as Bo Rothstein has pointed out, this gesture of goodwill toward the welfare state was relegated to a footnote (Rothstein 1994).
4. These articles were collected in a book soon after the last of the four debates was over; see Antman (1993).
5. See also Dahlkvist (1995) for analysis of this fundamental mutation in civil society theory, which also takes the form of a sharp critique of the concept as such in Sweden at that time, i.e. 1994.
6. For an account of the history of ideological shifts in SSU, see Håkan A. Bengtsson 1992.
7. I have taken this reference to the Swedish Government's statement from Amnå (2005, 20).
8. In Swedish, it has been designated as it own *område* (area) with a *områdesgrupp* (area group) created to inventory existing research and identify areas of potential future interest, and stimulate new research.
9. For a discussion of the literature, including both the labor movement and the religious groups, see Vetenskapsrådet 2003, 165ff. Also see Amnå 2005 for a useful discussion of the development of research into the civil society sector.
10. One scholar who early on used the concept of civil society was Michele Micheletti, an American political scientist who moved to Sweden in 1975. However, while using the concept she by and large operated within the tradition of classical research into the popular movements and the question of corporatism (Micheletti 1994).
11. Blennberger, personal communication. Also see Blennberger 1993 for an early discussion of emerging conceptual categories that could be used to capture the new object for study.
12. See also Busch Zetterberg 1996.

13. The concept *Folkstat*, i.e. "people's state" was used by leading Social Democrats in Sweden, influenced by the Germans, before it was replaced by the "warmer," more communitarian notion of *folkhem*.
14. This is not to say that Swedish leftists are particularly comfortable with being branded as nationalists. Indeed, the nationalism of the Swedish left is largely unspoken, even invisible, hidden behind a discourse on the welfare state, *folkhemmet*, solidarity, equality, etc.

References

Amnå, Erik. 1995a. *Handlingsprogram för forskning: Ideell verksamhet, förutsättningar, organisering och betydelse.* DS 1995: 20.
———. 2005. *Civilsamhället: Några forskningsfrågor.* Stockholm: Gidlunds.
Amnå, Erik, ed. 1995b. Medmänsklighet att hyra? Åtta forskare om ideell verksamhet. Örebro: Libris.
Antman, Peter, ed. 1993. *Systemskifte.* Stockholm: Carlssons.
Antman, Peter. 1994. "Inte utan jämlikhet" i Peter Antman och Karl-Petter Thorwaldsson, *Hur förena jämlikhet med individens frihet.* Stockholm: Utbildningsförlaget Brevskolan.
Aronsson, Peter. 1992. *Bönder gör politik.* Lund: Lund University Press.
Arvidsson, Håkan, and Lennart Berntson. 1980. *Makten, Socialismen och Demokratin: Om det förstatligade samhället.* Lund: Zenit.
Arvidsson, Håkan, Lennart Berntson et al. 1990. *Det civila samhället.* Stockholm: Timbro.
Arvidsson, Håkan, Lennart Berntson, and Lars Dencik. 1994. *Modernisering och välfärd.* Stockholm: City University Press.
Bellah, Robert, et al. 1985. *Habits of the Heart.* Berkeley: University of California Press.
Bellah, Robert, et al. 1991. *The Good Society.* New York: Knopf.
Bengtsson, Håkan. 1992. *Vägval: Idéutvecklingen i SSU.* Stockholm: SSU.
Berger, Peter, and Richard John Neuhaus. 1977. *To Empower People: The Role of Mediating Structures in Public Policy.* Washington, DC: American Enterprise Institute.
———. 1996. *To Empower People: From State to Civil Society.* Washington: American Enterprise Institute.
Berggren, Henrik, and Lars Trägårdh. 2006. *Är svensken människa? Oberoende och gemenskap i det moderna Sverige.* Stockholm: Norstedts.
Blennberger, Erik. 1993. "Begrepp och modeller." In *Frivilligt socialt arbete. Kartläggning och kunskapsöversikt.* SOU 1993: 82.
Busch Zetterberg, Karin. 1996. *Det civila samhället i socialstaten.* Stockholm: City University Press.
Cohen, Jean, and Andrew Arato. 1992. *Civil Society and Political Theory.* Cambridge, Mass: Harvard University Press.
Coleman, James. 1988. "Social Capital in the Creation of Human Capital." *American Journal of Sociology* 94.
———. 1990. *Foundations of Social Theory.* Cambridge: Belknap.

Dahlkvist, Mats. 1995. "'Det civila samhället' i samhällsteori och sam-hällssdebatt. En kritisk analys" in *Civilt samhälle kontra offentlig sektor*, ed. Lars Trägårdh. Stockholm: SNS.

Djilas, Milovan. 1957. *Den nya klassen.*

Eneroth, Tomas, and Jan Olsson. 1993. *Egenmakt och social ekonomi.* Stockholm: SSU och KOOPI.

Etzioni, Amitai. 1993. *The Spirit of Community. Rights, Responsibilities and the Communitarian Agenda.* New York: Crown Publishers Inc.

Fukuyama, Francis. 1992. *The End of History and the Last Man.* New York: Free Press.

———. 1995. *Trust: The Social Virtues and the Creation of Prosperity.* New York: Free Press.

Gittell, M. 2001. "Empowerment Zones: An Opportunity Missed: a six-city comparative study." New York: The Howard Samuels State Management and Policy Center, The Graduate School and the University Center of the City University of New York.

Habermas, Jürgen. 1989. *The Structural Transformation of the Public Sphere.* Cambridge, Mass: MIT Press.

———. 1996. *Between Facts and Norms: Contributions to a Discourse Theory of Law and Democracy.* London: Polity.

Havel, Václav. 1988. "Anti-Political Politics" in John Keane (ed.) *Civil Society and the State.* London: Verso.

Hegel, G.W.F. 1991. *Elements of the Philosophy of Right*, ed. Allen W. Wood. Cambridge: Cambridge University Press.

Jeppsson Grassman, Eva, and Lars Svedberg. 1993. "Frivillig verksamhet på fältet – en närstudie av sju organisationer." In *Frivilligt socialt arbete – Kartläggning och kunskapsöversikt.* SOU 193: 82

———. 1995. "Frivilligt socialt arbete i Sverige – både mer och mindre." In *Medmänsklighet att hyra? Åtta forskare om ideell verksamhet*, ed. Erik Amnå. Örebro: Libris.

———. 1999. "Medborgarskapets gestaltningar. Insatser i och utanför föreningslivet." In *Civilsamhället*, ed. Erik Amnå. SOU 1999: 84.

Karlson, Nils. 1990. "Det goda samhället." In *Det civila samhället*, Håkan Arvidsson, Lennart Berntson et al.. Stockholm: Timbro.

Keane, John. 1988. *Democracy and Civil Society.* London: Verso.

Keane, John, ed. 1988. *Civil Society and the State.* London: Verso.

Koselleck, Reinhart. 1988. *Critique and Crisis.* Cambridge, Mass: MIT Press.

Lasch, Christopher. 1991. *The True and Only Heaven: Progress and Its Critics.* New York: Norton.

Lidskog, Rolf. 1995. "Sociologins objekt eller politikens begrepp? Reflektioner kring begreppet civilt samhälle." Sociologisk forskning 1: 31–54.

Linder, P. J. Anders. 1988. *Demokratins små plattformar.* Stockholm: Timbro.

Lundström, Tommy, and Filip Wijkström. 1997. *The Nonprofit Sector in Sweden.* Johns Hopkins Nonprofit Series 11. Manchester and New York: Manchester University Press.

Maktutredningen. 1990. *Demokrati och makt i Sverige: Maktutredningens huvudrapport.* SOU 19990: 44.

Michelletti, Michele. 1994. *Det civila samhället och staten.* Stockholm: Fritzes.

Moderata samlingspartiet. 1990. *Idéer för vår framtid*. Stockholm : Moderata samlingspartiet.

Murray, Charles. 1984. *Losing Ground: American Social Policy 1950–1980*. New York: Basic Books.

Östberg, Kjell. 2002. *1968 när allting var i rörelse: sextiotalsradikaliseringen och de sociala rörelserna*. Stockholm: Prisma.

Petersson, Olof, Anders Westholm, and Göran Blomberg. 1989. *Medborgarnas Makt*. Stockholm: Carlssons.

Petersson, Olof, Jörgen Hermansson, Michele Micheletti, Jan Teorell and Anders Westholm. 1998. *Demokrati och medborgarskap*. Stockholm: SNS.

Pocock, J.G.A. 1975. *The Machiavellian Moment*. Princeton: Princeton University Press.

Putnam, Robert. 1993. *Making Democracy Work: Civic Traditions in Modern Italy*. Princeton: Princeton University Press.

———. 1995. "Bowling Alone: America's Declining Social Capital. *Journal of Democracy*, vol 6, no 1.

———. 2000. Bowling Alone. The Collapse and Revival of American Community. New York: Simon & Schuster.

Putnam, Robert, ed. 2002. *Democracies in Flux? The Evolution of Social Capital in Contemporary Society*. Oxford: Oxford University Press.

Rothstein, Bo. 1994. *Vad bör staten göra?* Stockholm: SNS.

———. 1995. "Svensk välfärdspolitik och det civila samhället." In *Civilt samhälle kontra offentlig sekton*, ed. Lars Trägårdh. Stockholm: SNS.

———. 1998. "Social Capital in the Social Democratic State: the Swedish Model and Civil Society" forthcoming in Robert Putnam (ed) *A decline of Social Capital? Political Culture as a Precondition for Democracy*. Under publicering.

———. 2002. "Sweden: Social Capital in the Social Democratic State." In *Democracies in Flux? The Evolution of Social Capital in Contemporary Society*, ed. Robert Putnam. Oxford: Oxford University Press.

Rousseau, Jean-Jacques. 1968. *The Social Contract*. New York: Penguin

SOU 1993: 82. *Frivilligt socialt arbete. Kartläggning och kunskapsöversikt.*

Salomon, Kim. 1996. *Rebeller i takt med tiden: FNL-rörelsen och 60-talets politiska ritualer*. Stockholm: Rabén Prisma.

Seligman, Adam. 1992. *The Idea of Civil Society*. New York: Free Press.

———. 1997. *The Problem of Trust*. Princeton: Princeton University Press.

Somers, Margaret. 1995a. "What's Political or Cultural about Political Culture and the Public Sphere? Toward a Historical Sociology of Concept Formation." *Sociological Theory* 13, no. 2: 113–144.

——— 1995b. "Narrating and Naturalizing Civil Society and Citizenship Theory: The Place of Political Culture and the Public Sphere." *Sociological Theory* 13, no. 3: 229–274.

Sommestad, Lena. 1995. "Civilsamhället: En utopi för medelklassens män?" In *Civilt samhälle kontra offentlig sekton*, ed. Lars Trägårdh. Stockholm: SNS.

Thorwaldsson, Karl-Petter. 1994. "Att bryta vanmakten" i Peter Antman och Karl-Petter Thorwaldsson, *Hur förena jämlikhet med individens frihet*. Stockholm: Utbildningsförlaget Brevskolan.

Trägårdh, Lars. 1997. "Statist Individualism: On the Culturality of the Nordic Welfare State" i Øystein Sørensen och Bo Stråth, *The Cultural Construction of Norden*. Oslo: Scandinavian University Press.

―――. 1999. "Det civila samhället som analytiskt begrepp och politisk slogan." In *Civilsamhället*, ed. Erik Amnå. SOU 1999: 84.

―――. 2000. Empowerment och egenmakt. Stockholm: Timbro.

―――. 2002. "Welfare State Nationalism: Sweden and the Spectre of 'Europe'." In *European Integration and National Identity: The Challenge of the Nordic States*, ed. Lene Hansen and Ole Wæver. London and New York: Routledge.

Trägårdh, Lars, ed. 1995. *Civilt samhälle kontra offentlig sektor.* Stockholm: SNS.

Vajda, Mihály. 1978. "The State and Socialism." *Social Research* 45, no. 4.

Vetenskapsrådet. 2003. *Svensk forskning om demokrati, offentlig förvaltning och folkrörelser.* Stockholm: Vetenskapsrådet.

Walzer, Michael. 1991. "The idea of Civil Society." *Dissent* (Spring).

Wijkström, Filip, and Tommy Lundström. 2003. *Den ideella sektorn.* Stockholm: Sober förlag.

Wolfe, Alan. 1989. *Whose Keeper? Social Science and Moral Obligation.* Berkeley: University of California Press.

Wood, Allen W. 1991. "Editor's Introduction." In *Elements of the Philosophy of Right*, Hegel, G.W.F., ed. Allen W. Wood. Cambridge: Cambridge University Press.

Zaremba, Maciej. 1987. "Byalagets diskreta charm eller folkhemmets demokratiuppfattning." In *Du sköna gamla värld*, ed. Sekretariatet för framtidsstudier. Stockholm: Liber Förlag.

Zaremba, Maciej. 1992. *Minken i folkhemmet.* Stockholm: Timbro.

Zetterberg, Hans. 1992. *Den svenska socialstaten – ett forskningsprojekt.* Stockholm: City University Press.

Zetterberg, Hans. 1993. "Var tid har sina reaktionärer" i Peter Antman (red), *Systemskifte*. Stockholm: Carlssons.

Zetterberg, Hans. 1995. "Civila samhället, demokratin och välfärdsstaten." In *Civilt samhälle kontra offentlig sekton*, ed. Lars Trägårdh. Stockholm: SNS.

Zetterberg, Hans, and Carl Johan Ljungberg. 1997. *Vårt land – den svenska socialstaten.* Stockholm: City University Press.

Chapter 2

CIVIL SOCIETY AND GLOBALIZATION: RETHINKING THE CATEGORIES

Jean L. Cohen

The discourse of civil society has "gone global." Now one of the most widely utilized concepts by politicians, academics, and political activists around the world, "civil society" is invoked to describe everything from civic initiatives, voluntary associations, and nonprofit organizations to global networks, NGOs, human rights groups, and transnational social movements. Indeed, the idea of a transnational or global civil society has become the twenty-first century's key contribution to civil society talk. As in the past, this discourse for the most part construes civil society both as the key to democracy and democratization and as *the* source of social solidarity and social integration (Arato 2000; Cohen and Arato 1992; Cohen 1999b; Putnam 1993, 2000). However, the new context in which civil society talk has exploded, and the target of democratization and integration, is no longer the state, but rather the emergent global order.

The reason for this shift is obvious: processes of globalization are seen as undermining the capacity of states to exercise the crucial functions of control and regulation over economic and social developments. States seem to be adapting to rather than shaping economic and market imperatives. Economic globalization, which includes the staggering expansion of trade, accelerated capital flows, increasingly autonomous financial networks, and the enormous power of transnational corporations, based of course on the new electronic technologies of communication, seems to replace the "rulers of territory" by the "masters of speed" (Habermas 2001: 67).

Other developments associated with globalization also tend to diminish the importance of the state and hence national political society's relevance as a referent or target of influence for civil actors. The transnational character of "risks"—ranging from ecological and environmental problems (nuclear accidents, acid rain), health issues (AIDS, SARS), and transnational criminal organizations trafficking in drugs, sex, and arms to burgeoning immigration-cum-refugee crises, global terrorism, and unilateral military and imperial projects—highlights the vulnerability of the modern nation-state and its lack of control over its own territory, borders, resident population, as well as the internal hazards that threatens its citizens. Indeed, the boundary between the domestic and transnational spheres seems to be evaporating, placing the sovereignty of the state in doubt (Cohen 1999; Sassen 1996; Strange 1996).

Meanwhile there is the notable emergence of a variety of supranational institutions engaged in regulation and rule making, like the IMF, World Bank, WTO, and EU, as well as a plethora of private global authorities such as standards and trade associations (Cutler 2001; Rosenau 1997, 1998; Teubner 1997). This multiplication of the sources of law above the state level, and the apparent uncoupling of law from the territorial state, suggests that the latter has lost legal as well as political sovereignty. The new forms of governance, however, are not democratically structured, being neither accountable to nor representative of any citizenry or demos. In short, the democratic, constitutional, sovereign nation-state no longer seems to make the only legitimate, collectively binding decisions that matter; elected legislatures no longer monopolize or hierarchize the creation of law; national courts or parliaments are no longer supreme in the legal hierarchy; territorial and political/legal sovereignty have become uncoupled; and sovereignty itself has become disaggregated, shared, and complex (Cutler 2001; Haufler and Porter 1999; Jayasuriya 2001). But the structures that do wield power, make binding decisions, create effective law, and engage in regulation are imbued with a managerial ethos: they cannot claim to be internally democratic, transparent, or accountable.[1] The terminological shift from the concept of government to governance captures this state of affairs (Hirst and Thompson 1996; Rosenau 1998).[2]

Small wonder that democratic theorists have placed their hopes once more on civil society to generate solidarity, publicize problems, and democratize the emergent global order. Civil society on the global level supposedly can make up for the democratic deficit in the new global order.[3] However, the meaning of civil society it is often unclear, as are the ways it can play these roles in this new context. In some accounts, empirical descriptions of transnational organizations, movements, and networks are fused with normative theories of an emergent global civil society as the potential site for global democracy, construed as the functional equivalent of the national state (Held 1995; Kaldor 1999). Global civil society, it is alleged, steps in where states can no longer tread, providing new sources of identity, solidarity, coordination, regulation, and control (Linklater 1999; Pasha and Blaney 1999). In other accounts, a transnational civil society composed of networks, NGOs and movement actors is construed more as a key vehicle than as a site for democratizing global and local governance. In this approach, civil society is seen as a source of democratic and liberal norms or moral principles that inform, orient, or constrain other actors, institutions, and power holders (Falk 2000; Kaldor 1999; Thoma 2001).

Thirdly, there are the managerial models of the dispersion and dissolution of powers of governance into institutions in "civil society" as well as the economy. From this perspective, "civil society" refers to the enforcement role of private agencies and organizations mobilized to monitor compliance with rules and/or to carry out functions of governance articulated on multiple levels (Jayasuriya 2001: 457). If such governance abandons the statist command and control approach to regulation in favor of adaptive learning, experimentation, and collaboration with relevant nonmanagerial groups, "civil society" allegedly fosters innovation and inclusion (Dorf and Sabel 1998; Sirianni and Friedland 2001: 23). In my view, the latter of course is hardly equivalent to democratization or critique: indeed this "civil society" approach could be seen as a cover for the privatization of formerly public mechanisms of regulation and policing. In the light cast by managerial models, the global civil society project looks like "pie in the sky," while the international norm-generating model seems too weak and amorphous to sanction powerful actors and too prone to become an ideology justifying very uncivil actions, instead of a means of even indirect control.[4]

This is the catch: Without a map to guide us between these conflicting discourses and models of civil society, we risk developing a naive optimism or becoming downright ideological about the democratizing capacity, nature, and global role of civil society. What is missing is a careful, systematic reflection on the ways in which globalization has transformed the key parameters of civil society and how such changes affect the potential impact of civil society on national, regional, and transnational structures. Without careful reflection, one will not be able to perceive what is new or what is possible. The risk is that the concept of civil society will become overburdened, saddled with tasks of regulation and/ or democratization that it cannot possibly fulfill.

This chapter intends to provide just such a reflection. I will first describe the concept of civil society that evolved in the context of the national state. I will then present a conception of the key parameters of my version, developed with Andrew Arato, of what has today become an "essentially contested concept" (Cohen and Arato 1992). I then turn to the issue of how these parameters must be rethought in the context of globalization. I want in particular to assess the chance of "globalizing" civil societies to help foster rights, democracy, and social justice in the contemporary context while avoiding the trap of the domestic analogy.

One caveat: I do not subscribe to the "strong" globalization thesis that has relegated the national state to the dustbin of history. I prefer a "weak" understanding of globalization, one that still ascribes to the state important aspects of sovereignty, and that still sees national political society as a crucial referent for civil actors. However, state sovereignty is partially disaggregated, with elements pushed upward toward regional, international, and/or global bodies and downward toward private and local actors. In short, there are additional layers of important political and legal institutions independent from the state, but these supplement, rather than replace, the national state.

The Concept of Civil Society in the Context of the "Sovereign" State

I understand civil society as a sphere of social interaction differentiated from the economy and the state, and composed of three analytically distinct parameters—plurality, publicity, and privacy. Modern "autonomous" civil society is created through processes of self-constitution and self-mobilization. It is institutionalized and generalized through laws and sets of subjective rights, which in turn stabilize social differentiation. It is thus important to stress that the emergence of civil society goes hand in hand with the development of the modern territorial sovereign state.

In other words, it was the coupling of law and the state and the development of internal legal sovereignty and constituitonalism that allowed for the emergence of the three-part model. Constitutionalism and representative government, i.e. the emergence of a responsive and accountable political society (parties) and an autonomous legal society (jurists, courts) became the sine qua non for the modern state's stabilized differentiation from both civil society and the market economy. Recognition by "international society" as a sovereign state in a system of states was of course also crucial: internal sovereignty went hand in hand with external sovereignty, although it is also true that the development of civil society did not depend on full "Westphalian" external sovereignty being ascribed to a state (Krassner 1999; Sorensen 1999).

The key nineteenth-century theorists of civil society understood the three parameters mentioned above in a particular way (Cohen 1999b; Cohen and Arato 1992). *Plurality* meant voluntary association involving face-to-face interactions and national organizations built upon the initiatives of such local groups. *Publicity* involved civil publics gathering in such "public" spaces as the coffeehouses, taverns, clubs, parks, libraries, lodges, and town halls to articulate common concerns, and their interconnection through the mass media of communication of the time, namely print. *Privacy* referred to the personal autonomy ascribed to the individual, institutionalized by sets of rights, ranging from habeas corpus and due process to the privacies of home and marriage, freedom of conscience, and market freedoms.[5] Higher law, in the sense of the overall set of constitutionalized subjective rights guaranteeing the structure of personal and public autonomy as well as the differentiation of civil society from the state and the economy, secures the institutionalization of civil society (Habermas 1996). The constitutionalization of the state thus entailed the self-limitation of the polity vis-à-vis civil society, thereby protecting civil society against being swampied by the state via overpoliticization. In other words, rights constitutionalize the differentiation of civil society (with its informal organizations, internal plurality, and civil publics), from the state's political and administrative systems, which are oriented to making collectively binding decisions and organized by the power medium.

A legal system (including the police) oriented by rule-of-law principles and a legal culture committing practitioners to the norms of impartiality are crucial to the process by which the particularistic projects of associated, communicating individuals within civil society are able to become informed by, and be made compatible with, the universalistic principles of modern constitutional democracies (Cohen 1999b: 212–214; Cohen and Arato 1992: 1–117). They are also crucial to the generalization of social trust.

These three dimensions of civil society were construed by earlier theorists to have a reciprocal relationship to the institutionalized political publics of the political and legal system (parliaments and courts) mediated by organizations of "political society" (parties) and legal society (lawyers and jurists generally), that are oriented to the acquisition and exercise of power and the making of society-wide binding collective decisions. A relationship combining influence—coming from civil society to the political system via political society—with mediation—flowing from representative organizations (parties engaged in formation of collective will and interest aggregation) and representative bodies (parliaments engaged in legislative will formation)—was central to this overall conception.

As I have pointed out elsewhere, twentieth-century European analysts of civil society added three crucial components to this understanding (Cohen and Arato 1992: 1–117). The first, stressed by Gramsci, was an emphasis on the cultural and symbolic dimension of civil society and the role it plays in generating consent (hegemony) and hence, in integrating society (Anderson 1977: 5–78; Cohen and Arato 1992: 142–159; Gramsci 1971: 206–277). His key contribution was to see civil society as both a symbolic field and a set of institutions and practices that are the locus for the formation of values, action-orienting norms, meanings, and collective identities. Accordingly, the cultural dimension of civil society is not given or natural; rather, it is a site of social contestation: its associations and networks are a terrain to be struggled over, and an arena wherein collective identities, ethical values, and alliances are forged. Indeed, competing conceptions of civil society are deployed in a continual struggle that pits dominant groups striving to maintain cultural hegemony against subordinate collective actors fighting for counter-hegemony. Thus no conception of civil society, including Gramsci's own, is neutral; any such idea is always part of a project to shape the social relations, cultural forms, and modes of thought of society.

The second major contribution, made by Touraine, Melucci, and others, was to emphasize the dynamic, creative, and contestatory side of civil society—informal associations and social movements as distinct from the more formalized voluntary associations and institutions and from class organizations (parties, unions) (Cohen and Arato 1992: 492–564; Melucci 1980, 1985; Touraine 1981). Recognition of this dimension allows one to articulate and shift between two perspectives: civil society as a dynamic, innovative source for thematizing new concerns, articulating new projects, and generating new values and new collective identities; and civil society as institutionalized civic autonomy. It also allows one to see how in its dynamic capacity (collective action), the institutional shape of civil society as well as the polity can be targeted in struggles over democratization. Thus the key twentieth century addition to the conceptualization of societal plurality was the stress on *social movements* as an important source of innovation, experimentation, and civic participation, which have an important signaling function for the political system in that they foster awareness of new issues and problems.

The other key contribution I have in mind is the deliberative conception of the public sphere developed primarily by Jürgen Habermas and his followers (Calhoun 1992; Cohen and Arato 1992; Habermas 1989). The category of the public sphere was already present in earlier understandings of civil society, but its role in mediating between the particular and the general was not clarified until relatively recently. In civil publics people can discuss matters of mutual concern as peers, learning about facts, events, and the opinions, interests, and perspectives of others. Discourse on values, norms, laws, and policies generates politically relevant public opinion. Moreover, through its generalized media of communication—in the first two thirds of the twentieth century these were print, radio, and TV—the public sphere can mediate among the myriad minipublics that emerge within and across associations, movements, religious organizations, clubs, local organizations of concerned citizens, and simple socializing.

There are, of course, differentiated and institutionalized civil and political publics, weak and strong.[6] In any liberal-democratic conception, however, discursively generated public opinion is meant to influence the debates within decisional political and legal publics proper (legislatures, constitutional courts) and to bring under informal control the actions and decisions of rulers and lawmakers, in conformance with the principle of responsiveness. Openness of access and parity of participation (equal voice) is the regulative ideal underlying every institutional arrangement claiming democratic legitimacy. All citizens subject to the law should have the right to participate, to articulate their views, and to try to exercise influence, and all participants should be able to do so on equal terms.[7] Together with democratic elections, this idea, in the twentieth century at least, involved a proceduralized conception of popular sovereignty: influence via communication and accountability via the electoral sanction are the mechanisms for insuring that representative government is representative (Cohen 2005; Habermas 1996: 462–490).

In my theoretical work with Arato on the concept of civil society, I attempted to account for and justify the tripartite conception inherited from the key nineteenth- and twentieth-century authors through reliance on the Habermasian distinction between system and life-world and its institutional implications (Cohen and Arato 1992). Accordingly the institutions and actors within the two subsystems that are coordinated through the media of power and money—the state and the capitalist market economy—are subject to a set of constraints that civil society actors do not face. In short, actors within these institutions are directly involved with state power and economic production, which they seek to control and manage. They cannot afford to subordinate strategic and instrumental criteria to the patterns of normative and social integration or the open-ended communication characteristic of civil society.

Thus, although we speak of "political society" and "economic society" as mediating between civil society and the state or economy respectively, and although these certainly involve publics within them—political parties, parliaments, labor unions, structures of collective bargaining and codetermination, etc.—they act under imperatives other than those of civil society institutions. Decisional publics in the state are under formal and temporal constraints (they must cut off debate at some point and decide). Economic publics in a corporation, no matter how much they discuss internal concerns and such things as social or environmental impact, cannot avoid the imperatives of profitability and productivity. Even as the legalization of trade unions, collective bargaining, codetermination, and so on attest to the development of economic society, the limits imposed by the effective use of power and money cannot be ignored. Civil society actors, by contrast, are not oriented to the conquest of state power or the organization of production but rather attempt to generate influence through the life of democratic associations, movements, and the media of the public sphere. Of course, this assumes that the institutions and organizations of political and economic society are receptive to the influence of civil society, i.e. that they establish "sensors" within the state and economy that make this possible. By sensors we mean institutionalized public spaces within the state and corporations respectively that are open to the input of relevant actors: the citizenry for the former, workers and employees, or more indirectly consumers, in the latter.

By construing communicative interaction rather than money or power as *the* coordinating mechanism of civil society, and by seeing communicative autonomy—the freedom of actors in society to articulate, criticize, and reaffirm norms, values, identities, and meanings through communicative interaction—as the defining feature of civil society we sought to highlight the critical potential of the latter regarding norms and projects, its ability to exert influence on political society, and the importance of protecting civil society from "colonization" by the media of money and power. A recent restatement of our position shows how this differs from the liberal understanding of civil society (Chambers 2002: 94), for the latter construes individual choice and voluntary association, rather than communicative interaction and autonomous civil publics, as the defining feature of civil society. To be sure, we also include voluntary association but as one among other parameters. But the liberal framework screens out the problem of colonization, whereby money or political instrumentalization overwhelm the character of civil society (Chambers 2002). It also screens out the democratizing role of civil actors: a role for which the public sphere of civil society, hardly conceivable as a voluntary association or understandable in terms of individual "choice," is crucial. It is the communicative interaction of civil actors—not their atomistically construed private choices—that is relevant here.[8]

Thus, as the opening sentence in our 1992 work stated, our model of civil society was meant as a contribution to democratic theory (Cohen and Arato 1992: vii). Indeed, we argued for shifting the core problematic of democratic theory to the issue of the channels of influence between civil and political society. Of course, our model also directed attention to the institutional makeup and internal articulation of civil society itself. We argued for the democratization of civil society (of, e.g., the family, associational life, and the public sphere) in the sense of rendering its core institutions more just, egalitarian, and open. Finally, our model aimed at a "reflexive continuation" of the welfare state, as against its replacement with neoliberal economics (Cohen and Arato 1992: 464–487).

We acknowledged the gravity of the neoconservative/neoliberal attack on the welfare state and the truth content of the left critique of the debilitating kinds of dependency and social fragmentation certain features of welfare systems created (colonization of the life-world). Nevertheless, we rejected the claim that state-mandated provision or procedures for conflict resolution (collective bargaining, codetermination, etc.) ipso facto undermine civil society's autonomy or associational spontaneity. By "reflexive continuation of the welfare state," we meant that alternatives to ineffective or destructive means used to foster growth can and should be found. In other words, the regulatory dilemmas caused by top-down command and control regulation by the state must be taken seriously, as must the fragmenting effect of certain kinds of interventions. To do so, however, one would have to disaggregate the term "welfare state" to see precisely which sorts of legal and administrative practices, regulations, provisions of "welfare," have which sorts of effects.

As already argued in 1992, provisions such as social security, health and unemployment insurance, job training programs, family supports such as day care or paid parental leave, and laws establishing collective bargaining and other procedures providing for participatory conflict resolution do not undermine civil society. Far from creating dependency and fragmentation, the procedural provisions help constitute economic society (civilizing the economy) and the substantive ones provide the basic preconditions for autonomy *and* solidarity within civil society. I also argued that other features, especially of the American welfare state, such as means-tested social policies and paternalistic quid pro quos like the "man-in the house" rule that predicates family assistance on the absence of an able-bodied male adult in the household, do, on the other hand, humiliate, fragment, and create dependencies. As Linda Gordon, Robert Lieberman, and later Bo Rothstein have shown, the core distinction is that between universal benefits and intrusive means-tested social policies. Gordon and Lieberman have revealed the gendered and race-based assumptions behind the means-tested provisions informing American welfare policy since the New Deal, while Rothstein has argued that it is the means-tested rather than universal social policies that "colonize" the lifeworld, fragment actors, and undermine social trust and social capital in civil society (Fraser and Gordon 1994, Lieberman 2001, Rothstein 2002). Thus sorting out which state regulations, benefits, and protections foster or undermine civil society and democracy is a complex issue.

In later work, Andrew Arato and I have each taken up the idea of a reflexive legal paradigm as a way to avoid the "regulatory tri-lemmas" that emerge when top-down state regulation occurs in areas to which it is unsuited.[9] Here too the idea is that state regulation is indispensable to a vital civil and economic society, but the issue is the form such regulation takes. Unlike the systems theorists from whom we borrow the term, we avoid evolutionism by arguing for a reflexive relationship to reflexive law itself. In other words, we argue that reflexive forms of legal regulation should replace the command and control approach to welfare state regulation in key areas but certainly not everywhere.[10] That we can choose among legal forms and types of "welfare interventions" in order to empower civil society, secure social justice, and protect against negative side effects is the point of the reflexive paradigm. There is, as it were, a *Wahlverwandtschaft* (affinity) between the civil society approach and the reflexive paradigm of law. Nevertheless, basic universalistic provisions by the state like universal health insurance or the idea of a basic minimum income cannot be and should not be replaced either by privatization or by reflexive law.

This fits with the claim that certain forms of relationship between the state and civil society are better than others from the perspective of the vitality of civil society itself. Rothstein's analysis of the "Swedish Model" makes this point. He shows that the relevant forms of "neocorporatism" that fostered vertical trust and self-limitation on the part of the social partners and the state, did not undermine horizontal trust crucial for civil association or for its emergence in a variety of spheres (Rothstein 2002). Government played an important facilitating role but it did not replace social actors with itself: it did not swamp economic society.[11] Apparently once the limits on the role of government were abandoned and the political system began to intervene more directly, the vertical trust built up in the earlier model evaporated. This had effects on horizontal trust, to use the Putnam lingo. This analysis seems to confirm the insights of the model of reflexive law and of the idea of the "reflexive continuation of the welfare state" as crucial for maintaining a vital civil society.

However, clearly the model developed by myself and Arato presupposed the sovereign state as a crucial referent and target, tacitly assuming that civil society and the state are coterminous. The individuals to whom plurality, publicity, privacy, subjective rights, and the protections of the rule of law (legality) are ascribed are tacitly assumed to be citizens of the state under whose jurisdiction and within whose territory they live. Their civic activity is oriented toward influencing, and rendering accountable, the political decisions made by their respective state. Citizens construed as authors and addressees of the law, subject to the same jurisdiction and rules, are presumed to share a certain community of fate. Citizenship was also seen as the basis for welfare state solidarity and social justice: "we" insist that "our" representatives make laws, policies, and regulations that provide the social basis for meaningful citizenship, for social justice and social solidarity.

Thus, while "civil society," unlike the nation-state, is *not* a membership organization, and while the parameters (and rights) of civil society need not be ascribed only to citizens, it is nevertheless true that in the modern conception of civil society that we theorized, this was nonetheless the underlying assumption. Accordingly, actors in civil society address and are the addressees of their state; associations are organized locally, regionally, and nationally, but not supra-nationally; and participation in public discourse, dissent, and critique is construed as part of a process of collective opinion and will formation of the citizenry (the popular sovereign) aimed at influencing the legislation and policy of "their" sovereign representative state. Indeed, an active and vigilant civil society, participating in these ways in addition to voting in periodic elections, is what makes government representative, democratic, and just (Manin 1997: 6, 161–193).

Despite important differences from ours, the competing conceptions of civil society that emerged in the last quarter of the twentieth century all shared the same presupposition, namely that the actors in a given civil society are the citizens of the sovereign state in whose territory they reside.[12] This is equally true of the liberal approach alluded to above and the neocommunitarian approach to civil society that focuses above all on reinforcing social integration and proper values through voluntary association (especially religious), volunteering, and self-help organizations, as it is of the neorepublican rational choice approach of the Putnam school concerned with the generation of trust, social capital, and civic virtue (construed as privileging public over private ends and the willingness/ability to cooperate).[13] Indeed, in the neo-Parsonian approach of Jeff Alexander, this tacit assumption becomes explicit. Alexander translates the concept of civil society into the structural-functionalist framework, equating it with the "societal community"—the sphere of social integration. He thus conceives of civil society as a membership organization, in short, as the nation—a bounded societal community coterminous with the state—characterized by trust, solidarity, and identity among members, as well as by distrust, lack of solidarity, and difference in relation to non-members. His work focuses on the dynamics of inclusion and exclusion within American civil society, so conceived. With this approach the elision of any difference between the concept of civil society and the nation as a bounded community of citizens of the sovereign state is finally accomplished.

Since I have subjected several of these models to critical scrutiny and described the differences between them and our own conception elsewhere, it is not necessary to rehearse these arguments here (Cohen and Arato 1992, Cohen 1999c). Let me simply note that I also disagree strongly with the neo-Parsonian approach because it is based on a category mistake: civil society is not conceptually equivalent to the nation or to the societal community, for it is not a bounded membership organization, not a totalized community (Cohen and Arato 1992: 118–142). Rather, the parameters of civil society and the concept itself are open-ended: none of the rights, activities, associational forms, or publics comprehended by them need be restricted to citizens or presuppose the sovereign state as the only political referent or target of civic action. It is true that even in our model, the tacit assumption was that the members of civil society associations are the citizenry of a particular state, which they target and whose laws and rights are reciprocally constituted by the communicative relations and complex interdependencies between them. However, this assumption is not inherent in our model but only articulates the historical form of civil society with which we were at the time preoccupied.

The Impact of Globalization on the Parameters of Civil Society

My claim is that our analysis of the parameters of civil society is abstract enough to permit other content and other institutionalizations of each dimension, which can apply to supra- as well as subnational levels. Let me now turn to the impact of globalization on the specific parameters of our original model. I do so, as already indicated, in order to avoid the pitfalls of the "domestic analogy," which would simply transpose an unchanged analysis of the parameters of a nationally oriented civil society to the global level, a serious mistake in my view. Rather I want to show that the transformation of the parameters of civil society in the contemporary context of globalization requires a decentered understanding of "globalized" civil society. I also want to assess the strengths and weaknesses of civil society actors vis-à-vis different subsystems of world society on the global level, i.e. regarding their role in fostering rights, democracy, and social justice. I will consider each parameter in turn.

Plurality

In our 1992 book, we construed the "new social movements" that emerged in the late 50s and early 60s, ranging from the civil rights movement to feminist, environmental, antiwar, consumer, and community organizing movements, as a new type of plurality and civic engagement paradigmatic of the twentieth century. All of them involved participation in myriad small-scale groups on the local level with face-to-face interaction (from consciousness-raising to self-help groups), the development of oppositional publics (newspapers, journals, radio stations, etc) and the more visible large-scale mobilizations that converged on Washington and other major cities. Our point was that these new forms of plurality indicate vitality in civil society, involving modes of civic engagement quite capable of generating social capital and quite important to projects of democratization. I believe the same analysis would apply throughout Western Europe for the respective period. However, these "new social movements" were locally and nationally but certainly not internationally organized, despite the fact that waves of protest occurred simultaneously all over the West in the 60s and 70s, and that the "new social movement" type emerged all over the globe.

The twenty-first century is seeing yet another shift in the form of plurality. Whether one thinks of the activists converging on the cities of Seattle and Genoa or of the protests in cities all over the world on 15 February 2003 against the war in Iraq, it is clear that the presence of actors from many parts of the globe in the first two, as well as the coordinated nature of collective actions in all three cases, means that plurality and potentials for organization have to be understood in new ways. The *transnational network* is the key innovation here. Transnational networks are becoming the paradigmatic form of civil society plurality (mode of association and solidarity) for the first part of the twenty-first century. I do not mean that older forms of plurality and movement organization have disappeared, but rather that a new form has emerged and another layer of "associational activity" has been added to the repertoire.

Much has been written on the concept of the network so I will only give a working definition here. According to Keck and Sikkink's study of activists beyond borders, a "network" consists of communicative structures in which differently situated actors participate in order to influence the public policy, discourses, norms, and decision-making procedures of powerful entities (Keck and Sikkink 1998). Typically networks are characterized by voluntary, reciprocal, horizontal patterns of communication and exchange. From a different perspective, they can also be seen as structures that develop an agency that is more than the sum of its parts (Keck and Sikkink 1998: 1–38). They certainly involve face-to-face interaction in local groups. Yet their communicative structures make use increasingly of the new electronic media, allow for the intertwining of "local" and nonlocal actors who connect and discuss in cyberspace through message exchanges instantly received and replied to. The Internet facilitates communicative interactions on a vastly expanded scale (global).

In my view, the transnational network is a new form of plurality that makes possible a new form of social connectedness, new forms of collective action and a more extensive "solidarity among strangers" than ever before. I am not referring to "collective action" or connectedness occurring exclusively on the Internet, such as an email campaign or chat room contacts.[14] Rather I refer to the combination of local groups interrelated via networks, and communicating in part via the new media. It is this combination that leads to a whole that is more than the sum of its parts.

Of course this position is contested. Some maintain that there have always been networks, and that there is no innovation here; others insist that we are confronting something radically new. In part, one's position on this issue is an artifact of the type of analysis one is using. Social network analysis finds the network to be among the oldest forms of social organization; technological analyses focusing on the use of the new media find networking to be radically new. Meanwhile organizational theories of networks lie somewhere in between, acknowledging that networks have existed in the past, yet allowing one to grasp the new without falling into a false evolutionism.[15] I prefer the latter approach as an improvement upon Keck and Sikkink's rather general definition provided, noted above.

Organizational theory differentiates the network form of organization from that of hierarchy and market exchanges. This has permitted three different types of network designs to be identified: the chain, the hub, and the all-channel net, which vary according to whether and how members may act autonomously, where leadership resides and/or is distributed, who can communicate with whom, and whether and how hierarchical dynamics may be mixed in with network dynamics. Moreover, there can be hybrids of the three basic designs as well as hybrids of network and hierarchy (Arquilla and Ronfeldt 2002: 325).

But organization is only one of five levels of analysis from which to examine the network form. What also matter to the strength of a network are its narrative, the doctrinal, the technological, and social levels. A network will be stronger if there is a story that convinces and integrates members, if there are collaborative strategies and methods backed up by a well-defined doctrine, if it can make use of advanced communications systems, and if it rests on strong personal and social ties at the base. Pace Putnam, even the global network form does not dispense with the associative dimension on the local level. If it does, it will prove ephemeral and rather weak.

It should be clear, however, that the narrative is not simply spin, but a real story that provides a convincing expression of peoples' experiences, interests, and values; that is, bringing to the fore and maintaining a sense of identity, a cause, a purpose or mission (Arquilla and Ronfeldt 2002: 328). New and old media are used for transmitting these narratives. On the doctrinal or strategic level, leaderlessness and the use of swarming strategies are the key innovations. This was especially effective in the Seattle confrontation with the WTO in 1999 (Arquilla and Ronfeldt 2002: chapter 7). While networks can operate without access to the Internet or other advanced technologies, the turn to the new technologies, especially by civil society activists at the end of the twentieth and the beginning of the twenty-first centuries, is noteworthy. It helps catalyze rapid spontaneous protests and it also helps publicize (see below) the desired image of the network's identity or goals. However, despite the importance of impersonal communications, personal relations of trust develop from "communities of practice" made up of local groups of people who know one another.

Contemporary transnational civil society activists make robust use of the cyber realm, globalizing local solidarities but vis-à-vis discrete issue areas, involving specific values and concerns: human rights networks evoke different solidarities, issues, and values from those of, say, environmentalist or feminist groups, or for that matter business networks. Thus the emerging multiplicity of globalized civil society networks address different "subsystems," not one single global civil society. Moreover, it cannot be stressed too much that the network form has also been adopted by the most uncivil of nonstate actors—transnational terrorist networks, transnational criminal networks, and the like. The network is thus a neutral form that can be used for manifold purposes.

I want to emphasize that the network form transcends national borders, constructs transnational civil society associations, and even straddles the line, in terms of participation, between civil and state actors. As Keck and Sikkink have argued, major actors can range from local social movements, foundations, international and domestic nongovernmental research and advocacy organizations (NGOs), parts of regional and international intergovernmental organizations, and even parts of the executive and/or parliamentary branches of government, as well as churches, consumer organizations, intellectuals, and trade unions (Keck and Sikkink 1998; Arquilla and Ronfeldt 2002: 9). To be sure, there have been transnational movements using networks in the past: the communist cell linked to the international communist movement is the most obvious example. The key difference in my view between these and the newer network form is the horizontal nature of the linkages and the flexibility of the latter compared with the hierarchical organizational structure and relative rigidity of the international ties characteristic of the former. Also key in the twenty-first century is the increasingly important role of the electronic media, as already indicated. Recall that a network is not a membership organization: while organizations may be components of networks, the word does not characterize their overall structure or the ties linking nodes to one another.

I do not want to deny the continuities between the network form and the structure of the 1960s type of "new social movement" or earlier transnational movements like pacifism. I simply want to indicate that the new technologies of communication make possible new forms of social connectedness and political contestation. The developing repertoire of new actions include "virtual marches," on-line petitions, and other such assemblages facilitated by the Internet, which allows linkages of like-minded local "groups" and extremely rapid, simultaneous mobilizations in a multiplicity of locales.

The influence they exercise is aimed at issue creation and agenda setting, and at securing their input on discursive positions of states and international organizations, on institutional procedures, and on policy change. The targeted entities may be states, international organizations, political bodies, or private organizations on local, regional, and transnational levels. Globalized networks participate in domestic and international politics simultaneously, shifting their focus and locus according to the matter at hand. Whatever the target—be it a state, the WTO, the UN, or a multinational corporation—the referent of such collective action is now something called "world public opinion." What does this mean and how does it work?

Publicity

It is obvious that new technologies of communication herald the arrival of new forms of publicity. The major recent technological innovations are the electronic media (the worldwide web e-mail, chat rooms), cable and satellite TV, and the 24-hour "global" news program. These technologies of communication are the terrain on which a new figure has emerged or is being constructed: "world public opinion" (Jaeger forthcoming). In describing the February 15 2003 anti-war protests, a *New York Times* reporter recently quipped that there are two superpowers in the twenty-first century: the US and world public opinion. This was meant as a jest. Yet there is something to it, for the key transformation of the public sphere in this century is indeed the shift from national to international and now to "world public opinion," made possible by the new media of communication mentioned above and evoked in the discourses of activists as well as political elites.

As in the case of the new forms of plurality, "world public opinion" is an additional layer and referent that does not replace national public opinion or the myriad small civil and counter-publics that crop up on local levels.

It is possible to theorize the porousness of partial and general publics vis-à-vis one another in two ways. Drawing on the insights of network analysis, one can see publics not only as enclaved within associations or specific milieus, but also as interstitial: as sets of communicative interactions that ease transitions between specific domains by decoupling actors from the pattern of particular relations and understandings embedded within any given public (White 1995, 1996). As such they serve crucial bridging functions between distinct network domains, allowing for "cross-cutting solidarities."

One can also draw on the concept of a more abstract, general civil public sphere of readers, listeners, viewers, and now cyber-communicators scattered throughout world society to articulate what it is that brings together the participants in partial publics and constitutes more generalized forums: i.e. the new mass media of communication. These enable socially distant interlocutors to come into contact impersonally, or virtually, to formulate collective orientations and alliances in the effort to exercise political influence. They also allow members of partial publics to understand themselves as part of a larger public and as contributors to "world public opinion."

The speed of the new communications is crucial here. But the network form and the new media of communication also facilitate a new pattern of influence by civil society. The capacity to engage in leverage politics is now developed on the part of those who are not necessarily citizens of the polity or members of the organizations that are targeted. "Activists across borders" mobilize "world public opinion" through what has been dubbed, quite aptly, the *boomerang effect* (Keck and Sikkink 1998: 12–14). The boomerang pattern involves a process by which domestic NGOs or civil society associations bypass their state and directly connect with transnational allies to try to bring pressure on their states (or on other target states) from the outside or "from above." A form of triangulation, the boomerang pattern can also involve local people's demands to participate in development projects that will affect them and that may be initiated by or dependent on external sources and pressures. Linkages through transnational networks provide local actors with access, leverage, and information that can then be used to pressure the relevant governmental and then nongovernmental agencies, from the outside in. The boomerang effect thus involves the bypassing of a local state, activation of a transnational network to publicize an issue, a drive to create "world public opinion," and a focus on invoking norms and principles articulated on the supra-national level to bring pressure on other states, regional bodies, or other third-party organizations, which in turn pressure the local state whose policies are at issue.[16]

Transnational publics get created, issues get put on agendas, "world public opinion" is formulated and invoked, new norms are articulated, influence exerted, pressure exercised from the outside onto the relevant powerful state (or nonstate) actor. This model applies to transnational human rights, environmental and women's networks, and the world public opinion created by anti-war activists hostile to the US intervention in Iraq. These activists within the US were able to link up with similarly minded groups all over the world, who in turn exercised influence on what became the relevant "political society," the UN Security Council. The US was not prevented from pursuing its aims, but it certainly lost legitimacy, for the younger Bush's administration, unlike that of his father, was never able to claim that world public opinion was on its side. The effects of this legitimation failure are still being felt.

Four aspects of publicity are involved in the new politics of world public opinion: *information politics*, predicated on the ability to quickly and credibly generate politically usable information where it will have the most impact; *symbolic politics*, or the invocation of symbols, and stories that make sense of a situation for local and distant audiences; *leverage politics*, or the ability to call upon powerful actors to affect a situation where weaker members of a network have little influence; and *accountability politics*, the effort to hold powerful actors to principles articulated previously on the local national level or on the level of world public opinion.[17] The level of reflection and self-reflection around the articulation of new norms, the mobilization of publics, and the construction and invocation of "world public opinion" by political entrepreneurs of transnational civil society is truly remarkable.

However, one also has to see the downside of all this. There is obvious potential for states and powerful economic organizations to instrumentalize "world public opinion" in order to justify unjust or illegitimate practices. Recent efforts to invoke "humanitarian" norms or democratic principles as a cover for projects of intervention and domination by powerful governments are obvious examples. Since there are as yet no global opinion polls, claims about "world public opinion" cannot be tested. On the other hand, such claims do not go uncontested. The new media of communication become sites where struggles to influence "world public opinion" occur.

Privacy

As indicated earlier, "privacy" refers to the personal autonomy ascribed to the individual, institutionalized by sets of rights ranging from habeas corpus and due process to the privacies of home and intimate association, freedom of conscience, and market freedoms (to acquire private property and freedom of contract). There have been many changes in this parameter, modiying how privacy securing personal autonomy is understood and to whom it is accorded. I will focus in turn on two main areas: privacy and autonomy regarding "intimate association," and the ascription of legal personhood and the rights associated with it to all individuals, whether or not they are citizens of the polity in which they reside.

In my view, some of the most important transformations have been in the "domain of intimacy," the quintessential private sphere. The declining importance of marriage with regard to the onset and pursuit of intimate relationships, the rise of the recombinant family, the shift in society's view of reproductive sex from a moral imperative to an ethical choice, and the massive entry of women (married, single, with and without young children) into the labor force and into public life are some of the relevant processes. An overall process of individualization has occurred in this domain (as in others), which constructs the individual rather than the family as the referent of privacy and as the bearer of privacy rights (Cohen 2002). A major shift in the status of women deriving from the recognition of claims to their full legal personality and the civic equality informs this trend. This is becoming a globalized principle despite resistance on the part of patriarchal power.[18] Pluralization of the forms of legitimate intimate association is one of its effects.

Entity privacy, which accorded autonomy and control to the male head of household and shielded the family as a "love community" from outside interference, has been displaced by privacy rights construed as securing the decisional autonomy and personhood of the individual (male or female) not only in forming intimate associations but also within the family and with regard to intimate concerns. Once women are ascribed full legal personality and construed as persons meriting equal concern and respect, whether or not they are married, it is no longer possible to ignore issues of justice arising in the domestic sphere by ascribing privacy to the family as a unit. Nor is it acceptable for the state to prohibit non-marital intimacies on the grounds that these are by definition immoral. The assumption that there is one morally correct way to form intimate relationships has been undermined along with the raison d'etre of a large part of states' morals legislation. In other words, the "naturalness" of the old public/private distinction, along with the gendered assumptions that informed previous forms of legal regulation, among them the creation of special statuses to which privacy attached, has been undermined.

Certainly women's struggle for gender equality has been a key force behind these transformations. Indeed, the meaning of the freedom of intimate association and of the right to privacy has radically shifted away from the right to marry or divorce and toward the equal right of all adult individuals to form and conduct their intimate associations as they wish, whether or not these entail marriage, provided that these are conducted in ways that do not violate the equal freedoms or basic needs of others (children).

I have written extensively on this topic (Cohen 2002). In particular I have challenged the claims of those who view the pluralization of the forms of intimacy and the individualization of the referent of privacy rights in this domain as synonymous with the disintegration of family values and as the cause of an alleged rise of an atomistic, egoistic, irresponsible, and overburdened individualism (Cohen 1999b: 235–238). What has disintegrated is not "the family" but the consensus on what a proper family is, on what form a good intimate relationship must take, and the understanding of women's and men's status and gender identity. Moreover, individualized privacy rights in the domain of intimate association do not undermine community or mutual responsibility. Rather, they protect individuals from the ill effects of breakdown in the solidarity of the love and against the unjust use of power by the stronger party.

To be sure, there are enormous pressures on families today. If processes of individualization occur without the necessary social and institutional supports, then the individual partners in an intimate association are bound to become overburdened. Privatization of care work—the work of providing for education, child care, after-school activities, care for the elderly, the sick—does create unfair and impossible responsibilities for those who do it (still mostly women) and can put enormous stress on intimate relationships. The problems and insecurities plaguing intimate associations arise from institutional change, individualization, economic uncertainty, and dislocation on the one side, and expanded gender equality, mobility, and opportunities on the other. Unless appropriate social supports are in place, the looser and more fragile family ties can come apart. While such supports must involve financial aid and remuneration for care work, as well as equal opportunities for women, the negative dimensions of privatization and individualization can be alleviated only if forms of solidarity and community are created on the local level with national resources allocated to them (such as day care centers in every neighborhood and workplace, services for the elderly and home care provided by professionals, community centers, a shortened work week for all, etc.).

The second trend I want to discuss under the parameter of privacy is the disaggregation of legal personhood from national citizenship and the ascription of legal rights and protections to resident noncitizens—a process that has accompanied the transformation of state sovereignty discussed earlier. The granting of a legal persona—i.e. protection of the law, including the right to sue in court—to resident noncitizens is the major development here. This parallels the transformation in the intimate domain: it acknowledges the equal moral worth, dignity, and integrity of all humans regardless not only of their gender but also of their citizenship status. The enormous growth of international law and the treatment of key human rights concepts as "jus cogens" is part of this transformation. As we have seen, states are coming under increasing pressure from international agreements and transnational institutions to protect the human rights not only of their own citizens but also of resident (even illegal) aliens in their territories. This emergent "cosmopolitan" globalized legal regime signals that governments and national courts are no longer the highest authority or sole source when it comes to basic rights.

I draw a theoretical conclusion from these changes: the status of legal personhood should be disassociated from citizenship status as a principle of membership in a discrete state, and it should be protected by multiple levels of legal jurisdiction and sanction. Indeed, vis-à-vis supra-national courts (from the ECJ to the ICC) and governmental bodies of regional federations (the EU), "citizenship" has come to mean "legal personhood" and legal standing, not membership in a demos delimited by national identity. One aspect of this complex situation is the ability of persons to enjoy a wide range of rights in states in which they are not citizens.[19] Another is the right of individuals who are citizens to appeal to supra-national courts to protect their rights against their own polities. The "direct effect" of regional courts on individuals in the member states of the E.U. and the emergence of global courts make this possible. These legal protections ascribe the protective cover of legal personhood and hence the personal autonomy and privacy crucial to a civil society to *everyone*, although just what content is given to the rights in question is politically contested and differs in different contexts.

That said, it would be irresponsible not to mention the serious threats to privacy and personal autonomy that are posed by globalization and the new electronic media (surveillance techniques, monitoring of the net, etc.). Civil liberties are under serious attack in the post–11 September context, states are suddenly reasserting a dangerous, uncontrolled form of sovereignty in this domain in the name of "national security." Some powerful states are dismantling the due process and privacy rights, habeas corpus rights, and rights to sue in court, especially but not only of noncitizens. In short, we may be facing the beginning of a counter-trend to the important globalized legal developments protecting privacy, plurality, and publicity. Yet the positive trend is still alive and constitutes the basis for resistance and legal challenges by civil society actors and by jurists.

Legality and Globalization

Although law is not a parameter of civil society, it is the medium through which civil societies are institutionalized. In the late twentieth and early twenty-first centuries, however, the dimension of legality has also undergone important changes that have repercussions for civil society. Here too the shifts are captured in new terminology: the replacement of the term government by "governance" for transnational ordering, and the new legal discourses of "soft law" and "societal constitutionalism" (Teubner 1997). What is involved is partly a shift of regulatory functions from public to semiprivate institutions, and partly a shift in regulation from the level of the national state to trans-national public institutions. Whether the new *Verrecthlichung* (juridification) secures the autonomy voice and solidarity of civil society actors is the key question.

"Governance" refers to systems of rule involving control mechanisms that are consistently exercised and that generate patterned compliance without requiring formal legal or political authority—"government"—and without necessarily involving hierarchy.[20] Goals are framed, directives issued, policies pursued, rules articulated that are minimally dependent on command-based hierarchical arrangements or reference back to a "sovereign legislator." Nongovernmental institutions and associations become an increasingly important source of law. "Governance" thus refers to many dimensions of the emergent global system as well as important developments on local levels. New forms of governance entail the proliferation of organizations to address the needs, challenges, and opportunities people face in everyday life, which are generated by the new interdependencies that global capitalism creates and enables.

Some claim that globalization of governance and the emergence of soft law forces us to rethink the traditional doctrine of the sources of law, according to which the distinction between law and non-law is based on a hierarchy of legal rules. On this model the constitution of a national state is the highest rule, which refers back to democratic political legislation (the will of the sovereign) as the ultimate source of legal validity (Rosenau 1998: xiii–xiv). Other normative, rule-based phenomena must be conceived as delegated law-making dependent on recognition by the official legal order; otherwise they are not law. Globalized governance seems to break this frame of rule hierarchy. That rule making by public or private instances escapes the control of sovereign states in the context of an increasingly fragmented "heterarchic" global society is the new conundrum (Black 2001). Legal pluralism allegedly replaces legal sovereignty and hierarchy in the globalized world society.

Hence the new discourse of "societal constitutionalism" (Teubner 1997). The basic intuition here is that we have to sever the idea of constitution from its historical tie to the state and generalize it to non- and supra-state entities if we are to keep abreast of contemporary developments. The claim is that the development of world society, functionally differentiated into a plurality of globalized, globalizing subsystems, involves the emergence of constitutions that constitute and have constitutionalized each domain. There is, in short, not only soft law and governance but constitutional law too in each of the globalizing subsystems.

But what is a constitution, in this approach? What criteria permit us to say that a field is constitutionalized? The answer implied in this approach is that a constitution is a matter of structural coupling between the subsystems' specific structures and legal norms.

For those of us used to the concept of constitutionalism as applied to states, this definitional claim sounds rather murky. Systems theorists insist that even on the state level, the core function of constitutions is to guarantee the multiplicity of social differentiation. From this perspective the point of constitutionalization is to liberate the dynamism of each subsystem, while institutionalizing mechanisms of self-restraint against their society-wide expansion, to prevent swamping.

"Structural coupling" allegedly exists between law and each globalizing subsystem: politics, economics, etc. But are we really in the presence of constitutionalism, rather than merely abundant regulations or sets of law? This matters for civil society theory because it is the constitution rather than the legislation that is crucial to protecting and institutionalizing civil society. Recall that Hart argued that in order for a legal order to exist there must be a differentiation between primary and secondary rules, between rules of conduct and rules for the production of law. A constitution is part of a legal order, comprised in part of secondary rules or the rules for change, including rules for changing the secondary rules themselves. Equally important, to tell participants in the legal system, especially courts, how to know whether something is valid law there must be a rule of recognition—i.e. a rule that can be invoked to settle disputes over this and over jurisdictions, and that indicates what the primary and secondary rules are and who can make them. In other words, reflexivity is crucial to a legal order and even more so to a constitution, which confers powers in addition to imposing duties. There can be multiple sources of law but something has to unify and hierarchize them for a legal order and a constitution to exist. In short, there is no legal order and certainly no constitution unless there are secondary rules that specify the ways in which the primary rules may be conclusively ascertained, introduced, eliminated, and varied and the fact of their violation conclusively determined (Hart 1961).[21]

To date there has been no overarching global constitution for world society that comes anywhere near meeting these criteria; nor is there a single global civil society. Indeed from the systems-theoretical perspective it would make no sense to argue for such a thing, because the guiding principle is that world society is radically decentered: no single subsystem among the functionally differentiated subsystems can stand for the whole. The entire thrust of contemporary systems theory is that it is a very bad idea to claim *pars pro toto* either for the state within national society or for international politics. Globalization and constitutionalization in world society is a polycentric process.

Thus, the discourse of "societal constitutionalism" involves a slightly different claim, namely that there exists a global constitution for each globalized subsystem of international society, including the political subsystem of international society. Societal constitutionalists point to the heterarchical organization of courts at the center of the new global law regime, as well as to centralizations of global remedies in supra-national instances like the ECJ, ICTY, ICTR, ICC, and truth commissions installed by the UN, along with regional human rights courts, etc., all of which have their legal basis in international public law treaties (Fischer-Lescano 2003; Slaughter 1997). They also point to the increasingly "hard" character of international human rights law *(jus cogens)* that renders invalid any law permitting such things as torture, genocide, disappearances, extralegal killing, crimes against humanity, etc.[22] The claim is that there thus already exist constitutional rules of jurisdiction, global remedies rules, courts, and formal constitutional law (norms regarding the legal formation of norms, with treaty law binding even non-signatories) in the global political arena. To be sure, in view of the infamous democratic deficit no one claims that the global political constitution is complete. Without a *pouvoir constituent*—a global political representation—of democratic legitimacy is missing. Rather, the claim is that there exists a constitution that is global and political, but not democratic.

Let me signal the hazards of this discourse of societal constitutionalism. The idea that globalized law mediates and institutionalizes civil society in a global political subsystem that tempers state sovereignty through direct effect and other mechanisms is an important one. However, it is dangerous and apologetic to assert that a global *constitution* already exists in this realm. The absence of the principle of the separation of powers (e.g., regarding the UN Security Council) and the limited jurisdiction of, say, the ICJ mean that there are important legal gaps, not to mention lack of clarity, regarding the higher-law status ascribed to human rights as hard law. It remains unclear what the rule of recognition is in this globalized domain, and what secondary rules exist regarding change on the higher-law level. Nor is there a consensus regarding the basic parameters of the lawmaking process that leads to preemptory rules.

The claim that a global constitution already exists on the global political level can tempt the powerful states—alone or in alliances of several states—to invoke the cover of law by invoking human rights principles to justify violent and even nonviolent but harsh forms of intervention in weaker states. In other words, here the discourse of constitutionalism could provide the cover of legality for unprincipled action and invites the symbolic abuse of the idea of constitutional law. Thus I recommend caution here. I am not arguing that intervention in the name of human rights is never necessary or legal, but rather that we are not yet at the point where it is clear what the rules or meta-rules are. Indeed, whereas the discourse preempts the important task of constitutionalizing the various globalized domains, it remains a *vérité-à-faire:* we are not there yet. Let me close with this problematic.

Conclusion

I am convinced that the globalization of civil society has led to very important successes in the domain of human rights, the genesis of global law, sensitivity to ecological issues, and to fostering of the democratization of national societies, in part via the boomerang effect discussed above. Civil society continues to play a key role in the further juridification of international society. There is a great deal of law on the international and global level, but it is not yet constitutionalism. In some respects the role of globalized civil society actors is greater here than it is on the national level because globally there is no equivalent political society, no equivalent accountable representative bodies making collectively binding decisions yet subject to the sanction of election in the way that national legislatures and executives are, so that civil society actors must do more here than on the national level.

Nevertheless, it would be a mistake to see the nongovernmental organizations, local associations, and networks that populate transnational civil society as functional equivalents of the representative institutions and political society (parties, unions) that operate on the domestic level in constitutional democracies. Civil society cannot monitor the new powerful governance institutions on the supra-national or on the subnational level, on its own—indeed, civil society itself requires monitoring. Civil associations and networks can be exclusionary, unjust, anti-egalitarian, and antidemocratic. Moreover, well-funded NGOs may foster the development of local, indigenous, autonomous civil societies in developing countries—or, they might substitute themselves and their funds for local initiatives, thereby undermining rather than reinforcing moves towards democratization, horizontal trust, and social solidarity. The monitors must, in short, be monitored.

The role of civil society in each globalized domain is not to substitute for a missing representative political society (government), for this would overburden civil society actors whose role it is to exert influence, not exercise power or make collectively binding decisions. That is the error of the idea of a globalized civil society, alluded to in the introduction to this paper. But neither can one restrict the function of globalizing civil society actors to norm creation (the transnational civil society model).[23] Rather, civil society actors in each globalized domain have the extra tasks, as it were, of helping to create their interlocutors, i.e. the functional equivalent of a responsive political society, and pressing for the institutionalization of political society as well as for mechanisms of accountability. This would involve the constitutionalization of each globalized domain in the Hartian sense, so that those making collectively binding decisions are rendered representative and accountable as well as receptive to the influence of civil society. In other words, constitutionalization of supra-national governance and the creation of representative and accountable institutions; including the separation and balance of powers, is not accomplished, it is the task ahead. Those advocating a constitution for the European Union have understood this desideratum. Only if this were accomplished, could one speak of the rule of law and end the "democratic deficit" of supranational governance.

The regulation of self-regulation by a public, accountable, responsive, representative political society that makes collectively binding decisions is indispensable to a global democratic future. Political society must be created on the global and regional level and be strengthened on the national level, even as the sovereignty of states is partially disaggregated and even as civil society actors manage to trigger the imposition of human rights principles, ecological concerns, and the like onto all political actors.

The politics of global civil society, with its new forms of plurality, publicity, and privacy can no longer be described in the same terms as its predecessor, national civil society. With respect to some issues, the new formation is politically stronger than many states. Few states (perhaps not even the United States) can fully escape and resist the pressure of targeted, international mobilization around human rights, ecological, labor, and cultural issues. This is the case because civil actors can mobilize states and regional organizations to participate in their communication processes and to exert pressure. Thus for the new global civil society, the politics of influence is supplemented by the use of some forms of power. Constitutionalization of global regimes would help establish legitimacy and legality.

This is especially important in the area of the global economy. Here global and even regional civil society actors are much much weaker than their national counterparts. As we all know, a neoliberal consensus has been hegemonic in this domain, and although there have been important challenges by civil society actors, global economic institutions from the IMF to the World Bank have not been very responsive to the demands for socioeconomic justice, or to the demands that those who are affected by the relevant decisions be included in deliberations. Without the institutionalization of a fair, inclusive political society in the public bodies that make global economic decisions, networks of civil society actors and "world public opinion" will have little chance to exert influence or control. Noting that it may be ironic to close a paper on civil society in this way, I would argue that today the main tasks are to construct a responsible and accountable political society in global institutions and to reconstruct the national-level political societies and institutional designs that seem to be in crisis (especially in the US) in order to secure a healthy and effective relationship between civil society, human rights, the rule of law, democracy, and social justice.

Notes

1. On the managerial nature of this approach to civil society see Jayasuriya (2001).
2. On emergent networks of regulatory agencies transforming international rules away from state-to-state relations, see Slaughter (1997) and Jayasuriya (2001).
3. Rosenau (1998) cites global cities along with civil society as a functional equivalent to control by states. We are not yet convinced about the equivalence idea here. It is not yet clear that public functions and democratic forms of participation and accountability can be put in place without the relevant developments in political society.
4. See Carl Schmitt's critique of humanitarianism and human rights discourse in Schmitt (1976 and 2003).
5. Of course, freedom to marry was restricted to heterosexuals while personal autonomy within marriage was restricted to the male head of household. Many restrictions existed regarding the marital relationship and sex outside of marriage was condemned.
6. On the distinction between civil and political publics see Cohen and Arato (1992). On 'weak' and 'strong,' see Fraser (1992). One must think of the distinction between civil, weak, political, and strong publics as a continuum. Weak publics are relatively speaking more deliberative and open to fewer constraints on deliberations. Strong decisional publics are more constrained both qualitatively and quantitatively (time for deliberation is shorter). A consciousness-raising group in a feminist movement is an example of a weak un-institutionalized civil public open to all sorts of statements and reasoning. A jury is an example of an institutionalized civil public that is "strong" in the sense that its deliberations lead to politically binding decisions. A parliament is an

even stronger institutionalized political public, legislating for the whole of society. For another way of distinguishing between the various constraints on different sorts of publics see Rawls (1993: 212–254).

7. This way of conceptualizing the public sphere precludes granting legitimacy to any group or institution claiming to embody or represent the public, or to be endowed with the authority to define what a matter of public concern is. Moreover, the line between public and private, along with the question of who is to be included in the public, cannot be decided once and for all.

8. For a rethinking of the privacy component of civil society see Jean L. Cohen (2002).

9. For an analysis of the regulatory paradoxes that occur in the regulatory state see Arato (1998), (2002) and Sunstein (1997). For the concept of regulatory tri-lemma see Teubner (1993).

10. Reflexive law is a new form of regulation that should supplement, not replace, the other legal forms. When and where a type of law or mode of regulation is suitable is an empirical question. Reflexive law is a form of regulation of self-regulation, not privatization. It is meant to steer self-regulation toward public purposes and to foster the creation of procedures of conflict resolution and decision-making that facilitate the participation, equality, and influence of the relevant stakeholders. See Cohen (2002), chapter 4.

11. How transparent these arrangements were and what degree of exclusion they fostered is another issue.

12. This is also true of the anti-politics model of civil society developed in the east. See Arato (2000: 1–81). Then of course there was the additional problem of the needing to reconstruct a representative political society receptive to the input of civil society.

13. For a discussion and critique of these two schools, which emerged in the US in the 1990s, see Cohen (1999c: 262–291).

14. Such contacts are indeed ephemeral and unstable. Perhaps the Putnam point works best regarding these types of "networks."

15. For a discussion of these issues see Arquilla and Ronfeldt (2001), chapters 1 and 10.

16. For a diagram see Keck and Sikkink 1998, 13.

17. I am paraphrasing Keck and Sikkink (1998: 16). This part is heavily reliant on their excellent analysis.

18. The various successes in framing women's concerns as health issues, as issues against violence, as human rights issues (rape), and as development issues on the global level bears witness to this. See Keck and Sikkink (1998: 165–198) for a discussion.

19. This was the trend before 11 September 2001.

20. I am relying on Rosenau (1998: 28–57) for this definition.

21. The issue before us is not that of efficacy of law or the availability of sanctions (the usual frame of reference vis-à-vis the deficiencies of inter- or supra-national law vs national state law) but rather one of validity.

22. Citing article 53 of the Vienna Convention on Human Rights.

23. Nor should the managerial model be bought into: while inclusion in deliberations in economic arenas is an important desideratum for taming globalized capitalism, civil society actors are not in the business of making profit any more than they are in the business of governing.

References

Anderson, Perry. 1977. "The Antinomies of Antonio Gramsci" in *New Left Review* 100.

Arato, Andrew. 1998. "Procedural Law and Civil society: Interpreting the Radical Democratic Paradigm." In *Habermas on Law and Democracy: Critical*

Exchanges, ed. Michel Rosenfeld and Andrew Arato. Berkeley: University of California Press.

Arato, Andrew. 2000. *Civil Society, Constitution and Legitimacy.* Lanham, MD: Rowman and Littlefield Publishers.

Arquilla, John, and David Ronfeldt, eds. 2001. *Networks and Netwars: The Future of Terror, Crime and Militancy.* Santa Monica, CA: Rand Corporation.

Black, Julia. 2001. "Proceduralizing Regulation: Part II." *Oxford Journal of Legal Studies* 21: 33–58.

Calhoun, Craig, ed. 1992. *Habermas and the Public Sphere.* Cambridge, MA: MIT Press.

Chambers, Simone. 2002. "A Critical Theory of Civil Society." In *Alternative Conceptions of Civil Society,* ed. Simone Chambers and Will Kymlicka. Princeton, NJ: Princeton University Press.

Cohen, Jean L. 1999a. "Changing Paradigms of Citizenship and the Exclusiveness of the Demos" in *International Sociology* 14, no. 3.

———. 1999b. "Trust, Voluntary Association and Workable Democracy: the Contemporary American Discourse of Civil Society." In *Democracy and Trust,* ed. Mark Warren. Cambridge: Cambridge University Press.

———. 1999c. "Does Voluntary Association Make Democracy Work?" In *Diversity and Its Discontents: Cultural Conflict and Common Ground in Contemporary American Society,* ed. Neil J. Smelser and Jeffrey C. Alexander. Princeton: Princeton University Press.

———. 2002. *Regulating Intimacy: A New Legal Paradigm* (Princeton, N.J: Princeton University Press.

———. 2005. "The Self Institution of Society and Representation: Can the Circle be Squared?" in *Thesis Eleven* 80, No. 1: 9–37.

Cohen, Jean L., and Andrew Arato. 1992. *Civil Society and Political Theory.* Cambridge, MA: MIT Press.

Cutler, A. Claire. 2001. "Late Capitalist Merchant Rule." *Constellations* 8, no. 4.

Dorf, Michael, and Charles Sabel. 1998. "A Constitution of Democratic Experimentalism." *Columbia Law Review* 98, no. 2.

Falk, Richard. 2000. "Global Civil Society and the Democratic Prospect." In *Global Democracy: Key Debates,* ed. B. Holden. New York: Routledge.

Fischer-Lescano, Andreas. 2003. "Die Emergenz der Globalverfassung." *Zeitschrift für ausländisches öffentliches Recht und Völkerrecht – (Heidelberg Journal of International Law)* 63, no. 3: 717–760.

Fraser, Nancy. 1992. "Rethinking the Public Sphere: A Contribution to the Critique of Actually Existing Democracy." In *Habermas and the Public Sphere,* in Craig Calhoun. Cambridge: MIT Press, 1992).

Fraser, Nancy, and Gordon, Linda. 1994. "A Geneology of Dependency: Tracing a Keyword of the United States Welfare State." *Signs* 19, no. 20: 309–333.

Gramsci, Antonio. 1971. "State and Civil Society." In *Selections from the Prison notebooks of Antonio Gramsci,* ed. and trans. Quintin Hoare and Geoffrey Nowell Smith. New York: International Publishers.

Habermas, Jürgen. 1989. *The Structural Transformation of the Public Sphere.* Cambridge, MA: MIT Press.

———. 1996. *Between Facts and Norms.* Cambridge, MA: MIT Press.

———. 2001. *The Postnational Constellation.* Cambridge: Polity Press.

Hart, H.L.A. 1961. *The Concept of Law.* Oxford: Clarendon Press.

Haufler, Virginia, and Tony Porter, eds. 1999. *Private Authority and International Affairs.* New York: SUNY Press.

Held, David. 1995. *Democracy and the Global Order: from the Modern State to Cosmopolitan Governance.* Stanford, CA: Stanford University Press.

Hirst, Paul, and Grahame Thompson. 1996. *Globalization in Question: The International Economy and the Possibility of Governance.* London: Polity.

Jaeger, Hans Matin. "World Opinion and the Transformation of International Governance." PhD diss., Columbia University, forthcoming.

Jayasuriya , Kanishka. 2001. "From Political to Economic Constitutionalism." *Constellations* 8, No. 4.

Kaldor, Mary. 1999. "Transnational Civil Society." In *Human Rights in Global Politics,* ed. T. Donne and N.J. Wheeler. Cambridge: Cambridge University Press.

Kaldor, Mary, Helmut Anheier, and Marlies Glasius, eds. 2003. *The Global Civil Society Reader.* Oxford: Oxford University Press.

Keck, Margaret E., and Kathryn Sikkink. 1998. *Activists Beyond Boarders: Advocacy Networks in International Politics.* Ithaca, NY: Cornell University Press.

Krassner, Steven. 1999. *Sovereignty: Organized Hypocrisy.* Princeton: Princeton University Press.

Lieberman, Robert. 2001. *Shifting the Color Line, Race and the American Welfare State.* Cambridge, MA: Harvard University Press.

Linklater, Andrew. 1999. "The Evolving Spheres of International Justice." *International Affairs* 75, no. 3: 473–482.

Manin, Bernard. 1997. *The Principles of Representative Government.* Cambridge: Cambridge University Press.

Melucci, Alberto. 1980. "The New Social Movements: A Theoretical Approach." *Social Science Information* 19.

Melucci, Alberto. 1985. "The Symbolic Challenge of Contemporary Movements." *Social Research* 52, no. 4.

Pasha, Mustapha Kamal, and David L. Blaney. 2001. "Elusive Paradise: The Promise and Peril of Global Civil Society." *Alternatives* 23, no. 4.

Putnam, Robert. 1993. *Making Democracy Work.* Princeton, NJ: Princeton University Press.

Putnam, Robert. 2000. *Bowling Alone.* New York: Simon and Schuster.

Rawls, John. 1993. "The Idea of Public Reason." In John Rawls, *Political Liberalism.* New York: Columbia University Press.

Rosenau, James. 1997. *Along the Domestic/Foreign Frontier: Exploring Governance in a Turbulent World.* Cambridge and New York: Cambridge University Press.

Rosenau, James. 1998. "Governance and Democracy in a Globalizing World." In *Re-Imagining Political Community,* ed. Daniele Archibugi, David Held and Martin Köhler. Stanford, CA: Stanford University Press.

Rothstein, Bo. 2002. "Sweden: Social Capital in the Social Democratic State." In *Democracies in Flux? The Evolution of Social Capital in Contemporary Society,* ed. Robert Putnam. Oxford: Oxford University Press.

Sassen, Saskia. 1996. *Losing Control? Sovereignty in an Age of Globalization.* New York: Columbia University Press.

Schmitt, Carl. 1976. *The Concept of the Political.* New Brunswick, N.J: Rutgers University Press.

Schmitt, Carl. 2003. *Nomos der Erde.* New York: Telos Press.

Sirianni, Carmen, and Lewis Friedland. 2001. *Civic Innovation in America.* Berkeley: University of California Press.

Slaughter, Anne Marie. 1997. "The Real New World Order." *Foreign Affairs* 76, no. 5.

Sorensen, Georg. 1999. "Sovereignty: Change and Continuity in A Fundamental Institution." In *Sovereignty at the Millennium* ed. Robert Jackson. Oxford: Blackwell.

Strange, Susan. 1996. *The Retreat of the State: The Diffusion of Power in the World Economy.* Cambridge: Cambridge University Press.

Sunstein, Cass. 1997. *The Partial Constitution.* Cambridge: Harvard University Press.

Teubner, Gunther. 1993. "Substantive and Reflexive Elements in Modern Law." *Law and Society Review* 17, no. 2.

Teubner, Gunther, ed. 1997. *Global Law without a State.* Aldershot and Brookfield: Dartmouth Publishing Co.

Thoma, Daniel C. 2001. *The Helsinki Effect: International Norms, Human Rights and the Demise of Communism.* Princeton: Princeton University Press.

Touraine, Alain. 1981. *The Voice and The Eye.* New York: Cambridge University Press.

White, Harrison. 1995. "Where do languages come from? Part 1." Pre-print series Lazarsfeld Center for the Social Sciences, Columbia University, no 4.

White, Harrison C. 1996. "Network Switchings and Bayesian Forks." *Social Research* 62.

Chapter 3

VOLUNTARY ASSOCIATION INVOLVEMENT IN COMPARATIVE PERSPECTIVE

Douglas Baer

From two very divergent theoretical perspectives, the last decade has witnessed a resurgence in interest in the study of participation in voluntary
associations.[1] Tracing its lineage to Coleman (1988, 1990) but energized
by Putnam's recent work (1995, 1996, 2000), the literature on *social capital* (Dekker and Uslaner, 2001; see also Portes 1998) views voluntary associations as critical in the development of the political competencies
necessary for a society to function democratically (see Fung 2003), as well
as in the construction and maintenance of dense social networks, which
are in turn seen as the glue that binds a society together and creates positive social and political outcomes. In this literature, organizations need
not be political or have political objectives to have a positive effect on
civic competence and participation (see de Ulzurrun 2002: 498), and
could be as diverse as recreational bowling leagues, religious groups and
philanthropic organizations (Putnam 2000). Most contemporary writers,
either working in this tradition (Paxton, 1999; Rotolo 1999) or criticizing
it (Baer et al. 2001; Levi 1996; Fine 2001) focus in some way on Putnam's belief that civic engagement in the United States, and by implication in other Western industrialized societies, is in a long period of
secular decline (see also Skocpol 2003). Putnam's writing thus stands out
as a lament for the disappearance of the "long civic generation"—a post
World War II cohort of individuals with high levels of civic engagement
that have not been replicated in subsequent generations.

   The literature on *new social movements* (Carroll 2002; Laraña et al.
1994) also sees voluntary associations as politically important, albeit with

an emphasis on the transformational potential inherent in some, but not all, types of organizations. Social movement associations stand against "older" forms of organizations such as conventional political parties, which are seen as unresponsive to emerging social needs that come to the fore as individuals and groups seek to establish identities and articulate grievances in a sphere of social action that is not totally encumbered by the state or by the market (Wuthnow 1991; Cohen 1985). But while social movement associations constitute a politically important social form existing within civil society—especially from the standpoint of democratic participation—they represent only one particular sector (Carroll 2002: 144) in a space that is also inhabited by "old" voluntary associations such as traditional political parties, religion, and voluntary associations that do not incorporate "movement activism." Movements typically referred to as NSMs in the literature, include the "urban social struggles, the environmental or ecology movements, women's and gay liberation, the peace movement, and cultural revolt linked primarily to student and youth activism" (Boggs 1986: 39–40), as well as anti-poverty organizations (Carroll and Ratner 1996: 411).

Generally, NSMs and social movement associations are held to be more prominent in Western "post-industrial" economies such as the United States, Canada or Europe (see Boggs 1986; Inglehart 1997; Larana et al. 1994; Offe 1985; Touraine 1981). Some writers believe that NSMs and the more or less formal organizations that have developed around them have emerged mainly because of the change to a "post-industrial" economy, suggesting that these movements and organizations will be particularly numerous, and participation in them more common, in the more advanced industrial societies, including the United States, Canada, and certain European nations.

Neither Putnam's social capital approach nor new social movement theories provide us with a clearly deterministic formulation. While Putnam emphasizes, over and over, that we are in a period of secular decline in voluntary association involvement, he tacks on the idea that reversing this trend is not beyond the ability of human actors (2000: 402–414). And, whereas social movement theorists would generally argue that social movement associations are of increasing importance, their own formulations do not preclude the possibility that a variety of constraining factors might prevent the dream of greater democratic participation—let alone social transformation—from coming into play. Still, there is clearly at least an implied position in each of these respective research traditions, and these contradict each other. Following Putnam, broad declines in organizational involvement might be expected, but following new social movement perspectives one might expect to see increases, at least in those forms of organization that might warrant the label of new social movement (the prognosis for the "old" organizations is somewhat ambiguous).

If there is discussion within the social movement literature of a radical disjunction between old-style associations and social movement associations, it speaks more to the relationship between movements and traditional holders of power in the state and the economy than it does about relationships with organizations in other sectors of civil society, though it is clear that traditional political parties are set off in strong relief against the practices of social movement associations, whose activities entail a strong component of "resistance" to the practices of both capital and the state (see Carroll 2002; Adam 1993: 327ff.) as well as an orientation to "new needs" that are neither articulated nor met in the conventional spaces of the state and the economy (Melucci 1989; Cohen 1985). At the very least, this suggests that the social and political orientations of NSM association participants will be different from those of other organizations, but it also suggests that social movement associations will attract more members among groups that have been marginalized by existing social relations, younger individuals (given that student groups are themselves either defined as social movement associations or are seen to take a role that is closely aligned to them), and those who are more likely to find themselves outside the traditional economy (for example, women). Whether the difference extends to differences in education is a bit less clear, but there is a strain of thought that suggests that the strong democratic norms and egalitarian orientations of NSM associations arise in part from the role of intellectuals (see Gouldner 1979).

If the literature on social movement associations points to differences between "old" and "new" voluntary associations with respect to the types of persons who are likely to be members and association activists, it also suggests that between-country differences do not necessarily follow parallel trajectories: those countries in which conventional associations are strong may or may not provide fertile ground for the development of NSMs. Even in countries with relatively weak associational bases, NSMs may be mobilized by political crises in so far as the formal political system is weakened and room for political innovation is created (Kreisi 1995; Skocpol 1979; Kitschelt 1986). It is thus possible for active voluntary association activity to take place not just in spite of widespread public non-confidence in government and other social institutions, but precisely because this non-confidence mobilizes individuals and groups to engage themselves politically. This stands in stark contrast to the postulated relationships seen in the literature on social capital, where social movement associations constitute but one of many "types" of voluntary associations, with membership levels in all of these driven by generalized interpersonal trust.

The two divergent perspectives raise the question of just how "new" or unique organizations that have been labeled new social movement associations actually are.[2] This question in turn relates to the longstanding issue of the relationship between types of political regimes and the strength of voluntary association involvement within different countries. While much of the earlier literature on voluntary association involvement took the form of an extended elaboration of a thesis of American exceptionalism (Lipset 1994; 1996; also see Curtis et al. 2001: 784), more recent discussions regarding citizenship regimes, civil society and participation in democratic regimes have tended to divide countries into various "regime types," within which countries display similarities and differences with respect to welfare state service provision, corporatist accommodation structures for labor and capital, levels of political rights, origins of the contemporary form of the state in relation to the historical development of popular movements, the extent of state involvement in the economy, and degree of state centralization (Esping-Andersen 1990; Janoski, 1998; Jepperson, 2002). Esping-Andersen's formulation was based on three welfare state characteristics that were labeled "liberal," "traditional" (or "conservative"), and "social democratic" (or "socialist"). This formulation is by now very well known though, as Janoski points out (1998: 21), it concentrates more on variables of differentiation and on ideal types than it does on the exhaustive classification of each Western democracy into one of the three types. In this analysis, traditional regimes arise from Catholic political party strength and a history of strong absolutist and authoritarian statehood; they focus on extensive systems of social rights, which are nonetheless segmented. Liberal regimes are characterized by the prominence of means-tested welfare provision and the reliance on private markets in the economy. (Esping-Andersen 1990: 133–135; Janoski 1998: 21) Finally, social democratic regimes are based on universalism and equality as principles of "welfare-state solidarity" (Esping-Andersen 1990: 136). The archetypal cases identified by Esping-Andersen were: for the liberal type, the United States, Canada, and Australia; for the corporatist/traditional type, Austria, France, Germany, and Italy; and for the social democratic type, Sweden, Denmark, Norway and Finland (1990: 17–20).

Janoski's revision of Esping-Andersen's theorizations follows closely from the latter, but makes a few changes. The most important one in the context of the present discussion is that the Netherlands, which on some of Esping-Andersen's criteria seems to accord more closely with the social democratic type than with other welfare regime/polity types and which is categorized by Janoski (1988: 23) as social democratic. This makes it the only non-Nordic country in this category, and also implies that the label "Scandinavian" is not an exact description of the category.[3]

As applied to American exceptionalism arguments, most regime type classifications can be seen as providing an implicit critique of the idea that there is only one available path to a society with a high degree of civic involvement and engagement. Left on its own, a comparison between the

United States and Western European countries might lend credence to the exceptionalism thesis, since in aggregate US rates of voluntary involvement are well higher than the *average* rates of involvement in most European countries. But, in light of earlier work demonstrating the existence, at least in the 1980s, of high rates of involvement in countries other than the United States, regime typologies can be helpful not only in identifying alternative paths to high levels of associational involvement, but also in isolating some of the mechanisms under which these might work.

While some of the more recent studies construct typologies that do not fully correspond to the division between Scandinavian and other societies, they will provide some measures that will identify the extent to which social democratic countries—as a type that includes Sweden, Norway, Iceland, Finland, Denmark and the Netherlands—are and remain unique in the world of voluntary association involvement. The strength and stability of voluntary association involvement, and of civil society in general, in these countries is of particular interest in light of conflicting claims in recent literature regarding the relationship between a strong welfare state and the health and vitality of civil society (see Rothstein 2001; Rothstein and Stolle 2003). These debates apply generically to social democratic countries, not just to those that are "Nordic." Is it the case, Rothstein (2001: 208) asks, that high levels of public spending and strong welfare state programs have reduced the social space available for voluntary associations or other forms of networking? In this perspective, Sweden is an ideal test case, though the arguments used in support of the case apply to a considerable degree to other countries with the "social democratic" label (Norway, Finland, Iceland, Denmark, the Netherlands).

Against the backdrop of a scholarly exchange on the relationship between welfare regimes and civic engagement, and a second exchange dealing with differentiations between *types* of voluntary associations with varying levels of political and social engagement, this chapter sets out to construct a comparative cross-national analysis of voluntary association involvement, paying particular attention to an assessment of similarities and differences in cross-national patterns across different types of organizations. The focus will be on membership and participation across entire societies. In the 1990s, large cross-national datasets useful for the purpose of studying cross-national differences in voluntary association involvement first became available. One of the most prominent of these is the World Values Survey, which now includes over 50 countries. This source has informed the study of overall association membership involving 30 countries (Curtis, Baer, and Grabb 2001; Schofer and Fourcade-Gourinchas, 2001) and in the analysis of change over the 1980–1990 period involving 15 countries (Baer, Curtis, and Grabb 2001). It will be used here to further investigate between-country differences in the context of the question of how NSM associations differ from older types of associations, and to supplement the earlier work with some new data taken from the 2000 World Values Survey.

World Values Survey Data on Membership and Voluntary Association Participation

In most of the countries covered by the World Values survey in 1990, respondents were asked about association membership in sixteen possible organizational categories: charities and social welfare, churches or religious organizations, education or arts groups, trade unions, political parties or groups, community action groups, human rights organizations, conservation or environmental groups, animal welfare groups, youth work groups, sport and recreation organizations, professional associations, women's groups, peace groups, health organizations, and "others." Two questions were asked for each of the association types: "Which, if any, of the following do you belong to?" and later, a second question was asked for each association type: "Do you currently do any unpaid voluntary work for any of them?" Elsewhere, Baer et al. (2001) distinguish between *nominal* and *active* membership types, suggesting that the latter are probably more important from the standpoint of theoretical concerns about civic engagement and participation. In the analyses reported here, a distinction is made between social movement associations and "non-NSM" associations; as in earlier work by Curtis et al. (2001) and Baer et al. (2001), religious-affiliated organizations are not included in either of these two measures.

For the 1990 World Values Survey data, social movement memberships involved membership in one or more of the following types of organizations: human rights, environment and conservation, women's, peace, and animal rights organizations. The category of non-social movement membership included all other organization types except unions (since union membership is usually not voluntary) and religious organizations (which are dealt with separately). In the 2000 World Values Survey data, only four items were available for social movement memberships; animal rights were instead included in wording for the "conservation and ecology" question. Multiple memberships are not coded separately, focusing the interest on whether or not an individual participates in *any* association of a given type.[4] For all of the analyses reported here, individual-level social background differences were controlled for: education, occupation, gender, marital status, age, and if available, community size.[5]

The sample sizes for the World Values Survey project are fairly large, if totaled together. Data from approximately 1,000 surveys (occasionally, somewhat more) were available in each of the 30 countries that were used in the analysis reported here for 1990 (total N of approximately

39,464, varying somewhat according to the particulars of the analysis), and the same applies to the 35 countries that were used in analyses for 2000 (total N of approximately 46,552).

Methods

Since the major focus of the analysis is to describe and examine between-country differences in voluntary association involvement, tables presenting comparative results for all available countries form the core of the results reported here. For each of the years 1990 and 2000, logistic regression models are used to show these differences. The dependent variables are yes/no indicators of whether individuals are members of (a) religious voluntary associations, (b) unions, (c) any one of the social movement association types outlined above, (d) any one of the other (non-social movement) types of voluntary associations included in the surveys, as identified above. Since log-odds coefficients are difficult, intuitively, to interpret, the results have been translated in Tables 1 and 2 into "expected probabilities" (Long 1997).[6] Expected probabilities are also used to show the across-country (pooled) effects of social characteristics of respondents (Table 5).

More complex "multiple-level" models are used later on to examine the relative effects of factors that operate at the level of entire countries as opposed to the level of individuals. These models are similar to logistic regression models in that they assess the effects of various individual background factors on whether or not the individual is a member (or active member) or not. But, instead of yielding individual results for each country, they provide summary measures for the effects of certain *country attributes* (in the case of the present study, number of years of continuous democracy, size of gross domestic product,[7] type of polity, and type of collective religious heritage). The two typologies that are used to describe the type of country are polity/regime type (social democratic; liberal democratic; former Eastern bloc European and all others) and type of religious heritage (mixed Christian; Protestant; Catholic; other).[8] The coefficients from these models are given as "log-odds" coefficients.[9]

For the final portion of the analysis, membership rate changes in countries where comparative data exist—1980 versus 1990 or 1990 versus 2000—are tabulated, with controls for within-country differences in education, age distribution, and other relevant factors. For this portion of the analysis, logistic regression models are again employed. The idea here is to assess changes in involvement after factoring out the extent to which changes over time can be attributed to *compositional* changes (a better educated citizenry, shifting age distributions so that the average age in some countries is slightly older ten years later, and so on). The coefficients presented in Tables 8 through 10 are "odds multipliers," which provide an indication of whether the odds of being a member of a given association type went up or down over time in each of the countries studied. An odds multiplier of 1.0 would imply that there has been no change.[10]

Between-Country Differences in Social Movements, Religious-Affiliated Organizations, and Other Organizations

Table 3.1 reports between-country differences in expected probabilities of voluntary association involvement for 1990, with controls for between-country differences in social background variables. This table uses a format similar to the one found in Curtis et al. (2001) using the same data, but now differentiates between social movement and non-social movement organizations. It also adds separate columns for (a) voluntary associations associated with religion and (b) unions. The numbers adjust for between-country differences in age, occupation, marital status, education, community size and gender. Overall, the expected probabilities are very similar to the "zero-order" probabilities that would have been obtained if differences in background attributes had not been controlled for.

The four columns on the left of Table 3.1 are for all memberships (active and inactive together). For non-social movement associations (leftmost column in the table), countries with high levels of participation are the Netherlands (.745), Norway (.669), Germany (.607 for residents of the former West Germany and .582 for the residents of the former E. Germany) and Denmark (.581). Slightly lower but still above average participation rates are found in Canada, the United States, Belgium, Northern Ireland, Britain, Ireland, and Austria. Almost all former Eastern bloc countries (except the former East Germany) have low levels of involvement, as do Japan, Argentina, Spain, and Mexico.

For social movement associations (column 2), very similar patterns obtain: once again, the Netherlands shows the highest participation rate and the countries with the four highest participation rates (Netherlands, .468; Belgium, .309; Sweden, .270; and Denmark, .253) are fairly highly ranked in terms of their non-social movement association participation rates as well. In general, countries with high rates of non-social movement involvement have high rates of social movement involvement, and vice versa. Norway is a bit exceptional in that it has a high level of non-social movement involvement (.669) yet only an average level of involvement (.154).

From the standpoint of overall numbers, roughly two to three times as many individuals are involved as members in "conventional" (non-social movement) associations as are involved in social movement associations, though the expected probabilities shown in Table 3.1 may not fully reflect the full range of possible formal associations (let alone infor-mal networks and groupings), given the fact that only six such types were identified in the 1990 World Values questionnaire. Among those countries with moderate to high overall levels of voluntary association member-ships, the *ratio* of social movement organization proportions to conven-tional association membership proportions is higher in some countries (especially Belgium, .309 to .468, but also the Netherlands, .468 to .745) than others, while countries with low rates of conventional membership involvement tend to have very low social movement involvement rates.[11]

The third column in Table 3.1 shows the expected probabilities for union membership in 1990. Some of the variability between countries might result from different regulatory regimes surrounding the compul-sory nature of membership (membership compulsory to work at a given location; dues check-off compulsory but membership optional) but some additional variability might correspond to systematic differences in the respondents' perceptions as to whether they constitute "members" even if, in fact, they are nominally members. It is clear from this table that unions do not provide a strong basis for organizational involvement in the United States (.089) or, for that matter, in Canada (.124), while they might do so in Scandinavian countries (Sweden, Norway, Denmark), and in some for-mer Eastern bloc countries (East Germany, Estonia, Russia, Latvia).

The pattern for religious/church associations (column 4) is not so directly tied to the patterns for NSMs and non-social movement (exclud-ing religious) memberships. First, Brazil, Chile, and Mexico have above-average church/religious membership rates, yet have below-average rates for other types of association memberships. These countries have a com-mon Catholic orientation, yet this is also the case with a large number of other countries that, in Table 3.1, display low rates of church/religious membership (France, Spain, and Italy, for example). As noted earlier (Cur-tis et al. 2001: 799), the United States ranks highest among 30 countries (.489) when it comes to association memberships that are related to church or religious organizations; the country with the next highest ex-pected membership rate is the Netherlands (.369), with a considerably lower level of membership involvement. Here, at least, the literature on the exceptional nature of American voluntary association involvement is supported, but as noted above, the United States is not unique for most other forms of voluntary association involvement. Thus far, there is little to suggest to us that, across countries, social movement membership forms a special pattern that is different from the pattern observed with conven-tional non-social movement associations. Affiliation with religious/church organizations is a different story, as they are some interesting divergences from the overall pattern, as noted above.

Column 5 of Table 3.1 shows the expected probabilities for active non-social movement memberships. The Netherlands, which had the highest

Table 3.1. Comparative Rates of Voluntary Association Involvement, 1990

Country	All Memberships				Memberships Reporting Voluntary Unpaid Work			
	Excluding rel, union soc. mov.	Social Movements	Union	Religious	Excluding rel, union soc. mov.	Social Movements	Union	Religious
Argentina	0.182 **	0.030 **	0.015 ***	0.082 **	0.134 **	0.021 **	0.007 *	0.061 **
Austria	0.405 **	0.157 **	0.249 ***	0.138 **	0.205 **	0.067 **	0.033	0.052 **
Belgium	0.468	0.309 **	0.196 ***	0.129 **	0.242 **	0.117	0.027	0.074 **
Brazil	0.336 **	0.186 *	0.079	0.288 **	0.220 **	0.098	0.023	0.175 **
Britain	0.446 *	0.180 **	0.165 ***	0.183 **	0.139 **	0.037 **	0.018	0.065 **
Bulgaria	0.241 **	0.099 **	0.194 ***	0.024 **	0.133 **	0.075 *	0.053 ***	0.026 **
Canada	0.510	0.230	0.124 ***	0.260 **	0.350 *	0.124	0.043 ***	0.166 **
Chile	0.296 **	0.114 **	0.064 **	0.211 **	0.220 **	0.073 **	0.026	0.153 **
Denmark	0.581 **	0.253	0.564 ***	0.065 **	0.208 **	0.045 **	0.040 **	0.024 **
Estonia	0.294 **	0.113 **	0.641 ***	0.039 **	0.206 **	0.084 *	0.123 ***	0.012 **
France	0.320 **	0.122 **	0.061 *	0.061 **	0.204 **	0.073 *	0.030	0.050 **
Germany (E)	0.582 **	0.205	0.616 ***	0.225 **	0.330	0.091	0.132 ***	0.096 **
Germany (W)	0.607 **	0.233	0.175 ***	0.174 **	0.277	0.091	0.021	0.077 **
Hungary	0.207 **	0.069 **	0.336 ***	0.120 **	0.113 **	0.040 **	0.058 ***	0.029 **
Ireland	0.446 *	0.142 **	0.103	0.143 **	0.251 *	0.067 **	0.015	0.071 **
Italy	0.316 **	0.110 **	0.088	0.092 **	0.230 **	0.061 **	0.031	0.077 **
Japan	0.177 **	0.052 **	0.083	0.064 **	0.098 **	0.033 **	0.016	0.025 **
Latvia	0.287 **	0.116 **	0.560 ***	0.030 **				
Mexico	0.239 **	0.140 **	0.050 ***	0.179 **	0.180 **	0.088	0.028	0.134 **
N. Ireland	0.465	0.160 *	0.141 **	0.276 **	0.244 *	0.062 *	0.028	0.117 **

Country	All Memberships				Memberships Reporting Voluntary Unpaid Work			
	Excluding rel, union soc. mov.	Social Movements	Union	Religious	Excluding rel, union soc. mov.	Social Movements	Union	Religious
Netherlands	0.745 **	0.468 **	0.210 ***	0.369 **	0.290	0.091	0.014	0.102 **
Norway	0.669 **	0.154 **	0.474 ***	0.109 **	0.283	0.037 **	0.077 ***	0.057 **
Portugal	0.296 **	0.050 **	0.063 *	0.113 **	0.172 **	0.024 **	0.021	0.069 **
Romania	0.098 **	0.029 **	0.223 ***	0.048 **	0.100 **	0.023 **	0.184 ***	0.045 **
Russia	0.220 **	0.074 **	0.761 ***	0.012 **	0.144 **	0.048 **	0.094 ***	0.010 **
Slovenia	0.222 **	0.097 **	0.212 ***	0.026 **	0.108 **	0.045 **	0.022	0.017 **
Spain	0.203 **	0.059 **	0.049 ***	0.053 **	0.066 **	0.025 **	0.011 *	0.026 **
Sweden	0.586 **	0.270 *	0.630 ***	0.096 **	0.310	0.079 *	0.068 ***	0.026 **
Switzerland	0.339 **	0.177 *	0.095	0.112 **				
United States	0.493	0.233	0.089	0.489	0.306	0.109	0.021	0.301

Evaluated at age=35–44; Occup=White-collar

Marital status=married; Sex=Female; Educ=Age 16–20; Commsize=>500,000

* Different from U.S. at p<.05

** Different from U.S. at p<.001

involvement rates when counting all memberships, whether involving unpaid work or not, still has high involvement rates (.290), but Canada (.350), Germany (.330), Sweden (.310) and the United States (.306) have higher expected probabilities. Notable for its low level of active involvement is Britain (.134), which, because its electoral system, political economy, language, and cultural traditions resemble those in Canada and the United States, would be expected to have higher rates of voluntary association involvement. The post-hoc explanation for this cannot reside solely in the fact that Britain's state sector has historically been larger than those in the other Anglophone democracies, since other countries with large state sectors (Sweden, for example) have high rates of active association involvement.

Social movement association active membership rates (column 6) are the highest in Canada (.124), Belgium (.117) and the United States (.109)—all countries with high rates for active membership in traditional association—but also in Brazil (.098). Earlier, Curtis et al. (2001: 802) invoked an explanation for higher association involvement rates in Brazil, relating this to church-based associations. It is indeed the case that working involvement in church/religious associations is very high in Brazil; only the United States has higher rates of involvement (see column 7, second from right). And it is also the case that NSM working membership involvement still represents small overall proportions of the populations, even in countries with the highest levels (less than 10% in all but three countries). Still, Brazil, and for that matter Mexico, can be seen as having much higher rates of involvement than would be expected (Argentina, by contrast, has an expected probability of active involvement of .021). While there are no "reversals"—countries near the bottom of one rank-ordered list but at the top of the other—when comparing social movement and non-social movement working memberships, there is not nearly so strong a connection between the two types of membership rates here as there was in the case of "total memberships." To be sure, some of this discrepancy may lie in sampling variability given the smaller proportions involved, but with sample sizes of at least 1,000 in most countries, the difference between, say, Brazil (.098) and Denmark (.045) cannot be attributed to chance.

It could be argued that, in the immediate post-cold war period, some residue of social movement activity might have been seen across Eastern Europe in the 1990 survey. This might explain high rates of social movement involvement in Estonia (.084), the former East Germany (which, in other terms, seems to have assumed the patterns of the former West Germany), and Bulgaria (.075), but it does not explain why some former Eastern bloc countries have low rates of involvement (e.g., Hungary, .040; Romania, .023).

As with social movement involvement, active involvement in religious and church organizations does not fall into a pattern that is consistent with the overall pattern for other non-social movement associations. The expected probabilities reported in column 8 of Table 3.1 (rightmost) further confirm what has been reported elsewhere (see Curtis et al. 1992, 2001): United States exceptionalism is in large part related to very high rates of religious involvement in that country. Active involvement in unions as unpaid volunteers does not incur the same interpretational difficulties, whereas regular membership (which is non-voluntary in some cases) does. Unions provide a basis for active involvement in Estonia (.123), Russia (.094), Romania (.184), and East Germany (.132) as well in two Scandinavian countries, Sweden and Norway (.068 and .077 respectively). For former Eastern bloc countries, unions represented in 1990 a relatively important vehicle for organizational involvement, considering the low levels of involvement with other types of associations.

The between-country comparisons ten years later, in 2000, are shown in Table 3.2. Some of the countries included in the 1990 analysis in Table 3.1 (Brazil, Norway, Switzerland) are not included in Table 3.2 due to the lack of available data, and data tabulated separately for the former East and West Germany are also unavailable. There are, however, more countries in the 2000 World Values data set, so the following countries are now included: the Czech Republic, Greece, Iceland, Luxembourg, Poland, and the Slovak Republic.[12]

Once again, the United States stands out as a country displaying high rates of voluntary association involvement, for both total memberships and memberships involving unpaid work. But, as will be seen, it is not alone. For non-social movement organizations, the United States has a high expected proportion of members among its population (.815), but the proportion is slightly higher in the Netherlands (.855), and also fairly high in Sweden (.761) and Iceland (.724). Relative to other countries, the remaining countries identified variously as Social Democratic, Scandinavian, or "Nordic" all show high rates of involvement (Finland, .626, Denmark, .659), and the pattern where two liberal democratic countries (the US and Canada) and all of the social democratic countries have higher rates than all other countries repeats itself in 2000, though the United States rises in the rankings. Canada also remains relatively high in involvement (.672).

Non-social movement, non-religious-affiliated, and non-union membership levels involving over half the population can be seen in many of the other countries shown in Table 3.2. These include Austria, Belgium, the Czech Republic, Germany, Ireland, Korea, Luxembourg, and the Slovak Republic. While these countries have lower expected proportions than the two highest liberal democratic countries, Canada and the United States, and lower expected proportions than social democratic countries, the

Table 3.2. Comparative Rates of Voluntary Association Involvement, 2000

Country	All Memberships				Memberships Reporting Voluntary Unpaid Work			
	Excluding rel, union soc. mov.	Social Movements	Union	Religious	Excluding rel, union soc. mov.	Social Movements	Union	Religious
Argentina	0.417 **	0.035 **	0.019 **	0.124 **	0.201 **	0.024 **	0.010 *	0.078 **
Austria	0.599 **	0.132 **	0.145 **	0.166 **	0.244 **	0.050 **	0.024 n	0.045 **
Belgium	0.579 **	0.206 n	0.124 **	0.067 **	0.258 **	0.077 **	0.024 n	0.032 **
Bulgaria	0.170 **	0.022 **	0.047 **	0.011 **	0.110 **	0.020 **	0.039 n	0.010 **
Canada	0.672 **	0.159 **	0.092 n	0.209 **	0.389 **	0.086 **	0.036 n	0.130 **
Chile	0.439 **	0.099 **	0.019 **	0.161 **	0.348 **	0.094 **	0.028 n	0.132 **
Czech Republic	0.546 **	0.083 **	0.069 n	0.039 **	0.266 **	0.041 **	0.032 n	0.017 **
Denmark	0.659 **	0.147 **	0.483 **	0.069 **	0.286 **	0.035 **	0.040 n	0.020 **
Estonia	0.267 **	0.030 **	0.029 **	0.039 **	0.128 **	0.023 **	0.005 n	0.016 **
Finland	0.626 **	0.134 **	0.281 **	0.357 **	0.325 **	0.070 **	0.053 *	0.053 **
France	0.411 **	0.041 **	0.029 **	0.028 **	0.228 **	0.021 **	0.018 n	0.022 **
Germany	0.551 **	0.065 **	0.054 *	0.090 **	0.182 **	0.028 **	0.005 **	0.038 **
Greece	0.484 **	0.137 **	0.056 *	0.046 **	0.288 **	0.122 n	0.045 n	0.045 **
Hungary	0.208 **	0.022 **	0.054 *	0.076 **	0.120 **	0.025 **	0.018 n	0.037 **
Iceland	0.724 **	0.138 **	0.511 **	0.620 **	0.281 **	0.040 **	0.029 n	0.030 **
Ireland	0.582 **	0.095 **	0.085 n	0.107 **	0.277 **	0.047 **	0.024 n	0.054 **
Italy	0.394 **	0.056 **	0.042 **	0.061 **	0.200 **	0.035 **	0.026 n	0.042 **
Japan	0.355 **	0.058 **	0.039 **	0.066 **	0.121 **	0.025 **	0.005 **	0.020 **
Korea, Rep.	0.527 **	0.068 **	0.042 **	0.336 **	0.259 **	0.057 **	0.021 n	0.222 *
Latvia	0.187 **	0.014 **	0.084 n	0.032 **	0.155 **	0.010 **	0.029 n	0.024 **

Country	All Memberships				Memberships Reporting Voluntary Unpaid Work			
	Excluding rel, union soc. mov.	Social Movements	Union	Religious	Excluding rel, union soc. mov.	Social Movements	Union	Religious
Lithuania	0.118 **	0.010 **	0.013 **	0.030 **	0.069 **	0.007 **	0.016 n	0.026 **
Luxembourg	0.588 **	0.186 *	0.090 **	0.053 **	0.262 **	0.093 **	0.033 n	0.037 **
Mexico	0.428 **	0.099 **	0.046 **	0.179 **	0.307 **	0.082 **	0.032 n	0.168 **
Netherlands	0.855 *	0.484 **	0.144 **	0.246 **	0.431 *	0.068 **	0.020 n	0.075 **
Poland	0.182 **	0.021 **	0.076 n	0.034 **	0.082 **	0.009 **	0.028 n	0.024 **
Portugal	0.241 **	0.015 **	0.013 **	0.033 **	0.105 **	0.008 **	0.005 n	0.017 **
Romania	0.130 **	0.014 **	0.071 n	0.024 **	0.072 **	0.010 **	0.071 **	0.022 **
Russian Federation	0.111 **	0.010 **	0.174 **	0.014 **	0.033 **	0.006 **	0.040 n	0.003 **
Slovak Republic	0.513 **	0.082 **	0.105 *	0.101 **	0.364 **	0.064 **	0.064 **	0.085 **
Slovenia	0.451 **	0.044 **	0.127 **	0.038 **	0.222 **	0.038 **	0.041 n	0.028 **
Spain	0.300 **	0.066 **	0.031 **	0.041 **	0.142 **	0.037 **	0.018 *	0.028 **
Sweden	0.761 *	0.207 n	0.577 **	0.641 **	0.390 **	0.073 **	0.091 **	0.178 **
United Kingdom	0.359 **	0.046 **	0.059 **	0.029 **	N/A	N/A	N/A	N/A
Northern Ireland	0.433 **	0.073 **	0.053 *	0.161 **	0.159 **	0.030 **	0.016 **	0.068 **
United States	0.815	0.233	0.084	0.472	0.517	0.140	0.030	0.293

n   Not significantly different from US

*   Significantly different from US at p<.05 but not p<.001

All other estimated proportions significantly different from US at p<.001.

differences are not as pronounced as they were in 1990. With the exception of the Czech Republic, Slovakia, and Slovenia, membership rates in non-social movement associations are extremely low in Eastern bloc countries (Bulgaria, Estonia, Latvia, Lithuania, Poland, Romania, and Russia).

The pattern in 2000 for social movement association memberships (column 2 under "All memberships" in Table 3.2) is very similar.[13] Again, the Netherlands (.484) and then the United States (.233) have the highest expected proportions. The values for Sweden (.207) and Belgium (.206) are not significantly different from those of the United States. Canada, Denmark, Finland, and Iceland are among the remaining countries with expected proportions greater than 10%, as might be expected, but Luxembourg and Greece are also included in this group. It is difficult to make distinctions among the remaining countries; levels of involvement are fairly low due to the small number of cases involved.

Sustained high voluntary association involvement in the United States has been connected with the continuing strength of its (especially Protestant) religious support (see Uslaner 2001; Ladd 1999; Lipset 1994), and from this it might be easy to predict the high rates of membership in religious-affiliated organizations in the US (.472). Other countries with apparently high rates include Korea and the Netherlands. The membership question for religious associations is somewhat susceptible to interpretational differences across countries (in some countries, respondents may have interpreted the question to include regular church membership), and there is some evidence that this may explain some of the higher numbers in some countries.[14]

The high reported rates of union membership seen in the 1990 data in many former Eastern bloc countries is no longer present in 2000, when the big distinction is between social democratic countries, with the exception of the Netherlands, and all other countries. Rates of union membership identification are high in Sweden (.577), Denmark (.483), and Finland (.281). The next highest countries are Russia (.174), Austria (.145), and the Netherlands (.144). Hungary, Estonia, and Latvia, which had very high levels of membership in 1990, now have comparatively low levels—or at least levels that are very close to those of the United States.

For active memberships, in 1990 the Netherlands stood out as having higher membership rates and, to a lesser extent, fairly high active membership rates. In 2000, the Netherlands, again, had the highest overall membership rate for total memberships ("all memberships" in the table), and a fairly high, though not the highest, rate of volunteering (that is, memberships voluntary reporting unpaid work). In 2000, the United States had the highest expected rate of active membership (.517), followed by the Netherlands (.431), Sweden (.390), and Canada (.389). Just behind these, in order, were Slovakia (.364), Chile (.348), Finland

(.325), and Iceland (.281). As was the case with total memberships, the Czech Republic, Slovakia, and Slovenia form exceptions to the general pattern of very low active involvement within former European Eastern bloc countries.

For NSM associations in 2000, working membership numbers are too small to make accurate comparisons, but the countries with the highest expected proportions include the United States (with the highest), Greece (at .122, unexpectedly high and not significantly different from the United States), Chile (.094), Luxembourg (.093), Canada (.086), Mexico (.082), and Belgium (.077). NSM associations—at least using the limited measures available here—remain much less important than conventional associations in terms of the number of citizens actively involved in them (see the relative proportions in the columns). The patterns do not always clearly match those patterns observed for non-social movement organizations, but once again we are pointed to Belgium and Luxembourg as exceptions to the "liberal democracy/social democracy" rule.

In an earlier discussion of overall association involvement using the 1990 World Values data, Curtis et al. (2001: 802) identified higher participation rates in Brazil (especially), Chile, and Mexico as being related to the role of recent Protestant religious activity in these countries, but not in Argentina where Protestantism remained relatively weak (see Martin 1990). At the time, the analysis did not include separate tabulations for social movement and non-social movement involvement. The findings presented here reinforce the suggestion made earlier. In Table 1, using 1990 data, Brazil ranked fairly high in terms of active social movement association involvement and active religious association involvement, but closer to average for non-social movement associations. The same applied to Mexico, and to a lesser extent Chile, but not Argentina. In Table 2, using 2000 data, Argentina again shows low levels of active social movement involvement (.024), but Chile (.094) and Mexico (.082) show relatively high levels.[15] Unlike 1990, the pattern for Chile does not include low involvement in non-social movement associations; as mentioned above, Chile shows relatively high rates of involvement (.348).

For active involvement in unions, countries with the highest levels of involvement, in order, were Sweden (.091), Romania (.071), the Slovak Republic (.064), and Finland (.053). Reflecting lower rates of union density, the active involvement rates in Canada (.036) and the United States (.030) are somewhat lower. They are exceedingly low in Germany, Estonia, Japan, and Portugal (all .005). For active involvement in religious associations, the United States stands out as fairly exceptional (.293), but Korea (.222), Sweden (.178), and Mexico (.168) also have high rates of involvement.

Across the entire table, the three Latin American countries (Mexico, Chile, Argentina) stand out as having rates of voluntary association involvement—both total memberships and memberships involving unpaid voluntary work—that are as high if not higher than those found in some European countries such as Spain, Greece, or most Eastern bloc countries. This applies especially to total non-social movement memberships (Argentina, .417; Mexico, .428; Chile, .439; compare with Italy, .394; France, .411; Portugal, .241; Spain .300) and to working non-social movement memberships (Argentina, .201; Chile, .348; Mexico, .307; compare with Italy, .200; France, .228; Portugal, .105; and Spain, .142).

Overall, some general conclusions emerge from both the 1990 and the 2000 findings, as do some interesting exceptions to the patterns. While there were some modest shifts in rank-order among them, social democratic countries and the two North American democracies consistently rank high, especially when one focuses on the major types of organizations giving rise to the vast majority of voluntary association participation in most countries—the "conventional" or non-social movement associations not associated with religion. Belgium and Luxembourg stand out as interesting exceptions whose national contexts warrant further discussion and investigation. In most political typologies, these two countries are not classified as "social democratic" (at best, they form part of a "left Catholic" category that is shared, variously, with countries such as Germany), and they can be considered of Catholic religious heritage. They thus break the "Catholic origin/low involvement" mold that was described earlier. As was reported earlier in Curtis et al. (2001), former Eastern bloc countries have low to very low rates of involvement, yet here too there are two or perhaps three important exceptions that might be worthy of further investigation: the Czech Republic, Slovenia, and Slovakia. Union memberships may continue to form a basis for associational involvement in Scandinavian countries, but their importance is small and possibly diminishing elsewhere. In the United States, the pattern is one where religious-affiliated voluntary associations remain important, though this comes in the context of high involvement in all association types (non-social movement, social movement), except for unions.

Tracking Systematic Patterns of Difference: Hierarchical Models for Voluntary Association Involvement

Research using multiple-level models to examine both individual- and contextual-level effects in the study of voluntary association involvement is fairly new. They first achieved prominence with the precursor to the present analysis (Curtis et al. 2001) and with a related work in the same issue of the *American Sociological Review* using the same data (see Schofer and Fourcade-Gourinchas 2001). The method involves the use of "level-1" (for individuals) and "level-2" (for countries) equations, where some or all of the coefficients in the level-1 equations themselves become the basis for equations at a higher level (see Raudenbush and Bryk 2002; Hox 2002). A major advantage of this technique is its ability to properly estimate both "context" and "individual difference" effects, but a disadvantage is that level-2 inferences can be based on fairly small numbers of cases when the grouping factor is "country." Even with the 30-plus countries available in a rich dataset such as the World Values Study, there are some major limitations on the number of alternative explanations that can be simultaneously investigated.

In the previous published work in this area, both Curtis et al. and Schofer and Fourcade-Gourinchas use similar respondent background measures (age, education, gender, etc.) at the individual level and then use measures of "state type" at the aggregate level, though their labels are slightly different. Both articles conclude that the "state types" represented by Scandinavia and by liberal democracies (the United States, the UK, and Canada) have higher rates of voluntary association involvement. Curtis et al. do not report findings with respect to NSM associations but Schofer and Fourcade-Gourinchas do. On the other hand, Schofer and Fourcade-Gourinchas do not evaluate the influence of religious tradition (as did Curtis et al.) and do not report findings for working memberships (only total memberships are modeled). Arguably, the study of working memberships provides a better indication of the involvement of citizens in public life or at least helps to dismiss the claim that some or all of what is being investigated amounts to little more than a token annual membership dues payment, readership of association literature, and little else.[16] To be sure, the measures that are available in the World Values Study might understate the extent of active involvement, since participation in association meetings, engagement in public debate, attendance at rallies, and various forms of solidaristic acts consonant with an association's orientation might not be construed by some respondents as representing "unpaid work." Still, they are probably a better indication of the potential of association involvement for the development of a vigorous civil society (however this is defined) than simple measurement counts.

Tables 3.3 and 3.4 provide results for the "level-2" variables in hierarchical models for the 1990 data, with association involvement modeled (as involved/not) for each of non-social movement, social movement, and religious/church related associations. The 6 columns in each of these tables cover the dependent variables that were dealt with in Table 3.1, but with the presentation of aggregate-level equations, where the effects of country characteristics and differences between "types" of countries appear as coefficients in the table instead of separate estimates for each country. To conserve space, Tables 3.3 and 3.4 do not show any of the individual-level effects from the Hierarchical Linear Model (HLM) model,

Table 3.3. Characteristics of Countries as Predictors of Voluntary Association Memberships, 1990 (Level-2 HLM Equation Results, Binomial Logit Models)

Level-2 Variables Modeled One at a Time

	Total Memberships			Working Memberships		
	Non-NSM	NSM	Religious	Non-NSM	NSM	Religious
	[1]	[2]	[3]	[4]	[5]	[6]
GDP (log base e)	0.494 **	0.369 **	0.168 *	0.214 **	0.081	0.168 *
Years of democracy	0.0156 **	0.014 **	0.002	0.01 **	0.006 **	0.002
Religion Type						
Mixed Christian	0.993 **	1.314 **	1.511 **	0.806 **	0.170	1.371 **
Protestant	1.188 **	0.951 **	1.583 **	0.919 **	0.151	-0.107
Catholic	0.099	0.301 *	1.036 **	0.145	0.246	0.408 *
Other (reference)						
Political Type						
Social dem.	1.325 **	0.701 **	0.179	1.325 **	0.075	-0.477 **
Liberal dem.	0.470 **	-0.396 **	0.386 *	0.47 *	0.283 *	0.678 **
Eastern bloc	-0.257	0.211	-0.863 **	-0.257	-0.297 *	-0.648 **
Other democracies (ref)						
Block chi-sq tests						
Religion Type (df=3)	38.570 **	24.76 **	31.41 **	43.73 **	1.770	29.97 **
Political Type (df=3)	60.054 **	12.84 **	17.86 **	60.05 **	9.15 *	30.56 **

* p<.05 ** p<.01

but the general effect of these variables will be discussed later and outlined in Table 3.6 below.

In Tables 3.3 and 3.4, the variables working at the "aggregate" level are
the same as those reported in Curtis et al. (2001): GDP per capita, years
of continuous democracy, religious composition (with four groupings:
mainly Protestant, mainly Roman Catholic, mixed Protestant and
Catholic, others), and political type. For political type, the classification
closely followed Janoski (1998), and classified countries into liberal
democracies, social democracies, a third category for former Eastern bloc
socialist nations, and a fourth group of other democracies (most of which
would be described as "traditional" polities). Social democracies include
Norway, Sweden, Denmark, and the Netherlands; liberal democracies include Canada, the United States, and Great Britain.

This formulation, following Janoski, is slightly different from the formulation used by Schofer and Fourcade-Gourinchas. Based on Jepperson
and Meyer's work (1991; see also Jepperson 2002), their classification
places the United States, Canada, and Great Britain in one cell (low corporateness, low statism); Scandinavian countries in another (low statism,
high corporateness); France, Italy, Spain, Portugal, and Latin America in
a third (low corporateness high statism); and Germany, Austria, Central and
Eastern Europe, and Japan in a fourth (high corporateness, high statism).
The location of the Netherlands in the scheme is ambiguous, though one
writing (Jepperson 2002: 70) suggests that it would be classified as "liberal" (hence, in the same cell as Canada, the US and the UK). The main
conceptual difference between the classification based on Janoski and
the classification used by Schofer and Fourcade-Gourinchas is one of
focus: Janoski focuses on rights (citizenship rights, welfare rights), while
Schofer and Fourcade-Gourinchas focus more on institutional process
(decision-making structures in the state), though one is never very far from
the other in either scheme.

One final remark is in order with respect to the relationship between
the scheme used by Schofer and Fourcade-Gourinchas and the one employed here. While the "statism versus corporateness" scheme involves
four cells (2001: 817, Table 3), the model that was elaborated by these
authors was limited in the sense that it imposed an implicit constraint
that the effect of statism must be consistent across categories of corporateness and the effect of corporateness must be consistent across categories of statism. If we can take the "ideal type" country in each of the
four cells, what this means is that the model assumed that the difference
between the US (low corporateness) and Scandinavian countries (high
corporateness) would be the same as the difference between France (low
corporateness) and Germany (high corporateness). In statistical parlance,
the model did not include an interaction term. The models used in the

analysis reported here conceptualize regime type as a single categorical variable, but allow for unconstrained differences of any sort among the four major categories.

Janoski's typology did not incorporate countries from Latin America or the former Eastern bloc of Europe, although they initially had been coded as separate categories. Later, due to the small number of countries in Latin America and the relative similarity, with control variables, between these countries and other "traditional" countries, the separate classification was collapsed to keep the number of variables in the model reasonable.

In addition to regime type and religious heritage, Inglehart's (1997) measure of "number of years of continuous democracy" was used as a control variable. There are high correlations among these level-2 variables, and given the small number of units in the level-2 equations, it is important to understand that it may not always be possible to separate out effects where overlaps exist. For example, all but one of the "mainly Protestant" states are social democratic states. The measures of GDP (log) and years of continuous democracy are also highly correlated (r=.85). For this reason, models are estimated both on a "one variable at a time" basis and with all variables entered as a set.

Table 3.1 shows the effect of the aggregate variables. The first three columns suggest that systematic between-country differences play a major role in predicting membership rates for all of the different total membership types. Taken individually, each of the four predictor variables has a significant effect upon membership rates for non-social movement, social movement, and religious associations, with only one exception: years of democracy does not affect religious membership. The level of economic development has a positive effect in all three cases, as does years of democracy for non-social movement and social movement (but not religious associations). The size of the coefficients must be interpreted in light of the metric of each of the variables: the (log) GDP measure has a range (minimum to maximum) of 3 and a standard deviation of 1, while years of democracy has a range of 71 and a standard deviation of 32. For two nations at either extreme of the GDP range, we would expect the higher GDP country to have an odds ratio (members : non-members) 4.4 times higher than the odds ratio for the lower GDP country.[17] A similar difference would be observed between a social democratic country and a former Eastern bloc country. Finally, if the years of democracy variable has a coefficient of .02, then the "odds ratio multiplier" representing the multiplicative difference in odds ratios between the two countries with a 30-year difference in democratic experience will be 1.8.[18] How, approximately, these ratios work for particular countries is illustrated by the expected probabilities shown in Table 3.1.[19]

For country religious type, mixed Christian and Protestant countries are not substantially different, but both have much higher membership rates for both non-social movement and social movement associations. Only in the case of religious and church associations is there a convergence between Catholic and non-Catholic countries. In all cases, countries identified as "other" are substantially lower in membership levels.

Table 3.4 shows the models with each of the level-2 variables entered simultaneously. In some cases, overall models are highly significant but individual variables are considerably less so; this is a function of the high correlations (overlaps) among variables. For non-social movement associations (column 1), political type seems to hold up with controls for other variables, with the major finding being the higher membership rates in social democratic countries. For social movement association memberships (column 2), years of democracy has a positive effect on membership, and there is also a significant effect of religion type: mixed Christian countries have higher membership rates, controlling for differences in individual-level respondent attributes and for the country-level effects of other variables (polity type, GDP, years of democracy). Finally, for religious associations, the variable that remains significant with controls for other variables is religion, and its effect basically amounts to a difference between all three Christian types (which are similar to each other) on one hand, and non-Christian countries on the other.

Considered one at a time at the aggregate level—that is, not controlling for other aggregate factors, but controlling for individual-level attributes— GDP, years of democracy, country religion type, and country political type affect working membership probabilities, though the effects appear to be far less pronounced in the case of social movement associations. Briefly, high GDP has a positive effect on non-social movement and religious working memberships, but is not a significant predictor of social movement activity. The years-of-democracy variable has a positive effect on non-social movement and social movement working membership probabilities, but not on religious association working memberships.

The effect of political type is significant for non-social movement and religious associations, though the pattern differs from that in the case of total memberships. For non-social movement associations, the major division is between social democratic countries and the other country types. The coefficient of 1.325 works out to an odds ratio multiplier of 3.76, which means that social democratic countries have "odds" that are 3.76 times as high as those for the "other" country types. Liberal democracies have somewhat higher probabilities of involvement than other, non-social democratic country types (+.47, which works out to an odds ratio multiplier of 1.60). By implication, if social democratic countries have 3.76 times the odds of membership as "other" countries, and if lib-

Table 3.4. Characteristics of Countries as Predictors of Voluntary Association Memberships, 1990 (Level-2 HLM Equation Results, Binomial Logit Models)

Level-2 Variables with Added Controls for other Level-2 Variables

	Total Memberships			Working Memberships		
	Non-NSM	NSM	Religious	Non-NSM	NSM	Religious
	[1]	[2]	[3]	[4]	[5]	[6]
GDP (log base e)	0.198	0.033	0.120	-0.112	-0.149	-0.258
Years of democracy	-0.003	0.013 **	-0.001	0.009 *	0.010	0.002
Religion Type						
Mixed Christian	0.235	0.744 *	1.473 **	0.591 **	-0.203	1.235 **
Protestant	-0.132	-0.098	1.533 **	0.922 *	-0.789	0.715
Catholic	-0.235	0.131	0.947 **	0.255	0.006	0.472
Other Religious Types						
Political Type						
Social democracy	1.200 **	0.529	-0.279	-0.12	0.451	-0.571
Liberal democracy	0.122	-0.281	0.198	0.088	0.067	0.134
Eastern bloc	-0.400	0.125	-0.402	0.343 *	-0.069	-0.893 **
Other Democracies						
Block chi-sq tests						
Model (df=8)	115.040 **	47.75 **	43.51 **	68.62 **	13.3	51.42 **
Religion Type (df=3)	6.87	8.68 *	12.77 **	10.21 *	3.02	14.24 **
Political Type (df=3)	26.59 **	4.99	2.43	5.92	1.44	13.32 **

* p<.05 ** p<.01
Note: All models involve level-1 controls for age, religion, gender, marital status, and education.

eral democracies have 1.60 times the odds, then social democratic countries have 2.35 times the odds of membership as liberal democratic countries, all other things being equal. For religious associations, active involvement rates are elevated considerably in liberal democratic states (+.678), but reduced in social democratic (−.477) and former Eastern bloc states (−.648).

Finally, the dominant religion of a country cannot be said to affect active involvement in social movement associations since the test statistic in this table is not statistically significant,[20] but years of continuous democracy and political type both have an effect: countries with longer histories of democracy have higher involvement rates, and there is a slight tendency for liberal democratic countries to have higher rates and for Eastern bloc countries to have lower rates. These effects are not nearly so substantial as they are in the case of active (working) involvement in non-social movement or religious associations. In this table, it is possible, in a rough fashion, to compare the magnitudes of the coefficients for any given independent variable across different dependent variables (and to a lesser extent, to compare coefficients that involve dummy variables—religion and political type).[21]

With controls for other level-2 (country-level) variables, the overall model for active social movement association memberships (column 5) is not statistically significant. When it comes to non-social movement associations, religion and years of democracy remain significant; with controls, the difference between mixed Christian and Protestant countries is reversed (now mixed Christian countries, .591, are slightly lower than Protestant countries at .922), but both still have significantly higher rates than countries of other religious types. Finally, for religious associations, country religion type and country political type remain significant when adjusting for the effects of other level-2 variables: mixed Christian countries have higher rates of active involvement, and Eastern bloc countries have lower rates.

What bearing do these findings have on our questions regarding differences between social movement and non-social movement volunteering? For total memberships, the patterns we see for social movement associations do not appear to be much different from those for non-social movement associations. But for working memberships, systematic between-country variations, if they exist at all, are not covered very well by the standard country-level variables of religious type, political type, level of economic development (GDP), and number of years of continuous democracy.

Table 3.5 provides a replication using data from 2000. Since level-2 equation results can depend critically on the presence or absence of particular aggregate "cases" (countries), this replication is important not only as an examination of the possibility that relationships observed in 1990

Table 3.5. Characteristics of Countries as Predictors of Voluntary Association Memberships 2000 (Level-2 HLM Equation Results, Binomial Logit Models)

	Total Memberships				Working Memberships			
Model 1								
Polity Type Only	Non-NSM	NSM	Union	Religious	Non-NSM	NSM	Union	Religious
Polity Type								
Social dem.	1.0382 ***	0.8548 *	2.4008 ***	1.4924 **	0.5275 **	-0.0529	0.9779 **	0.1429
Liberal dem.	0.3234	0.1983	0.1957	0.978	0.6013	0.539	0.1297	0.853
Eastern bloc	-0.8688 **	-1.1811 **	0.355	-0.577 **	-0.5372 *	-0.930 **	0.4715	-0.618 *
Reference: others								
Block test:								
Polity (chi-sq)	35.49 ***	26.830 ***	47.01 ***	29.190 ***	17.35 ***	18.970 ***	12.58 **	11.940 **

	Total Memberships				Working Memberships			
Model 2								
Polity + GDP	Non-NSM	NSM	Union	Religious	Non-NSM	NSM	Union	Religious
Polity								
Social dem.	0.7379 **	0.6428	2.1782 ***	1.610 **	0.4577 *	-0.090	1.0502 **	0.483
Liberal dem.	0.079	0.0321	0.0558	1.079	0.5487	0.513	0.1744	1.146 *
Eastern bloc	-0.140	-0.6325	1.2202 ***	-0.820 **	-0.3841	-0.867	0.2711	-1.184 ***
Reference: others								
GDP (ln)	0.487 ***	0.3691 *	0.491 **	-0.166	0.1063	0.052	-0.1189	-0.419 **
Block test								
Polity (chi-sq)	9.137 *	4.325	60.9 ***	24.87 ***	8.706 *	9.430 *	11.27 *	17.530 ***

Model 3

Polity + Religion	Total Memberships				Working Memberships			
	Non-NSM	NSM	Union	Religious	Non-NSM	NSM	Union	Religious
Polity								
Social dem.	1.489 ***	1.8301 ***	1.8411 ***	2.385 **	0.3152	-0.3552	0.8141	0.7787
Liberal dem.	0.2317	0.3053	0.1149	0.9686 *	0.3602	0.2914	0.4957	0.8272
Eastern bloc	-0.8708 **	-1.192 ***	0.3536	-0.593 **	-0.5423 *	-0.941 **	0.4702 *	-0.625 *
Religious Heritage								
Protestant	-0.6188	-1.3874 ***	0.7085	-1.1692	0.1974	0.3399	0.2502	-0.8694
Mixed Christian	0.5492	0.190	-0.1239	0.237	0.3557	0.222	-0.6374	0.210
Block tests								
Polity (chi-sq)	109.100 ***	165.200 ***	18.99 ***	35.650 ***	5.843	16.950 **	8.766 *	13.090 **
Relig (chi-sq)	43.510 ***	77.100 ***	3.941	3.984	1.293	0.504	10.64 **	5.697
Excluded variables (t-values for inclusion)								
GDP [ln] chi-sq	1.486	1.116	1.484	-0.512	0.359	-0.406	0.338	-1.242
Yrs. Democracy	1.146	1.045	1.681	0.431	0.320	0.338	-0.406	-0.930

* p<.05
** p<.01
*** p<.001

Note: All models involve level-1 controls for age, religion, gender, marital status and education

may have changed over time, but also as a source of slightly different data points against which basic findings can be tested. Unfortunately, the newer data share with the 1990 data one important limitation: the ability to evaluate the separate effects of polity type and religious heritage is restricted by the fact that all of the social democratic countries except the Netherlands have Protestant cultural heritages (as does the UK, which is not social democratic).

Table 3.5 provides the results of a parallel analysis using data from the 2000 World Values Survey dataset. Ten years later, findings are similar, though not quite as consistent across the application of controls at the aggregate level. Left on its own, without controls for other aggregate-level variables, polity type has a contextual influence on voluntary association involvement for all of the dependent measures found in the table (see Model 1 at the top of the table). For total memberships, social democratic polities have considerably higher rates of involvement than other types, and Eastern bloc countries have rates that are considerably lower. For non-social movement working memberships, the rate for social democratic countries (coefficient of .5275, which translates to an odds multiplier of 1.7) is hardly different from the rate for liberal democratic countries (coefficient of .6013, which translates into an odds multiplier of 1.82), but it is significantly higher than that of former Eastern bloc countries (−.5372, or an odds multiplier of 0.58) or of "other" countries (the "reference category" which represents the baseline odds multiplier of 1.0). For social movement total memberships, compared to other polities the social democratic countries have considerably higher (coefficient of +.8548, which translates into an odds multiplier of 2.35) and the former Eastern bloc countries considerably lower rates of involvement than other countries (the coefficient of −1.1811 in the table translates into an odds multiplier of .307). As for social movement working memberships, Eastern bloc countries again have significantly lower involvement rates. Although significance tests results are not shown in the table, the coefficient for social democracies (−.0529) is significantly lower than the coefficient for liberal democracies (.539).[22] This is consistent with Table 3.3 (1990 data), where the expected rate for liberal democracies was higher than that for social democracies (.283 vs. .075), but where the difference was not statistically significant.

For religious association memberships, social democratic countries have the highest overall membership rates (coefficient of 1.4924), but for working religious associations liberal democracies have the highest rates (coefficient of .853), though the difference between social democratic and liberal democratic countries is not statistically significant. For union memberships, it should be no surprise that, given the nature of institutional support for labor in the social democratic countries, union membership rates are higher than in any other regime type. The same is true for "working" union memberships (that is, memberships involving unpaid voluntary work), where the .9779 coefficient in the table represents an odds multiplier of 2.48. Again, this means that the odds of being a working union member are 2.48 times higher in social democratic countries than they are in "other" countries. The comparison of social democratic countries with liberal democratic countries on the one hand and former Eastern bloc countries on the other is almost as extreme.

The "polity type" effects observed in Table 3.5 (see Model 1) are less clear when per capita GDP is added as a level-2 predictor (see Model 2), though itself this variable has a statistically significant effect only on (a) non social movement total memberships, (b) social movement total memberships ($p<.05$ but not $p<.01$), (c) union total memberships, and (d) working religious memberships. With GDP controlled for, polity type continues to have a statistically significant contextual effect (at $p<.05$) in all cases except for total social movement memberships. For total non-social movement memberships, social democratic countries have higher expected rates, with a coefficient of .7379 (which translates into an odds multiplier of 2.10), than "other" polity types (mostly countries described as "corporatist/traditional"). Again, this means that, in relation to the "other" country category (the "reference" in the table), the odds of membership for those living in social democratic countries are 2.10 times higher. For associations affiliated with religions, both social democratic and liberal democratic countries have high rates (coefficients of 1.610 and 1.079 respectively; these translate into odds multipliers of 5 and 2.9 respectively), while former Eastern bloc countries have lower rates (coefficient of –.820; this translates into an odds multiplier of .44).[23] Finally, social democratic countries have higher total membership rates for unions (2.1782, which translates into odds that are eight times (!) as high as those in "other" countries and 2.6 times as high as those in former Eastern bloc countries [coefficient of 1.22]). The differences are not quite so dramatic with respect to working union memberships, but it is still the case that social democratic countries have working membership odds that are 2.8 times as high as those in "other" countries and 2.4 times as high as those in liberal democratic countries.

The portion of Table 3.5 labeled "Model 3" adds religious heritage to Model 1 to replicate the analysis originally conducted with the 1990 data. Given the low degree of freedom in these models, GDP and years of democracy are initially left out of the model rather than included but are then tested against the model residuals; as shown in the table, in no case would the addition of either variable contribute significantly to the model once religious heritage and polity type are included (the t-value would need to exceed approximately 2.05 for this to be the case). The findings for polity type in Model 3 suggest patterns that are similar to those discussed in earlier models, though in the case of working non-social movement associations, neither religion nor polity type was statistically significant. For all dependent variables, rates were lower in former Eastern bloc countries (though not significantly so in the case of working non-social movement associations, as mentioned above), and for all total membership variables social democracies had substantially higher rates.

The "effect" of Protestant heritage on voluntary association involvement appears to be negative, which is counterintuitive given earlier findings. Note, however, that most social democratic polities are also of Protestant heritage, so the "net" effect is the sum of the two. Thus, Sweden (Protestant; social democratic) would have an expected log-odds coefficient of +.8702 (odds multiplier of 2.387), which is still very high. The negative coefficient representing the difference between Protestant and other countries really mostly reflects on the fact (as observed in Table 3.2, where individual country results are presented) that the total membership rates in the Netherlands (a social democracy with a mixed religious heritage as opposed to a Protestant one) are higher than those in Sweden, Finland, and Iceland (where they are still, nonetheless, high). The negative coefficient will also reflect the fact that membership rates among the liberal democracies are lower in Great Britain (Protestant) than they are in Canada or the United States (mixed).[24] Thus, the *total* impact of country being both Protestant and social democratic will be that membership rates are higher than in most other countries, even thought the coefficient for "Protestant" is negative in parts of the table (note the even higher positive coefficient for "Social democratic"). Since most Protestant countries are also at the same time social democratic (excepting the Netherlands), these countries will have higher rates of involvement than most other countries.[25]

The hierarchical models in 2000 have been useful for replicating earlier 1990 findings with respect to the differing contextual affects associated with the major polity types identified in Curtis et al. (2001), but they have not been particularly helpful in isolating the aggregate effects of the dominant religious form or heritage. An alternative measure, employed in models that already contain polity type, involves the use of *present* aggregate religious identification rates, which provide for a greater amount of discrimination than simple mutually exclusive categorizations (instead, two variables, percentage Protestant and percentage Catholic, were used).[26] In only one of the models were these new variables statistically significant at $p<.10$. For total religious-affiliated memberships, an overall significance test for *both* the percentage Protestant and the percentage Catholic variables yielded slightly significant results ($p<.043$). The coefficient for percentage Protestant was +.01362 ($p<.021$), but the coefficient for percentage Catholic was not significant, implying that, controlling for the religious affiliation of individual respondents, as the proportion of a country's citizens who are Protestants increases, so does the expected probability that an individual will be a member of a religious-affiliated voluntary association.

Other than this, these two measures of aggregate-level religious composition have no discernible effect upon voluntary association participation. Meanwhile, at the individual level, across all countries, the average expected differences between individuals who were Protestant, Catholic, or neither were strong for most of the voluntary association measures. Not shown in Table 3.5, these will be briefly outlined. It is no surprise, first, that there is a strong difference between Protestant and Catholics, on the one hand, and "others" (often nonreligious) on the other, when it comes to religious-affiliated association memberships (both total and working memberships). For non-social movement memberships, Protestants are significantly different from others, having expected odds than are 1.2 times as high as those of other groups. Translated into probabilities for, say, a country with a .600 probability of membership (for example, Finland at .626 as shown in Table 3.2), this would mean that we would expect Protestants to have a .646 probability and Catholics or others to have a .605 probability of non-social movement membership. As for total social movement memberships, the effect is in the same direction for Protestants (more participation; odds ratio of 1.14 but not statistically significant at p>.10), and in the opposite direction for Catholics (less participation; odds ratio of .89, significant at p<.015). Finally, for working non-social movement memberships, Protestants (odds ratio 1.2, p<.015) and Catholics (odds ratio 1.11, p<.04) have higher odds of participating than others. There are no significant differences in the case of working social movements (p>.176).

Does this signify a declining importance of religion—even the historically long-lasting forms of surviving traditions and norms established prior to desecularization processes but still held if not cherished among those who have long since abandoned formal religion? This conclusion may be premature since, among other things, the tests employed here may not be sufficiently sensitive to separate out effects at the aggregate level (at the individual level, there are still hints that religion affects participation), especially given the fact that in most countries the social movement variables had fairly low probabilities in the first place. On the other hand, it is possible that the once-prominent "long arm" of religious heritage extending to participatory norms and patterns of voluntary participation could be fading over time in many countries, or showing itself mostly through intermediate organizational consequences (forms of governance, group interaction, and interpersonal networking that might, or might not, possibly, have been affected by prior patterns of religious observance over generations).

The analysis thus far has proceeded on the premise that when it comes to social movement organizations there may be something new and different about patterns of involvement that might place them out-side the model of conventional volunteering. To further explore this ques-tion, non-social movement and social movement association involvement patterns will be compared compositionally (that is, the social backgrounds of members will be compared and examined).

Before leaving the hierarchical models, though, some additional obser-vations are warranted. Because of the politicized nature of social move-ment organizations—even in those cases where organizations eschew the formality of traditional politics and deliberately remain outside the am-bit of conventional political parties—we might expect involvement lev-els to be more connected to the country-level factors such as "political opportunity structure" (Kriesi 1995) which measures the degree of cen-tralization/decentralization in the state, and the responsiveness of the political system to new political party formation. Kriesi argues that "a weak state provides a more favourable setting for collective action" (1995: 172), but this variable can work, as he notes, in both directions: strong states can act on movement demands but may not be inclined to do so, while weak states may be more likely to "give in" to demands but may in turn not have the power to push through policies demanded by social movements. To a very limited degree, some distinctions may have been captured by the difference between the social democratic political type and other country types: for example, liberal democratic countries in our model all have first-past-the-post constituency democracies, whereas the social democratic states rely on some form of proportional representa-tion. It is clear, however, that these distinctions are not sufficient to ex-plain variations in social movement activity.

Who Joins?

Table 3.6 provides calculations for the expected probabilities of associa-tion membership—both total memberships and working memberships—for different levels of variables representing the structural location of respondents. Across all of the countries that were studied, voluntary as-sociation involvement is stratified by age, occupation, gender, education, and to a lesser extent, marital status. What is striking in this table are the similarities between non-social movement and social movement involve-ment. First, there is an almost linear pattern of association between age and any of the measures of association involvement (non-social move-ment; social movement; religious): older people are more involved. To be sure, the line dips back very slightly after age 65 and then a bit more af-ter age 75 (undoubtedly as a result of physical mobility, health, and other age-related issues), but the pattern is remarkably consistent. For all mea-sures other than religious-affiliated associations, the highest probabilities

are in the 55–64 age group, while the 65–74 age group has expected proportions that are only nominally lower. For religious-affiliated organizations, this slight deviation from the linear pattern starts at an older age:
the highest involvement levels are at 65–74 (for working memberships)
or both 65–74 and 75 and over (for total memberships).

Not shown in Table 3.6 are parallel results from the 1990 World Values
Survey: in the earlier surveys, the peak age group for both non-social
movement and social movement associations (working and total memberships) was in the 35–54 age range. This has now shifted upward, by
approximately ten years. Putnam (2000: 254ff.), referring to the United
States, describes a "long civic generation" born between 1910 and 1940
that, owing to a variety of factors (including a high likelihood of wartime
military service) represents a high-involvement cohort never duplicated
by other "postcivic generation" cohorts. Of course, there can be some debate as to whether the social conditions described by Putnam in the case
of the United States apply elsewhere in the world (Putnam did not generalize this claim beyond the US.). The youngest individual in this cohort
would have been 60 years old when the World Values Survey data were
collected in the year 2000. There is no discernible (major) downtrend
below this age, however. Rather, the pattern is more suggestive of some
combination of secular trend and aging processes.

Across all three non-union association types, and for both total and
working memberships, individuals who are professionally employed or
who are owners/managers tend to have higher participation rates, and
those who are not in the workforce have the lowest participation rates or
are close to the next-lowest group, blue-collar workers. While students
do not stand out as a high involvement group for any of the other association types—either in terms of working memberships or in terms of total memberships—they are tied for the highest rate of involvement when
it comes to working social movement memberships (.188 for students;
.189 for owners/managers).

Males were considerably more likely than females to be members of
non-social movement organizations in 1990 (.611 vs. .493; figures not
shown in Table 3.6) and to be active in these organizations (.389 vs. .306).
Only ten years later (see Table 3.6), this had largely shifted except in the
case of overall memberships in conventional (non-social movement) organizations (.815 for males; .769 for females). Otherwise, substantial
gender differences exist in the opposite direction: women are more likely
than men to be social movement members (.351 versus .233), to be active in social movement associations (.208 versus .140), and to be active
non-social movement members (.403 versus .300). The social movement
comparison is, however, affected by the fact that one of the handful of
organizational types included in the list on the World Values Survey was
"women's" organizations. Women are also more involved in religious-

Table 3.6. Expected Probabilities of Membership by Social Characteristics of Respondents

	Total Memberships				Working Memberships			
	Excluding rel. union soc. mov.	Social Movmt	Union	Religious	Excluding rel. union soc. mov.	Social Movmt	Union	Religious
Age								
18–24	0.815	0.175	0.142	0.412	0.229	0.117	0.029	0.227
25–34	0.794	0.191	0.222	0.413	0.247	0.111	0.058	0.230
35–44	0.815	0.233	0.264	0.472	0.300	0.140	0.090	0.293
45–54	0.822	0.266	0.296	0.511	0.343	0.160	0.071	0.334
55–64	0.835	0.325	0.295	0.563	0.403	0.204	0.086	0.393
65–74	0.831	0.319	0.211	0.612	0.394	0.189	0.070	0.431
75 and over	0.800	0.281	0.178	0.614	0.351	0.163	0.047	0.364
Occupation								
Not in workforce	0.795	0.231	0.084	0.514	0.294	0.134	0.023	0.344
Student	0.898	0.276	0.100	0.555	0.342	0.188	0.039	0.395
Owner/manager	0.873	0.304	0.108	0.506	0.382	0.189	0.044	0.341
Professional	0.897	0.280	0.255	0.495	0.345	0.167	0.069	0.350
White collar	0.861	0.266	0.273	0.493	0.329	0.155	0.071	0.323
Blue collar	0.815	0.233	0.264	0.472	0.300	0.140	0.071	0.293
Marital Status								
Married	0.815	0.233	0.264	0.472	0.300	0.134	0.264	0.244
Wid,sep,div	0.798	0.215	0.234	0.425	0.277	0.143	0.234	0.268
Single	0.820	0.240	0.239	0.445	0.306	0.140	0.239	0.293
Gender								
Male	0.815	0.233	0.264	0.472	0.300	0.140	0.264	0.293
Female	0.769	0.351	0.213	0.560	0.403	0.208	0.213	0.366

	Total Memberships				Working Memberships			
	Excluding rel. union soc. mov.	Social Movmt	Union	Religious	Excluding rel. union soc. mov.	Social Movmt	Union	Religious
Education								
< Elem	0.532	0.082	0.146	0.387	0.120	0.056	0.146	0.193
Elem	0.602	0.111	0.204	0.410	0.155	0.058	0.204	0.215
Some High sch	0.677	0.145	0.213	0.409	0.195	0.085	0.213	0.225
High sch. Grad	0.733	0.176	0.228	0.445	0.235	0.106	0.228	0.255
Some post Sec	0.815	0.233	0.264	0.472	0.300	0.140	0.264	0.293
Univ grad	0.823	0.253	0.247	0.498	0.325	0.148	0.247	0.307
Comm. Size								
<20,000	0.850	0.267	0.267	0.580	0.342	0.165	0.267	0.380
20–100,000	0.837	0.245	0.290	0.538	0.309	0.139	0.290	0.338
100–500,000	0.841	0.247	0.297	0.546	0.322	0.134	0.297	0.361
Over 500,000	0.815	0.233	0.264	0.472	0.300	0.140	0.264	0.293
Wald Tests								
Age (df=6)	51.2	153.9	186.9	197.5	80.1	82.1	54.5	170.7
Occup (df=6)	446.1	40.1	1010.4	21.8	178.0	29.7	147.1	26.8
Marstat (df=2)	10.8	5.27n	15.3	22.2	11.2	.73n	6.2	21.5
Sex (df=1)	130.4	237.6	67.4	121.5	47.8	97.6	37.1	67.6
Educ (df=5)	818.2	292.6	47.0	53.6	424.5	147.0	55.3	62.6
Commsize (df=4)	44.2	12.3	15.7	81.7	91.1	16.8	7.2n	46.5

n=NS at p<.05

Evaluated at Country=USA; Age=35–44; Occup= Blue-Collar

Marital status = married; Sex=Male; Educ=Some post sec; Community size=>500,000 affiliated organizations, though not in unions. In 1990, the only membership/organization category for which women had higher involvement rates was active memberships in social movement associations.

For all association types, across both total membership probabilities and working membership probabilities, those with higher levels of education are more likely to be involved.[27] The significance test results provided at the bottom of the table ("Wald" tests) can be used in an approximate fashion to judge the comparative size of the effects of different variables. They suggest that, among all of the variables studied here (except the "country" variable used as a control in this analysis), education's effect is strong for both social movement and non-social movement associations but not for religious associations.

It would be tempting, given these findings, to ask, "What is new about New Social Movements?" The patterns of joining are, across all 30 countries studied here, very similar to the patterns observed for non-social movement associations. This does not, of course, point to ideological homogeneity or cultural affinity, since respondents of a given background choosing to join and then work in social movement associations might be quite different from those involved with more traditional associations. What can be said, however, is that across all countries in the World Values Survey, there is no evident surge on the part of the youngest age cohort (which generally exhibit lower rates of participation) toward social movements as an organization form that is compatible with anti-system sentiments. While this is possibly true for small pockets of individuals in particular social movements organizations, across large numbers of individuals involved in associations, social movement association participation takes on a very "conventional" form. From the standpoint of the impact of social movements and the networks they generate, either most of what is important happens outside the context of formal organizations (to the extent that survey respondents are unable to recognize what they do as "membership" or as "doing unpaid voluntary work"[28]) or there are strong parallels in the involvement patterns of social movement and non-social movement associations.

The statistical model presented in Table 3.6 made a critical assumption regarding the homogeneity of effects: basically it suggested that, across all or most countries, patterns were similar. In a model with over 30 countries, it would be difficult to test for interactions between country and the social characteristics of survey respondents—and almost impossible to make sense of them. This is where the hierarchical models discussed earlier can be helpful. Using as an organizing basis the polity type distinction, and controlling for the (aggregate-level) effects of economic wealth (log-GDP), tests were conducted to ascertain if the effects of three factors—age, community size, and education—differed by polity type. The results of these tests, and the estimated effects in each country type, for all cases where effects were not consistent across country type, are shown in Table 3.7. The model estimated here is sometimes referred to as a *varying slopes* or *slopes-as-outcomes* model (Raudenbush and Bryk 2002: 27–28, 117ff.).

The major differences between country types observed in Table 3.7 relate to the effects of age and community size on non-social movement association involvement. Age is measured in ten-year units (in this table not collapsed, but as age in tens of years), and community size is measured

---

Table 3.7 Variations in the Effect of Background Variables According to Polity Type

(Polity Type × Age; Polity Type × Community Size and Polity Type × Education Interactions)

Dependent Measure:

A. Non-NSM, non religious association memberships

Effect of **Age** in:	log	Odds ratio
1. Social democratic countries	0.0722	1.0749
2. Liberal democratic countries	0.1083	1.1144
3. Former East bloc countries	−0.0504	0.9508
4. All others	0.0231	1.0234
Chi-sq=20.63, df=3, p<.0003		

Effect of **Community Size** in:		
1. Social democratic countries	−0.0254	0.9749
2. Liberal democratic countries	0.0032	1.0032
3. Former Eastern bloc countries	0.0050	1.0050
4. All others	−0.0373	0.9634
Chi-sq=13.52, df=3, p<.0040		

B. Non-NSM, non religious association *working* memberships

Effect of **Age** in:	log	Odds ratio
1. Social democratic countries	0.075	1.0779
2. Liberal democratic countries	0.0887	1.0928
3. Former Eastern bloc countries	−0.0541	0.9473
4. All others	0.0393	1.0401
Chi-sq=22.03, df=3, p<.0002		

Effect of **Community Size** in:		
1. Social democratic countries	−0.0778	0.9251
2. Liberal democratic countries	−0.0271	0.9733
3. Former Eastern bloc countries	−0.0191	0.9811
4. All others	−0.0652	0.9369
Chi-sq=18.04, df=3, p<.0007		

on an 8-point scale (from rural to "over 500,000"). As can be seen in the table, there is one exception to the pattern of involvement increasing with age: in former Eastern bloc countries, if anything, the opposite is true. It is also the case that the age gradation is far less strong in countries that are neither social democratic nor liberal democratic. Just how strong is this difference in the effect of age? In a liberal democratic country where a 20-year-old would have a .39 probability of participating in non-social movement associations,[29] a 60-year-old would have a .60 probability. In a social democratic country, the probability would range from .43 for the 20-year-old to .57 for the 60-year-old. But in an Eastern bloc country, the ratios would be reversed: if the probability for the 20-year-old were .55, for a 60-year-old it would be .44. Finally, the probability would remain fairly close to .50 in "other" countries: .48 for the 20-year-old and .52 for the 60-year-old. So, in countries with the highest levels of voluntary association involvement, the age gradient is much stronger than it is elsewhere. To put it another way, social democratic and liberal democratic countries differ most from other countries in the older age cohorts.

A similar pattern occurs with respect to working non-social movement association memberships; indeed, the numbers are sufficiently similar to those found in the case of overall (total) non-social movement association memberships that the hypothetical example provided above could be applied equally (except that the overall proportions would be lower in all cases). The chi-square significance tests provided in Table 3.7 refer to a test for whether the slopes differ by polity type.[30]

Differences in the effect of community size across polity types follow a different pattern. For overall membership levels in non-social movement associations (Panel A), individuals in larger communities are *less* involved in social democratic and "other" countries (−.0254 and −.0373 respectively), whereas the effect of community size is very small (if anything, individuals are *more* involved) in the case of former Eastern bloc and liberal democratic countries. A full interpretation of this difference might require a more detailed country-by-country understanding of whether large cities are often comprised of smaller-size suburbs (as is the case with the United States) where "urban residence" takes on special meaning. But for now, a decline in participation would be the predicted effect of a movement to urban centers in social democracies, but not in liberal democracies. For working non-social movement memberships (Panel B), the effects are all in the direction of less involvement on the part of those living in larger centers, but this gradient is far more pronounced in social democratic and former Eastern bloc countries.

For social movement association involvement (both total membership and working membership), the effects of age, education, and community size, were not contingent on polity type (p>.10). For total religious-affiliated association memberships, the education effect shown in Table 3.7

did not apply at all to former Eastern bloc countries and applied slightly less to social democratic countries; otherwise, higher education implied more involvement. There was no significant variation for working religious-affiliated associations.

Changes Over Time

Research on the composition of associations addresses in part the question of how NSM associations might or might not differ from conventional voluntary associations with regard to the types of individuals who become involved. Stable compositional patterns do not, of course, signify an absence of change. At the societal level, cultural shifts (see Inglehart 1997) can lead to major changes in the ways in which people volunteer and the purposes for which they do so, even if individuals from certain status groups still tend to be more participatory. Moreover, while pointing to important differences between men and women, between professionals and those in other occupations, and between people at different age levels, the previous discussion on the social bases for voluntary association involvement failed to uncover any radical separation that appears consistently across countries: the participation rate of a group with a "low" level of involvement is rarely lower than one-half of the rate of a group with a "high" level of involvement (see Table 3.5). Cross-nationally, the real story is that of differences between countries, and not so much differences within countries.

As a leading exponent of the social capital approach, Putnam argues that voluntary association involvement is more or less in secular decline; that is, if we are to characterize differences between the "civic" generation of those who were raised in the Depression and World War II and subsequent cohorts, the trend is one of "civic disengagement" (Putnam 1995, 1996, 2000). Explanatory factors include increased female participation in the labor force (but note our finding, from Table 3.6, that those in the workforce participate more than those outside of it), declining extended family networks, greater demands on people's time and money, the rise of the welfare state (but note our findings, from Tables 3.1 and 3.2, that social democratic states have high rates of voluntary association involvement), the greater use of television (and possibly home computing), and generational effects (see Baer et al. 2001: 251).

While writers in the NSM tradition (Boggs 1986; Larana et al. 1994) would hardly place a determinist cast on the expectation that social movement activity is on the rise, it is clear from these writings that there is little place for ideas such as "civic disengagement" (Putnam 2000) or even "civil privatism" (Habermas 1976) in their writings. This literature is joined in some senses by "postmaterialist" writers such as Inglehart

(1997), even though Inglehart himself has often been considered to have an affinity with "social capital" writers (see Jackman and Miller 1998: 48, 50, et passim). This section extends and elaborates on previous research reported by Baer et al. (2001) which examined changes in voluntary association participation rates over the 1980 to 1990 period. Using items that had parallel wordings in the 1980 and the 1990 World Values Survey, the study looked at fifteen countries that were included in both surveys with voluntary association questions in both years. The membership definitions were constructed to create a new category particularly germane to the discussion of civic disengagement: the "nominal" membership. This is defined as a membership in which a respondent indicates membership in a group but answers "no" to the "Did you do unpaid work for...?" question. Working memberships are defined, as in previous work, as those "yes" responses to the unpaid work question.

Using overall rates of nominal and working memberships, both with and without church and union memberships, the previous work concluded that "there is little support for Putnam's hypothesis that voluntary association activity has declined in this period" (2001: 268). Putnam's work was centered on the United States, where indeed, a decline in *nominal* memberships was observed, at least if one includes religious association memberships. But if one extends this to other countries, the pattern was mixed, with most countries showing increases in nominal memberships in associations, excepting religious organizations (Belgium, Italy, and the Netherlands, especially, but also Sweden and West Germany) while significant overall declines were observed only in Spain. Including church association memberships in the count, the pattern was a bit more mixed, with significant declines observed in Ireland, Northern Ireland, Spain, Sweden, and the USA. The research modeled counts as opposed to probabilities of association involvement. Thus, if the type of person who belonged to both a church/religious organization and another association type in 1980 belonged only to the nonreligious association type in 1990, we would see a decline in the count from 2 to 1, which would affect the results.

Table 3.8 reports changes in membership levels for the five of the six individual association types discussed briefly in Baer et al. (2001). Union memberships are excluded as not constituting "voluntary" participation in most cases. Table 3.8 also includes statistics for a sixth category labeled "Conservation, ecology". In the 1981–1983 World Values Survey study, a single item concerning "conservation, environmentalist or animal welfare groups" was included, while in 1991–1993 the survey asked two questions, on "conservation, the environment, ecology" and "animal rights." The fact that responses are distributed across two questions in the 1991–1993 version of the survey might lead to a small increase in response rates for this item. Otherwise, the items are identical from the 1980 survey to the 1990 survey. Table 3.8 includes education, occupation, age, community size, marital status, and gender as control variables to adjust for changes in occupational composition and differences in the education levels of respondents; a parallel analysis without controls (not reported here) yielded fairly similar results. In this table, an odds ratio multiplier of 1 would signify no change; significance tests for are for the difference between the odds ratio reported in the table and the null hypothesis "no change" parameter value of 1.0.

It should come as no surprise that significant declines in church/religious voluntary association "nominal" memberships were recorded in a number of countries. The most pronounced declines were in Northern Ireland (.221), Ireland (.255), and Spain (.329), but significant declines were also seen in Great Britain (.539), the US (.529), and Canada (.488). On the other hand, significant *increases* in the odds that individuals will be involved in nominal religious memberships could be seen in the former West Germany (2.001), Italy (2.285), Denmark (2.348), and Norway (2.069). For working religious memberships, a significant increase was to be found only in France (1.718), while declines were reported in Spain (.347), Northern Ireland (.366), Ireland (.596), and especially, Sweden (.166). Thus, while the overall picture might be one of decline in participation, this decline is not universal: in some countries, participation in church/religious voluntary associations actually increased from 1980 to 1990.

The results for political party participation are important because of the connection between this activity and the thesis that civic participation has been on the decline. While researchers interested in the vibrancy and health of the institutions of civil society may not be concerned about those associations that are more "recreational" in nature (bowling leagues, sports, etc.), reduced formal political party participation would, in the absence of other forms of involvement, signal a worrisome decline. While political parties are more closely aligned to the state than other forms of associations—there can, indeed, be some debate as to whether they are properly conceptualized as part of "civil society"—the will to engage discursively in the formation of public policy represents a form of engagement that is far more "civic" than is the case with local organizations designed to gratify individual members (for example, sports leagues). Though all associations involve non-privatized interaction among members to varying degrees, some ought to be privileged as more important than others from the standpoint of the "civic disengagement" thesis.

For political parties, there is no clear pattern of increase or decline when it comes to nominal memberships. Within this overall pattern, there are some countries showing significant declines (Spain, Ireland, Sweden) and one showing significant increases (Belgium). In the Swedish case, the decline may in part be attributable to a move into working membership, where there was a pronounced increase from 1980 to 1990. If people

Table 3.8. Changes in Nominal and Working Membership Odds, 1980–1990 (with controls)

Odds ratio for change from 1980 to 1990 (multiplicative)—with controls

Country	Church, relig.		Educ, arts, cultural		Professional associations		Unions	
	Nominal Odds ratio	Working Odds ratio	Nominal Odds ratio	Working Odds ratio	Nominal Odds ratio	Working Odds ratio	Nominal Odds ratio	Working Odds ratio
France	1.085	1.718 *	1.131	1.180	1.071	1.406	0.460 ***	0.687
Britain	0.539 ***	0.715	1.219	1.770	0.816	0.914	0.616 ***	0.971
West Germany	2.001 ***	1.318	3.156 ***	2.832 ***	1.546	1.514	0.984	1.230
Italy	2.285 *	1.436	4.908 ***	0.903	3.237 ***	1.489	0.894	0.443 ***
Netherlands	1.178	1.080	4.525 ***	2.814 ***	2.135 ***	1.414	1.209	1.605
Denmark	2.348 **	1.561	1.807 **	4.448 ***	0.759	0.450	1.157	1.124
Belgium	0.897	1.250	1.852 ***	1.050	1.820 *	1.010	0.992	1.456
Spain	0.329 ***	0.347 ***	1.058	0.567 **	0.626 *	0.457 **	0.408 ***	0.475 **
Ireland	0.255 ***	0.596 **	1.517 *	2.061 *	1.005	0.631	0.538 ***	0.439 *
Northern Ireland	0.221 ***	0.365 ***	2.239	1.916	1.159	1.536	0.714	1.450
USA	0.529 ***	1.019	1.299 *	2.158	0.732 *	0.848	0.464 ***	1.717
Canada	0.488 ***	0.788 *	1.642 **	1.682 ***	1.071	1.012	0.813	2.100 **
Japan	1.111	0.546 *	1.496	1.720	0.665	0.446 *	0.678 *	0.467 *
Norway	2.069 **	1.165	1.838 **	3.680 ***	1.418 *	1.097	0.992	0.846
Sweden	1.298	0.166 ***	0.501 **	0.763	0.559 *	0.332 **	1.810 ***	5.453 ***

Country	Political parties		Conservation, ecology		Youth work	
	Nominal	Working	Nominal	Working	Nominal	Working
	Odds ratio	Odds ratio	Odds ratio	Odds ratio	Odds ratio	Odds ratio
France	1.374	0.733	4.582 **	2.107	0.314 *	0.466 **
Britain	0.964	1.148	1.312	1.590	0.756	0.589 *
West Germany	1.243	1.089	2.959 ***	3.605 ***	1.505	2.026 *
Italy	1.110	0.761	4.382 ***	2.202 *	3.133	1.995 *
Netherlands	1.132	1.235	2.635 ***	2.794 **	1.065	0.928
Denmark	0.840	0.787	2.519 **	2.793	0.430 **	0.445 ***
Belgium	2.884 ***	1.030	8.067 ***	2.318 **	1.128	1.402
Spain	0.313 ***	0.382 ***	1.204	1.109	0.481 *	0.338 ***
Ireland	0.492 *	1.106	1.684	0.467	0.967	0.638 *
Northern Ireland	0.348	0.240	1.020	1.092	3.002	1.317
USA	0.973	1.166	1.688 ***	3.510 ***	1.058	1.140
Canada	1.341	0.930	1.576 *	2.181 **	0.892	0.840
Japan	1.725	0.651	1.899	4.864 **	0.759	0.426
Norway	1.082	0.972	1.157	0.758	1.302	0.731
Sweden	0.569 *	4.278 **	7.028 ***	0.334 **	0.457 *	1.783

* p<.05
** p<.01
*** p<.001

were less inclined to be "nominal" members in Sweden, this is in part because they were *more* inclined to participate actively as unpaid volunteers (odds ratio multiplier of 4.278). For working memberships, the only other significant change from 1980 to 1990 was in Spain, where a decline was observed (odds ratio multiplier of .382).

Two important patterns in Table 3.8 can be found in the results associated with education, arts, and cultural organizations and those associated with conservation and ecology groups. Overall, the pattern for the former is one of increase, both in the case of nominal memberships and in the case of working memberships. The only significant decrease occurred in Sweden (.501). Some of the odds ratio multipliers for this type of association are substantively very large. For working memberships, only three countries (Spain, Italy, Sweden) had coefficients of less than 1.0 (signifying decline), and of these only the Spanish case was significantly different from 1.0 (.567, p<.001).

For unions, the picture is one of significant declines in nominal memberships in France, Great Britain, Spain, Ireland, the United States, and Japan, while for other countries the declines either are statistically insignificant or represent increases—at least in terms of those who identify themselves as members—as opposed to declines.[31] There were also significant declines in working memberships in Italy, Spain, Ireland, and Japan, with a significant increase in Sweden.

Environmental groups ("conservation, ecology" in Table 3.8) showed a general increase in involvement between 1980 and 1990. No country showed decreases in nominal memberships for this type of association. In some countries, the increase in nominal memberships was immense: France (4.582), Italy (4.382), Belgium (8.067), and Sweden (7.028) all showed very large membership increases for this association type.[32] We thus have some support for the idea that there has been a shift in voluntary association participation rather than a secular decline. Surveys that emphasize "traditional" voluntary association activity will not, of course, reveal this. We are limited in our comparisons for the 1980 to 1990 period to one social movement association type, and we are further limited because of a slight difference in the way in which the question was asked in the 1980 World Values Survey. Still, if this single indicator can be used with a modicum of caution, it seems appropriate to suggest that both traditional investigators of voluntary associations, whose interest is in what drives people to "join," and social theorists, whose concern is more broadly based in conceptual concerns surrounding the future of civil society in processes of social transformation, have a joint interest in the shifts in association involvement that we see across many advanced industrial countries.

Putnam, though, tends to dismiss the observation that we can look to social movement associations for a promising future in the realm of civic participation and involvement. He first suggests that these movements may not survive long (2000: 153–154) because we are now past the period of "uncommon social and political mobilization" of the 1960s and 1970s, when most such associations were created, and then notes that it is still in question whether such organizations have created a "long wave" of involvement as opposed to changes that are ephemeral in nature. This, of course, does not explain the substantial growth into the 1980s that is shown by the World Values Survey data; and while the argument that the 1980s were "too close" to the 1970s for us to make definite conclusions about the longevity of this newly appearing increase in NSM involvement helps to explain the absence of a decrease, it does not explain an increase.

Putnam acknowledges the "explosive" growth in national environmental organizations in the United States from 1960 to 1998 (2000: 156) but dismisses this as fairly unimportant on a number of bases. First, because these organizations allocate large percentages of their budget to fundraising and advertising, many "members" are more likely to be considered "donors" as opposed to members per se: "most affiliates ... do not even consider themselves 'members'" (2000: 158). This latter point is, of course, addressed in the World Values Survey, where respondent identification, rather than membership list numbers, is used to estimate involvement rates. Still, Putnam's point is that many members are so by "mail" and that this form of activity hardly can be equated with civic engagement.

Our distinction between nominal and working memberships, though, covers this objection. If one focuses on the results in Table 3.8 dealing with *working* memberships (the criterion of "doing unpaid work" is more stringent even than some criterion such as "attending meetings regularly"), we find declines in only 3 countries (Ireland, Norway, Sweden); for only one of them (Sweden, .334) the drop is statistically significant. On the other hand, there are substantial increases in many countries.

Tables 3.9 and 3.10 extend this analysis into the period between 1990 and 2000. The focus is on working memberships to conserve space. Overall, across all of the membership types that were included in both the 1990 and the 2000 surveys, statistically significant increases were observed in 12 countries and statistically significant declines were observed in 8 countries. One social democratic country (Finland, .646) exhibited overall decline, but most (Sweden, Denmark, Netherlands) showed substantial gains. Liberal democratic countries generally showed increases as well. Former Eastern bloc countries that showed fairly low levels of involvement in 1990 often showed even lower levels in 2000: these include Hungary (.623), Romania (.470), Russia (.317), and Estonia (.372). All three of the Latin American countries included in the comparison (Mexico, 2.463; Argentina, 1.499; Chile, 1.900) show substantial and statistically significant increases.

Table 3.9. Changes in Working Membership Odds, 1990–2000 (with controls)

Odds ratio for change from 1990 to 2000 (Multiplicative—with controls)

Country	All except rel. unions	Social movmt.	Religious	Social Welfare	Arts, Culture
Argentina	1.499 **	2.744 *	1.996 ***	1.300	0.908
Austria	1.232 *	1.124	1.198	1.341	1.355
Belgium	1.008	0.855	0.710	0.787	1.034
Britain	4.887 ***	N/A	1.048	2.934 ***	0.672
Bulgaria	1.046	0.492 **	0.612	1.059	1.129
Canada	1.172 *	0.964	1.240 *	1.441 **	1.094
Chile	1.900 ***	2.578 ***	1.439 **	1.656 **	1.028
Denmark	1.838 ***	1.844 *	1.195	1.833 *	1.832*
Estonia	0.372 ***	0.594 *	2.194 *	2.219 *	0.776
Finland	0.636 **	0.550	0.876	0.542 *	0.457*
France	1.073	0.378 ***	0.721	0.735	1.067
Hungary	0.623 **	0.971	2.107 **	1.319	1.507
Iceland	0.919	0.679	1.449	0.899	1.260
Ireland	1.125	1.258	1.328	0.548 **	1.107
Italy	0.972	1.037	0.822	1.251	1.439
Japan	1.253	0.901	1.143	2.357 **	1.125
Latvia	0.646 **	0.135 ***	0.913	0.525	1.377
Lithuania	0.295 ***	0.261 ***	1.234	0.838	0.444 **
Mexico	2.463 ***	1.802 **	1.928 ***	2.028 **	1.937 ***
N. Ireland	0.531 ***	0.680	0.703	0.543	0.709
Netherlands	1.787 ***	0.943	1.174	1.062	1.815 ***
Portugal	0.862	1.072	0.523 **	0.749	0.695
Romania	0.470 ***	0.674	0.754	0.452	1.281
Russia	0.317 ***	0.360 ***	0.509	0.348 **	0.159 ***
Slovenia	2.282 ***	1.849 *	2.725 ***	3.367 ***	2.470 ***
Spain	1.994 ***	1.688 **	1.653 **	1.709 **	1.608 **
Sweden	1.492 ***	1.079	N/A	2.418 ***	3.353 ***
USA	2.177 ***	1.684 ***	1.431 ***	2.363 ***	1.764 ***

* p<.05
** p<.01
*** p<.001

Examining the different types of associations for which we can directly compare data from 1990 to 2000, a few observations are worth noting. First, the decline in church/religious-affiliated association involvement observed from 1980 to 1990 does not seem to have been replicated over the next decade: if anything, there are statistically significant (and substantial) increases in active religion-affiliated associations in Argentina, Canada,

Chile, Estonia, Hungary, Mexico, Slovenia, Spain, and the United States, and significant decline in only one country (Russia), though low initial rates in some Eastern bloc countries provide a "floor" effect. Union involvement appears to be on the decline in some countries, most notably in Estonia (where the coefficient implies a virtual collapse), Finland, Hungary, Latvia, Lithuania, Portugal, Romania and Russia. Significant increases were, however, observed in Spain and Sweden. It should be noted that, for individual types of associations with fairly low probabilities, the magnitudes of the coefficients must be fairly high before they become statistically significant. An increase from a probability of .02 to .04 may represent an odds ratio multiplier of approximately 2.0, but the initial probabilities are so low that differences, even in samples of 1,000, could easily be attributable to chance. This is why it is that only in the most extreme cases that the "change" odds ratios are significant past the first two columns (all memberships except church and union; social movement association–type memberships).

As was the case from 1980 to 1990, in many countries arts and cultural organizations are once again on the increase, though in a few (particularly Estonia and Finland) they are on the decline. Sports organizations, not included in the 1980 to 1990 comparison, seem in general to have increasing participation rates (significantly so in Chile, Mexico, Slovenia, Spain, and the United States, and trending upward in most other countries). If these two types of organizations represent areas of growth in voluntary involvement, political party involvement is clearly on the decline except in Mexico. At the same time the other organization type that is involved in wide-ranging discourse involving society goals—the very thing that would signify the emergence of a vital and active public sphere—is also on the wane: in most countries, with the notable exception of the United States, Great Britain, Argentina, and Sweden, active involvement in conservation and ecology groups is down. While only one social movement association type was available for the 1980–1990 comparison, more association types were included in the 1990 and 2000 surveys, making it possible to construct a binary measure indicating whether respondents were involved (and actively involved) in four social movement association types identified earlier (women's, peace, human rights, ecology/conservation). Changes in this measure over time are shown in the second column of Table 3.9. In six countries (Argentina, Chile, Mexico, Spain, the US, Denmark) there were significant increases from 1990 to 2000, and in five cases there were significant and substantial decreases (Bulgaria .492; Estonia, .594; France, .378; Russia, .360; Finland .550). Of the countries experiencing significant increases, Spain had had very low levels of involvement in 1990 (thus, an increase simply placed it closer to the norm), as did Argentina. All of the countries experiencing significant declines had had fairly low levels of social movement involvement in 1990, except France, which was closer to the average.

Table 3.10. Changes in Working Membership Odds, 1990–2000 (with controls)

Odds ratio for change from 1990 to 2000 (multiplicative)— with controls

Country	Political		Professional		Sports		Conserv. Eco.		Union	
Argentina	3.634	***	3.585	#	1.391		7.256	*	1.412	
Austria	0.926		1.313		1.124		1.026		0.735	
Belgium	1.582	*	1.126		1.207		0.806		1.142	
Britain	0.731		4.377	***	1.555		5.596	***	1.177	
Bulgaria	0.633		0.853		1.010		0.419	**	0.808	
Canada	0.786		1.004		1.175		0.842		0.843	
Chile	0.770		1.530		2.072	***	1.325		1.174	
Denmark	1.241		2.086	*	1.562	**	1.936		1.161	
Estonia	0.321	***	0.700		0.393	***	0.548		0.040	***
Finland	0.276	**	0.327	*	0.775		0.288		0.497	***
France	0.324	**	0.411	**	1.422	*	0.357	**	0.589	
Hungary	0.512		0.977		1.332		1.042		0.230	***
Iceland	0.798		1.021		0.838		0.453		1.037	
Ireland	0.857		1.901		1.880	***	0.929		1.536	
Italy	0.428	***	1.766	*	1.097		0.835		0.818	
Japan	0.819		0.935		1.120		0.920		0.417	*
Latvia	0.194	***	0.440		1.321		0.087	***	0.230	***
Lithuania	0.434	**	0.229	*	0.425	***	0.253	**	0.136	***
Mexico	1.744	*	1.646		2.486	***	1.343		1.350	
Northern Ireland	1.477		0.373		0.678		0.280		0.654	
Netherlands	1.053		1.567		1.709	***	0.629		1.498	
Portugal	0.400	*	0.862		1.161		0.601		0.220	*
Romania	0.843		0.646		0.344	**	0.465		0.377	***
Russia	0.072	***	0.517		0.369	***	0.288	***	0.387	***
Slovenia	1.017		1.283		3.170	***	1.718		1.916	*
Spain	1.560		0.868		2.257	***	0.843		1.674	*
Sweden	0.930		1.492		1.205		1.486		1.756	***
United States	1.231		1.623	**	2.138	***	1.403	*	1.569	

Discussion

The first major set of findings pertains to the differences among the countries that have been studied here. As expected, the United States shows high and sustained levels of voluntary association involvement in non-social movement associations, social movement associations, and religious-affiliated associations, but not with respect to union membership. There is little evidence of decline in the period from 1980 to 1990 or from 1990 to 2000. Just behind the United States, Canada too falls into a pattern of "liberal democracies" with high levels of involvement, though the Canadian level of government involvement in the welfare state is somewhat higher than that in the United States.[33] Unfortunately, comparable data were not available for Australia, another Anglophone liberal democracy. Finally, where they are available,[34] data from the UK suggest that it does not quite fit the same "high involvement" pattern.[35]

But it is not just the North American liberal democratic countries that display high levels of associational involvement. In the multiple-level analysis, the one regime "type" that consistently ranks high in terms of involvement is the social democratic polity type, a category comprising Sweden, Norway, Finland, Iceland, Denmark, and the Netherlands (excluding the Netherlands from this group would not alter the result, since the Netherlands is, across the various association types, a country with very high levels of involvement). This finding may well understate the relative standing in at least one case, that of Sweden. One of the limitations of the World Values Survey data is that respondents are asked whether or not they are members of types of associations provided in a list. This has the advantage of enabling cross-national comparability, but how a country ranks in comparison to other countries can hinge critically on the types of associations that are included in the list. For instance, earlier work (Curtis et al. 1992, 2001) has established that the "exceptional" nature of US voluntary association involvement becomes less so when counts of membership types exclude church-related membership and volunteering.

To be sure, at least at the level of voluntary unpaid work, it is hard a priori to exclude *any* type of voluntary association involvement as an indicator of civic engagement, but it must be noted that the United States has particularly high involvement in religious-affiliated voluntary associations, as reported here. Thus, according to the same logic that includes religious affiliated organizations in the membership variables used in this analysis and elsewhere, if types of associations that are prominent in Sweden but not so prominent in the United States were included in the analysis, it is conceivable that the main finding with respect to Scandinavian countries—that as part of the "social democratic" type, they display high levels of voluntary association involvement—would be even stronger. Specifically, it is unlikely that the World Values Survey question fully captured membership and involvement in two types of organizations identified by Rothstein (2001: 216) as the third and fourth most important type of voluntary association in Sweden: consumers' cooperatives and tenants' organizations.[36]

Another factor that may result in the over-reporting of differences between the United States and other countries may relate to the fairly high estimates of US voluntary association involvement in the 2000 World

Values Survey. While the World Values Survey is an important source of comparative data, in which reasonable diligence seems to have been applied in each of the countries were samples were drawn, the major increase in US association involvement reported in Tables 3.2 and 3.8 has not been confirmed by data obtained elsewhere. In Table 3.2 the rate of involvement in unpaid work for non-social movement associations *alone* (.517 for the United States) is higher than the response obtained to the question "Did you do any volunteer work in the past year?" posed in the U.S. election studies of 2000 and 2002, where the "yes" responses were 40.7 percent and 42.1 percent respectively. Of course, the sequence of questions in the World Values Survey can also be expected to lead to higher affirmative response rates where series of questions assist respondents in identifying the various types of involvement that are possible (and might have been forgotten by respondents when they answer a single question). So, while it seems reasonable to support the claim that the US ranks among the highest in the world when it comes to voluntary involvement in all association types except union activity, it may be premature to suggest that membership involvement is increasing in that country.

Whether it makes sense to talk about a social democratic regime "type" when discussing voluntary association involvement, or whether instead there are notable if perhaps subtle differences between patterns of involvement in the Netherlands as opposed to other Scandinavian countries, remains an open question. Though noting that the nonprofit sector workforce as a share of the economically active population is very high in the Netherlands (and Belgium to a lesser extent), Salamon et al. (2004: 19–21) report much higher ratios of unpaid to paid staff in the nonprofit sector in Sweden (75.9% voluntary), Norway (63.8 percent) and Finland (54.3 percent) than in the Netherlands (37.1 percent) or Belgium (21.7 percent). If the nonprofit sectors of these countries are more "driven" by state funding, though, this has not had a negative effect on actual voluntary participation; clearly, organizations with paid staff can mobilize volunteers and engage members as much as they can dissuade individuals from participating because "someone else is doing it already."

Thus far, the discussion has centered on high-involvement countries. At the other end of the continuum, many Eastern bloc countries display low to very low levels of association involvement. Unions, which in 1990 formed almost the sole basis for civic participation in some countries, underwent a major decline in all of these countries in the 1990–2000 period, and as a result most countries have rates of voluntary association involvement that are lower even than those found in the handful of Latin American countries studied here. Three exceptions to this pattern are the Czech Republic, Slovakia, and Slovenia. This might, in some senses, be seen as a continuation of the vigorous civic participation observed in at least the former Czechoslovakia in the post-1989 period, though it should be noted that it is only in the area of non-social movement associations—not NSM associations—that these countries' involvement rates are more typical of those found in Western Europe (see Table 2).

Three Latin American countries were studied in 2000: Mexico, Argentina, and Chile. A fourth country was included in the World Values dataset in 1990 but not in 2000. By 2000, the levels of voluntary involvement in non-social movement associations in these countries were similar to the levels of involvement experienced in France, Greece, and Italy and actually higher than those in Spain, Portugal, and most former Eastern bloc countries. The same applies to religious-affiliated associations (but not so much for social movement associations). In earlier work, Curtis et al. (2001: 802) commented on the higher-than-expected working membership involvement in Latin America, noting that when religious associations are excluded from the counts of memberships, this pattern is not pronounced. They then relate this finding to earlier literature involving Christian community involvement in Latin America. In 2000, the "unexpectedly" high levels of involvement apply even when church-affiliated memberships are excluded, though they are not equally applicable to NSM activity.

It is possible, of course, that the legacy of church-based association involvement continues, having expanded into nonsectarian associational forms, but it is also possible that involvement in these countries arose before Latin America' major shifts toward neoliberal economic policies in the late 1980s and the 1990s. Prior to these changes, Roberts (2002) identifies countries where the polity was dominated by what he characterized as a "mass-based, labor-mobilizing" party; these countries were Argentina, Bolivia, Brazil, Chile, Mexico, Peru, and Venezuela. By contrast, other Latin American countries experienced less in the way of class-based cleavages because their polities emphasized "elite-based forms of political competition" (Roberts 2002: 12). Those countries that had mass-based parties experienced more difficulty in the economic transition as well. What this might imply, then, is that a confluence of circumstances (prior active engagement of the population as a result of the participatory orientation of governing parties as movements, and the reaction to rapid economic change) could have led to higher levels of involvement in these countries in a way that it did not in other economies experiencing major disruption during this period (notably, most of Eastern Europe). It also implies that the findings reported here may not be generic to all of Latin America, and may at most be applicable to those countries identified by Roberts as having "Labor Mobilizing Party Systems."

Among the non-social democratic European countries, Belgium, Luxembourg, and to a lesser extent Austria and Ireland stand out as having participation rates that are *slightly* higher than those found in Germany, and rates that are considerably higher than those found in Spain, Portugal, France, and Italy. Belgium is noteworthy because it has recently undergone a constitutional realignment that has had the effect of creating a federal state out of what had formerly been a unitary state in 1993, to some extent transforming the political system in that country (see Hooghe, 2004). Austria, also a state with multiple ethnic groups that are more or less segmented in geographic terms, has a history that Wilinsky (2002) describes as "left-Catholic." If ethnic (as opposed to religious) plurality is the dominant factor, though, the explanation for reasonably high rates of involvement in Luxembourg (aside from a diffusion effect from neighboring countries) and Ireland is less clear, though one could argue that Ireland now archetypically fits the "liberal democratic" polity type (Wilensky 2002, categorizes Ireland as "least corporatist" along with the US, the UK, New Zealand, Australia, and Canada).

If anything, the more recent 2000 findings with respect to Belgium, Luxembourg, and Ireland cast some doubts on the earlier assumptions that voluntary association involvement is suppressed in Catholic countries or, conversely, that it is the Protestant and "mixed Christian" religious types that lead to high association involvement (Curtis et al. 2001). In the analysis using 2000 data, it no longer appears to be the case that the type of religious heritage plays a statistically significant role in predicting a country's voluntary association involvement (see Table 3.4) or in an unexpected decline thereof.[37] This may not necessarily mean that religious pluralism or Protestant heritage plays no role in the development of active political cultures with high levels of civic engagement, but it at least implies that this does not represent a singular "path" to such an outcome. The findings do seem to reaffirm, in a strong way, the importance of the type of democratic political regime on civic participation outcomes.

There are both continuities and discontinuities in voluntary participation in NSM associations and traditional voluntary associations, though the main message seems to be one of similarity in patterns, where these are discernible. Countries that rank high for "social movement" association involvement also tend to show high involvement in conventional associations, although the reverse is not necessarily the case. In many countries, most individuals who are members of social movement associations are also members of non-social movement associations at the same time. In the United States, fully 92.3 percent of social movement association members fit this pattern; in Sweden it is 86.3 percent, in the Netherlands 85.4 percent, and in Canada it is 77.0 percent.

As for religious and union memberships, patterns diverge more from those observed in the case of other membership types. For the most part, countries with high levels of religious association involvement also show high levels of involvement in other areas (non-social movement and social movement); these include the United States, Canada, and Sweden.

There are cases, however, where high levels of involvement in non-religious associations do not correspond with high levels of involvement in religious associations (Belgium and Denmark, for example). Finally, the connection is the weakest for union membership, where involvement levels are fairly high in social democratic countries (which are also highly involved in other association types) but not elsewhere.

If there is one thing that the cumulation of comparative cross-national studies on voluntary association involvement, including the present exercise, should by now have accomplished, it is to have put to rest "American exceptionalism" arguments that attribute the outcome of high association involvement to an individualistic culture, a neoliberal economic structure, and a weak and highly restricted welfare state. While these factors are all coincident in the case of the United States, they do not coincide with the structural features of other countries that have experienced and continue to experience high rates of active voluntary association involvement. This "multi-path" explanation for differing levels of civic participation does not fit easily with aggregated quantitative models that seek to identify variables with linear effects (for example, the proposition that less government involvement in the economy leads to more voluntary activity). In the present exercise, this problem was dealt with primarily by way of using multiple classifications (liberal democratic, social democratic, etc.), but other methods may be possible.

It remains to be seen which form—the liberal democratic form or the social democratic/Scandinavian form—is the most resilient to the features of individualized life (Bauman 2001) that work against the collective definition of problems and the engagement of individuals in associational life. Nonetheless, there is as yet no compelling evidence that the form of associational involvement in the social democratic country type in general and Scandinavian countries in particular is inherently weaker than the form observed in the case of the United States.

Notes

1. This is a revised version of a paper originally prepared for the Studies in Civil Society and Its Social Implications seminar held at Ersta Sköndal University College, Stockholm, 12–13 June 2003. Thanks to (the late) James Curtis and Edward Grabb for earlier collaborations that ultimately led to the production of this work, and to the Social Sciences and Humanities Research Council of Canada for financial assistance.
2. Note that in rest of this this chapter, I will use the phrases "new social movements" "NSM", and "social movements" interchangeably.
3. Another variant in terms of regime-type classifications can be found in Wilensky (2002), who classifies Sweden, Norway, Israel, Denmark, and Finland as "left corporatist" while classifying the Netherlands, Belgium and Austria as "left-Catholic corporatist" on the basis of the strong systems of worker participation observed in these as opposed to other Catholic corporatist countries such as Italy and Germany.

4. Other models, using counts of membership types as opposed to yes/no "binomial" models of involvement, are possible for some of the organization types explored here (though not, obviously, for those where only one yes/no measure was available on the World Values Survey), but most of the results reported here change very little with these alternative models.

5. Occupation was broken into six categories: managers, professionals, other non-manual, manual, students, others not in the workforce. Age was categorized in ten-year increments (see tables, below), and marital status: married (including common law); widowed, separated or divorced; and single. In the 1990 World Values Survey, the only available education measure asked respondents how old they were when they finished school, and then ranged them on a 1–10 scale (age 21 = 10) with response truncated at 21 years of age. This variable was categorized as less than 16, 16–20, and 21 in analyses using the 1990 survey and analyses combining both the 1990 and the 2000 surveys. For the 2000 survey, a slightly better measure of education was available, providing the following response categories: less than elementary, elementary, some high school, high school grad, some post secondary, and university grad. For more complex hierarchical models, age (in years) and education (six levels) were treated as linear terms.

6. These basically represent the probability that an individual in a given country will be a member of a voluntary association of the given type, with adjustments for between-country differences in background variables such as education, age range, marital status, and occupation. Expected probabilities can also be read as percentages when multiplied by 100: a value of .304 in one of the tables would indicate that 30.4 percent of respondents are expected to be members of a particular association type or set of types. Significance tests in these tables are used to show whether each country is significantly different from the United States, which in many tables is the country with the highest level of voluntary association involvement. To calculate the expected probabilities, values of other variables must be "held constant" at a particular level. These levels are identified in the tables (for example, in Table 1, at age 35–44, white-collar occupation, community size of over 500,000 and education completed at ages 16–20). Changing the levels would change the expected probabilities but would not change the rank ordering of countries, and changes would be roughly proportional. Technically, changing the "level" at which other variables are held constant approaches but does not exactly preserve proportionality of results, since the equation being estimated (in "log-odds") is a non-linear function of probabilities.

7. The value of per capita GDP is logged.

8. These labels will be familiar to North American readers. For European readers in countries with political parties formally calling themselves "Social Democratic," etc., it must be remembered that there is no necessary correspondence between *regime type* and *political party names*. Regimes will be called social democratic, for example, even if they only sometimes have social democratic parties in power.

9. These do not have the same intuitive interpretation as the expected probabilities presented in the earlier tables. They can, however, be interpreted in terms of direction and relative magnitude, and significance tests are provided. The *extent* of differences between countries of different types can, of course, be gauged by the results of the earlier tables, which show expected probabilities for each country.

10. This is not quite a "probability" multiplier, though across most values it is close; if the probability of membership is .10, then the odds are .10 / .90 = .111. Multiplying the odds by 2.0 would result in an expected probability of .182, and multiplying the odds by 0.5 would result in an expected probability of .053. As mentioned earlier, odds (really, odds "multipliers") are also used in Tables 3 and 4 (multi-level model tables) to describe differences between categories. The tables themselves use "log-odds" coefficients that can then be converted back into "odds" for some improvement in interpretation. The tables themselves produce coefficients that represent the relationship

between each of four categories (in the case of polity type: social democratic, liberal democratic, former Eastern bloc, other) and express this relationship in relation to the last category in the table (in the parlance of dummy variable models, this is called the "reference category"). The interpretation of the coefficients is facilitated by providing "odds." If the odds "multiplier" for the social democratic category is calculated at 2.8, what this means is that, in relation to the "reference category," people in social democratic countries have 2.8 times the odds of being members. If the odds multiplier for liberal democratic countries is calculated at 1.4, this means that (a) liberal democratic countries have 1.4 times the odds of "other" countries, but (b) social democratic countries have 2.8 / 1.4 = 2.0 times the odds of liberal democratic countries. How "odds" translate into probabilities will depend somewhat on the marginal distribution of the variable (are 10 percent of the people currently members or are 50 percent?), but at a 50 percent probability, an odds multiplier of 2 will increase the probability to 67% and at a 10 percent probability, an odds multiplier of 2 will increase the probability to 18 percent). For readers used to working with probabilities but not with odds, the odds multipliers may seem to work on a metric that states effects more strongly than would be the case if expected probability increases were examined.

11. Not shown in any of the data presented here is the fact that there is considerable overlap between involvement in the two different types of associations. For example, in the United States, only 2 percent of respondents belong to social movement associations but not to any conventional association; in the Netherlands, which has the highest percentage of "social movement only" members, this figure is still only 8 percent.

12. In addition to these, surveys from a large number of developing countries in Africa and Asia are also available as part of the publicly available World Values Survey dataset. These countries, with generally low levels of reported association membership, have not been included in the present analysis for reasons of comparability (with 1990 results), consistency and possible concerns about the quality of data.

13. Because of some differences in the coding of the background variables available in each of the two time periods (1990 and 2000), and because of differences in the number of association types counted in columns other than "union" or "religious," expected proportions in Table 3.1 (1990) cannot be compared directly to those in Table 3.2 (2000), though it is of course appropriate to compare relative standings of countries.

14. Data from Sweden and Iceland have been excluded from the analysis since they both exhibit extremely high rates of expected membership (.641 and .620 respectively) yet at the same time show more moderate levels of working memberships (see the far left column in Table 3.2).

15. To conserve space, standard errors are not supplied in the table (in any event, these would apply to the original "log-odds" coefficients and not the expected probabilities). As an example, though, for Chile, with an expected probability of .094, the 95% confidence interval is .073 to .135, and for Argentina, with an expected probability of .024, the 95% confidence interval is .016 to .037.

16. Skocpol (2003) and Putnam (2000) both make this argument for some (or, in Skocpol's case, most) types of voluntary associations. See Edwards (2004: 82) for a response that argues that many "new" organization types do, in fact, entail strong levels of engagement.

17. This is calculated as exp(.494 × 3). Odds ratios are not quite probabilities, but are close. So, when an odds ratio of .20, representing a probability of .25, is multiplied by 4, it yields an odds ratio of .80, which is a probability of .44.

18. Calculated as exp (.02 × 30).

19. The between-country differences in Table 3.1 are not adjusted for differences in the individual-level variables (that is, compositional differences) or for other competing aggregate-level explanations.

20. Chi-square=1.77, p>0.5

21. Since the binary dependent variable equations include an intercept that factors in differences in marginal distributions, it is possible to compare other coefficients in the model across dependent variables.

22. The chi-square test for the difference is 3.901 (df=1, p<.045).

23. Given the small number of countries in the analysis, effects must be fairly large to be statistically significant.

24. Japan, which is neither of Protestant heritage nor mixed-(Protestant) is also included in the liberal democratic category.

25. In cases where the coefficient for the Protestant category is negative, the coefficient for social democratic countries is larger than in models with religion not present. For example, for total non-NSM memberships, a coefficient of 1.0382 in Model 1 now rises to 1.489 at the same time that a negative coefficient is estimated for the Protestant category (–.6188). The *sum* of the two is not much different: 1.038 versus 1.489 – .6188 = +.8702. The "sign reversal" for the Protestant category is an indication of the high degree of collinearity between the polity type and the religion variables.

26. These two variables were only modestly correlated as a result of the fact that other religions (including "no religion") are present in many countries.

27. The one minor exception to this pattern is that the highest level of education is slightly less involved in unions than the second highest education level, but the more educated group is still more involved—both as members and as active members—than most other education levels.

28. See Fine and Harrington (2004) for a much more extensive discussion of this theme.

29. This number does not represent an exact computation for any particular country, but an approximation for a country at roughly a .500 overall level of participation.

30. They are not a general test of whether any or all slopes are significantly different from zero).

31. An alternative explanation for the apparent finding that nominal membership rates have gone up in Sweden is that workers are now more likely to identify themselves as union members or to see themselves as part of a work organization than they were in the past.

32. These odds ratios can be affected by small starting proportions. Thus, the odds ratio for a change from .03 to .07 is 2.4, while the odds ratio for a change from .12 to .16 is 1.4.

33. In 2000, government consumption as a percentage of GDP was 14 percent in the United States and 18 percent in Canada, compared to 27 percent in Sweden (World Bank data). These numbers do not factor in the ratio of military spending (high in the US) to welfare provision.

34. Not all membership questions were asked in each of the World Values Surveys in the case of the UK.

35. For an examination of British data using mostly non-World Values data, see Hall (2002), who argues that voluntary association involvement in the U.K. has been sustained at reasonably high levels over the past fifty years. No comparisons with other countries are made, however.

36. If these are captured at all in the World Values Survey, it is when some respondents might answer in the affirmative to the category "local community action on issues like poverty, employment, housing, racial equality," having in mind tenants' organizations. Still, it appears highly likely that large numbers of members would answer negative to the World Values Survey questions.

37. This finding applies to total memberships for non-social movement associations and to total memberships in social movement associations in Table 3.4. As noted earlier, the *total* effect of being at once in a Protestant heritage country and a social democratic country is that of an increase in association involvement relative to most other types. The problem is one of *disaggregating* effects, given the fact that most Protestant countries are social democratic and vice versa.

References

Adam, Barry. 1993. "Post Marxism and the New Social Movements." *Canadian Review of Sociology and Anthropology* 30, no. 3: 316–336.

Baer, Douglas, James Curtis and Edward Grabb. 2001. "Has Voluntary Association Activity Declined? Cross-national Analysis for Fifteen Countries." *Canadian Review of Sociology and Anthropology* 38, no. 3: 249–274.

Bauman, Zygmunt. 2001. *The Individualized Society*. Cambridge: Polity.

Boggs, Carl. 1986. *Social Movements and Political Power*. Philadelphia: Temple University Press.

Carroll, William. 2002. "Social Movements." In *Political Sociology: Canadian Perspectives*, ed. Doug Baer. Don Mills: Oxford.

Carroll, William and Robert Ratner. 1996. "Master Frames and Counter-Hegemony: Political Sensibilities in Contemporary Social Movements," *Canadian Review of Sociology and* Anthropology 33, no. 4: 407–435.

Coleman, James. 1988. "Social Capital in the Creation of Human Capital." *American Journal of Sociology* 94: 94–120.

———. 1990. *Foundations of Social Theory*. Cambridge, MA: Harvard University Press.

Cohen, Jean. 1985. "Strategy or Identity: New Theoretical Paradigms and Contemporary Social Movements." *Social Research* 52: 663–716.

Curtis, James, Edward Grabb, and Douglas Baer. 1992. "Voluntary Association Membership in Fifteen Countries: A Comparative Analysis." *American Sociological Review* 57, no. 1: 139–152.

Curtis, James, Douglas Baer, and Edward Grabb. 2001. "Nations of Joiners: Explaining Voluntary Association Membership in Democratic Societies." *American Sociological Review* 66, no. 6: 783–805.

de Ulzurrun, Laura. 2002. "Associational Membership and Social Capital in Comparative Perspective: A Note on Problems of Measurement." *Politics and Society* 30, no. 3: 497–523.

Dekker, Paul, and Eric Uslaner, eds. 2001. *Social Capital and Participation in Everyday Life*. London: Routledge.

Edwards, Michael. 2004. *Civil Society*. Cambridge: Polity.

Esping-Andersen, Gösta. 1989. "Three Political Economies of the Welfare State." *Canadian Review of Sociology and Anthropology* 26, no. 1: 10–36.

———. 1990. *The Three Worlds of Welfare Capitalism*. Cambridge: Polity.

Fine, Ben. 2001. *Social Capital Versus Social Theory*. London: Routledge.

Fine, Gary Alan, and Brooke Harrington. 2004. "Tiny Publics: Small Groups and Civil Society." *Sociological Theory* 22: 341–356.

Fung, Archon. 2003. "Associations and Democracy: Between Theories, Hopes and Realities." *Annual Review of Sociology* 29: 515–539.

Gouldner, Alvin. 1979. *The Future of Intellectuals and the Rise of the New Class*. New York: Seabury Press.

Habermas, Jürgen. 1976. *Legitimation Crisis*. Trans. Thomas McCarthy. Boston: Beacon Press.

Hall, Peter. 2002. "Great Britain: The Role of Government and the Distribution of Social Capital." In *Democracies in Flux*, ed. Robert Putnam. Oxford: Oxford University Press.

Hooghe, Liesbet. 2004. "Belgium: Hollowing the Centre." In *Federalism and Territorial Cleavages*, ed. Ugo Amoretti and Nancy Bermeo. Baltimore: Johns Hopkins.

Hox, Joop. 2002. *Multilevel Analysis.* Mahwah, NJ: Lawrence Erlbaum.

Inglehart, Ronald. 1997. *Modernization and Postmodernization: Cultural, Economic and Political Change in 43 Societies.* Princeton: Princeton University Press.

Jackman, Robert, and Ross Miller. 1998. "Social Capital and Politics." *Annual Review of Political Science* 1: 47–73.

Janoski, Thomas. 1998. *Citizenship and Civil Society.* Cambridge: Cambridge University Press.

Jepperson, Ronald. 2002. "Political Modernities: Disentangling Two Underlying dimensions of Institutional Differentiation." *Sociological Theory* 20, no. 1: 61–85.

Jepperson, Ronald, and John Meyer. 1991. "The Public Order and the Construction of Formal Associations." In *The New Institutionalism in Organizational Analysis*, ed. Paul DiMaggio and Walter Powell. Chicago: University of Chicago Press.

Kitschelt, Herbert. 1986. "Political Opportunity Structures and Political Protest: Anti-Nuclear Movements in Four Democracies." *British Journal of Political Science* 16: 57–95.

Kriesi, Hanspeter. 1995. "The Political Opportunity Structure of New Social Movements: Its Impact on Their Mobilization." In *The Politics of Social Protest*, ed. J. Jenkins and B. Klandermans. Minneapolis: University of Minneapolis Press.

Ladd, Everitt C. 1999. *The Ladd Report.* New York: Free Press.

Laraña, Enrique, Hank Johnston, and Joseph Gusfield, eds. 1994. *New Social Movements: From Ideology to Identity.* Philadelphia: Temple University Press.

Levi, Margaret. 1996. "Social and Unsocial Capital." *Politics and Society* 24: 45–55.

Lipset, Seymour M. 1994. "The Social Requisites of Democracy Revisited." *American Sociological Review* 59, no. 1: 1–22.

———. 1996. *American Exceptionalism: A Double-Edged Sword.* New York: W.W. Norton.

Long, J. Scott. 1997. *Regression Models for Categorical and Limited Dependent Variables.* Thousand Oaks, CA: Sage.

Martin, David. 1990. *Tongues of Fire: The Explosion of Protestantism in Latin America.* Cambridge, MA: Basil Blackwell.

Melucci, Alberto. 1989. *Nomads of the Present: Social Movements and Individual Needs in Contemporary Society.* Philadelphia: Temple University Press.

Offe, Clause. 1985. *Disorganized Capitalism.* Cambridge: Polity.

Paxton, Pamela. 1999. "Is Social Capital Declining in the United States? A Multiple Indicator Assessment." *American Journal of Sociology* 105: 88–127.

Portes, Alexandro. 1998. "Social Capital: Its Application and Origins in Modern Sociology." *Annual Review of Sociology* 24: 1–24.

Putnam, Robert. 1995. "Bowling Alone: America's Declining Social Capital." *Journal of Democracy* 6: 65–78.

————. 1996. "The Strange Disappearance of Civic America." *American Prospect* 24: 34–48.

————. 2000. *Bowling Alone: The Collapse and Revival of American Community.* New York: Simon and Schuster.

Raudenbush, Stephen, and Anthony Bryk. 2002. *Hierarchical Linear Models.* Thousand Oaks, CA: Sage.

Roberts, Kenneth. 2002. "Social Inequalities Without Class Cleavages in Latin America's Neoliberal Era." *Studies in Comparataive International Development* 36, no. 4: 3–33.

Rothstein, Bo. 2001. "Social Capital in the Social Democratic Welfare State." *Politics and Society* 29, no. 2: 207–241.

Rothstein, Bo, and Dietlind Stolle. 2003 "Social Capital in Scandinavia." *Scandinavian Political Studies* 26, no. 1: 1–26

Rotolo, Thomas. 1999. "Trends in Voluntary Association Participation." *Nonprofit and Voluntary Sector Quarterly* 28: 199–212.

Salamon, Lester, S. Wojciech Sokolowski, and Associates. 2004. *Global Civil Society: Dimensions of the Nonprofit Sector.* Bloomfield CT: Kumarian Press.

Schofer, Evan, and Marion Fourcade-Gourinchas. 2001. "The Structural Contexts of Civic Engagement: Voluntary Association Membership in Comparative Perspective." *American Sociological Review* 66, no. 6: 806–828.

Skocpol, Theda. 1979. *States and Social Revolutions.* New York: Cambridge University Press.

————. 2003. *Diminished Democracy: From Membership to Management in American Civic Life.* Norman: University of Oklahoma Press.

Touraine, Alain. 1981. *Voice and the Eye: An Analysis of Social Movements.* New York: Cambridge University Press.

Uslaner, 2002. *The Moral Foundations of Trust.* Cambridge: Cambridge University Press.

Wilensky, Harold. 2002. *Rich Democracies: Political Economy, Public Policy and Performance.* Berkeley: University of California Press.

Wuthnow, Robert. 1991. "Tocqueville's Question Reconsidered: Voluntarism and Public Discourse in Advanced Industrial Societies." In *Between States and Markets: The Voluntary Sector in Comparative Perspective,* ed. R. Wuthnow. Princeton: Princeton University Press.

Chapter 4

CIVIC PARTICIPATION IN
A SCANDINAVIAN WELFARE STATE:
PATTERNS IN CONTEMPORARY SWEDEN

Eva Jeppsson Grassman and Lars Svedberg

Introduction

The discussion and debates surrounding Swedish civil society throughout the 1990s up to the present day have been an arena for mostly ideological, and to a lesser extent theoretical, investment. The concept of
civil society is a borrowed one. But although its historical roots lie in
other societies with different political traditions, views on Swedish civil
society have been formulated both in Sweden and abroad, often in highly
charged political terms (see Trägårdh 1995 and 1999). The concept is
complex and in actual usage at times contradictory, since it has sprung
from different debates and discourses stressing sometimes democracy,
sometimes the provision of care and welfare services, and most recently,
social capital. The many different versions of the concept nonetheless
have one thing in common—an interest in the present position and the
future of civil society in a Scandinavian-type welfare state. The purpose
of this chapter is twofold: to present and discuss trends and patterns in
discourses about civil society and civic participation in Sweden and the
assumptions they build on; and to evaluate these assumptions through
an analysis of actual data on Swedish civil society and patterns of civic
participation. These data, which come from empirical studies conducted
by the authors and by other scholars, allow for a broader exploration and
more complex discussion aimed at adding more shades to the picture
than are usually presented.

It is not only the articulated assumptions concerning Swedish civic participation and social capital in the past fifteen years that appear partly contradictory. The same goes for our research results, when viewed in the light of results from other studies. This has, among other things, to do with the ambiguity of the civil society and civic participation concepts. The underlying questions are not only whether there can be a strong civil society in a Scandinavian-type welfare state, but how to measure it, and not only whether it shrinks or expands, but also what "it" really is.

The issue of civil society, its present state, and possible weakening has in recent times been much discussed, and not only in Sweden. Skocpol (1999, 2003), for example, reflects on the divisive debate on American civil society, and Lorentzen (2001) and Wijkström (2001) discuss the Scandinavian situation at the turn of the millennium. The core of civil society is generally taken to be the voluntary sector, with its wide range of organizations and activities and accent on civic participation. This is also the point of departure for this chapter. Yet, we agree with Gundelach and Torpe (1997), Janoski (1998), and Wijkström (1998), who underline the need for a more in-depth, more differentiated analysis of how the concept of civil society is defined and delimited. What to include and what to exclude from the civil society sphere is not obvious. Nonetheless, for the purpose of this chapter our definition of the term civil society will include the variety of *informal* networks that exist outside formal organizations and *non-organizational informal helping*.[1] We argue that by doing this, we are able to include aspects and dimensions of Swedish civil society that become invisible when only participation in formal organizations is considered. One acknowledged risk of this approach is that by adding complexity we may in fact also contribute to increasing the ambiguity of the concept.

Civic involvement can be understood from both a conflictual and a consensual perspective. It can be the expression of resources, social capital, or instrumentality. The most common point of view is that civic participation is "a good thing." A good example of this is what one could call Putman's first position (1993). Although this stance has been nuanced and problematized by a number of other scholars, for example Berman (1997), Schlozman, Verba, and Brady (1999), Lorentzen (2000), Wijkström and Lundström (2003), and Jeppsson Grassman (2004), civil society and citizenship have often been linked in the discussions during the past decade. Citizenship in this context has been given a wider interpretation, and has been loaded with meanings that go beyond formal rights and obligations vis-à-vis the State (Butcher and Mullard 1993; Janoski 1998; Rees 1996). In this wider definition, citizenship combines a number of individual roles and identities not least in regard to being an active citizen in civil society. Active citizenship in this sense can thus assume many forms, depending on the definition of civil society and how its boundaries are drawn.

Civil society is also, however, often treated as a *sphere of society*. Most often civil society is intended to denote a public but autonomous sphere in which citizens' organizations and associations occupy the core space. In this view, national associations, grassroots associations, and other groups in the local social fabric function as arenas for action in a space devoted to the practice of active citizenship. Civic participation in its various forms thus, from this perspective, is seen as linked to a particular sphere of society. This sphere constitutes a prerequisite: it must have a certain scope in terms of organizations and activities, in order to provide citizens with the space in which to participate and act. The size of this space, in turn, has to do with the division of responsibilities between the different spheres of society. The idea of a social sphere and space for civic action is important for an adjacent "family" of concepts that has gained ground in Sweden in the past two decades. This school of thought conceives of society as consisting of *four sectors*, where civil society is most often identified with the "non-profit sector," or—the term that we mainly use here—the voluntary sector.[2]

Civic participation is also connected to *civicness*, which in its wider sense has to do with community spirit but also stands for attitudes and characteristics of the citizens—their commitments and actions and the quality of these (see also Lorentzen 2001; Skocpol 2003). That civicness in this sense can be exercised and expressed anywhere, but can perhaps best be learned and mediated through activities in civil society, is the often underlying assumption. Without vivid civic participation and activism, civil society may be regarded as underdeveloped, according to this view.

Civil society is thus both a social sphere, a home for independent organizations not controlled by the state, and a designation for the single or collective efforts through which people learn and pass on virtues that are of benefit to the entire society. Furthermore, civil society has not only democratic dimensions and implications but social and economic ones as well, not least in the welfare domain. This has come vividly into focus during the past fifteen years. The meanings attributed to the concepts of civil society and civic participation also tend to be time-bound, with reference both to concrete social change and to ideologically related shifts in the discourse. All these different interpretations of the concept of civil society have to be taken into account when we look into the assumptions about Sweden and Swedish civil society. In this chapter we intend to take a closer look at some of these assumptions, which fall into two general areas:

I. Countries like Sweden with a "strong State" and comprehensive state welfare arrangements largely financed by public means and administered by public agencies, tend to have an underdeveloped civil society in terms of density of voluntary organizations and civic participation within and outside organizational frameworks. The assumption would be that "the state has taken over." Here "underdeveloped" suggests an implicit comparison to other countries. Consequently, an international empirical comparative perspective ought to shed some light on this issue.

In the logic of the assumption above, the retrenchments of the welfare state in the past decade and the increasing demand for welfare services that is not met by the state welfare arrangements—ought to lead to increased private initiatives, most of all in professional for-profit and non-profit welfare organizations, but also to more unpaid, civic involvement—more responsibility for civil society. The relevance in this kind of thesis should be tested in comparisons over time.

II. Another assumption is strongly attached to the political and democratic side of the civil society concept and connected to a Swedish and Scandinavian debate:

Civic participation is steadily falling as a result of the way the Swedish society is developing *now*. The Swedish model was, at its height, characterized by a vibrant, inclusive civic participation. However, in present-day Sweden this has fallen victim to a drastically shrinking interest in traditional politics and political parties. Among other things, this loss is held to be an effect of the ongoing individualization processes in the Western world, where citizens have increasingly come to see themselves as mere consumers.

This chapter is composed of four sections that address these contradictory assumptions in two ways. First, we analyze the discourses and the assumptions they build on concerning the present state of civil society and its future scope in the Swedish context, reviewing them within a broad frame of reference, including the research traditions and scientific perspectives from which they have emerged; then we go on to reformulate these assumptions as questions. In the second and third sections, we use results from current research and especially our own studies from the 1990s and on to examine the following questions:

1) Do welfare states such as the Swedish one necessarily have a poorly developed civil society in terms of a sphere of associations and different forms of civic participation? Are there aspects of civic participation that are not addressed—not "seen"—in the current dominating discourses on Swedish civil society? We assess the magnitude of associations, as well as of different kinds of civic activities, and examine their character, roles, and functions in Swedish society.

2) What has happened to civic involvement in view of the relatively extensive changes that took place in Sweden during the 1990s? What

changes in civic involvement have taken place and in what areas of civil society? Based on the results of our repeated surveys over time, we discuss patterns of change with reference to results from other studies.

In the final section of the chapter we make some concluding remarks on civic participation as an indicator of the continuing liveliness of civil society in Sweden, i.e. its importance and function in a transitional stage of the societal development. We will argue that the Swedish state and civil society exert influence on each other, but the mutual relations are complex and ambiguous. This is important for understanding what in some quarters is seen as a paradox—that Sweden, with its welfare model, does have a vibrant civil society, measured in terms of organizational affiliation and civic participation both within and outside the boundaries of these organizations.

Civil Society in the Swedish Welfare State: Frames of Reference and New Discourses

The idea that a society of the Scandinavian/Swedish type, or in fact Sweden itself, should have a poorly developed civil society, at least if measured in terms of voluntary associations and civic participation, does not fit either the Swedish self-image or the traditional standpoint of the long ruling (Social Democratic) political party. On the contrary, the modern history of Sweden is viewed as "a history of popular mass movements." This tradition, with its wide range of popular organizations demanding the broad involvement of the people, has been a source of great pride in Sweden and has shown by international comparison to be unique in character (see e.g. Jeppsson Grassman and Svedberg 1996; Lundström and Svedberg 2003; Salamon et al. 1999; Wijkström and Lundström 2003). Therefore, when it was asserted at the beginning of the 1900s that the Swedish civil society was probably stunted in its growth and even shrinking, the reaction of many Swedes was bemused surprise.

By tradition and not least through consistent government backing, membership in associations has been seen both as a basic component and a necessary condition for a functioning democracy in Sweden and therefore of very direct importance. The associations have provided individuals with a medium for the exercise of political citizenship. They are looked upon as "schools for democracy," where democratic values and patterns of behavior are taught or handed down to the advantage of the society as a whole (see e.g. SOU 1987: 33). Nevertheless, in recent years political commentators and academic researchers, starting from different viewpoints, experiences, and empirical data have come to ask whether and to what extent Swedish and Scandinavian popular organizations still fulfill this fundamental role (see e.g. Lorentzen 1998; Petersson, Hermansson, Michelletti, Teorell, and Westholm 1998; Selle and Öymyr 1995; SOU 2000: 1; Torpe 2001; Vogel, Amnå, Munck, and Häll 2003). The associations most often at the center of attention have been those with *political* orientation, and the focus has been from a citizen's political resource perspective.

Welfare Production and the Obligation to Help

At the beginning of the 1990s, Swedish associations and their activities were articulated in a way entirely new for Swedish conditions. By connecting with the international debate and international research, the notion of the four sectors of society was introduced (see e.g. Blennberger 1993 and Pestoff 1991). In this system, the voluntary/non-profit sector became the sphere most identified with so-called civil society, that is, the sphere of society that is not the state, the market, or the family. What was radically new in the Swedish context about this modern, international research was partly the clear boundaries drawn between the various sectors of society and partly the highlighting of the division of responsibilities. Thus, the world of associations was identified and defined as a distinct and separate sector. This was new and not at all in line with an old and well-established Swedish corporatist tradition that blurs the boundaries between organizations and the state, both in theory and practice. The Anglo-American tradition of conceptualizing the voluntary sector in terms such as "production," "service," "contribution," and "core areas of welfare," was introduced.[3] Our own research from those years can partly be placed in this context. The spotlight was suddenly focused upon an area that up until then had been as good as invisible, at least in post-war Sweden.

In this international research on the voluntary sector, with its emphasis on the production of services, there was clear skepticism about the chances of Sweden having a voluntary sector of any importance (see e.g. Boli 1992; James 1989). This viewpoint emerged from two streams of thought. One, based on economic public-goods theory, maintained that the more heterogeneous the society, the more important its voluntary sector. Historically homogeneous countries such as Sweden, Denmark, and Norway "ought" therefore to have small voluntary sectors. The other started with the assumption that in a welfare state of the Swedish type the state is prone to "crowd out" the voluntary sector (cf. Lundström 2004). Both assumptions are so common and so deeply rooted, not least in the US tradition, that they have continued to exert an impact, even after new research results have complicated that version of reality and other views have emerged (see e.g. O'Connell 1998 and Weissbrod 1997). To this should be added that researchers, out of habit and ethnocentricity, have been looking for big, professionally run nonprofit organizations, which are fairly few in the Swedish and Scandinavian contexts.

In fact, metaphors such as "crowding out" and "colonization" also appeared on the Swedish discursive scene at the beginning of the 1990s and had their defenders in certain circles (see e.g. Zetterberg 1995). On the whole in Sweden at this time, there was increased interest in welfare-oriented voluntary organizations and, not least, in their potential for service provision through unpaid work. "The crisis of the welfare state"—with demands for cuts in public spending in a neoliberal climate that intensified criticism of the Swedish welfare state as bureaucratic and inefficient—was the background of this situation (Jeppsson Grassman and Svedberg 1999). At the same time, certain conservative ideas were launched and added to the new welfare discourse. One sought to promote the close, organic, caring neighborhood steeped in community spirit, which had been invaded and weakened not only by the state but also by the market (Ljungberg 1992; Zetterberg and Ljungberg 1997). This "small world" idea, represented by the family and networks close to home, had an ideological connection to the communitarian discussion in the US (see Etzioni 1993). The personal moral obligations to one's community that were imposed by citizenship were thus brought into focus in a new way, where helping and caring became key words (Lundström and Svedberg 1998; Svedberg 1995). In texts on civicness another shift was effected in the early 1990s along this line: from "active membership," which is the Swedish civic participation tradition to, "volunteering" in the Anglo-American mold. The core of the volunteering paradigm is not collective action but the deeds of the individual actor and his or her voluntary, often help-oriented work (Habermann 2001; Jeppsson Grassman 1998; Van Til 1988).

Towards the end of the 1990s, it seemed a gradual ideological silence was spreading with regard to the moral aspects of unpaid help work. Instead, the message of the public agenda was transformed into one of pure instrumentality, underlining the need for citizens to contribute to welfare through unpaid work. This was particularly true of the discourse concerning the need for citizens to get involved in *informal helping*, particularly caring for frail family members (Jegermalm, 2002; Jegermalm and Whitaker, 2000; Jeppsson Grassman 2001, 2003).

To sum up: during the 1990s the need for a "helping-out" civil society was articulated in various ways in Sweden (see Jeppsson Grassman 1993, 2001, 2003; Svedberg 1996). This emphasis on civic participation as helping was grounded in the assumption that Swedish citizens, made passive by their welfare state, did not have an active involvement in this type of activity (cf. Ljungberg 1992; Zetterberg 1995). This rather depressing picture of Swedish civil society seemed strange to the common Swedish self-understanding (Jeppsson Grassman 1993).

However, at the same time, a different discourse was gaining ground in Sweden, based on other assumptions but with the shared idea of a problematic Swedish civil society.

The Swede as a Politically Active Citizen: A Constant Source of Anxiety

The moral evaluations of (the lack of) civic involvement among Swedish citizens that burgeoned at the beginning of the 1990s continued to inform the entire decade and the 2000s as well, but more as an internal Swedish debate and more often specifically focused on political involvement and the ultimate effects for democracy, that is, on the consequence of declining civic participation in political life. This "deficit" is said to be created by both falling election rates and shrinking membership in political parties and the traditional popular mass movements, i.e. by reduced direct participation by citizens in the democratic process.

Swedish research on democracy, meanwhile, most often starts out with another image of Sweden: it is a "land of popular mass movements" that used to have a lively, widespread organizational life but has gradually lost it in recent decades, especially the 1990s (Petersson 2000; Vogel et al. 2003). The assumption is that Swedes view themselves as consumers of a ready-made system rather than as equal actors in a political process. In the words of one group of researchers commenting on political participation in the 1990s: "The Swedish interpretation of democracy tends to dilute the meaning of citizenship by reducing the social role of the individual. The emphasis is now definitely on what the country can do for you and no asking what you can do for your country" (Petersson et al. 1998: 17, our translation). Judging by their results, there was every reason to worry. The group found that between the late 1980s and the late 1990s civic participation through active membership had fallen off or stagnated in several areas. The same alarming situation was revealed with regard to passive memberships in organizations, where, according to their results, the level of activity had fallen drastically in the ten years studied. What had been referred to as the "land of popular mass movements," was evidently coming apart at the seams.

These two discourses, expressed repeatedly during the past fifteen years, paint a rather bleak picture of recent trends in Sweden. According to the "helping discourse," involvement in community and welfare through voluntary or informal caring/helping barely ought to exist in this state-dominated country where civil society is poorly developed. Decreasing involvement by the state might consequently increase citizens' involvement in unpaid work. The "political involvement discourse" argues that participation in associations in Sweden has fallen or stagnated in several areas, leading to the weakening of an earlier, stronger civil society. But maybe there is more to it. Perhaps some aspects of civil society have not been articulated in these time-bound discourses. In the following sections we go on and confront these arguments. By incorporating different types of information the picture takes on additional shades that problematize and broaden the perspectives outlined above.

Sweden: A Land of Associations and Civic Involvement?

The assumption that a democratic country like Sweden has a poorly developed civil society implies a weak sphere of associations for people to be active in. A logical point of departure must then be: Does Sweden have a weak civil society, measured in terms of its voluntary organizations? In order to get a relevant answer to this question a comparison to other countries must be made.

Size and Economy

In fact, Sweden has a strong tradition of popular organizations. Comparative studies carried out in the 1990s (e.g. Jeppsson Grassman and Svedberg 1996; Lundström and Wijkström 1997; Lundström and Svedberg 2003) actually confirm the image of a "land of associations." With its approximately 200,000 associations in a population of nine million inhabitants and just under three association memberships per head, Sweden stands out in an international comparison as better endowed in this respect than most other countries (Curtis, Grabb, and Baer 1992; Curtis, Baer and Grabb 2001; Lundström and Wijkström 1995).

New interest in the Swedish voluntary sector prompted Swedish researchers to participate in a large comparative research project that measured the importance of the voluntary/nonprofit sector in a number of countries.[4] The size and composition of the Swedish sector was investigated and compared to that of other Western countries, mainly in economic terms. Contrary to preconceived ideas, Sweden turned out to have a voluntary/nonprofit sector comparable in size and economic importance (measured as percent of GNP) to other Western European countries (Lundström and Wijkström 1997; Salamon and Anheier 1994). This is illustrated in Table 4.1. Regarding the role of the sector in total employment, Sweden breaks with the pattern in an interesting way. Only two percent of all wage earners are found in the non-profit sector, a much lower figure than in other, comparable countries. This suggests that the Swedish

Table 4.1 Size and Economic Importance of Voluntary Sector by Country

Annual voluntary sector operating expenditures by country as percentage of GDP.
Voluntary sector employment as percentage of total employment

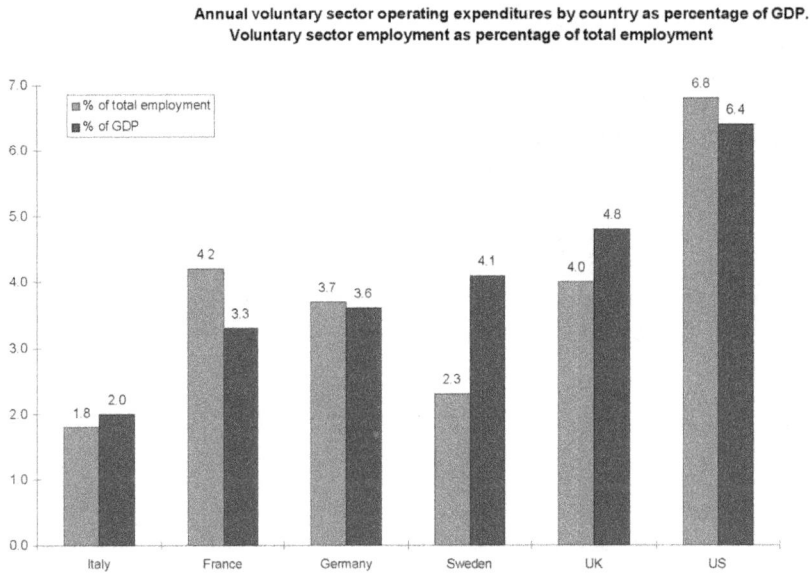

Sources: Lundström and Wijkström 1997; Salamon and Anheier 1994.

sector is of a comparatively "non-professional" and "popular" character and that activities are run on a genuinely voluntary basis, which is wholly in line with the Swedish tradition of popular movements and the self-image generated by this. Following this, the character of the Swedish sector is that it is member-based and has a voluntary orientation as opposed to a service-based, professional orientation (see Lundström and Svedberg 2003).

The popular image of the Swedish voluntary/nonprofit sector appears to be closely connected with the geography of the sector: It is dominated by sports and recreation, culture, and labor market organizations; only to a small degree is it made up of social welfare organizations (which often are areas heavy on staff). While, by contrast, activities in the core areas of welfare stood for 68 percent of total turnover of the voluntary/nonprofit sector in France and 85 percent in the United States, the corresponding figure for Sweden was 27 percent (Salamon et al. 1999; cf. Jeppsson Grassman 1999).

We found no support for the idea that welfare states of the Scandinavian/Swedish type necessarily have a voluntary sector that is economically negligible or that the state has crowded out the sector, as a vital part of civil society in any general sense. The voluntary sector in Sweden has partly developed in quite another direction to fulfill functions it does not address in many comparable European countries (for a further discussion see also Janoski 1998). It is clear that the Swedish welfare model, along with a general pro-state tradition (including strong processes of integration between the voluntary sector and the state), has had an important effect on the present-day profile of the voluntary sector, as has the Swedish tradition of popular mass movements. However, these factors can only partly explain the size of the sector (see Jeppsson Grassman and Svedberg 1996; Lundström and Wijkström 1997; Lundström and Svedberg 2003).

Taking as a point of departure this refutation of the assumption that Sweden has a low density of voluntary organizations, let us now discuss the first question posed at the beginning of the chapter in connection to Assumption I: Is civic participation poorly developed?

Civic Participation in Sweden:
A Multitude of Unpaid Activities

Here we will explore civic participation in the areas of volunteering, access to informal networks and informal helping, and the connection between these different types of activities. We will also try to uncover and articulate aspects and roles of these activities that, in our understanding, have been overlooked by current discourses and research. For instance, we examine the multifaceted social meanings that civic participation may have, such as offering "togetherness" and shared leisure time. Our analysis builds on the results of three comprehensive population studies of civic participation in Sweden carried out in the 1990s, both nationally and as part of European-wide, comparative surveys.[5] In addition, results from an in-depth survey on informal helping carried out in the year of 2000 are to some extent discussed.[6] The extent among the Swedish population of organized volunteering, informal helping outside voluntary organizations, and access to informal networks (only measured in 1998) is summarized in Table 4.2.

Table 4.2 Volunteering, Informal Helping, and Informal Networks in Sweden during the 1990s: National Results.

Percentage of the population aged 16–74 involved in each activity.

	1992			1998		
	Total	Men	Women	Total	Men	Women
Volunteering	48	52	44	52	53	50
Informal helping	28	29	27	30	28	31
Informal networks				48	47	50
BASE (Sample size)	1,045	524	521	1,104	568	536

According to the results in Table 4.2, approximately half of the Swedish population aged 16–74 had volunteered in the past twelve months. A slight increase can be noted between beginning and the end of the decade. Approximately half of the population regularly participated in informal networks, and about a third of the population did informal helping on a regular basis. How are these results to be interpreted and how do they compare to data on other countries?

In the following, we will first discuss volunteering—voluntary work in an organizational setting—and then go on to examine access to informal networks and finally, non-organizational informal helping.

Volunteering in Organizations

Involvement in the voluntary sector and participation in its activities is, as already pointed out, often seen as a "main indicator" of civic participation. Of the three forms discussed here, volunteering is also the one most often referred to in discourses on civil society. Organizational affiliation can take many forms and have varying degrees of intensity. There is membership—passive and active—and unpaid volunteering. In the Anglo-American research tradition the focus has generally been on unpaid volunteering. The empirical studies presented here follow this tradition. Unpaid, voluntary work in organizations, whether it is called active membership or volunteering, is generally seen as the truest expression of "civicness" in the organizational context, in the sense of benefiting others as well as the actor himself. There is no single definition of volunteering. The definition we have used in our own population studies as well as in the European comparative study is commonly used.[7]

Our first investigation of civic participation in the form of volunteering and informal helping was carried out in 1992 and covered the entire Swedish population aged 16–74. Contrary to predictions—given the debates—our results showed that volunteering was widespread in Sweden at the beginning of the 1990s. This situation remained stable during the decade, as shown by a repeat survey carried out in 1998/1999 (patterns of change are further discussed in the third section of this chapter). At the end of the 1990s Sweden was still characterized by broad participation in voluntary organizations in the form of voluntary work. The results also show that volunteering was most common in the 45–59 age group. However, Swedish people did not seem to be volunteering in organizations of "the right sort": the most common area of voluntary involvement was not social care and welfare but sports and leisure organizations, followed by cultural organizations, and housing associations. Organizations for social care and welfare attracted a small share of the volunteers. The same goes for political organizations. One exception was volunteer involvement in trade unions (Jeppsson Grassman and Svedberg 1999).

In traditional Scandinavian style, organized volunteering has been very strongly coupled to membership. Consequently, Sweden also rates high in an international comparison when it comes to the share of active persons who are members of the organization where they make their contribution as volunteers (see e.g. Gaskin and Davis Smith 1995; Jeppsson Grassman and Svedberg 1995).

Comparing and Understanding Volunteering

The extent of voluntary involvement in Sweden during the 1990s revealed in our data must be viewed as surprisingly high in itself and seems, at least partially, to refute the kind of assumption presented at the beginning of the chapter—that a country with a strong and comprehensive public sector of the Swedish type should choke that part of civil society expressed through unpaid work in organizations. However, the high level of participation in voluntary organizations cannot simply be related to the Swedish model of the welfare state only. Explanations must be sought in the more complex picture created by historical, political, and cultural traditions, as the results of a ten-country European comparative study of the voluntary sector have made clear (Gaskin and Davis Smith 1995; Jeppsson Grassman and Svedberg 1995, 1996).[8]

Table 4.3 shows results for six of the participating countries: Belgium, Germany, Ireland, the Netherlands, Sweden, and the UK. These are all well-developed West European countries, but they differ with regard to welfare regime types, relations between the state and the voluntary sector, labor market conditions, and historical traditions.

Table 4.3. A Comparison of Volunteering in Six European Countries

Significance tests of odds ratios show deviation from the value for the UK, which is the reference category

	Volunteering	Volunteering in care and welfare	Volunteering in sports and leisure	Volunteering in cultural associations	Volunteering in trade unions
Belgium	0.865	0.550**	1.067	0.472	0.451
Ireland	0.655***	0.765	1.410*	0.655	0.401
Netherlands	1.168	0.788	2.181***	1.791	0.661
Sweden	1.112	0.418***	2.315***	2.442**	3.442**
Germany	0.494***	0.508***	0.863	0.581	0.885
UK	1	1	1	1	1

*p<.05 **p<.01 *** p<.001.

Column 1 in the table shows that volunteering in general was most common in the Netherlands followed by Sweden, the UK, Belgium, Ireland, and Germany in that order. This reinforces the view that variations in welfare arrangements are a basis, albeit a complicated one, for understanding the differences in extent of volunteering between the countries. The results are nevertheless in line with an analysis of citizenship and civil society presented by Janoski (1998). He proposed a framework for understanding the balance of rights and obligations in systems of restricted or generalized exchange by focusing on differences between regime types. Partly on the basis of comparative results from the World Values Survey of 1990 in a study by Curtis, Grabb, and Baer (1992), he suggests that whereas civic participation through organizations differs according to the type of welfare regime, the explanations for this are related to specific characteristics of each regime type. Civic participation is thus most pronounced in countries with "social democratic" regime types, followed by countries with a "liberal" regime type. Last of all come the countries of the "conservative" regime type (cf. Curtis, Baer, and Grabb, 2001; see also Baer in this book). The results in Column 1 seem to illustrate this argument to a fairly high degree, perhaps with the exception of the Netherlands, which, although generally placed in the "conservative" regime type, takes the lead. However, the regime-type of the Netherlands is ambiguous, as pointed out by Esping-Andersen (1999), who refers to this country as a Janus-headed welfare regime, combining both social democratic and conservative regime attributes.

An analysis based on the latest round of surveys from the World Values Survey (2000), in which the same countries, along with the US, were included in the model, was conducted by the authors of this chapter.[9] In terms of volunteer work in general, the US takes the lead. Apart from this, the rank order of countries seen in Table 4.3 was confirmed: it turned out to be the same as in 1994, the year when the European comparative study was carried out.[10]

The next four columns group the voluntary organizations according to their main objectives and show the share of the population volunteering in each type of voluntary organization. These results give a clearer picture of the composition of activities within the sector. Column 2 shows the differences in regards to volunteering in organizations for social care and welfare. Here another pattern emerges: taking the lead is the UK, a country where unpaid, voluntary social work plays quite a central role. The same is true of Ireland. Also ranking high is the Netherlands, which together with the UK rates highest for volunteering in social care and welfare. Despite the large size of its voluntary sector and the broad extent of volunteering, Sweden comes last among the compared countries. This is not surprising, given the results from the national survey that were presented earlier.

The figures in Table 4.3 seem to indicate that the regime type—in the sense of welfare arrangements with their specific orientations and ambitions—is important for the general demarcation of the voluntary sector. In Sweden, in spite of certain cutbacks, welfare has remained predominantly a public-sector responsibility. The contribution by voluntary/nonprofit organizations, whether paid or unpaid, does not play the role within the core areas of welfare that it does in many other countries. Following Janoski's reasoning, one could say that because they need not deal with social services provision, Swedish voluntary organizations can direct their energies into other tasks. It is interesting to note, however, that the analysis of World Values Survey-data mentioned earlier indicated an increase of volunteer work in care and welfare in Sweden relative to the other countries in the model. Sweden now ranks higher than Belgium, Ireland, and Germany (with the UK, the Netherlands, and the US ranking highest). This may be an indication of patterns of change in Sweden discussed later on in the chapter.

The dimension of civil society represented by involvement in voluntary organizations mainly follows other lines in Sweden, where it is expressed in areas not covered by the welfare state. As the following columns indicate, these are volunteering in sports and leisure organizations as well as in culture. Sweden rates high in these areas, as its dominant position in Table 4.3 also clearly shows. Another dominant and exceptional pattern, relative to the other countries, emerges in the last column to the right— volunteering in trade unions—where no other country comes even close to Sweden. Results from our national surveys on volunteering confirm this specific pattern. The explanation for this is, partially, that trade union membership in Sweden is among the highest in the world. Membership is, as has already been pointed out, the typical bridge to unpaid, volunteer work in Sweden. This connection also seems to pertain to volunteer work in unions. This particular connection is also illustrated by the results of the analysis of the World Values Survey data of 2000, where the difference in trade union volunteering between Sweden and other countries turned out to be even more striking than in the European comparative study.

The Role and Function of Civic Participation

The patterns described raise the question of meaning of volunteering— that is, what are the different countries' attitudes to the role and function of civic participation, notably in relation to the welfare state? In the comparative European study on which the model in Table 4.3 is based, these attitudes were another area explored. They were investigated with an instrument containing five items.[11] Cluster analysis has revealed two separate dimensions of the role of volunteering in society (Jeppsson Grassman and Svedberg 1995). One dimension has to do with the value of volunteering as a "substitute for paid employment," reflecting an instrumental view of the character and role of volunteering, in relationship to the welfare state. The other dimension has to do with the intrinsic value of volunteering as an "independent force" in civil society, irrespective of any need for services that the welfare state might have. In the analysis, the attitudes captured were assumed to reflect historical, political, and cultural traditions, as well as more concrete, current conditions of the welfare state. In the results, the countries fell into different groups. Belgium and Ireland rated high on both dimensions. The Netherlands and the UK rated high on the substitution dimension but low on the intrinsic value dimension. The UK, with the marked liberal attributes of its regime type, has pursued a social policy in recent decades where significant volunteering efforts are expected to compensate for the slashing of public funds. The British result may thus be interpreted as reflecting this specific relation between the welfare state and civil society. Sweden alone among the compared countries rates low on volunteering as a substitute for public services but fairly high on volunteering as an intrinsic value and independent force.

Informal Networks: A Fabric for Civicness

Informal networks are considered to be the "cement" that constitutes the basic fabric of civil society, contributing to the creation of social capital (Coleman 1994; Putnam 1993), based on norms of reciprocity and trust (Putnam 2000). This reasoning has been criticized as being far too general and too uncritically based on positive assumptions. One problem is that the network concept is a broad and complex one; another is that it is given different meanings in different contexts. Finally, almost anything can in principle be analyzed as a network (Mizruchi 1994). This vagueness makes systematic comparisons and understanding of networks difficult, notably when considering the importance of networks from a "citizens' perspective." In discourses on Sweden, it has been suggested that the Swedish population have scarce and fragile informal networks. This has partly been coupled to specific conceptions of the Swedish national character (see Trägårdh 1995). Indeed, during the entire postwar period strong assumptions have been made, implying a connection between the welfare models of Sweden and the rest of Scandinavia, on the one hand, and the supposedly weak networks among their populations, on the other hand (see e.g. Austin 1970; Wolfe 1989). This type of argument has seldom been supported by empirical proof, however.

In Swedish general household surveys, "networks" are generally measured with family contacts, frequency of meeting friends, etc., as indicators. We wanted to explore networks as a more explicit ingredient of civil society, and the resulting measurement of the existence of networks in our 1998 survey is, as far as we know, the first of its kind carried out in Sweden. Our ambition was to chart the occurrence of informal networks of a certain type.[12] In-depth analysis of the data revealed that these networks could have an instrumental or a more social, supportive function, and that patterns varied between men and women (Jeppsson Grassman 2004).

Table 4.2 made clear that just under half of the Swedish population belongs to one or several such networks. According to our results, the most common purpose of these networks is to cultivate or carry out a shared leisure activity. If almost half of the population belongs—is that a high or a low figure in this context? And what does this tell us about Swedish society from a comparative perspective? As there are few comparable results from other countries, drawing a conclusion is difficult. One exception is a study by Wuthnow (1994), who looked into networks outside formal organizations in the US. He found that approximately 40 percent of the American population belonged to what he names "small groups"— i.e. a small number of people getting together regularly for the purpose of enjoying shared interest. The conclusion to be drawn is that Sweden and the US—two countries that generally project very dissimilar images with respect to civil society—seem to resemble each other when it comes to this particular form of involvement.

The gender differences were small, according to these results. There was also quite an even distribution among the various age groups. The distribution of this type of network between rural and urban areas also turned out to be relatively even. Multiple regression analysis revealed determinants for network affiliation that can be summed up as *traditions* and *resources*. Persons who had grown up in homes with parents active in associations had more frequent access to networks than others. Persons with access to networks also had more resources in other areas, e.g., they were more likely to have higher education and higher incomes than people without affiliation to networks. The statistical analysis furthermore indicated that the "joiners" were more likely to be active in volunteering than "non-joiners," a fact that agrees with the international research (see e.g. Wilson and Musick 1997a; Putnam 2000). The different activities through which civil society is expressed are not only seen to be linked to each other: access to informal networks is a resource—a personal capital—that as such increases the chances for other forms of civic participation. Or, from the adverse perspective, one could say that participation in associations may provide a space for the creation of networks that individuals can then use (Jeppsson Grassman and Svedberg 1999).

Informal helping

Civic participation as unpaid labor outside the home can take the form of volunteering within an organization, but can also be *informal help* to others. Carried out outside the home or organization, such work is also one expression of civicness and an important component in the dynamic of civil society. But while the act of helping is certainly a component of civicness, informal helping is unclear as a concept, having been given different definitions in different research traditions. In the discourse on civil society and civic participation, informal helping is mostly referred to in sweeping generalizations.

In recent years, the question of informal helping (often in connection with family care) has aroused increased attention in the Western hemisphere as well as in the Swedish debate, especially in view of the widening gap between the needs of the dramatically growing group of elderly people and the available care and welfare resources (see Esping-Andersen 1999, 2001; Hansson, Jegermalm and Whitaker 2000; Jeppsson Grassman 2003; Johansson and Sundström 2002). Often, not least in nursing and/or social care research, informal helping is not viewed from a civil society perspective at all; rather it is the family perspective that is implicit. Yet in international research on volunteering there is also a certain tradition of asking questions about unpaid work outside organizational frameworks, i.e. civic participation in a broader sense (see e.g. Anglo-American population studies). It is in this tradition that we have carried out our research, well aware of the fact that informal helping can denote different things—from helping neighbors on a mutual basis to everyday helping of an elderly, frail mother living by herself but in need of much help and care (Jeppsson Grassman 2001, 2003).

In both of the national surveys carried out during the 1990s, questions were asked about informal helping, with a broad, general approach. Table 4.2 indicated that roughly 30 percent of the population regularly assisted others in this way (outside their own home), a figure that, according to the results of our surveys, seems to have remained relatively stable during the 1990s. A more in-depth discussion about patterns of change will be presented in the third section of this chapter. The gender pattern is surprisingly even in the resulting percentages of the population regularly involved in this type of work. Women, however, do average a few more hours than men. The "care profile" of women was confirmed by Jeppsson Grassman (2001) in a survey of informal helping in the Stockholm region: The helping carried out by women was characterized by time-consuming care obligations toward frail relatives to a much greater extent, compared to that of men (cf. Jeppsson Grassman 2004). Of those who are involved in informal helping, just over 75 percent turned out to help relatives on a regular basis; friend, neighbors, and/or workmates were beneficiaries in 34 percent of cases.[13]

Is 30 per cent of the population involved in informal helping a large or a small proportion? What does this say about civicness and involvement in civil society? What does it say about the impact of the welfare state from a comparative perspective? Systematic cross-national studies of informal helping have not been performed until recently. National studies may give some indication of how to interpret the Swedish results. In Denmark, whose welfare model is similar to the Swedish one, informal helping outside the immediate family also engaged 30 percent of the population, and in as many as half of those cases for someone not a relative (Anker and Koch Nielsen 1995). A national survey of the UK (Davis Smith 1998) showed that about 30 percent of the population in the UK regularly devoted time to informal helping. Even given the relatively sparse data, one can still—if with some caution—draw the conclusion that informal helping in Sweden does not differ from that in several other European countries. In contrast, quite another pattern is found in the US, where a majority of the population tended to carry out some form of informal help for others on a regular basis (Wilson and Musick 1997a), even if—according to Putman (2000)—the numbers now seem to be declining.

Summary I

As a measure of the magnitude and liveliness of civil society in Sweden, we set out to examine three forms of civic participation: unpaid, voluntary work in an organizational setting, informal networks, and non-organized informal helping. We have found no support for the contention that a country such as Sweden should have an underdeveloped civil society in these respects. On the contrary, we have found that the voluntary sector, usually seen as the core of civil society, is quite comparable in Sweden and other countries in terms of civic involvement and economic importance. Volunteering in associations turned out to be more widespread than in many comparable European countries; indeed, Sweden ranks high even in a worldwide comparison, as pointed out by by Curtis, Baer and Grabb (2001; see also Baer in this book). However, the Swedish voluntary sector seems to differ in character from that in many other European countries. It is not volunteering in welfare organizations that Swedish volunteers are primarily involved in, although, as we shall see, there seems to be increasing interest in this field. Sport and leisure organizations and cultural associations attract far more volunteers. Welfare provision is, in general terms, not a salient feature of the sector.

The first of the two assumptions presented at the beginning of the chapter was that "the state has taken over." The most adequate answer to this assumption, and to the first adjacent question, seems to be: Yes, the state has itself either organized or taken over the organization and provision of *professional welfare services* to a great extent. This does not mean, however, that an extensive civil society cannot exist. Nor does it mean, that there is no need for voluntary/nonprofit welfare organizations or voluntary and informal activities in different welfare fields.

Organizations solely dedicated to provision of social services are not very common in Sweden (see e.g. Jeppsson Grassman and Svedberg 1993; Svedberg 1993, 2001). Any such provisions are mainly a positive side effect of organizations' regular operations, where the boundaries between core activities, activities to boost community spirit, and activities catering to individual members' social needs are fairly blurred. This is a salient feature, for example, of associations for patients, pensioners, and the disabled. Social support or mutual help seems to be more or less integrated into different organizational activities and to consist largely of non-professional efforts. What is "social" in the context of Swedish voluntary organizations is therefore often difficult to pinpoint (Jeppsson Grassman and Svedberg 1996). As pointed out earlier, from an international perspective the Swedish voluntary sector accounts for a small share within the more strict area of core social services. Still it is far from negligible, contrary to what one might have assumed from the discussion in this text so far. Social work, delivered by professionals as well as by volunteers, is of crucial importance in certain specific niches (Svedberg 2001).

The idea that access and belonging to social networks is less common in Sweden than in other comparable countries does not seem to be supported by the findings presented in this chapter. Social networks of the kind mapped in our study can be assumed to have a supportive as well as an enabling function. Our results show strong evidence that there are linkages between different types of civic involvement: people who volunteer are also more likely to be involved in informal helping, and to have access to social networks, etc. In other words, there are reasons to speak about a *cumulative pattern* in civic participation. The contention that the Scandinavian/Swedish type of welfare state makes people passive when it comes to informal helping finds no empirical support in our population studies. Paradoxically, these kind of arguments have indirectly been supported by the internationally recognized Scandinavian welfare research tradition. In this tradition, it is striking how systematically the voluntary and the informal sectors have been overlooked or ignored when analyzing welfare (see for example Esping-Andersen 1990, 1999; Palme et al. 2000, 2001).

Patterns of Change in Civic Participation in the 1990s

Our starting point for this third part of this chapter is: What happened to civil society during that era of transition that was the 1990s? We will take a closer look at some specific areas of civic participation to see what changes did—or did not—take place during the decade. We shall particularly address the following questions: Did civic involvement increase during the decade? If so, what about the area of care and welfare? Or, did civic participation, on the contrary, decrease during the decade?

Let us first present some of the changes in socioeconomic conditions that may have affected Swedish civil society, or at least the parts relevant to our discussion. First, it is important to underline that the 1990s were in many ways a turbulent period for the country, not only ideologically, but also because of an economic and labor-market crisis, the worst since the 1930s. Unemployment was—from a Swedish viewpoint—uniquely high during the first part of the 1990s. The economic crisis hit families with small children, young people, and immigrants especially hard. The 1990s even saw shifts in welfare policy, with regard to both ideological position—that is, a new market orientation—and actual policies. These changes mostly amounted to certain cutbacks, e.g., reduced chances of getting certain types of help and support, and lower compensation levels for certain types of income loss. When the worst crisis had blown over and a retrospective assessment could be made, there did not seem to strong reasons to speak of a *fundamental* shift in the welfare model itself. (see e.g. Palme et al. 2002). Yet, the changes cannot just be discarded. Looking back at the 1990s from a vantage point some years into the 2000s, the balance sheets of the 1990s indicate that, in terms of professional welfare provision, it was primarily the for-profit organizations, and not the nonprofit ones, that gained some ground (Trydegård 2001)—and in Sweden more than in the other Scandinavian countries (Rostgaard and Lehto 2001).

Let us now go back to our original discussion concerning the assumptions that have commonly been made about Swedish civil society in order to make a few more comments regarding the types of changes that are implied by or inherent in them. The starting point for the first assumption was that a "strong state" would discourage all forms of civic involvement. Adding fuel to this viewpoint—and indeed to much of the debate in Sweden and other Scandinavian countries during the 1990s—is the idea of a zero-sum game between the sectors of society. It follows from this logic that a shrinking state, in terms of its welfare system, ought to lead to a corresponding increase in the civil society sector, including more unpaid civic involvement among other activities. We saw in the second section of this chapter that the first part of the assumption, from a general point of view, was not supported by empirical findings. Later on in this part of the chapter we will consider the second part of this assumption, namely the implication that retrenchment of the welfare state inevitably will lead to growth in the civil society sector.

The second assumption, meanwhile, at first sight has an unmistakable Swedish or Scandinavian touch, yet connects to an international tradition of differing groups of conservatives, post-Marxists, and communitarians coming together to share a dark view of modernization, post-modernism, and individualism, which are "supposed to hamper pro-social behaviour in general and volunteering in particular" (Decker and van den Broek

1998; cf. Berger and Neuhaus 1977, 2001; Keane 1988; Lasch 1991; Offe 1985).

In Sweden, the assumption builds on the idea that there was indeed once—certainly for two to three decades beginning in the 1960s—a powerful and functioning tradition of social movements and civil society organizations.[14] This was expressed in both strong, stable popular organizations and a widespread inclination among the public to take part in different forms of sociopolitical activities. The contention now is that since the late 1980s the position of these groups and organizations have consistently been undermined from two directions: from above, by the growing fossilization of political parties and popular mass movements no longer able to capture and utilize the political potential of the public, and from below, by the average Swede's increasingly emaciated interest in direct political involvement. Swedes are now said to have become quite passive, not only regarding political involvement but generally speaking, and their social capital is held to be eroding (see e.g. Petersson et al. 1998; Petersson 1999). In fact, there is no doubt that the Swedish political parties are experiencing a difficult time. Swedish citizens view them with growing mistrust, which is furthermore reflected in a steeply decreasing number of members.

From the point of view of maintaining and renewing Swedish democracy, these tendencies are certainly worrying. Studies over time show that during the past twenty-five years the political parties have lost half of their membership. The same goes for the number of volunteers serving on committees. This seems to be a striking parallel to what happened in the US during the same period (see Putnam 2000: 40–47). The question is, however, how far this trend in politics goes toward assessing and predicting developments in the entire Swedish voluntary sector, and whether it is the most powerful measure of vanishing social capital. The incompatibility between the different assumptions presented in the introduction becomes apparent here: according to the first one, civic participation in the 1990s ought to have increased, in response to the crisis of the welfare state. According to the second assumption, the decrease in civic participation ought to be ongoing, due to the crisis of democracy. Thus it is urgent to discern what changes in the civic involvement studied here actually took place in the 1990s.

Stability and Change in Volunteering

Swedish involvement in volunteering, as captured in our studies, remained high during the decade.[15] This was clearly illustrated in Table 4.2. But some changes have taken place and others are clearly on the way. What are these changes? If we go back to Table 4.2, two patterns are clear. One has to do with a general increase in volunteering, slight but statistically significant. The other relates to gender. Although men still dominate volunteering in Sweden, women account for the increase in participation.

Experiences of repeated surveys in other countries with a high incidence of volunteering warrant a certain caution about drawing rapid or definite conclusions from moderate fluctuations at any one time of measurement. The results of studies from Great Britain and the US suggest that from a long-term perspective, volunteering is characterized by a remarkably high level of stability (see e.g. *Giving & Volunteering in the United States* 1994, 1999; Jarvis and Hancock 1997). Nevertheless, in the following discussion, we shall come back and consider to what extent the noted increase in volunteering is related to the second part of the first assumption: that reduced welfare state commitments lead to more civic participation, for instance in the form of volunteering.

Another important change to note is the increase in the share of women in volunteering. In Sweden, as in Denmark, more men than women have traditionally been active in volunteering. The evidence of recent decades is that this pattern is disappearing. This development has usually, from a "citizens' resource perspective," been interpreted as an effect of greater gender equality (Anker and Nielsen 1995; Vogel et al. 2003). However, from a "helping out" perspective the emancipation hypothesis becomes questionable (Jeppsson Grassman 2004). It is interesting to note that in another Scandinavian country, Norway, the pattern of development has gone in quite the opposite direction. There, the previous dominance of women in volunteering has lessened, and now the percentage of men in volunteering is greater (see Wollebaek, Selle, and Lorentzen 2000). The UK and the US have long had a greater share of women in volunteering (see e.g. Jarvis and Hancock 1997; *Giving and Volunteering in the United States* 1999). These different conditions seem to depend both on the specific profile of the voluntary sector in each country and on its role in women's lives, as well as on the general status of women in those countries (see Jeppsson Grassman 1998, 2004). This may suggest that the development visible in the 1990s is an expression of a more long-term trend of Swedish women taking a more dominant role in a hitherto male-dominated bastion—the Swedish voluntary sector. This trend may, however, be interpreted in several other, contesting ways (Jeppsson Grassman 2004).

What types of organizations attracted the most volunteers at the end of the 1990s? Were there changes? The basic pattern is one of stability: at the end of the 1990s, just as at the beginning of the decade, sports and leisure organizations attracted most volunteers among men as well as among women. Participation in cultural associations, trade unions, and housing associations also appears to have remained stable at a high level. Parallel with this stable trend, however, there are some small, but interesting patterns of change. Humanitarian organizations, together with pensioners' organizations, make up the category that has increased most in relative terms (in attracting volunteers). These increases prove to be statistically significant. Next to sports and leisure organizations, the humanitarian organizations (i.e. organizations with a welfare objective) are the ones that now attract most female volunteers. Activities within the Church of Sweden also attracted many more volunteers at the end of the 1990s than at the beginning of the decade.

Civil society expressed in the form of volunteering seems to be facing a development where the main tendency to focus on sports and leisure activities not only is sustained but even strengthened. At the same time, in a broad sense we find a certain increase in volunteering in the area of welfare. From the traditional, popular Swedish/Scandinavian perspective, with its ideological emphasis on the role of the organization as advocate, its function as mediator between citizen and state, and its role as a democracy school, neither the apolitical sports and leisure volunteering trend nor the recent surge of volunteering in social welfare appears particularly appealing. Nevertheless, civic participation in the form of volunteering in organizations with a welfare objective increased in the 1990s. This pattern is confirmed by the comparative analysis of Sweden, other European countries, and the US, based on World Values Survey data (2000), referred to in this chapter's first section. More involvement from women, as we have seen, as well as from retired people, seems to account for this increase. This finding is in line with the assumption concerning consequences of welfare state changes—that is, that cuts in public welfare lead to more volunteering in welfare organizations. An additional and complementary interpretation might be that, owing to the welfare discourse described at the beginning of the chapter, the new groups attracted to volunteering—women and older people—simply are interested in volunteering in the sphere of welfare, which then shows in the number of volunteers.

The second assumption presented initially takes its starting point in the *decrease in civic participation*, more specifically, in the fact that membership rates are falling drastically in the traditional Swedish political parties. However, if we examine this occurrence from the viewpoint of our interest in volunteering, another picture emerges. The percentage of the population that actively volunteers in political organizations did not in fact diminish during the 1990s. At the end of the decade this amounted to around 3 percent of the adult population, making it still one of the major forms of volunteering. In view of the dwindling membership in political organizations, our conclusion is that an increasing share of those who remain members have become active as volunteers. This taken into account, and considering that volunteering is not seldom coupled with wider political involvement and interests, the picture is perhaps not as unequivocally negative as often presented.

Ages or Cohorts?

Closely connected to the argument in the previous section is the notion that whereas older persons perhaps continue to be active, younger persons definitely do not. We found no evidence of this. On the contrary, what we have observed is a slight increase in volunteering in the 16–29 age group. Age patterns vary between countries, however. In the case of the UK, for instance, the lack of involvement among the youngest citizens in the late 1990s was so drastic that the British government saw fit to intervene (Davis Smith 1998; *Giving Time, Getting Involved* 1999). Yet widespread volunteering took place in all age groups, and the pattern observed at the beginning of the 1990s remained relatively stable. It is the "middle-aged" who are most often involved in the volunteer work of Swedish voluntary organizations.

A tendency could nevertheless be observed in 1998 toward a higher average age for the most active group, compared to 1992. Volunteering was now most common in the 45–59 age group, and it was this group and the older one that accounted for most of the increase. These are the largest cohorts of the twentieth century: the postwar "baby boomers." Theirs was the first generation to benefit from higher education irrespective of socioeconomic background. Further, more than any earlier generation, this group has had the chance to influence societal developments, which promoted volunteering in this age cohort (see Pettersson 1992; Häll 1994). Putnam conducted a broad empirical study of civic participation in the US, in which he showed that the American generation born between 1910 and 1940 belong to what he calls "a long civic generation" (2000: 132) that has been exceptionally involved in unpaid civic work. We may have something of an equivalent in the 1940s generation in Sweden.

A comparison of results from our 1992 and 1998 surveys concerning persons in the 60–74 age group shows that the share of those actively involved increased during the 1990s. In 1992, 37 percent were engaged in volunteering; by 1998, the figure had risen to 44 percent—an increase both among men and women—a percentage slightly greater than that for the equivalent age group in the US at the same point in time (*America's Senior Volunteers* 1998). Among Sweden's elderly the largest relative increases have taken place in organizations with a welfare objective, i.e. the humanitarian organizations, pensioners' organizations, and the Church of Sweden or other Christian congregations. In 1992, 12 percent of the population aged 60–74 were engaged in one or several of these organizations. In 1998, the corresponding figure was 22 percent—a significant increase. The tendency distinguished earlier toward increased involvement in welfare organizations is even stronger here.

Patterns of change in informal helping

In 1998, we found that 30 percent of the adult population did some kind of informal helping. This is a rather high percentage and slightly above the 28 percent of 1992. Table 4.4 indicates that the share of the population doing informal helping is large and stable, though with a slight upward tendency. It is important to note, however, that we measured informal helping in a very broad sense. Cuts in welfare budgets may well have increased the need for and the extent of informal helping. Indications are strong that informal care has increased to meet the needs of particularly vulnerable groups among the elderly (see Jeppsson Grassman 2001; Johansson and Sundström 2002). According to Table 4.4, there is hardly any difference with regard to average time spent per month on informal helping at the beginning compared to the end of the decade. Those involved in informal helping still spend, on average, 12 hours per month doing this type of unpaid work. The share of women performing it seems to have increased, however, while the share of men has remained the same. At the end of the 1990s men seemed to spend more hours on average in informal helping and women less hours than at the beginning of the decade. These are only trends, and the changes are not statistically significant. The total effect, however, is somewhat more hours spent in informal helping than at the beginning of the decade.

Informal helping can be seen as an expression of resources as well as of a sense of duty. It is especially important to pay attention to the latter aspect since there have been fears that groups that already carry out a great deal of unpaid work will be asked or "forced" to do even more as public resources become more constrained. The share of the population who devote a large part of their time to helping, in a broad sense, has not increased during the decade, either among men or among women. This is worth emphasizing. Yet, in spite of the obvious stability in the extent of this type of informal helping and even in view of what has been said above, it should nevertheless be stated that the small increase we have found possibly speaks in favor of an emerging pattern that in a longer-term

Table 4.4. Informal Helping in Sweden in 1992 and 1998: Total Percentages of the Population Aged 16–74 and by Gender

	1992			1998		
	Total	Men	Women	Total	Men	Women
Informal helping (%)	28	29	27	30	28	31
Hours/month	12	9	15	12	11	13
BASE (Sample size)	1,045	524	521	1,104	568	536

perspective may support the thesis that reduced commitments on the part of the welfare state lead to greater substitutional efforts on the part of citizens in terms of unpaid work. At least, this seems to be true in the case of support and care for the frail elderly.

Informal Networks: Patterns of Change

When it comes to informal networks, we know from other research that both the number of friendships and the time spent in being with friends and socializing seems to have increased in general in the postwar period, especially in recent decades (see e.g. ; Perlinski 1990; Statistiska Central-byrån 1997). In our 1992 survey we had no question on informal networks of the kind referred to here, which made a comparison impossible. Therefore, in the 1998 survey, we included a question asking respondents to assess for themselves whether their participation in informal networks had changed during the decade. No change was indicated by roughly half of the respondents. About 25 percent stated that they now belong to fewer networks than before, while the last 25 percent stated that they belonged to more networks than at the beginning of the decade. The youngest group, the 16–24-year-olds, were likely to belong to more networks now, while the 25–34-year-olds were likely to be involved in fewer. These facts seem reasonable from a life-cycle perspective.

Summary II

Civic participation is still widespread and in a process of change. In this third part of the chapter we have explored patterns of stability and change in civic participation among the Swedish population during the 1990s. Based on our empirical findings we have argued that civic participation has continued to be high and relatively stable with regard to the forms of participation we have studied—high in both absolute and relative terms and stable especially with regard to scope. We have found no proof that *volunteering* as an expression of civic participation is on its way to being eroded in contemporary Sweden. Instead, our research indicates that there is a continued high level of traditional activities. But they continue mainly not to be of the "right kind": sports and leisure organizations have continued to be, by far, the most common area of involvement, which also reflects the composition of the voluntary sector. Another very common area continues to be cultural organizations.

In the 1998 survey, 52 percent of the Swedish population aged 16–74 stated that they had participated in some form of volunteering, and 30 percent had carried out informal helping on a regular basis for someone outside their own household. This means that *two-thirds of all citizens in Sweden carry out such unpaid work outside their own households.* This is a very high share, especially in an international comparison, and must refute the assumption that Sweden is characterized by a poorly developed civil society.

At the other end of the spectrum we find the barely 25 percent who are not engaged in any of these forms of activities or belong to any networks. What are the characteristics of this group? The pattern is the expected one from our previous results, but here, at the turn of the millennium, it is more clearly outlined. The dominant profile is of a low-educated, low-income, big-city dweller whose parents have not been active in any kind of organization. Even if there are no patterns of pure misery, there is nevertheless some cause for alarm. All the data we have to date (which cover but a short period of time) suggest a reinforcement of the mentioned pattern, and that contemporary Swedish and Scandinavian civil society may be veering in a new direction, away from a tradition that has been a cherished part of the Swedish and the Scandinavian self-image. However, as we stated earlier in the chapter, up till now there has also been a successful modern Scandinavian and Swedish tradition of "catching up" with regard to quite a few of the disadvantaged groups in the longer run.

The small increase that we have seen in volunteering is attributable to more volunteer work performed in humanitarian and welfare organizations, and also mainly by women. This may be interpreted in favor of the argument that cuts in public welfare lead to more volunteering. At the same time we can see tendencies toward new forms of civic participation, mainly within but also alongside the traditional body of associations. The question is, how stable we can assume this situation to be? International and Swedish research show that people of the Western world are becoming increasingly individualistic in their values, to the detriment of norms and values stressing collectivity and membership (Halman and Nevitte 1996; Inglehart 1990; Pettersson 1992). This naturally also applies to Sweden and its volunteering population. Still, our results show that this development is not yet in serious conflict with a general preparedness to carry out either organized or informal helping. We could describe this as a sort of *"collective individualism,"* where there is scope for individuality and personal self-fulfillment, but in a collective context with a corresponding acceptance of collective responsibility.[16] By this we would like to stress the collective aspect and its ongoing influence even in the current period.

In line with other research, the results of our population studies show that the average age in volunteering is rising. A partial explanation for this is probably the life-cycle phenomenon. Just as important an explanatory factor may be the generation or cohort effect. Middle-aged and older generations, raised in a tradition of both duty and popular participation, continue to be active in the community to a very high age. The risk is there, however, that this pattern of behavior will not be repeated among younger generations. That said, we nevertheless do not share the pessimistic view expressed by Putnam (2000) when he describes a similar development in the US. He argues that "the growth of volunteering in recent years is real, but not really an exception to the broader general decline in social capital. At century's end we were enjoying not a springtime of volunteerism, but an Indian summer." (Putnam 2000: 132). This is indeed a striking way to express a dilemma, but it is hardly a convincing argument to predict the future.

Civic involvement in the forms we have studied evidently has to do with *affiliation*. This can take many different expressions. Our data shows that volunteering can provide such connections, but so does networking and informal helping. In our study, we have analyzed different kinds of civic participation and the connections between them. We have pointed out the interconnectedness in civic participation: every kind of participation can be a precondition for, or an effect of, other kinds of involvement. This is an important observation that has received hardly any attention in either Scandinavia or internationally. There is no doubt that *access to resources* and *access to social arenas* on the one hand, and *traditions* and *cultural and social factors* on the other, contribute to explaining how people become involved in various forms of volunteering. A clear picture also emerges of a *cumulative citizenship*, where those who already make large contributions show a propensity to do even more.

Conclusions

At the beginning of the twenty-first century, what is the state of civic participation in a Scandinavian type of welfare state such as Sweden, and how is this civicness expressed? These are the questions we have addressed in this chapter, starting from two assumptions about Swedish civil society that have dominated recent discourse. What *empirical* evidence have we found in support or refutation these assumptions? In brief, there is little evidence to sustain the view of a limited civil society in Sweden characterized by an insignificant voluntary sector with volunteering on a modest scale—the data point in quite the opposite direction, in fact. Furthermore, when it comes to informal helping and affiliation to informal networks, our conclusion is that this is at least as extensive in Sweden as in most other comparable countries.

Meanwhile, the idea of an inverse relationship between the size of the welfare state and the size of civil society as expressed through civic participation gets some support from our data. Concurrent with certain cutbacks in Swedish welfare commitments during the 1990s was a moderate rising tendency toward social volunteering and informal helping. The changes are small (though not negligible) and we do not know if there are any connections between these two trends. Other kinds of research over a longer period of time will be needed in order to substantiate this trend.

The first assumption about Swedish civil society that we confronted—that the state had taken over—was born out of the international research community's earlier lack of understanding of the particular traditions of Sweden and the Scandinavian countries. To some extent this formed the point of departure for our own research. The empirical and international comparative studies carried out by Swedish researchers, including ourselves, have played a fundamental role in clarifying the actual situation and revealing the similarities and discrepancies between our own and other countries.

The second assumption—that in contemporary Sweden civic participation is steadily falling—reflects a rather pessimistic overall cultural view of Sweden, contending that while Sweden once had a vital civil society with extensive civic participation, this is now in a process of advanced decay. We found scant empirical support for this either, in the types of data presented here.

This second assumption has a more Swedish or Scandinavian point of departure. However, we argue that this builds on a faulty premise—namely, that it is feasible to subject civic participation in general and the voluntary sector in particular to the same analysis that applies for the rapidly growing difficulties faced by the traditional political parties and others carrying out traditional political work. Given our empirical data, our view is that this will not work. It should be clear from this chapter that we have given the concept of citizenship a wide interpretation, going beyond the direct political meaning that has formed the basis for most research on active Swedish and Scandinavian citizenship. Instead we attempted to capture a broad spectrum of indicators of this phenomenon. By this it also follows that a narrow utility or service perspective on the nature and roles of civil society is too limited, and we would even venture to claim inadequate, when it comes to understanding the functions, importance, and meaning of what we in Sweden call civil society. In our view, the argument against the utility perspective is valid irrespective of whether the issue is activities to create welfare or activities that serve democracy. Moreover, these ideological effects should not be confused with another outcome of volunteering, the performance of integrative functions. Let us recall too the extensive social capital that is held to be created in the wake of the efforts and activities described. As pointed out earlier on, we assume that most such functions and effects are positive in a wider welfare perspective.

According to our results there is a high degree of stability, not only in scope but also in the character of the voluntary sector. A major finding of our research is that the Swedish voluntary sector is colored by a "lagging traditionalism." This fact acts both as a counterweight to rapid fluctuations in other areas of the society and as a concrete determinant of the direction and shape of the voluntary sector. In other words, the Swedish tradition of popular mass movements—i.e. membership and collective activism—continues to set its stamp on this central aspect of civil society.

What we have seen is that the Swedish people do not at all act as or experience themselves as mere consumers. They are prepared to become involved, though not in quite the same way as before or under the same conditions. Personal life projects seem to be coming to play an even greater role, leading to new and changed demands on both the forms and the content of involvement. All in all, we have found in our own and others' empirical research that an overwhelming part of volunteering activities are of a form and tendency clearly marked by the Swedish-Scandinavian tradition of popular mass movements. At the same time there is a clearly identifiable trend in contemporary Sweden of individualizing forces exerting a growing impact, at both the individual and group levels.

Wollebaek, Selle, and Lorentzen (1999) make an essential and fruitful partitioning of perspectives by choosing to view the different forms of affiliation to, and evaluations of, civil society through voluntary organizations and volunteering in terms of *integration, democracy,* and *economy.* This distinction enables us to separate the effects that are directly creative or supportive of democracy from other, often more loosely defined integration effects. When we separate the integrative functions and effects of the voluntary sector from the ones that create and support the democratic process, we find that much has happened in the past decades. We can discern a clear long-term development: the changing focus of voluntary organizations reduces their once-essential mediating function between the state and its citizens, as well as their function as "schools for democracy." We know nothing about what the effects of this might be, but let us invoke caution against an all-too-pessimistic view. In fact, one of our points of departure that is empirically supported by our results is that the kind of activities that we have explored may even be understood and justified *in their own right*—beyond the instrumental and utility perspectives most often applied. Precisely because of this, they are an important aspect of civil society. Our contention here thereby goes beyond, even breaks with, a Scandinavian tradition in which "the good of the state" almost always is implicit.

The kind of perspective presented in this chapter, which before now was almost totally ignored, partly reveals images of Sweden other than the rather dark one painted in recent years. What we argue is that civic participation *is not only about providing welfare, nor is it only about political activism.* It is also about being a volunteer in a cultural organization, a team leader in a local soccer club, or an unpaid assistant in a pensioners' organization—all three are examples of positions where the social capital is created in the Swedish civil society. In this chapter we have shown that different aspects of volunteerism can be accommodated under the same roof in the broader world of Swedish voluntary organizations because they often combine recreational activities and direct self-interest—activities only for the sake of members—with activities for people other than members, possibly also working to affect interests and values. All this seems rather evident in view of the last fifteen years of specific research, but in (scientific) debates and controversies these aspects and facts are still often ignored, in both the Scandinavian and the international context.

Notes

1. In the contemporary definitions of civil society one usually excludes the state, the market and most often the nuclear family; for a more in-depth analysis, see for example Keane (1988); Cohen and Arato (1992); Janoski (1998), and Giddens (1998). But there is disagreement over whether to include or exclude certain family- and relative-related activities. In the studies presented here, for example, we include informal help extended to family members and relatives outside one's own home.
2. In the Nordic tradition we tend to follow the terminology used in the UK, that is, to denote associations as voluntary organizations. However, the term "nonprofit organization" is becoming more commonly used in connection with, for example, foundations and larger, professional organizations with many employees. This means that in this text we mainly use the term "voluntary sector" except when speaking about professional service provision and employment in this particular sector.
3. Market oriented paradigms for analyzing divergent fields of activities focused on producers, service, and customers became popular at this time. This New Public Management-tradition was mainly and paradoxically introduced to the voluntary sector via the public sector, as have been shown by Wijkström (2001) and Lundström (2004).
4. This research project was initiated by a research team at Johns Hopkins University, Baltimore. It is the biggest and most significant comparative, empirically based research project on the international voluntary/nonprofit sector.
5. A first national mapping of both organized volunteering and informal helping among the Swedish population was carried out in 1992 (Jeppsson Grassman 1993). This survey was replicated in 1998, when we also measured the extent of access to informal networks in the population (Jeppsson Grassman and Svedberg 1999). In 1994, Sweden was also one of ten countries participating in the Eurovol Study, a European, comparative survey of volunteering (Jeppsson Grassman and Svedberg 1996).
6. The survey, carried out in 2000, was based on the population of Stockholm and its surrounding province (Jeppsson Grassman 2001, 2003).
7. "Volunteering is unpaid work that has been freely chosen by the individual, that is carried out within the framework of an organization, and that is not only to the benefit of the active individual himself" (see e.g. Cnaan, Handy, and Wadsworth 1996; Jeppsson Grassman 1998; Tilly and Tilly 1994; Wilson and Musick 1997a).
8. The participating ten countries were Belgium, Bulgaria, Denmark, France, Germany, Ireland, the Netherlands, Slovakia, Sweden, and the UK.

9. A logistic regression analysis was conducted, with significance tests of odds ratios and the UK as a reference category.

10. The World Values Surveys build on a two-step approach (for further explanation, see Baer in this book). Only those who report memberships are asked about their volunteer work. This implies that a certain caution is needed when comparing the results from the two different studies.

11. The five items were: (1) Active volunteers offer something different that could not be provided by paid professionals. (2) If the government took its full responsibility there would be no need for voluntary work. (3) Everyone has a moral responsibility to do unpaid work at some time in their life. (4) Voluntary work is a threat to paid work and is used to make cutbacks in public spending. (5) Engaging in voluntary work helps people to take an active role in a democratic society. The *substitute* factor was composed of items 2 and 4. The *intrinsic value* factor was composed of items 1, 3, and 5.

12. I.e. informal networks with a certain continuity, in which at least three persons who are all acquainted with each other regularly engage in some activity. Our definition excluded family relationships, close friendships between two persons, and the type of workplace relationships only manifested during working hours.

13. Because some of the respondents carried out informal work for relatives *and* friends, the number does not add up to 100 percent.

14. A fundamental problem is that we have very little robust comparable data from these decades and no population studies directed at volunteering.

15. Other indicators of the extent of volunteering are the average number of hours spent on such activities and the number of types of organizations that are worked for. These results show an even greater degree of stability: the average contribution of twelve hours per month was almost the same at the end as at the beginning of the decade, while the average number of organizations in which Swedes were actively engaged had grown somewhat to just under two.

16. For example, Renaut (1997) has used the concept "collective individualism" to characterize the activity patterns during the premodern and modern phases, and he argues that we now are entering a phase of "subjective individualism." We would tend to argue that this could mislead by being too individualistic a conceptualization, at least of the Scandinavian/Swedish circumstances.

References

America's Senior Volunteers. 1998. Booklet. Washington, DC: Independent Sector.

Anker, Jørgen, and Inger Koch Nielsen. 1995. *Det frivillige arbejde*. Copenhagen: Socialforskningsinstituttet.

Austin, Paul Britten. 1970. *The Swedes: How They Live and Work*. New York, Praeger Publishers.

Berman, Sheri. 1997. "Civil Society and the Collapse of the Weimar Republic." *World Politics* 49, 401–429.

Berger, Peter, and Richard John Neuhaus. 1977. *To Empower People: The Role of Mediating Structures in Public Policy*. Washington, DC: American Enterprise Institute.

Blennberger, Erik. 1993. "Begrepp och modeller." In *Frivilligt socialt arbete. Kartläggning och kunskapsöversikt*. SOU 1993: 82.

Boli, John. 1992. "Sweden: Is There a Viable Third Sector?" In *Between States and Markets: The Voluntary Sector in Comparative Perspective*, ed. Robert Wuthnow. Princeton, NJ: Princeton University Press.

Butcher, Hugh, and Maurice Mullard. 1993. "Community Policy, Citizenship and Democracy." In *Community and Public Policy*, ed. Hugh Butcher et al. London: Pluto Press.

Cnaan, Ram A., Femina Handy, and Margaret Wadsworth. 1996. "Defining Who Is a Volunteer: Conceptual and Empirical Considerations." *Nonprofit and Voluntary Sector Quarterly* 25, no. 3: 364–384.

Cohen, Jean and Andrew Arato. 1992. *Civil Society and Political Theory.* Cambridge, MA: The MIT Press.

Coleman, James S. 1994. *Foundations of Social Theory.* Cambridge, MA: The Belknap Press of Harvard University Press.

Curtis, James, Edward Grabb, and Douglas Baer. 1992. "Voluntary Association Membership in Fifteen Countries: A Comparative Analysis. *American Sociological Review* 57, no 1: 139–152.

Curtis, James, Douglas Baer, and Edward Grabb. 2001. "Nations of Joiners: Explaining Voluntary Association Membership in Democratic Societies. *American Sociological Review* 66, no. 6: 783–805.

Davis Smith, Justin. 1998. *1997 National Survey of Voluntary Activity.* London: The National Centre for Volunteering.

Dekker, Paul, and Andries van den Broek. 1998. "Civil Society in Comparative Perspective: Involvement in Voluntary Associations in North America and Western Europe." *Voluntas* 9, no. 1: 11–38.

Esping-Andersen, Gösta. 1990. *The Three Worlds of Welfare Capitalism.* Cambridge: The Polity Press.

———. 1999. *Social Foundations of Postindustrial Economies.* Oxford: Oxford University Press.

———. 2002. "Towards the Good Society, Once Again." In *Why We Need a New Welfare State*, ed. G. Esping-Andersen. Oxford: Oxford University Press.

Etzioni, Amitai. 1993. *The Spirit of Community. Rights, Responsibilities and the Communitarian Agenda.* New York: Crown Publishers Inc.

Gaskin, Katherine, and Justin Davis Smith. 1995. *A New Civic Europe?* London: Volunteer Centre UK.

Giddens, Anthony. 1998. *The Third Way: The Renewal of Social Democracy.* Cambridge: Polity Press.

Giving and Volunteering in the United States. 1994. Washington, DC: Independent Sector.

Giving and Volunteering in the United States. 1999. Washington: DC: Independent Sector.

Giving Time, Getting Involved: A Strategy Report by the Working Group on the Active Community. 1999. The British Government.

Gundelach, Peter, and Torpe, Lars. 1997. "Social reflexivity and new types of citizen involvement in Denmark." In *Private Groups and Public Life. Social Participation, Voluntary Associations and Political Involvement*, ed. J. W. Van Deth. London: Routledge.

Habermann, Ulla. 2001. *En postmoderne helgen?* Lund Dissertations in Social Work 3. Lund: Department of Social Work, Lund University.

Halman, Loek, and Neil Nevitte, eds. 1996. *Political Value Change in Western Democracies. Integration, Values, Identification and Participation.* Tilburg: Tilburg University Press.

Hansson, Jan-Håkan, Magnus Jegermalm, and Anna Whitaker. 2000. *Att ge och ta emot hjälp. Anhöriginsatser för äldre och anhörigstöd – en kunskapsöversikt.* Working Papers series 15. Stockholm: Ersta Sköndal University College.

Häll, Lars. 1994. *Föreningslivet i Sverige – en statistisk belysning.* Stockholm: Statistiska Centralbyrån.

Inglehart, Ronald. 1990. *Culture Shift in Advanced Industrial Society.* Princeton, NJ: Princeton University Press.

James, Estelle. 1989. "The Private Provision of Public Service: A Comparison of Sweden and Holland." In *The Nonprofit Sector in International Perspective,* ed. Estelle James. New York: Oxford University Press.

Janoski, Thomas. 1998. *Citizenship and Civil Society.* Cambridge: Cambridge University Press.

Jarvis C., and R. Hancock. 1997. "Trends in volunteering and the implications for the future." In *Dimensions of the Voluntary Sector,* ed. C. Pharoah. Kings Hill: Charities Aid Foundation.

Jegermalm, Magnus. 2002. *Anhörigstöd – en uppföljningsstudie av kommuners och frivilligorganisationers stöd till äldres anhöriga.* Working Papers series 25. Stockholm: Ersta Sköndal University College.

Jegermalm, Magnus, and Anna Whitaker. 2000. *Upptäckten av anhöriga?* Working Papers series 17. Stockholm: Ersta Sköndal University College.

Jeppsson Grassman, Eva. 1993. "Frivilliga insatser i Sverige - en befolkningsstudie." In *Frivilligt socialt arbete. Kartläggning och kunskapsöversikt.* SOU 1993: 82.

———. 1998. "Full sysselsättning! Frivilligt arbete och annat arbete i Sverige och andra europeiska länder." *Socialvetenskaplig Tidskrift* 5: 128–146.

———. 1999. "The Voluntary Sector in a Welfare Perspective: Sweden – with a Comparison to France." In *Comparing Social Welfare Systems in Nordic Europe and France.* Paris: MIRE, Drees.

———. 2001. *Medmänniska och anhörig. En studie av informella hjälpinsatser.* Occasional Papers series 17. Stockholm: Ersta Sköndal University College.

———. 2004. "Makt, socialt kapital och hjälpgivande. Om kvinnor och män i civilsamhället." In *Genus och civilt samhälle,* ed. Erik Blennberger, Ulla Habermann, and Eva Jeppsson Grassman. Occasional Papers series 23. Stockholm: Ersta Sköndal University College.

Jeppsson Grassman, Eva, ed. 2003. *Anhörigskapets uttrycksformer.* Lund: Studentlitteratur.

Jeppsson Grassman, Eva, and Lars Svedberg. 1993. "Frivillig verksamhet på fältet – en närstudie av sju organisationer." In *Frivilligt socialt arbete – Kartläggning och kunskapsöversikt.* SOU 193: 82

———. 1995. "Frivilligt socialt arbete i Sverige – både mer och mindre." In *Medmänsklighet att hyra? Åtta forskare om ideell verksamhet,* ed. Erik Amnå. Örebro: Libris.

———. 1996. "Voluntary Action in a Scandinavian Welfare Context: the Case of Sweden." *Nonprofit and Voluntary Sector Quarterly* 25: 415–428.

———. 1999. "Medborgarskapets gestaltningar. Insatser i och utanför föreningslivet." In *Civilsamhället*, ed. Erik Amnå. SOU 1999: 84.

Johansson, Lennarth, and Gerdt Sundström. 2002. "Anhörigvårdens omfattning i Sverige." *Socialmedicinsk tidskrift* 2: 119–130.

Keane, John, ed. 1988. *Civil Society and the State*. London: Verso.

Kuhnle Stein, and Per Selle. 1992. *Government and Voluntary Organizations*. Aldershot: Avebury.

Lasch Christopher. 1991. *The True and Only Heaven: Progress and its Critics*. New York: Norton.

Ljungberg, Carl Johan. 1992. "Ny syn på frivilliga insatser." *Uppsala Nya Tidning*. 24 December.

Lorentzen, Håkon. 1998. "Normative forståelser av sivile sammanslutninger." *Socialvetenskaplig Tidskrift* 5: 244–268.

———. 1999. "Civil Associations and Social Integration." Paper presented at the conference Civil Society Between Market and State, Lidingö, Sweden, 10–12 February 1999.

———. 2000. *Sivilitet, moral og felleskap*. Working paper 1.2. Oslo: Institutt for samfunnsforskning.

———. 2001. "Frivillighet i forandring. Om forholdet mellom sivile felleskap og moderniteten." In *Frivillighedens udfordringer*, ed. Lars Skov Henriksen and Bjarne Ibsen. Odense: Odense Universitetsforlag.

Lundström, Tommy. 2004. *Teorier om frivilligt socialt arbete. En diskussion om forskningens läge och organisationernas framtid*. Occasional Report series 22. Stockholm: Ersta Sköndal University College.

Lundström, Tommy, and Lars Svedberg. 1998. "Svensk frivillighet i internationell belysning – en inledning." *Socialvetenskaplig tidskrift* 5: 106–127.

———. 2003. "The Voluntary Sector in a Social Democratic Welfare State – The Case of Sweden." *Journal of Social Policy* 32: 217–238.

Lundström, Tommy, and Filip Wijkström. 1997. *The Nonprofit Sector in Sweden*. Johns Hopkins Nonprofit Series 11. Manchester and New York: Manchester University Press.

Mizruchi, Mark S. 1994. "Social network analysis: recent achievements and current controversies." *Acta Sociologica*, 37: 329–343.

O'Conell, Brian. 1999. *Civil Society. The Underpinning of American Democracy*. Hanover, NH: University Press of New England.

Offe, Claus. 1985. "New Social Movements: Challenging the Boundaries of Institutional Politics." *Social Research* 52: 817–868.

Palme, Joakim et al. 2000. *Välfärd vid vägskäl. Utvecklingen under 1990-talet*. SOU 2000: 3 .

Palme, Joakim. et al. 2001. *Välfärdsbokslut för 1990-talet*. Slutbetänkande, Kommittén Välfärdsbokslut. SOU 2001: 79.

Palme, Joakim. et al. 2002. *Welfare in Sweden: The Balance Sheet for the 1990s*. Ds 2002: 32.

Pestoff, Victor. 1991. "Social service i kooperativ regi." *Kooperativ årsbok 1991*.

Perlinski, Marek. 1990. "Livet utanför fabriksgrinden och kontorsdörren." In *Industrisamhälle i omvandling*, ed. Rune Åberg. Stockholm: Carlsson Bokförlag.

Petersson Olof. 1999 "Uttåget från det gemensamma." In *Demokratin är död. Leve demokratin!*, ed. C. Nergårdh and G. Hemberg. Stockholm: Ordfront.
———. 2000. "Det finns anledning till oro." In *Svenska Dagbladet*, 19 January.
Petersson, Olof, Jörgen Hermansson, Michele Michelletti, Jan Teorell, and Anders Westholm. 1998. *Demokrati och medborgarskap.* Demokratirådets rapport. Stockholm: SNS förlag.
Pettersson, Thorleif. 1992 "Välfärd, välfärdsförändringar och folkrörelseengagemang." In *Mot denna framtid. Folkrörelser och folk i framtiden*, ed. Axelson, S. och T. Pettersson. Stockholm: Carlssons.
Putnam, Robert D. 1993. *Making Democracy Work: Civic Traditions in Modern Italy.* Princeton, NJ: Princeton University Press.
———. 2000. *Bowling Alone. The Collapse and Revival of American Community.* New York: Simon & Schuster.
Rees, Anthony M. 1996. "T.H. Marshall and the Process of Citizenship." In *Citizenship Today: The Contemporary Relevance of T.H. Marshall*, ed. M. Bulmer and A.M. Rees. London: UCL Press.
Renaut, Alain. 1997. *The Era of the Individual. A Contribution to a History of Subjectivity.* Princeton, NJ: Princeton University Press.
Rostgaard, Tine and Juhani Lehto. 2001. "Health and Social Care Systems: How Different is the Nordic Model?" In *Nordic Welfare States in the European Context*, ed. M. Kautto, J. Fritzell, B. Hvinden, J. Kvist, and H. Uusitalo. London and New York. Routledge.
Salamon, Lester M. and Helmut K. Anheier. 1994. *The Emerging Sector. An Overview.* Baltimore: The Johns Hopkins University Institute for Policy Studies.
———. 1997. *Defining the Nonprofit Sector: A Cross-national Analysis.* Johns Hopkins Nonprofit Sector Series 4. Manchester and New York: Manchester University Press.
Salamon, Lester, S. Wojciech Sokolowski, and Associates. 1999. *Global Civil Society. Dimensions of the Nonprofit Sector.* Baltimore: The Johns Hopkins Comparative Center for Civil Society Studies.
Selle, Per, and Bjarne Öymyr. 1995. *Frivillig organisering og demokrati.* Oslo: Det Norske Samlaget.
Schlozman, Key L., Sidney Verba, and Henry E. Brady. 1999. "Civic Participation and the Equality Problem." In *Civic Engagement in American Democracy*, ed. Theda Scocpol and Morris P. Fiorina. Washington DC: Brookings Institution Press.
Skocpol, Theda. 1999. "Making Sense of the Civic Engagement Debate." In *Civic Engagement in American Democracy*, ed. Theda Scocpol and Morris P. Fiorina. Washington DC: Brookings Institution Press.
———. 2003. *Diminished Democracy: From Membership to Management in American Civic Life.* Norman: University of Oklahoma Press.
SOU 1987: 33. *Ju mer vi är tillsammans.* Betänkande från 1986-års folkrörelseutredning.
SOU 2000: 1 *En uthållig demokrati? Politik för folkstyre på 2000-talet.*
Statistiska Centralbyrån. 1996. *Politiska resurser och aktiviteter 1978–1974. Levadnadsförhållanden*, Rapport nr 90. (Statistics Sweden).
Statistiska Centralbyrån. 1997. *Välfärd och ojämlikhet i 20-årsperspektiv 1975–1995. Levnadsförhållanden*, Rapport 91. (Statistics Sweden).

Svedberg Lars. 1993. "Socialt inriktade frivilligorganisationer – några grundläggande karaktäristika." In *Frivilligt socialt arbete. Kartläggning och kunskapsöversikt.* SOU 1993: 82.

———. 1996. "Frivillighet som ideologiskt slagträ och faktisk verksamhet." In *Ojämlikhet från vaggan till graven – på väg in i 2/3-samhället.* Stockholm: FKF Fakta.

———. 2001. "Spelar ideella och informella insatser någon roll för svensk välfärd?" In *Välfärdstjänster i omvandling. Forskarantologi från Kommittén Välfärdsbokslut,* ed. M. Szebehely. SOU 2001: 52.

Svedberg, Lars, and Eva Jeppsson Grassman. 2001. Frivilliga insatser i svensk välfärd – med utblickar mot de nordiska grannländerna." In *Frivillighedens udfordringer- nordisk forskning om frivilligt arbejde og frivillige organisationer,* ed. L. S. Henriksen and B. Ibsen. Odense: Odense Universitetsforlag.

Tilly, Charles, and Chris Tilly. 1994. "Capitalist Work and Labour Markets." In *Handbook of Economic Sociology,* ed. N. Smelser and R. Swedberg. Princeton: Princeton University Press.

Torpe, Lars. 2001. "Folkets foreninger? De frivillige organisationers folkelige forankring i Skandinavien." In *Frivillighedens udfordringer – nordisk forskning om frivilligt arbejde og frivillige organisationer,* ed. L.S. Henriksen and B. Ibsen. Odense: Odense Universitetsforlag.

Trydegård, Gun-Britt. 2001. "Välfärdstjänster till salu – privatisering och alternativa driftsformer under 1990-talet." In *Välfärdstjänster i omvandling. Forskarantologi från Kommittén Välfärdsbokslut,* ed. M. Szebehely. SOU 2001: 52.

Trägårdh, Lars, ed. 1995. *Civilt samhälle kontra offentlig sektor.* Stockholm: SNS Förlag.

———. 1999. "Det civila samhället som analytiskt begrepp och politisk slogan." In *Civilsamhället,* ed. Erik Amnå. SOU 1999: 84.

Van Til, Jon. 1988. *Mapping the Third Sector. Voluntarism in a Changing Social Economy.* New York: The Foundation Center.

Vogel, Joakim, Erik Amnå, Ingrid Munck, and Lars Häll. 2003. *Föreningslivet i Sverige: Välfärd, socialt kapital, demokratriskola.* Örebro: Statistiska centralbyrån.

Weissbrod, Burton. 1997. "The Future of the Nonprofit Sector: Its Entwining with Private Enterprise and Government." *Journal of Policy Analysis and Management* 16: 541–555.

Wijkström, Filip. 1998. *Different Faces of Civil Society.* Stockholm: Stockholm School of Econimics.

———. 2001. "Socialt kapital och civilt samhälle i Norden." *Frivillighedens udfordringer- nordisk forskning om frivilligt arbejde og frivillige organisationer,* ed. L. S. Henriksen and B. Ibsen. Odense: Odense Universitetsforlag.

Wijkström, Filip, and Tommy Lundström. 2003. *Den ideella sektorn.* Stockholm: Sober förlag.

Wilson, John, and Marc Musick. 1997a. "Who Cares? Toward an Integrated Theory of Volunteer Work." *American Sociological Review* 62: 694–713.

Wilson, John, and Marc Musick. 1997b. "Work and Volunteering: The Long Arm of the Job." *Social Forces* 76: 251–272.

Wollebaek, Dag, Per Selle, and Håkon Lorentzen. 1999. *Frivillig insats.* Oslo: Fagboksförlaget.

Wolfe, Alan. 1989. *Whose Keeper? Social Science and Moral Obligation.* Berkeley: University of California Press.

Wuthnow, Robert. 1994. *Sharing the Journey: Support Groups and America's New Quest for Community.* New York: Free Press.

Zetterberg, Hans. 1995. *Before and Beyond the Welfare State. Three Lectures.* Stockholm: City University Press.

Zetterberg, Hans, and Carl-Johan Ljungberg. 1997. *Vårt land – den svenska socialstaten.* Stockholm: City University Press.

Chapter 5

ASSOCIATIONAL LIFE, YOUTH, AND POLITICAL CAPITAL FORMATION IN SWEDEN: HISTORICAL LEGACIES AND CONTEMPORARY TRENDS

Erik Amnå

In recent international debate on the social foundations of democracy and the market economy, scholars have stressed the importance of a vibrant civil society and the formation of social capital. This is an emphasis that is shared by public intellectuals and scholars of Sweden, and over the past decade the state of Swedish associational life has become the focus of a great deal of research as well as a subject for heated political debates. After an introduction on the common perception that associational life is central to Swedish democratic self-understanding, I will in this chapter first provide a summary and analysis of recent research on both the associations and their membership, including survey data from several projects on Swedish democracy and associational life. Next I will briefly engage this data in terms of the particular question of how the generation, as well as decline, of social capital at large relates more specifically to changes in political capital formation among Swedish adults. Against the backdrop of these preliminary sections, and the conclusions drawn in them, I will then analyze what I consider the key question, namely the decline of social and political capital among young people. More precisely, I will attempt to identify key dynamics and differences when it comes to social capital and political behavior of Swedish versus American youth, again based on several international large-scale datasets. An attempt will be made to assess the extent to which there is reason to believe that emerging new patterns of political behavior among the youth herald negative long-term prospects for the health and vitality of Swedish democracy.[1]

The Associational Base of Swedish Democracy

Swedish voluntary associations occupy a special place in the grand narrative on Swedish democracy. Along with schools, they are credited with being major fosterers of a democratic creed, in which voluntary membership is held to motivate and equip citizens to become politically involved: If individuals are engaged in collective endeavors to solve common problems, this makes for a more enlightened and active citizenry, among whom individual development, upward social mobility, and political stability go hand in hand. This Toquevillian assumption pertains to individual motivations and the values a citizen gets in return from its membership. Citizens who are active in associations are admired and respected. The opposite, passivity or non-membership, is viewed as "a threat to democracy" (Misgeld 2001: 126), according to the 1990 Swedish Social Democratic Party program. The associational life is assumed to provide a solid base for political life, a democratic infrastructure. This has been a leitmotif in Swedish political discourse throughout the twentieth century.

That voluntary associations in general, and in particular the labor and temperance movements and the free churches, known as the *folkrörelser* (people's movements), comprise a national treasure was also a theme in a recent report by the Swedish Commission on Democracy. Between 1997 and 2000 the commission was convened to analyze worrying trends in Swedish democracy mainly caused by globalization, EU membership, new media structure, and declining voter turnout. Probably most criticized and questioned was the commission's view of democracy as basically a moral and cultural order, which led it to stress the value of more participatory and deliberative features of democracy and of the private or nongovernmental spheres of civic life. In sharp contrast to a firm tradition of official investigations putting representative democracy and the well being of the public institutions at the center (Jacobsson 1999), it argued for the development of "more of participatory democracy with stronger deliberative qualities" (Demokratiutredningen 2000). Although appreciated by several political actors, the commission was criticized for marginalizing the value of political equality when advocating expanded participatory opportunity structures between the elections (Amnå 2006).

The commission wanted to shift the focus of the democracy debate from the output side of the welfare state to the input side, including a reorientation of the way the role of voluntary associations were conceived as well. It could be seen as nothing less than an attack on the predominant output orientation of the Swedish public discourse on democracy. Historically, the size of the public sector has been equated with the strength of the democracy, because "a proper expansion of the public sector extends the freedom of choice" (Tilton 1991: 268). The Commission, however, claimed that "the aim of the democracy is neither a big state nor big municipalities, but a society of individuals possessed by a citizen's spirit, upholding the faith in justice and solidarity" (Demokratiutredningen 2000: 31). Consequently a democracy should be assessed with respect to the quality of its common values, for example the way in which it treats ethnically diverse immigrants.

Its citizen-oriented approach furthermore led the commission to energetically argue for more direct participation. With reference to their own capacity for analysis and deliberation, the commission suggested that the citizens be given an expanded sphere of initiative and influence in relation to the institutions of representative democracy. Such statements by the commission can be regarded as the triumph of a non-statist view of the role of civil society, a conception that nearly always has lost out in the struggle against a more state-centered view during the never-ending internal ideological battle within the Social Democratic Party (Dahlkvist 1999). This was a vision that recalls a mostly forgotten bottom-up, social, or citizens' perspective of democracy that has often given way to the more dominant, top-down, professional, or "technocratic" view of democracy. Similarly, the commission's approach challenged to the dominant role played by a few large collective, or organized, groups in the Swedish democratic development.

It has been a long time since this tension between the two democratic ideals was demonstrated so clearly and publicly. Until recently, at least, the national welfare state retained its legitimacy, based on its ability to deliver social services and permit the conditions for economic growth, equitable income distributions, and a well-functioning democratic system (Strandberg 2006). Therefore, the democratic value of Swedish voluntary associations cannot be judged apart from their embeddedness in this political project. As in other small and ethnically homogenous states, Sweden has not suffered from much internal strife. Nor have the associations of civil society in general been viewed as antagonistic in relation to the state. Instead a strong sense of a shared interest in the nation's well being as whole, has given the interest groups a joint frame of reference (Olsen 1990).

Indeed, the organizations have been seen as partners with the state, and traditionally there has been widespread confidence in the associations' capacity to avert social and political problems by promoting civic education, thus preventing and counteracting asocial behavior. Indeed, in Sweden civic participation has been valued as "a cure-all ... that ... is said to instill civic values, enhance political behavior, and improve democracy and society" (Theiss-Morse and Hibbing 2005: 229–230), in the wording of a recent critical review of the social capital literature. During certain periods of Sweden's modern history, lack of involvement in associational life consequently has been regarded as the probable— and rectifiable—cause of social problems, a collective socialization failure. "Associationless youth" has even been the label commonly applied to a perceived problem that has at times caused a sort of moral panic (Olson 1992). Voluntary associations have been given access to generous public funds in exchange for their efforts at socializing youth and, at the same time, legitimating the state and established society in the eyes of the youth. That different political parties have been affiliated with and controlled different parts of this family of associations has, of course, facilitated a stabilizing political consensus (Micheletti 1995).

From Growth to Stagnation of Swedish Associational Life

The Swedish voluntary life often has been highly commended from a comparative perspective.[2] In *Democracies in Flux*, Robert Putnam expresses his admiration of Swedish associational life, especially the study circles. He is astonished that they continue to grow, managing to attract 40 percent of Swedish adults year after year. He is equally surprised that over half the costs of the study circles are borne by the state and municipalities, contradicting the worry that the existence of a large public sector could weaken civil society—of which study circles are a clear expression, although considerably overrated by Putnam (Putnam 2002).[3]

At the beginning of the twentieth century, approximately one in ten Swedes was involved in associational life. A century later, the ratio is exactly the opposite: only one in ten is *not* involved. Under the surface of the constant growth implied by those figures, however, lie major changes in the structure of associational life. The breakthrough for associations in Sweden came around 1830. This was followed in the second half of the nineteenth century by the growth of the labor, temperance, and free-church movements with their strong class basis and/or complex ideologies and belief systems. Somewhat later, the cooperative movement and the free adult education and athletic associations were established. Some organizations, such as labor unions and temperance societies, continued to expand until the mid twentieth century, as did religious associations such as free churches (Micheletti 1995).

In the second half of the twentieth century, gains were made by other interest associations, such as those serving patients, handicapped, and women, and by lifestyle associations such as those devoted to athletics and culture. New social movements also developed during the last few decades of the twentieth century; these included modern variants of the radical left, along with peace, environmental, and women's movements that challenged the older popular movements with their critiques of the established order (Micheletti 1995).

In this section we will take a close look at the state of Swedish associational life at the beginning of the new millennium. We will start with the associated and end up with the associations.

The Associated

Due to new official statistics, based on a repeated representative survey including panel data, we are able to investigate the trends in associational memberships in Sweden 1978–2000. Adult Swedes were asked about their associational relationships. We will try to see whether the global trends describing decreasing willingness to participate in traditional, long-term organizational activities in representative democratic organizations (Inglehart and Welzel 2005) also hit the historically strong Swedish voluntary associations.

Numbers of Members and Memberships

As seen in Table 5.1, there has indeed been a decline in association membership in the 1990s. The number of individuals who were members of

Table 5.1. Swedes 16 and over Who Are Members of at Least One Association[4]

Year	1978	1984	1992	2000
Age/gender				
Men	89 (46)	92 (47)	93 (56)	92 (48)
16–24	82 (49)	83 (49)	90 (65)	80 (43)
25–44	92 (50)	96 (52)	96 (59)	94 (51)
45–64	92 (45)	95 (45)	95 (57)	95 (52)
65 +	78 (34)	85 (34)	88 (41)	88 (40)
Women	81 (32)	90 (37)	91 (46)	89 (40)
16–24	70 (32)	80 (42)	83 (50)	73 (42)
25–44	88 (35)	95 (42)	96 (49)	93 (42)
45–64	84 (31)	92 (32)	96 (48)	95 (42)
65 +	70 (24)	84 (33)	82 (36)	82 (33)
All	85 (39)	91 (42)	92 (51)	90 (44)

Source: Statistics Sweden, *Survey of Living Conditions,* 1978, 1984, 1992, and 2000.

at least one association decreased by 120,000, or 1.7 percent, between 1992 and 2000; nearly 700,000 adults, roughly 10 percent, do not belong to any association. The vast majority of associations experienced membership declines in this period. Nevertheless, 90 percent of adult Swedes aged 16–84 (6.2 million) still are members in at least one association. The 1990s seem to have been an exceptional period in terms of high rate of memberships as well as of numbers of memberships and degree of activity.

Simultaneously a thinning of the ranks took place. The number of individuals who were members of several different associations was substantially higher in 1992. Between 1992 and 2000, the proportion of individuals that were members of least four associations had decreased by 20 percent, and the proportion holding only one membership increased significantly.

Degree of Activity
Parallel to membership declines in most types of association were reductions in the level of activity among the remaining members. The proportion of passive members, who "have not participated actively in any association during the preceding twelve months," increased by over 10 percent, and more members appeared to limit their involvement to moral and/or financial support without active participation. Voluntary, unpaid contributions of work also declined somewhat, due to an increased amount of paid professional service provision, according to what Jeppsson-Grassman and Svedberg demonstrate in their contribution to this volume. In addition, the data indicate that half a million members—roughly 12 percent of the total—withdrew from active involvement in associations over the eight years covered by the study. They remained members but have not actively participated in the association during the last twelve months.

There has also been a reduction, amounting to 7.5 percent of the adult population, in the proportion of active members. Nearly half of all members (46 percent) are passive. The number of passive members increased by roughly 400,000 (ca. 10 percent of adults) in the 1992–2000 period, while the proportion of active members declined to 44 percent of the adult population. As others have shown, passive membership has become the rule rather than the exception in organized civil society (Skocpol 2002; Wollebæck and Selle 2002).

A further tendency is for fewer members to carry a greater load. In 2000, every fourth adult Swede occupied a position of trust of some sort in one or more associations. Although high, that figure also represented a decrease since 1992, but not as great as the other downward trends noted. In any event, the work of associations has become more concentrated among fewer individuals. Compared with 1992, fewer officials spent a greater portion of their time on association duties in 2000. The average increase in time was about nine hours per month, representing a total approximately 20 percent greater than in 1992. Among association members in general, there was no apparent increase in activity level. A typical response was, "I do not have enough time or interest to devote more effort to any organization." This is consistent with the trends toward declining membership and fewer active members.

Generations

By the end of the twentieth century, more general problems among voluntary associations became obvious. The most remarkable has been youth's refusal to join established organizations, as has also been seen in other Scandinavian countries (Torpe 2003). More particularly the problems concern young males' hesitation to get involved in associational life, which furthermore goes hand in hand with a narrowing of their general, social relationships. Swedish voluntary organizations are dealing with severe problems of various kinds, among them the matter of aging members. In comparison with the 1980s, significantly fewer young people are now joining any association. The membership replacement rate has declined markedly within a very short period. Associational life has generally been sustained by a comparatively older segment of the population; consequently, pensioners comprised the only age group whose level of participation did not decline. In year of 1992 an the all-time high of about 90 percent of the Swedish men between 16 and 24 years old were members of at least one association, but by 2000 only about 80 percent were members. Active membership in this group, meanwhile, has fallen from about 65 percent to slightly over 40 percent (Amnå and Munck 2003; Vogel, Amnå, Munck, and Häll 2003).

Gender

Men, especially those aged 45–64, were proportionately more active than were women in 2000. They also more frequently occupied positions of trust, spoke at meetings, and attempted to influence decisions. However, the rate of membership declined more among men than among women, resulting in a more even gender balance overall. There were, meanwhile, distinct gender imbalances in specific types of association. Women's involvement was oriented more toward social care, culture, religion, and international solidarity, women being overrepresented in humanitarian and religious organizations and in consumer co-ops. In contrast, men predominated in associations concerned with lifestyle, motoring, athletics, hobbies, and civil defense. Males were also more active than females were in political parties, fraternal orders, and shareholders' associations.

Socioeconomic Recruitment

From the standpoint of occupational status, disposable income, and education, the data reveal a general pattern in which upper-level, white-collar employees, the highly educated, and those with high incomes are over-represented in associational life as a whole, while manual laborers, the poorly educated, and those with low incomes are underrepresented. This applies to associations concerned with politics, the environment, special interests, women's rights, housing, international solidarity, and lifestyles. Religious organizations are the only type of association in which white-collar employees are not overrepresented, while civil defense associations alone have a relatively high proportion of manual laborers. The distribution of membership by social class narrowed somewhat in the 1990s, because white-collar employees withdrew from associational life to a greater extent than did manual laborers.

Ethnicity

Like the growing hesitation of the young Swedes to be involved in associational life, the absence of ethnic minorities is a remarkable feature. Forms for civic participation offered by the established voluntary sector overall seem not to interest them. In fairly restricted numbers they have chosen to create their own voluntary organizations (SOU 2004:49). The public institutions demonstrate an obvious incapacity to deal with the distinctive variations of these citizen groups that can not necessarily be treated in traditional, socioeconomic terms. Indeed, the Commission on Democracy saw the general marginalization of "new Swedes" as the greatest failure of modern Swedish democracy (Demokratiutredningen 2000).

The Associations

Shifting our perspective from the members to their organizations will enable us to evaluate whether the current Swedish organizational landscape still can be seen as trustworthy when it comes to democratic development. Are associations operating as mediating channels between the local, national, and global political spheres? Do they offer the citizens arenas for civic education? Are they adapting to global value changes? Are they becoming more dependent on others' money and less varied with respect to their members' interests, ideas, and needs?

Political orientation

Comparison between earlier times and the 1990s reveals a general decrease in political involvement, especially with regard to two trends. One was that associational life in general came to provide fewer and fewer opportunities for specifically democratic training because the proportion of members actively participating and holding positions of political trust declined and that associational activities as such became less political in nature. I will return to this aspect later.

The second trend was that political parties lost members without being able to replace them completely. In political parties, the proportion of active members declined only slightly during the 1990s (by 0.6 percent), but there were sharp drops in total membership, especially among passive members. In 1968, 13 percent of the adult population belonged to a political party; twenty years later, that figure had risen to 15 percent. But by 2000, party membership had dropped by over half, to 7 percent. Altogether, Swedish political parties lost a quarter of a million members between 1992 and 2000—and this was after the sharp drop occasioned by the elimination of labor unions' collective membership in the Social Democratic Party (Gidlund and Möller 1999). Over the same period many local political positions were removed due to rationalization and amalgamation reforms of various kinds. About one-quarter of all municipal boards have disappeared since 1980, causing a loss of about 15,000 related positions of trust (Montin 2002; Montin and Amnå 2000).

National and Global Integration

According to Norwegian research into the development of associational life, organizations that are preoccupied with surviving, perhaps unaware that they are out of step with the times, have difficulty maintaining widespread belief in the legitimacy of their traditional goals. Furthermore, there has been a decline in the number of associations that resist social trends and that introduce alternative social projects (Wollebaeck and Selle 2002). Other Norwegian studies have also found that fewer associations are specifically concerned with political discussion and basic values of general interest; nowadays, there is a tendency towards associations that are more narrowly concerned with particular, special-interest activities. In short, there has been a weakening of associations' democratic-training function. Danish and Norwegian studies of volunteer work have found that today's associations place greater emphasis on individual choices and interests, and less on traditional and collective values and affiliations. At the same time, there is also a greater emphasis on self-interest, less continuity in associations, a weaker connection between the individual and the organization, and a growing tendency toward short-term involvement (Selle and Øymyr 1995).

Even if no Swedish studies have yet been published in this area, there is no reason to believe that the trends are specifically Norwegian or Danish. Moreover, I would argue that even if there are Swedish voluntary organizations that have been engaged in development programs in new EU member states, they hitherto have played a fairly marginal role in the European integration of the Swedish society. Even more noteworthy is the fact that most of them, in spite of international experiences in their past, have been unable to connect to the citizens' interest in global issues. There are few signs of any ambition to fulfill the promises often heard in cosmopolitan discussions about a global civil society.

External Democratic Dynamics

When social scientists argue that associational life is good for democracy, they are generally referring to its integrating and articulating functions. In associations, people develop the competence and virtues essential to joint decision-making, for example by learning to express themselves, to evaluate and present arguments, and to make decisions. Associations provide arenas, separate from the market and the state, in which people can develop the skills and virtues essential to both economic and social growth. Training in democracy is an extra benefit that accrues from pursuing the goals and interests of an association regardless of its specific goals. But it would be wise to consider the possibility that the changes described above have been so fundamental that they have weakened the political functions of established associations, and that the significance of associational life for democracy may no longer be as unequivocal as it once was.

Thus far, we have touched on only one democratic function of associations, that of meeting place and "training center." But they have another democratic function as well, that of providing society with social infrastructure in a free public space where alternative political agendas can be developed. This has the effect of augmenting members' freedom: through social organization, the authority of association members is increased, as is their ability to make their voices heard and their potential to exert direct or indirect political influence. In other words, this has to do with the *external* democratic function of associations, which consists of making social and political claims on the state (Hadenius 2004). Modern research into democracy has been primarily concerned with associations' *internal* function; their *external* aspects have not been dealt with as frequently in recent years.

The fact that an increasing proportion of members are becoming more passive does not necessarily have great significance for associations' success in promoting general welfare, or for their roles as political critics and links between the state and citizens. Nor do low levels of member activity per se constitute a great problem. The importance of face-to-face contacts may be overstated. Recent Norwegian studies thus play down the difference between the active and the passive members (Wollebæck and Selle 2002).

The selective recruiting by social class is, however, problematic. If mainly local service activities are stressed, it may lead to a weakening of ties between the local and national levels. As has been indicated by other Nordic studies, there could be consequences for associations' contribution to the nation-state's politics (Selle and Østerud 2006), notably a reduction in associations' ability to integrate citizens across social and geographic boundaries. From this standpoint, the growth of rural action groups during the 1990s is especially interesting, since they questioned the contract between large and centralized political institutions and big industry. They protested particularly against the structural transformation that fused a large number of layman-led municipalities—geographically spread out, but small in terms of population—into fewer, bigger, professionalized, and centralized organizations. Rural actions groups created local networks between new and old associations (Herlitz 1999), and they were among the few organizations that grew during the 1990s.

New Patterns of Institutionalization

In many respects, the profound changes in associational life reflect events in the two other major sectors of society, the labor market and the public sector. In traditional Social Democratic rhetoric, an expanded presence by the voluntary sector as a source of social service provision is construed as a weakness of the welfare state. Even as organizations have been celebrated as generating a general interpersonal and political infrastructure, they have been seen as unfit to become important providers of social assistance. But the 1990s public-sector cutbacks and social service privatization—especially in education, childcare, and healthcare—often resulted in responsibility for services being assumed by religious associations, temperance societies, co-ops, etc. It is, however, important to note that the extent of the shift was not all that great: by 2000, only some 13 percent of employees providing social services were hired within the private sector, including some corporations (Montin 2002).

Yet the rhetoric about "co-producing citizens" and cultural governance (Bang 2003) indeed paves the way for "bringing the civil society back in." The transfer of traditional social services to voluntary associations, though hard for many to ideologically put up with, signals a new epoch in the history of universalist welfare states that includes a reluctant, sometime painful recognition of the role played by voluntary associations. This shift represents a new, in some cases a restored, function of associational life. It is a process that, not least in a Scandinavian context, must accommodate ideological tensions ultimately rooted in the lack of a general recognition, in the case of social service provision, of the value of associations in comparison to the value of the general wage-earning sector (Torpe and Kjeldgaard 2003).

When associations are increasingly under contract with national and local authorities to provide certain services, the formerly general and imprecise contributions of associations have been replaced by specific tasks that are compensated on the basis of performance (Amnå, Lundström, and Svedberg 2000; Johansson 2005). This is part of a general trend by which associations have, to some extent, shifted in focus from giving members a political voice to providing services to clients (Wijkström and Lundström 2002). In the short term, at least this may spur an increase in activity level among the members, but it will not necessarily result in an expanded membership. Rather, it is more likely to lead to an expanded professional staff, which may challenge one traditional feature of Swedish voluntary/nonprofit associations, namely their large proportion of voluntary workers and low degree of hired personnel.

The financial demands upon the associations generally have become more burdensome. This may be disadvantageous, possibly resulting in higher costs for members and cutbacks in activities, both predictable responses to sharply increased meeting-hall rents, municipal cutbacks, and other budgetary strains. Although easy to defend from a tax payer's point of view, a more "New Public Management"-style of control notwithstanding, bottom/line decisions have led to a concentration on activities that impair internal democratic processes and external political activities. A transformation to publicly audited bureaucracies does promote the introduction of more professional criteria—but at the expense of less cost-effective democratic procedures. Increasing efforts must be devoted to fundraising activities, for example through the sale of lottery tickets. Another possible consequence is that the affected associations have come to be perceived as part of the public sector and the political establishment; if so, their former image as alternatives to the establishment may be weakened. Standardization appears to be the condition for their organizational survival. The Swedish Commission on Democracy expressed concern that political parties had become more dependent on central and local government resources and less reliant on their members for both financial resources and ideas (Amnå 2006).

In numerous ways the Swedish government has sought to mobilize the voluntary associations and put them to use so as to benefit itself. In the case of the Swedish development program elaborated in response to the United Nations' Millennium Development Goals, it tried to get the whole voluntary sector involved, one aim being to "give fire power" to Carin Jämtin, the minister for international development cooperation, as she expressed her interest in them. She arranged a "citizens' forum" in which matters of common concern were discussed. Many of the Swedish nonprofit organizations will work under contract to implement Swedish developmental policy (Amnå 2005a). Instead of leaving an organization free to distribute block grants by itself, the national government set up very specific criteria that direct the organization's activities to certain policy areas. For instance, in its appropriation to the Swedish Sports Confederation, an umbrella organization of the Swedish sports movement, the government's directive is composed of explicit, cost-related requirements that the organizations carry out the government policies on public health, social integration, gender equality, etc. At the local government level a parallel development seems to take place when citizens and citizen groups are invited to be "co-creators" or "co-producers" of public service in cultural governance-like alliances between the public sector and civil society (cf. Bang 2003).

The interests of the public sector and civil society do not, however, always go hand in hand. More often, public authorities and governmental ministries seem to co-opt public opinion activities that used to be performed by civil society organizations. For instance, when the government declared that it needed an organization to stimulate the Swedes' lack of interest in European affairs, the preparatory commission deliberately did not rely on the adult study organizations' capacity to distribute the grant, since they traditionally have been: "… free to decide how public funds will be used. Therefore it can be complicated to lay down conditions for the subsidies to groups that are used to setting their agenda according to the demands of the participants." (SOU 2004: 82: 70–1).

These examples illustrate that the public sector–civil society contract in Swedish politics is not fixed but subject to continuous renegotiation. The voluntary associations are not always valued as independent spheres of public deliberation but may instead be rewarded as trustworthy partners in governmental policy implementations.

Some organizations are able to handle this delicate governmental relationship. Others yield to the temptation to behave in a subordinated way, waiting for the government to tell them what do to in exchange for financial rewards. The CEO of the Swedish Absolutist Motorists' Association *(Motorförarnas Helnykterhetsförbund)* unintentionally illustrated the instrumental, if not obsequious, ingenuity that can result from a too-tight state-organization relationship when he argued for a cross-sectional national coalition for road safety: "The General Director of the Swedish National Road Administration has to formulate precise tasks, mandates and time tables. The Administration's project leader ought to have a clear national leadership as well as the authority to rapidly *purchase both ideological and practical services from the popular movement sector*" (*Motorföraren* 2003; my emphasis).

Simultaneously, several actors in the private sector have been trying to draw on the legitimacy of the voluntary sector by sponsoring it. Businesses have provided economic and professional support to a number of associations in exchange for goodwill and market exposure, among other things. One example is the "Ideas for Life" project of the Skandia insurance company, in which the company cooperates with municipal maternal healthcare programs, for example in parental education. The direct aim, of course, is to promote maternal health, but the desired indirect effects are to reduce the future costs of risk behavior and to create goodwill. Some private businesses, including IKEA, the global furnishing giant, have also started quasi-associations in the form of customer clubs that offer discounts and promote faithfulness but offer no particular ways of exerting influence. In addition, some associations have been affected by the neoliberal market philosophy that has gained ground since the 1980s. Consumer co-ops, for example, have been incorporated and restructured, radically altering the conditions for individual members' influence. Once a leading pioneer in the construction of democracy in Swedish society, the Swedish chain of co-operatives, COOP, may now be regarded as a supermarket chain like any other. In short, historic distinctions between very different kinds of associations have been gradually obscured and erased. Roughly speaking, the membership card has been devalued into a discount coupon.

At the same time, Swedish civil society organizations have chosen different strategies to promote their goals. Some of them have decided to include the corporations in their solutions to social and environmental problems. Different patient organizations have been supported, some almost founded, by pharmaceutical industry enterprises. The human-rights group Amnesty cooperates with the clothing company H&M. The Swedish section of World Wild Fund for Nature (WWF) cooperates with the car producer Volvo. Both organizations also work together with the grocery chain ICA. In contrast, others, like Attac Sweden and Jordens vänner (Swedish chapter of Friends of the Earth), prefer to treat private companies as ordinary, external targets when going about their own lobbying activities. That the voluntary organizations take the risk of being (perceived as) co-opted by the corporations is remarkable, since this can erode their value for democratic development, not least their reputation for providing an alternative when it comes to knowledge production and political perspectives (Cedstrand 2005). However, given that the option is continued heavy reliance on the public sector, it may also be that seeking partners in the private sector infuses new life into their external democratic role.

Increasingly, the historical contracts between state, market, and associations are under renegotiation, a process that was apparent as early as in the nineteenth century. Such renegotiation does not provide a basis on which to uncritically maintain a somewhat mythic rhetoric of associations and other popular movements. Traditional beliefs concerning associations and popular movements need to be demystified. Modern secular processes of institutional change affecting associations and society in general call for intellectual and political reassessment. This applies to both the general ideological and the financial support that local governments and the state provide to associational life on the assumption that it strengthens democracy.

Value Changes

It appears that the ideas represented by traditional associations do not always reflect current lines of conflict. The development of most Swedish voluntary associations has been closely linked to the development of the strong welfare state. In a time of globalization and related debates, isolation within national borders and fixed public-private relationships may be perceived as a weakness.

Swedish associationalism in the 1990s also showed signs of a major shift in values relating to the balance between individual and collective projects, short- and long-term perspectives, and material versus non-material interests (cf. Dalton 1996; Norris 2002; Inglehart and Welzel 2005). For the most part, associational life represents a special combination of these elements. The comparatively time-consuming, formally established procedures of associations could easily be perceived as boring and inefficient by those steeped in the apparently new values of the 1980s and 1990s. This is hardly a one-way process, but rather one of feedback. It is equally plausible that traditional Swedish popular movements may have failed to win support for their perspectives, procedures, and values. Other, more individualized, temporary, and less membership-based modes of action seem to expand, though this seldom occurs without network contacts with older associations or financial relationships with local and national governments, or both.

To sum up, there are still general reasons to have confidence in Swedish associational life and its ability to successfully perform the general-welfare and democratic functions that members its expect of it. Indeed, our analysis has shown that the voluntary sector still stands strong. Especially from a comparative point of view, in line with what Jeppson Grassman and Svedberg as well as Baer demonstrate in this volume regarding voluntary work, there is no overall crisis in terms of the Swedes' willingness to be involved in matters of common concern. However, our analysis also shows that Swedish associational life was generally weakened in the 1990s, as the proportion of both non-members and passive members increased. More and more citizens left their associations or never joined any. The class-related divisions within associational life remained. There is good reason to advise caution, lest the response to the trends outlined here be tardy and their significance for associational life downplayed.

The picture of associational life as it emerges from the 1990s is characterized by challenges similar to those facing national democracy and the welfare state at large: globalization; European integration; medialization; disengagement of citizens; rise of campaign parties without members; pauperization, isolation and commercialization of local government in relation to the citizenry. The legacy of the ambivalent, partly paternalist view of Swedish political parties is reflected in their views regarding the role of citizens in politics and public administration (Amnå 2006). Here the transformation of the Swedish associational life is, not surprisingly, largely tied to the weakening of the welfare state. The organizations are increasingly asked to compensate where the state is withdrawing. On the other hand, their role in autonomously manifesting alternatives and organizing conflicting perspectives and critical ideas does not seem to have strengthened. To a large extent the current transformation of Swedish civil society can be seen more as an aspect of the general problems facing democracy than a solution to them.

Perhaps the critical skills of the citizens are effectively developed in other arenas, both individual and collective. Besides homes, the arenas of school and peer groups, the Internet and other media spaces ought to be mentioned. Other types of involvement are signified by wearing particular brands of clothing, listening to certain styles of music, buying certified fair-trade products while boycotting goods produced under bad working conditions, or donating money to support an idealistic cause even though one is not a member of any solidarity organization (Micheletti 2003; Micheletti, Føllesdal, and Stolle 2003). However, not all early experiences from the new movements promote confidence in this optimistic vision of a progressive reproduction of old civic virtues in new forms. As is true for all voluntary organizations, neither the democratic goals nor the democratic methods should be taken for granted when it comes to the so-called new social movements (cf. Skocpol 2002).

It would be a mistake to underestimate the Swedish voluntary sector's capacity to adapt to new political, economical, and cultural circumstances. However, their demonstrated inability to integrate newcomers to Sweden indicates a structural dilemma, perhaps rooted in a historical legacy that associates narrow ethnic national identity with social citizenship in the welfare state. And one of the most significant findings, to which I will return later in my analysis, is that traditional associations are not attracting young people—especially boys and young men—in sufficient numbers to ensure their renewal. There are probably several reasons for this. For one, it is likely that the forms and methods of traditional associations, with their time-consuming democratic procedures, are perceived as impractical and inefficient.

Thus collective political activities are now developed to only a limited extent within the framework of traditional associational life. While it is true that some long-established associations and popular movements have attempted to modernize their activities and procedures, citizens are making increasing use of alternative modes of action provided by the media, the marketplace, and new social movements that not seldom are financially supported by national, county, and local governments. But before we are ready to draw conclusions about the correlation between strong associational presence and strong democracy, one assumption has to be more critically reviewed: how can we be so sure that associational life is good for democracy? Does it offer citizen groups interesting ways of cultivating political development and influence? The still-high total figure of memberships may be deceptive.

Does Voluntary Involvement Promote Swedish Adults' Political Involvement?

Leaving aside the numbers of memberships and the development of the organizations, we now will approach the critical question of how democratically productive an associational membership really is for the individual. The time has come for more precise statistical analysis of the available longitudinal data concerning adult associational life in Sweden, based on a model illustrated in Figure 5.1.[5]

My assumed, hypothetical point of departure is the following politically desirable mechanism. By joining a voluntary association people get socially involved by working together and sharing experiences that enrich them as social beings. They learn manners, how to deal with other people, and how you form contacts and friendships. This socialization process improves their feeling of efficacy (Bandura 1997). Voluntary associations, in other words, can both compensate for weaknesses in other spheres of life, and cultivate and strengthen existing social talents. As a side effect of associational membership or activity one grows as a political self. Associational activity is thus claimed to promote individual political efficacy (Warren 2001), which has long and repeatedly has been named as a significant factor in explaining political participation (Verba et al. 1995).

To test whether such a correlation actually holds, we have measured the individual's social capital, on the one hand, and what we prefer to call "political capital," on the other (Figure 5.1). The independent vari-

Figure 5.1. Model of Analysis

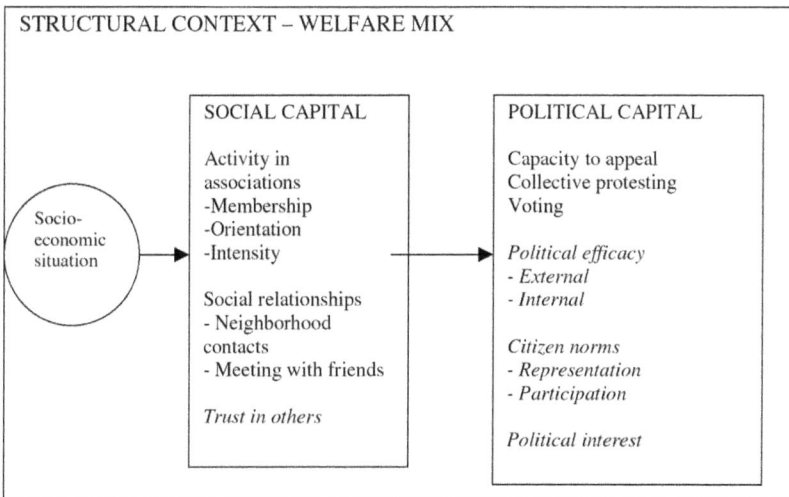

STRUCTURAL CONTEXT – WELFARE MIX

SOCIAL CAPITAL	POLITICAL CAPITAL
Activity in associations	Capacity to appeal
-Membership	Collective protesting
-Orientation	Voting
-Intensity	
	Political efficacy
Social relationships	*- External*
- Neighborhood contacts	*- Internal*
- Meeting with friends	
	Citizen norms
Trust in others	*- Representation*
	- Participation
	Political interest

Socio-economic situation

able, "social capital," is defined by the nature of the individuals' activity in associational life, i.e. its intensity (passive, active, engaged in leadership positions) and scope (number of memberships), and by the substantial orientation or type of organizations. This substantial aspect is differentiated according to political, interest, solidarity/religious, and lifestyle orientations. The nature of individuals' associational life is gauged by evaluating their social networks in terms of social relationships with friends outside the home and fellow workers; neighborhood contacts such as service exchanges, meetings, informal conversation, and neighborhood watch programs; and meeting with friends. In addition, general trust in others will be gauged later on.

The analysis is driven by a questioning of the potential of voluntary work to promote active citizenship as not necessarily superior but complementary to the socialization arena mentioned above. "Political capital" is the center of analysis. I want to test whether "belonging to voluntary associations is a woefully inadequate foundation for good citizenship" (Theiss-Morse and Hibbing 2005: 227). My aim is to investigate whether this kind of civic participation, purposely or not, may have spillover effect on political participation. By focusing on political capital, I ultimately will try to examine whether active citizenship is one of the most crucial individual factors for meaningful political participation. Agreeing with Theiss-Morse and Hibbing that "a successful approach for securing public participation in the first place has not been conceived," and that there is a lack of empirical evidence for the civic participation thesis, suggesting that civic participation should not necessarily be regarded as a cure-all, I am however not content with their claiming that "most people want to stay away from politics" (Theiss-Morse and Hibbing 2005: 227).

The variable "political capital" comprises two indicators. The first reflects a latent aspect of political activity in terms of individuals' self-reported capacity to appeal the decision of a public authority. This could be regarded as an aspect of civic knowledge, a prerequisite for attempting to win a case. The next indicator reflects a set of manifestations of individual political involvement, self-reported as experience of political action of various kinds, namely political discussions, speaking at public meetings, and other collective protesting actions. The third indicator, finally, is self-reported voting in the last election. Later in the analysis three further indicators of political capital will be introduced in the analysis, namely political efficacy, citizen norms, and political interest.

I will now examine three aspects of social capital's political relevance that have been touched on in the international debate on social capital. First, I would like to determine whether the active cadres of Swedish organizations belong to the ranks of those who have the most political capital.

As shown in Figure 5.2, active association members are mainly found in the groups with the most political capital. The greater the amount of

Figure 5.2. Political Capital of Swedes 16 and over, 2000[6]

Distribution of Political Capital among Citizen Groups
Number of people year 2000

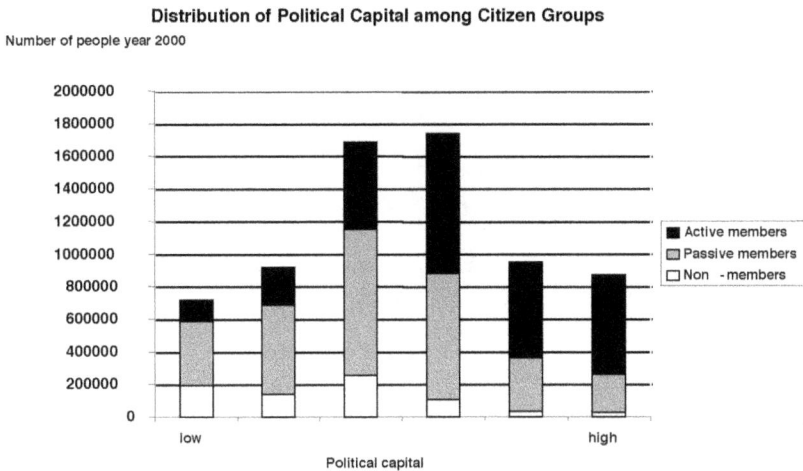

Source: Statistics Sweden, *Survey of Living Conditions,* sample *n*=5677 (year 2000).

political capital, the more probable it appears to be that any one person's associational involvement will be active. Yet, these organizations' active members are drawn from every population segment. Even among the about 700,000 citizens with the least political capital, there are about 100,000 active association members. In other words, active membership is not inherently a pathway to prominent political capital positions; nor does an associational connection directly generate a richness of political capital.

Maybe the plausible explanation of this result is that various organizations contribute unequally to individuals' political capital. Consequently, my second question addresses exactly this hypothesis.

As shown in Figure 5.3, political capital is distinctively distributed among the interviewed individuals. In contrast to what Putnam has suggested (Putnam 2000) but in line with Habermas's original conceptual work as well as recent Norwegian studies (Wollebaeck and Selle 2002), the goal and orientation of the organization seem to matter. Activity in a political association coexists with the highest amount of political capital, whereas activity in a lifestyle-oriented club seems to make a relatively low positive contribution. There appears to be a substantial difference in terms of accrual of political capital between activities in political versus non-political membership organizations.

Next, the intensity of associational involvement correlates with differences in levels of civic engagement. Following type, the second most important distinction is between those who are active and those who are

Figure 5.3. Political Capital Index and Associational Types and Participation among Swedes 16 and over, 2000[7]

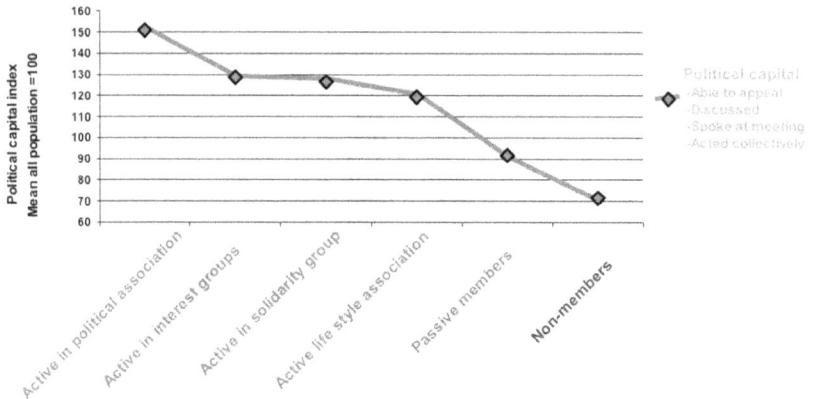

Source: Statistics Sweden, *Survey of Living Conditions*, sample n=5 677, year 2000

not. More precisely, the more active a citizen is in a voluntary organization, the greater his or her civic engagement, after controlling for social class, family background, and age (Amnå and Munck 2003). In contrast to findings in Norway (Wollebaeck and Selle 2002), this seems true not only of young people but of those of all ages. The level of activity per se appears to be significant. Although not as strong in terms of political capital as activists in political organizations, individuals who take active part in interest groups, solidarity groups, and lifestyle associations tend to have far more political capital than do passive members—not to mention non-members. Like other students of Swedish data (Teorell 2003), we furthermore confirm the impact of membership numbers. For the younger generation, after socioeconomic background and particular social circumstances, it is the intensity of organizational involvement that correlates most strongly with the level of political capital. Therefore, organizations' apparent and growing difficulties recruiting young people must be taken seriously, at least until we know more about the alternative ways young people may get politically involved.

To deepen our understanding of the interplay between various factors of significance for civic knowledge, voting, and collective protesting, we wish to observe whether factors other than organizational involvement are more powerful in determining the political capital position of an individual. The analysis is taken one step further to develop a structural equation model to estimate the total effects, after controlling for age and family situation. Thereby the significance of individual organizational involvement can be measured relative to a factor shown to be very powerful at explaining political participation, namely socioeconomic status (SES). The second latent independent variable, social capital, comprises associational activity, neighborhood contacts, and meeting with friends.

As shown in Table 5.2, the expected relative importance of SES is verified for all three modes of political participation: capacity to appeal (0.39), collective protesting (0.30), and voting in the last election (0.16). However, organizational activity seems to be influential for two of the above modes—collective protest, 0.31 and voting, 0.12—while its importance for a person's capacity to appeal seems to be marginal (0.05). Of the remaining social capital factors, only neighborhood contacts appears to be more powerful: the more neighborhood contacts you have, the more probable it is that you participate in some sort of collective political protest (0.12). In other words, associational life is generally more strongly correlated than are other social networks with voting and collective protest.

To sum up, organizational involvement and political capital appear to be linked. What matters for political capital is not only the association's substantial orientation but also the member's activity intensity and number of memberships. Thus, the decline of Swedish associations can be regarded as tending, on the whole, to weaken political capital for two reasons. First, the associations' overall capacity to give citizens a second chance to compensate for less privileged socioeconomic backgrounds became impaired, marginally, in the 1990s. In other words, it now runs a greater risk of reproducing political inequalities. Second, associations' capacity to recruit well-motivated youngsters, especially males, has been weakened. Young people may have chosen other ways to channel their interests; perhaps they have created other, equally powerful socialization arenas. Nonetheless, the theory-based modeling of a rich data source—

Table 5. 2. National-Level Model Explaining Political Participation: Swedes 16 and Over, Standardized Total Effects, Year 2000[8]

	SES	Organizational activity	Neighborhood contacts	Meetings with friends
Capacity to appeal	.39	.05	.08	.06
Participated in collective protests	.30	.31	.12	.02
Voted in last election	.16	.12	.05	.00

Source: Statistics Sweden, *Survey of Living Conditions, n* = 5677 (2000); for national register data, see http://www.ssd.scb.se/databaser/dbinfoeng.asp

the survey of living conditions in Sweden together with its panel data—has shown that the total capacity of voluntary associations to promote civic engagement, especially among youth, declined in the 1990s. Even factoring in the difficulties of gauging the impact of self-selecting mechanisms, organized Swedish voluntary life demonstrates a decreased capacity to pluralistically fertilize political participation. The associations have become less successful than before in convincing young Swedes that a membership offers meaningful opportunity structures.

Comparisons between Swedish and American Adolescents

For decades scholars have been claiming that major global changes in political participation are taking place (Barnes, Kaase, and Allerbeck 1979; Ichilov 1998, 2003; Inglehart 1977, 1997). Citizen actions are becoming less institutional and more individual, diverse, and "unconventional"—in other words, more postmodern. Overall, the repertoire of citizen activism is expanding, to take in non-political arenas as well (Dalton 1996, 2000; Leighley 1995; Norris 2002; Topf 1995). One main feature of citizens' multifaceted reappraisal of political participation seems to be a questioning of representative democracy as the natural political system (Inglehart and Catterberg 2003; Inglehart, Halman, and Welzel 2004).

Comparative research has also focused on youth, the segment of the population most intensely engaged in questioning or exiting the traditional patterns for political participation (Inglehart and Catterberg 2003). The young do not vote as willingly as their parents, nor do they take part in voluntary associations to the same extent as did older generations. They prefer other activities to reading newspapers—watching television, for example—and this is thought to cause a severe loss in terms of civic literacy (Milner 2002). Some scholars are tempted to blame youth for what is regarded as a crisis, or as a time bomb for democracy (Putnam 2000). Other scholars have curiously and self-critically reconsidered their own concepts of democracy as well as their methodological instruments for capturing political currents among youth (Bennett 2003; Norris 2004). New forms of political engagement are indeed being registered (Micheletti, Føllesdal, and Stolle 2003), although knowledge of the implications of these new forms and of the motivations for creating them, as well as of the character of their mechanisms, is still remarkably meager (Theiss-Morse and Hibbing 2005).

As seen in Figure 5.4, indeed there is reason for critical reflection on the intergenerational value difference, which we touched upon in an earlier section. Following Pettersson (2003), we distinguish between emancipative and conformity values. While the former seek to advance tolerance

Figure 5.4. Intergenerational Value Differences between Regions[9]

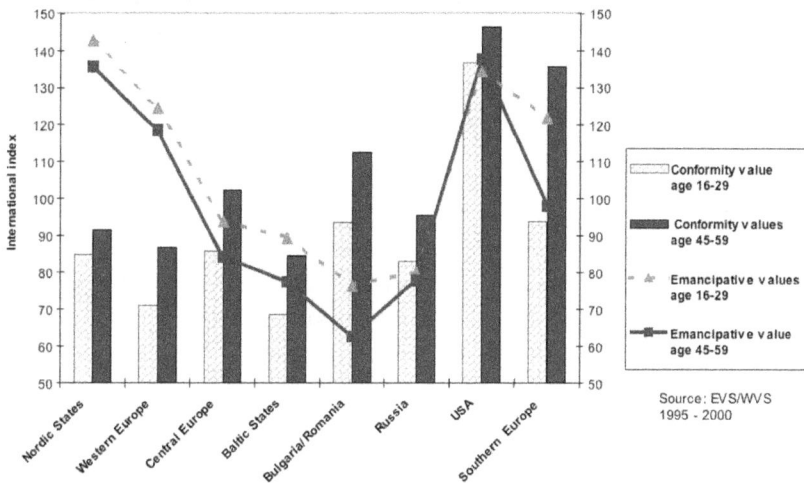

Source: EVS/WVS 1995 (Norway), 2000 (US) and all others 1999, available at www .uvt.nl/evs (in cooperation with Professor Thorleif Pettersson, Uppsala University).

of human diversity, aspirations to liberty, trust of and respect for others, and civic protest; the latter stress religious involvement, subordination, traditional family values, and nationalism as well as the values of obedience of and respect for authorities. Our analysis shows that youth generally express greater sympathy for emancipative values, while their parents lean more toward conformity values. Differently expressed, young people indeed seem to advocate democratic values to a somewhat larger extent than their parents. On the other hand, they also appear to be less loyal to the upholding of established institutions as their parents. However, it would be unimaginative to conclude that this necessarily constitutes a democratic problem per se.

Figure 5.4 also demonstrates an interesting difference in the balance between the two value sets in Nordic countries by comparison with the US. While the level of conformity values in the Nordic population is below the international mean, its level of emancipative values is far above the international mean. In the US the level of emancipative values is as high as in the Nordic countries; simultaneously, its conformity values turn out to be at the same high level. In other words, whereas Nordic youth and adults primarily uphold emancipative values, in the US emancipative and conformity values are upheld in equal measure, and radically when compared with other nations.

Will this regional difference in values also be mirrored in differing concepts of democracy and citizenship, and/or in differing prognoses of youth's and adults desire to take active part in politics? Will this make young people less inclined than their elders to take part in electoral politics as well as mid-term participative politics?

Fortunately, we have access to data collected in 1999–2000 by the International Association for the Evaluation of Educational Achievement (IEA) regarding 14-year-olds in twenty-three European democracies and the United States (Martin et al. 1999; Torney-Purta et al. 2001). By comparing Swedish and American adolescents' attitudes toward trust in others, political interest, political efficacy, and citizenship norms in the light of their associational involvement, we may be able to contribute to the debate on the future of these democracies. Granted, a report by a person in the midst of a dynamic life period, such as adolescence (Watts 1999), cannot be taken as a reliable predictor of future behavior: things will certainly happen during later adolescence to change the development of the political self in various ways (Galston 2001; Jennings and Niemi 1981; Niemi and Hepburn 1995). The statements of adolescents can, however, be treated as validly reflecting one important aspect of the political culture of a society, particularly from a comparative perspective.

Consequently, understanding the political development of youth is key to understanding the development of contemporary democracies (Jennings and Stoker 2001). Unfortunately, for decades international research has paid remarkably little attention to political socialization (Jennings 2001; Niemi 1999; Niemi and Hepburn 1995). Yet there is growing realization of both the necessity and the possibility of contributing theoretically and empirically to building understanding of the values and behavior of youth; this new awareness has come to inform the work by political scientists (Flanagan and Sherrod 1998; Galston 2001; Sapiro 2004; Stolle and Hooghe 2004), educationists (Ichilov 2003), and development theorists (Stattin and Kerr 2002).

American 14-year-olds are equipped with low trust in other people but substantial political capital and strong feelings of external efficacy. In sharp contrast, Nordic and Western European youth seem to trust fellow citizens, including political leaders, but not their own political resources; their sense of internal efficacy is thus the lowest. Like Eastern and Southern Europeans, American teenagers believe comparatively strongly in their own capabilities to contribute to political discussion, this being evident in terms of strong political self-efficacy. Most notably, American youth uniquely combine high external efficacy and political capital with the lowest level of trust in others. They express a mix of fairly widespread confidence in their politicians' responsiveness with very limited interpersonal trust. American 14-year-olds stand out as the exception to a general pattern valid for the twenty-three European countries examined.

Nordic adolescents, meanwhile, have comparatively greater trust in their politicians' responsiveness to the desires of ordinary people (external efficacy) as well as greater trust in their fellow citizens (social capital) (Amnå, Munck, and Zetterberg 2004). These differences cry out for deeper analysis, including also later adolescence. Since we do know that internal efficacy is a particularly significant motivator of political participation, we have reason to continue seeking the mechanisms of this very peculiar pattern.

As shown in Figure 5.5, a comparison of the four Nordic countries with the US presents a more nuanced inter-Nordic description. It depicts how the lowest levels of both representative and participatory norms are found in Finland, while the highest participatory norm level is found in Norway. Fourteen-year-old Danes more often say that they trust each other than do their peers in other countyries. American teenagers' level of trust in people is much lower than the Nordic mean level, as expected from comparative adult studies (Uslaner 2002). Nevertheless, American teenagers score high in both representative and participatative norms. In line with what we saw earlier (Figure 5.4), in the aggregate they seem able to combine internationally high values in both respects in their democratic understanding. At the age of fourteen they anticipate the widest repertoire of political action when becoming adults.

Having presented new evidence for a comparative pattern, we will of course attempt to seek explanation in terms of the theme of this book.

Figure 5.5. Attitudes to Citizenship Norms and trust in people: The Nordic Countries and the US, 14-year-olds (1999–2000)[10]

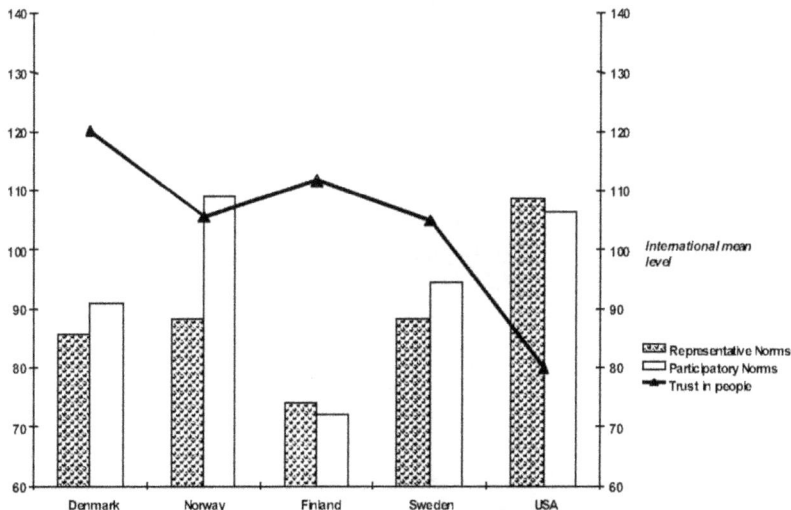

Sources: IEA Civic Education Study, 14-year-olds, data collection 1999–2000.

Perhaps country differences in associational involvement can throw a new light on the difference? Thus, our remaining analysis of 14-year-olds in Sweden and the US will be devoted to determining whether associational activity has any impact on the motivational factors we have thus far scrutinized on a per-country basis.

To determine whether the associational factors differ in terms of their impact on citizenship norms and motivational factors, our analysis again will make use of three dimensions, namely type of association, intensity of associational involvement, and scope of associational involvement across various association types (Wollebaeck and Selle 2002). However, because of the limitations of our data, the scope dimension will only be dichotomous (referring to members and non-members, respectively).

There are rather few comparative studies in the field of social capital (Prakash and Selle 2004). In order to contribute somewhat to a deepened contextual understanding a cross-country comparison will be made. Due to the pronounced differences between both the character of their polities (Jepperson 2002) and their voluntary associations (Salamon et al. 1997), young Swedes and Americans will be compared. Scandinavian countries have extensive, multiple memberships but low activity rates, while the US is characterized by strong ties with a few associations (Dekker, Koopmans, and van den Broek 1997).

The international rate of associational involvement is 88 percent for 14-year-olds. Both Sweden and the US exceed this mean, 96 percent and 95 percent of their 14-year-olds, respectively, being active participants in associational meetings. Only 4–5 percent of Swedish and American young adolescents have never joined an association, compared with an average of 12 percent for all twenty-four countries surveyed. Notably, in both these countries only 27 percent can be described as former participants. The contrast between the intensity of participation in the two countries deserves mention: among Americans as few as 13 percent are passive, while in Sweden up to 40 percent are. It seems to underline what was found in recent global studies (Dekker, Koopmans, and van den Broek 1997; Schofer and Fourcade-Gourinchas 2001). One explanation may be found in the political institutional contexts. The greater the degree of corporateness that characterized a country, the higher its level of associational activities will be—and the more passive members will be (Jepperson 2002). So the differences found here between Sweden, scoring high in corporateness, and the US, scoring low, might be explained by the historically institutionalized patterns embedded in the Swedish collective welfare system that stresses the socially expected membership more than the participants' activity.

Moreover, adolescents' associational life differs in an interesting way regarding type of association. In both countries recruitment to sports clubs is overwhelmingly dominant. However, we know of the adults that the structure and the volume of voluntary work mirror the different national

Figure 5.6.   Political Capital among Association Participants by Type of
Association, Passive Members, and Non-Members, Swedish
and US 14-Year-Olds (1999–2000)[11]

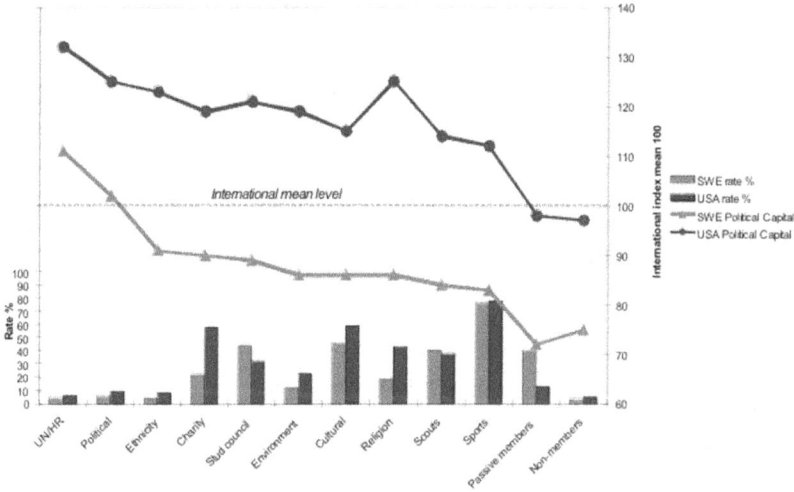

Sources: IEA Civic Education Study, 14-year-olds, data collection 1999–2000

welfare mixes and profiles (Salamon et al. 1997). American 14-year-olds
are much more oriented towards charity, cultural, and ethnic associations.
Maybe more unexpected is their higher overall level of involvement in
political and environmental groups.

Political impact appears to vary depending on associational type. We
can demonstrate that in comparison with an active membership, being a
former participant or a non-participant appears to correlate with significantly lower levels of political interest and sense of political efficacy, as
well as with the erosion of the citizenship norms developed earlier.

In analyzing Swedish adult data above we concluded that different
types of association are connected with different spillover effects on the
factors that motivate civic engagement. However, we cannot prove the
direction of the correlations found. As long as we cannot be decisive about
the selection of the association members, we always have to be cautious
(Rothstein and Stolle 2003) and be satisfied with claiming that there are
strong and similar correlations.

In line with figure 5.2, we finally want to summarize both the rate of
associational involvement of 14-year-olds (broken down by associational
type) and the level of political capital of Swedish and American 14-year-
olds affiliated with and spending part of their leisure time in voluntary
associations. The question that still awaits an answer is whether similar

associations generate political capital differently in different political cultural contexts.

The analysis confirms that associational involvement seems to contribute significantly across all countries and types of association. There are differences between those groups involved and those uninvolved in particular associational relationships Furthermore, within the respective countries, the same types of associations appear to promote political capital in a remarkably similar pattern. However, American association participants, former as well as active, retain more political capital than do the Swedes, as expected from the analysis above. Three pronounced levels of political capital are generally discernible. The greatest amount of political capital is found among participants in human rights, UN, and political organizations, and in the US, among participants in ethnic and religious-oriented organizations as well. Poorest in terms of political capital are non-participants and former participants. Participants in remaining associations are situated between these two extremes, with minor differences in terms of levels of political capital.

This interesting comparative pattern perhaps again can be understood in terms of the different structural contexts of civic engagement (Scofer and Fourcade-Gourinchas 2001). To be involved in associational life means different things in various societal and cultural contexts. In Sweden an associational membership linked to one's corporate status is something natural, and most individuals are members, although the membership is often passive. In the US, by contrast, an active associational life is regarded as somewhat more deserving and therefore individual characteristics have a stronger impact on whether one enters a voluntary association or not. The hypothesis is that the difference in civic engagement between participants and non-participants would be greater in the US than in Sweden. However, because very few of the adolescent respondents were non-participants, no statistical support for the hypothesis was found.

Regarding the necessity and morality of the various ways people articulate their needs and protests—what we call voice—being a non-member, a passive member, or less intensely involved in an organization is associated with weaker support for voice. As seen in Figure 5.6, both countries have a level of voice significantly above the international mean. Furthermore, UN/HR association members in US stand out sharply, as do scouts and sports group members in Sweden.

Finally, we would like to draw attention to one more finding captured in Figure 5.5, namely that the internationally highest level of trust among 14-year-olds is found in Nordic countries (about 65 percent positive), while the internationally lowest level is found in the US (about 35 percent positive). Since trust in people was captured by only a single question, its significance levels probably are underestimated due to measurement weaknesses. To an extent not accounted for in our analysis, Sweden and the

US are likely to differ in all researched aspects of associational life when it comes to trust in people: obviously, this powerful contextual feature has such a vast impact that no type of organizational membership in either country is capable of overriding it efficiently. Precisely how this will play out is, however, unclear. For example, it may be that there is a national level of interpersonal trust that remains unaffected by the associational involvements of the teenagers. We may also note that the members of cultural, charity, and religious associations seem to "bond" (Putnam 2000) to each as a bulwark against a significantly lower level of trust in people outside the association, while being involved in political activities appears, in the US, to act as a "bridge" (Putnam 2000) leading to greater trust in fellow citizens. Active members in political associations in Sweden are also more trustful than scouts or those active in outdoor associations.

With reference to what we found for the adult Swedish population above, the conclusion is that associational involvement seems to influence the amount of political capital. It does so in many ways; different organizations seem to matter differently within the countries but similarly between them. And the more associational involvement, the more efficient it appears to be for gaining political capital. Concerning at least 14-year-olds, whether one is active or not seems to be of decisive importance for the acquisition of political capital. Therefore political capital hypothetically can be seen as a function of the type of association and the intensity of involvement. Again opposing Putnam's suggestion (Putnam 2000) but confirming the findings of Norwegian studies (Wollebaeck and Selle 2002), our data suggest that the orientation of the organization affects the accumulation of political capital. As manifested in other studies, the impact is not exclusively limited to politically oriented organizations (Dekker and van den Broek 1998). As for Swedish adults, indeed we found that politically oriented associations attract those with the highest levels of political capital. Furthermore, we have empirically confirmed that this general pattern also applies, as of the turn of the millennium, to youth in Sweden and the US.

Meanwhile, the most remarkable nation-specific exception is that of the American religious denominations, in which the level of participants' political capital is found to be as high as it is among those active in political associations. This finding is also interesting in view of these denominations' demonstrated power to attract the participation of 43 percent of US adolescents, in comparison with the religious participation of 18 percent of Swedish adolescents. It also verifies the fruitfulness of including religious factors in comparative research into democracy (Verba et al. 1995; McDonough, Shin, and Moisés 1998). And regarding Swedish associations' problems dealing with an increased ethnical heterogeneity, the religiously more varied American associations may have something to teach.

What, Then, Can a Country's Associations Be Said to Contribute to Its Democracy?

The political ecology of Nordic countries is regarded as common and specific due to their distinctive welfare mix (Esping Andersen 1999; Powell and Barrientos 2004) and their combination of a comparatively low level of statism with a high level of corporateness (Schofer and Fourcade-Gourinchas 2001). It gives them on the one hand a specific balance between state, market, and civil society, and on the other specific structural contexts for civic engagement. The associational life's general state-friendliness, shown by a close relationship to the welfare state, also gives the Nordic democracies their characteristic institutional form and stability. As a consequence, the dividing line between civic and political participation has been less sharp than in the US. In fact, the Nordic civil society has been honored as a entryway into formal, participatory, and representative democracy. In the US, civic participation on the contrary appears to be cherished as an escape from the big, Leviathan democracy (Theiss-Morse and Hibbing 2005). Echoing the comparatively low voter turnout among young Americans in comparison with the Swedes, there seems to be something that hinders the cultivated political capital of the American adolescents active in voluntary associations to bloom later in formal democratic processes linked to the state.

However, the long-standing homogenous character of Scandinavian welfare state democracies may be coming to a relative close. If recently presented democratic audits of Denmark, Norway, and Sweden are put together, an emergent heterogeneity is revealed. It is still possible to praise the positive effect of broad-based voluntary organizations as vehicles for enhancing political equality, as the Danish Power Study recently did with typical Nordic rhetoric:

> Political participation in Denmark and the other Scandinavian countries is comparatively high. This is the legacy of the broad, class-based social movements, which at the end of the nineteenth century and the beginning of the twentieth century provided the setting for the political system we know today. Thanks to these movements we today have a society characterized by significant equality in terms of individual resources. Moreover, except in the case of party activities, the equality of participation has increased rather than decreased over recent years." (Togeby et al. 2003: 43, translation from Danish)

Yet, as we are arguing in this chapter, Nordic associational life now faces severe difficulties in upholding its proud tradition. The changes in more general cultural, economic, and institutional conditions are hard to handle within their national-welfare-state–based self-understanding. So when the Norwegian Power and Democracy Study put all their analyses together, they ended up with very worrisome conclusions. Not surprisingly, it greatly resembles the conclusion articulated in the contribution to this anthology by Tranvik and Selle, the latter himself a member of the study team:

> The turning point in the development of Norwegian organizational society is characterized by the breakdown of the traditional organizational model and the breakthrough of organizations oriented toward an immediate response to consumer demands "here and now" … Maybe we are witnessing the beginning of the end of the organizational society's dominant role in national democracy, particularly because associations no longer operate as local society's channels of communication with society at large. If so, this will weaken the most typical feature of Norwegian voluntarism—that low-status groups exert influence on public policy, locally as well as nationally, by participating in large, ideological organizations." (Makt- og demokratiutredningen 2003: 23–24, translation from Norwegian).

More careful reading of the two research groups' conclusions reveals not only that the Danes and the Norwegians emphasize different aspects of associations, but also that they differently discern the value of their contribution to democracy. They display two contrasting ideals of democracy. While the Danes praise associations for helping empower individuals, the Norwegians remind the reader of their function in giving underprivileged groups a collective voice. Where the Danes register progress in terms of political equality, the Norwegians notice loss of social inclusion. In light of the history of political ideas, the Danes stand closer to the liberal, British ideal of democracy with strong and autonomous individuals, while the Norwegians seem more allied to the collectivistic, French ideal of democracy in which representative actors are needed to realize the people's will. The commissions' diverse understanding of the voluntary associations and their role in individual and collective emancipation tellingly illustrates different embedded democratic accentuations that have too seldom been explicitly discussed. If there is increasing heterogeneity in the development of the Scandinavian democracies (Strandberg 2006), we have to determine the extent to which voluntary associations function as brakes, mirrors, or driving forces of this divergence.

When it comes to the question of the future of the Swedish democracy, the analyses have given us reason to affirm that associational life in Sweden is likely to offer its members, both youth and adult, added political value, probably also superior to that offered by other kinds of social intercourse. Differences in the associational involvement of youth likewise seem to persuasively explain disparities in political capital between countries. Nordic voluntary associations will probably continue to afford various opportunities for individual development of political significance. Before engaging with the obvious contentions of the rhetoric surrounding Scandinavian associational life, future research should first devote more attention to the different qualities of formally equal memberships.

By contrast, American associations likely accomplish the added political values more forcefully, due to their superior activity level in combination with their—probably interrelated—internationally high levels of political interest, internal political efficacy, and citizenship norms. The structural country context seems to matter. The Swedish associations may have something to learn from the American ones in coping with ethnically related variations.

Apart from the individual level, the Swedish voluntary associations' increased governmental dependency may shrivel their democratic role as autonomous sphere for public deliberation. More comparative research is needed to learn how shifting national political and cultural settings determine voluntary work, as well as what a membership means to an individual in different structural contexts.

The study also has implications for public policy. In Swedish politics there is a solid trust in the idea that voluntary associations can be used to fulfill political aims—at less expense and maybe with greater legitimacy than the public sector. To some extent this study may bring the political decision-makers to their senses, since the voluntary organizations appear to be operating neither as short-cuts nor as cure-all. Socioeconomic inequalities, such as those rooted in ethnic background, seem to be hard to overcome through increased public investments in voluntary association. But the study also calls for self-criticism among the organizations themselves for accommodating the welfare state's wish to standardize them for public use, for this may come at the expense of reduced potential to boost societal pluralism and civic education.

Swedish democracy is experiencing a phase of confusion, its electorate divided between erosion and consolidation as a means to reform its old design. The universal public services play a fundamental role in the Swedish model and its welfare-state democracy. At the same time, a policy window seems to have opened for a democratic turn from strengthening output-oriented legitimacy (by liberalization of welfare bureaucracy) to strengthening input-oriented legitimacy (by reinforcing deliberative participatory democracy), as well as a shift from collective consensual orientations to more individual empowerment orientations. The core question may no longer be whether or not voluntary work promotes Swedish democracy, but which choice it promotes at the crossroads that Swedish democracy is approaching. Is there at all a way beyond the European main road, where the institutional logic seems to prescribe that "individuals are represented more as valued members of the polity, bearing natural rights, rather than as empowered citizens with voluntarist responsibilities in a common spiritual mission" (Jepperson 2002:78)? Are Swedish associations doomed to remain mere subcontractors to representative democracy? Or is there a different grand narrative now waiting to be told by them, about new ways to take advantage of earlier successes while also setting the potential of their offspring free in order to attract new generations and ethnic citizen groups?

Notes

1. I wish to thank my colleague at Göteborg University, Professor Ingrid Munck, whose expertise made the advanced statistical analysis possible.
2. This section is mainly based on the author's contribution to Joachim Vogel, Erik Amnå, Ingrid Munck, and Lars Häll (2003), *Associational Life in Sweden. General Welfare, Social Capital, Training in Democracy, Living Conditions.*
3. Putnam's statement that 40 percent of Swedes are involved in study circles every year ought to be treated with care; approximately 20 percent may be more accurate (Amnå and Munck 2003).
4. Association membership: Self-reported active, passive, and non-membership, respectively, over the past 12 months in approximately 30 types of association (trade unions and political parties excluded).
   The oldest group in 1978 and 1984 comprises only people up to 74 years old; in other years the oldest group includes those up to 85 years old.
5. The data used in this research were derived from the annual surveys of living conditions conducted by Statistics Sweden (ULF). The surveyed population consists of residents of Sweden aged 16–84 years. Changes in associational life are described on the basis of: (a) a cross-sectional comparison of random samples of adults aged 16–84 years, selected in 1992 and 2000, and (b) a longitudinal study of a panel of adults interviewed in 1992 and 2000. Sample sizes for this study were 5,980 and 5,677. The non-response rate was approximately 20 percent. The sample design was based on mixed panel and cross-sectional samples. The sample of some thirty different associations is large enough to permit comparison of their development in relation to each other, both individually and sorted into categories based on primary activities (political, interest group, solidarity, religion, recreation, and lifestyle). For further information, see Vogel and Amnå (2003).
6. *Association membership:* self-reported active, passive, and non-membership, respectively, over the past twelve months in approximately 30 types of association (trade unions and political parties excluded)
   Political capital: four indicators: (1) ability to appeal; (2) collective action: "Have you ever tried to act in order to do something about a deficiency or incorrectness (in this municipality)?" or "Generally regarding political issues, besides the local ones in this community, have you at any time … ?" The answer format covers how often the respondent has contacted officials or politicians, written a letter to the editor, signed a petition, or participated in a demonstration; (3) "Have you ever spoken at a meeting of an association or organization?" (4-point scale); (4) "How do you usually behave if you are present at a party when the conversation turns to political issues?" 4-point scale ranging from "I normally don't listen when people start talking politics" to "I generally join the discussion and articulate my opinion."
   Political capital scale: six categories.
7. Index scale, mean all population = 100 and standard deviation = 50.
   Association membership: self-reported active, passive, and non-membership, respectively, over the past twelve months in approximately 30 types of associations (trade unions and political parties excluded).
   Associational types: (1) political associations, e.g. local action groups and environmental associations; (2) interest groups like consumer co-ops, parents', housing, ethnic, disabled, women's, temperance, shareholder, and pensioner organizations;

(3) solidarity groups, including international organizations, peace associations, and Christian denominations; (4) lifestyle associations promoting sports, culture, outdoors, hobbies, motoring, and voluntary defense, and interests.

Political capital: four indicators: (1) ability to appeal; (2) collective action: "Have you ever tried to act in order to do something about a deficiency or incorrectness (in this municipality)?" or "Generally regarding political issues, besides the local ones in this community, have you any time… ?" The answer format covers how often the respondent has contacted officials or politicians, written to the editor, signed a petition, or participated in a demonstration; (3) "Have you ever spoken at a meeting in an association or organization?" (4-point scale); (4) "What do you usually do if you are present at a party when the conversation turns into political issues?" Four-point scale from "I normally don't listen when people start talking politics" to "I mostly join the discussion and articulate my opinion".

Political capital scale: six categories.

8. Path model with political participation as outcome, SES as exogenous variable, and social capital as intervening variable.

Political participation: three of the self-reported outcome variables: (1) "capacity to appeal" a decision by a public authority, (2) "participation in collective protest" (contacted responsible politicians or civil servant, signed a petition or letter to the editor, or participated in a demonstration), and (3) "voted in last election."

SES: National Register data on education, income, and socioeconomic group.

Social capital: (1) "Activity in associations" (passive, active, and holding commissions of trust), (2) "neighborhood contacts" (exchange of services, meet and talk with neighbors, neighborhood watch programs) and (3) "meeting with friends."

9. International index scale is defined by mean = 100 and standard deviation = 50 across 23 countries.

Conformity values: captured by four components in the European/World Values Surveys: (1) importance of religious involvement and confidence in religious organizations; (2) family values (such as importance of the family in one's life, love and respect for parents, and the value of marriage); (3) national identity (national pride and belonging to a country); and (4) conformity norms (the obligation of a subordinate to follow a superior's instructions).

Emancipative values: measured by four indicators: (1) tolerance of human diversity (whether one would object to having homosexuals, immigrants, and people of another race as neighbors); (2) aspirations to liberty (preferences for giving people more to say in important decisions and for protecting of freedom of speech in comparison to preferences for fighting inflation and keeping law and order, respectively); (3) social trust and respect for others; and (4) inclination to social protest by signing a petition, joining a boycott, attending a lawful demonstration, joining an unofficial strike, or occupying a building or factory (Welzel, Inglehart, and Klingemann 2003)

Regions: The regions are comprised as follows: Baltic States (Estonia, Latvia, and Lithuania); Central Europe (Poland, Czech Republic, Slovakia, Slovenia, and Hungary); Southern Europe (Italy, Portugal, Cyprus, and Greece); Western Europe (Belgium (French-speaking), England, Germany, and Switzerland); Nordic Countries (Denmark, Finland, Norway, and Sweden) (cf. Berglund and Aarebrot 1997).

10. International index scale common for all dimensions is defined by mean = 100 and standard deviation = 50 across twenty-four countries.

Representative norms: factor score composite based on four items, each with four alternative responses from "not important" to "very important" to the following: "An adult who is a good citizen…" (1) "votes in every election," (2) "joins a political party," (3) follows political issues in the newspaper, on the radio or on TV," (4) "engages in political discussions."

Participatory norms: factor score composite based on four items each with four alternative responses from "Not important" to "very important" to the following: "An adult who is a good citizen..." (1) "would participate in peaceful protest," (2) "participate in activities to benefit people in the society," (3) "takes part in activities promoting human rights," (4) "takes part in activities to protect the environment."

Trust in people: based on a single item "How much of the time can you trust ... the people who live in this country?" Four-point scale, ranging from "never" up to "always".

11. International index scale for political capital is defined by mean = 100 and standard deviation = 50 across 24 countries.

Participants: Answered "yes" ≥ by choosing association type from 15 alternatives.

Former participants: Participants answering "never or almost never" to "How often do you attend meetings or activities of any or all of these organizations?"

Non-participants: None of the 15 alternatives selected.

Intensity: "How often do you attend meetings or activities for any or all of these organizations?" Four-point scale, ranging from "never or almost never" to "almost every day (4 or more days a week)."

UN/HR: "A UN or UNESCO club", "A human rights organization" (in Sweden: also "association ... for humanitarian aid").

Political: "A youth organization affiliated with a political party or union."

Ethnicity: "A cultural association (organization) based on ethnicity."

Charity: "A charity collecting money for a social cause" and "a group conducting voluntary activities to help the community."

Student council: "A student council/student government."

Environment: "An environmental organisation."

Cultural: "A cultural association/association based on ethnicity."

Religion: "An organization sponsored by a religious group" (in Sweden: "a group associated with a religious organization").

Scouts: "Boy or Girl Scouts" (in Sweden: also "other outdoor association (friluftsförening)").

Sports: "A sports organization or team."

Members: Answered "yes" ≥ association type among 15 alternatives.

Passive member: Members answering "never or almost never" to "How often do you attend meetings or activities for any or all of these organizations?"

Non-members: No "Yes" ticked for any of the 15 alternatives.

Political capital: Factor score composite based on four indicators: (1) political interest (single item: "I am interested in politics", four-point scale from "strongly disagree" to "strongly agree," (2) internal efficacy: factor score composite based on 3 items, each with four alternative responses (strongly disagree, disagree, agree, strongly agree) to "I know more about politics than most people my age," "When political issues or problems are being discussed, I usually have something to say," and "I am able to understand most political issues easily," (3) representative norms, and (4) participatory norms: see note 10 above.

References

Amnå, Erik. 2005a. "Cykelvinster, brukarråd i Rosenbad och onödiggjorda partier." In *Den tömda demokratin*, ed. A. Sörbom. Stockholm: Agora.

———. 2005b. "Scenöppning, scenvridning, scenförändring." In *Civilsamhället: några forskningsfrågor*, ed. E. Amnå. Hedemora/Stockholm: Gidlunds förlag i samarbete med Riksbankens Jubileumsfond.

———. 2006. "Playing with fire? The Swedish mobilisation for participatory democracy." *Journal of European Public Policy* 13, no. 4: 587-606.

Amnå Erik, Tommy Lundström, and Lars Svedberg. 2000. *Three essays on volunteerism and voluntary organisations, Sköndalsinstitutets arbetsrapportserie, 9*. Sköndal: Ersta Sköndal högskola.

Amnå, Erik, and Ingrid Munck. 2003. Socialt och politiskt kapital. In *Föreningslivet i Sverige. Välfärd, socialt kapital, demokratiskola*, ed. J. Vogel, E. Amnå, L. Häll, and I. Munck. Stockholm: SCB Rapport 98.

Amnå, Erik, Ingrid Munck, and Pär Zetterberg. 2004. *Meaningful Participation? Political Efficacy of Adolescents in 24 countries*. Paper presented at "Emerging Repertoires of Political Action: Toward a Systematic Study of Postconventional Forms of Participation." ECPR Joint Sessions of Workshops.

Bandura, Albert. 1997. *Self-efficacy: The Exercise of Control*. Basingstoke: W. H. Freeman.

Bang, Henrik, ed. 2003. *Governance as Social and Political Communication*. New York: Manchester University Press 2003.

Barnes, Samuel H., Max Kaase, and Klaus R. Allerbeck. 1979. *Political Action: Mass Participation in Five Western Democracies*. Beverly Hills, CA: Sage.

Bennett, W. Lance. 2003. "Communicating Global Activism: Strengths and Vulnerabilities of Networked Politics." *Information, Communication & Society* 6, no. 2: 143–168.

Berglund, Sten, and Sten Aarebrot. 1997. *The Political History of Eastern Europe in the 20th Century: The Struggle between Democracy and Dictatorship*. Cheltenham: Edward Elgar.

Cedstrand, Sofie. 2005. *Idealism till salu? Om ideella organisationers strategival och dess demokratiska betydelse*. Göteborgs universitet: Förvaltningshögskolan.

Dahlkvist, Mats. 1999. "Den instängda demokratin. Rörelsesocialism och stats-socialism i svensk arbetarrörelse." *Civilsamhället som demokratins arena*, ed. E. Amnå. Stockholm: Demokratiutredningens skrift nr 29, SOU 1999: 112.

Dalton, Russell J. 1996. *Citizen Politics: Public Opinion and Political Parties in Advanced Industrial Democracies*. 2nd ed. Chatham, NJ: Chatham House.

———. 2000. "Citizen Attitudes and Political Behaviour." *Comparative Political Studies* 33, no. 6-7: 912–940.

Dekker, Paul, Ruud Koopmans, and Andries van den Broek. 1997. "Voluntary Associations, Social Movements and Individual Behaviour in Western Europe." In *Private Groups and Public Life: Social Participation, Voluntary Associations and Political Involvement in Representative Democracies*, ed. J. W. van Deth. London: Routledge.

Dekker, Paul, and Andries van den Broek. 1998. "Civil Society in Comparative Perspective." *Voluntas* 8 no. 1: 11–38.

Demokratiutredningen. 2000. *En uthållig demokrati? Politik för folkstyrelse på 2000-talet*. SOU 2000: 1.

Esping-Andersen, Gösta. 1999. *Social Foundations of Postindustrial Economies*. New York: Oxford University Press.

Flanagan, Constance A., and Lonnie R. Sherrod. 1998. "Youth Political Development: An Introduction." *Journal of Social Issues* 54, no. 3: 447–457.

Galston, William A. 2001. "Political Knowledge, Political Engagement, and Civic Education." *Annual Review of Political Science* 4: 217–234.

Gidlund, Gullan, and Tommy Möller. 1999. *Demokratins trotjänare: lokalt partiarbete förr och nu*, Demokratiutredningens forskarvolym, 10. Stockholm: Fakta info direkt.

Herlitz, Ulla. 1999. "Bygdens organisering." In *Civilsamhället*, ed. E. Amnå. Demokratiutredningens forskarvolym VIII, SOU 1999: 84. Stockholm: Fakta Info Direkt.

Hadenius, Axel. 2004. *Social Capital and Democracy: Institutional and Social Conditions*. Thousands Oak, CA: Sage.

Ichilov, Orit. 2003. "Education and citizenship in a changing world." *Oxford handbook of political psychology*.

Ichilov, Orit, ed. 1998. *Citizenship and Citizenship Education in a Changing World*. London: Woburn Press.

Inglehart, Ronald. 1977. *The Silent Revolution: Changing Values and Political Styles among Western Publics*. Princeton, NJ: Princeton University Press.

———. 1997. *Modernization and Postmodernization: Cultural, Economic, and Political Change in 43 Societies*. Princeton, NJ: Princeton University Press.

Inglehart, Ronald, and Christian Welzel. 2005. *Modernization, Cultural Change, and Democracy*. New York: Cambridge University Press.

Inglehart, Ronald, and Gabriela Catterberg. 2003. "Trends in Political Action: The Development Trend and the Post-Honeymoon Decline." *International Journal of Comparative Sociology* 43, no. 3–5: 300–316.

Inglehart, Ronald, Loek Halman, and Christian Welzel. 2004. "Introduction." In *Human Beliefs and Values: A cross-cultural Sourcebook Based on the 1999/ 2002 Values Surveys*, ed. R. Inglehart, M. Basáñez, J. Díez Medrano, L. Halman, and R. Luijkx. Delegación Coyoacán: Siglo XXI Editores, Mexico.

Jacobsson, Kerstin. 1999. Den offentliga demokratisynen. In *Demokrati och medborgarskap*, ed. E. Amnå. Demokratiutredningens forskarvolym II, SOU 1999: 77.

Jennings, M. Kent. 2001. "Socialization: Political." *International Encyclopedia of the Social and Behavioral Sciences*, pp. 14522–14525.

Jennings, M. Kent, and Laura Stoker. 2001. "Generations and Civic Engagement." Paper read at American Political Science Association Meeting, San Francisco.

Jennings, M. Kent, and Richard G. Niemi. 1981. *Generations and Politics*. Princeton: Princeton University Press.

Jepperson, Ronald L. 2002. "Political Modernities: Disentangling Two Underlying Dimensions of Institutional Differentiation." *Sociological Theory* 20, no.1: 61–85.

Johansson, Staffan. 2005. *Ideella mål med offentliga medel*. Stockholm: Sober.

Leighley, Jan E. 1995. "Attitudes, Opportunities and Incentives: A Field Essay on Political-Participation." *Political Research Quarterly* 48, no. 1: 181–209.

Makt- og demokratiutredningen. 2003. *Makt og demokrati. Slutrapport fra Makt- og demokratiutredningen*. Vol. 2003: 19. Oslo: Norges offentlige utredninger.

Martin, Michael O., Keith Rust, and Raymond J. Adams, eds. 1999. *Technical Standards for IEA Studies*. Amsterdam: International Association for the Evaluation of Educational Achievement (IEA).

McDonough, Peter, Doh C. Shin, and José Álvaro Moisés. 1998. "Democratization and Participation: Comparing Spain, Brazil, and Korea." *The Journal of Politics* 60, vol. 4: 919–953.

Micheletti, Michele. 1995. *Civil Society and State Relations in Sweden*. Aldershot: Avebury.

———. 2003. *Political Virtue and Shopping: Individuals, Consumerism and Collective Action*. Basingstoke: Palgrave.

Micheletti, Michele, Andreas Føllesdal, and Dietlind Stolle. 2003. *Politics, Products, and Markets: Exploring Political Consumerism Past and Present*. New Brunswick, NJ: Transaction Publishers.

Milner, Henry. 2002. *Civic Literacy: How Informed Citizens Make Democracy Work*. Hanover, NH: Tufts University.

Misgeld, Klaus. 2001. *Socialdemokratins program: 1897 till 1990, Småskrifter utgivna av Arbetarrörelsens arkiv och bibliotek*. Stockholm: Arbetarrörelsens arkiv och bibl.

Montin, Stig. 2002. *Moderna kommuner*. Malmö: Liber ekonomi.

Montin, Stig, and Erik Amnå, eds. 2000. *Towards a New Concept of Local Self-Government?: Recent Local Government Legislation in Comparative Perspective*. Bergen: Fagbokforlaget.

Motorföraren. 2003: 3

Niemi, Richard G. 1999. "Editor's Introduction." *Political Psychology* 20 no. 3: 471–476.

Niemi, Richard G., and Mary A. Hepburn. 1995. "The Rebirth of Political Socialization." *Perspectives on Political Science* 24, no. 1: 7–17.

Norris, Pippa. 2002. *Democratic Phoenix: Reinventing Political Activism*. Cambridge: Cambridge University Press.

———. 2004. *Young People & Political Activism: From the Politics of Loyalties to the Politics of Choice?* Available from http://ksghome.harvard.edu/~pnorris/Acrobat/COE%20Young%20People%20and%20Political%20Activism.pdf.

Olsen, Johan P. 1990. *Demokrati på svenska*. Stockholm: Carlssons.

Olson, Hans-Erik. 1992. *Staten och ungdomens fritid: kontroll eller autonomi? Arkiv avhandlingsserie, 40*. Lund: Arkiv.

Pettersson, Thorleif. 2003. *Basic Values and Civic Education*. Available at http://www.worldvaluessurvey.org/library/index.html.

Powell, Martin and Armando Barrientos. 2004. "Welfare regimes and the welfare mix." *European Journal of Political Research* 43, no. 1: 83–105.

Prakash, Sanjeev, and Per Selle, eds. 2004. *Investigating Social Capital: Comparative Perspectives on Civil Society, Participation and Governance*. London: Sage.

Putnam, Robert D. 2000. *Bowling Alone: The Collapse and Revival of American Community*. New York: Simon & Schuster.

———. 2002. "Conclusion." In *Democracies in Flux*, ed. R. D. Putnam. New York: Oxford University Press.

Rothstein, Bo, and Dietlind Stolle. 2003. "Social Capital in Scandinavia: An Introduction to a Special Issue of *Scandinavian Political Studies*." *Scandinavian Political Studies* 26, no 1: 1–26.

Salamon, Lester M., Helmut K. Anheier, Tommy Lundström, and Filip Wijkström. 1997. *Defining the Nonprofit Sector: A Cross-national Analysis*, Johns Hopkins nonprofit sector series, 4. Manchester: Manchester Univ. Press.

Sapiro, Virginia. 2004. "Not Your Parents' Political Socialization: Introduction for a New Generation." *Annual Review of Political Science* 7: 1–23.

Schofer, Evan, and Marion Fourcade-Gourinchas. 2001. "The Structural Contexts of Civic Engagement: Voluntary Association Membership in Comparative Perspective." *American Sociological Review* 66: 806–828.

Selle, Per, and Bjarne Øymyr. 1995. *Frivillig organisering og demokrati : det frivillige organisasjonssamfunnet endrar seg 1940–1990*. Oslo: Norske samlaget.

Selle, Per, and Øyvind Østerud. 2006. "The Eroding of Representative Democracy." *Journal of European Public Policy* 13, no. 4: 551-568.

Skocpol, Theda. 2002. "From Membership to Advocacy." In *Democracies in Flux*, ed. R. D. Putnam. New York: Oxford University Press

SOU 2004: 49. *Engagemang, mångfald, integration*. Betänkande av Integrationspolitiska maktutredningen. Stockholm: Liber.

SOU 2004: 82. *Sluta strunta I EU!* Betänkande av EU 2004-kommittén. Stockholm: Liber

Stattin, Håkan, and Margaret Kerr. 2002. "Adolescents' Values Matter." *Navigating Through Adolescence: European Perspectives: The Michigan State University Series on Families and Child Development*, ed. J.-E. Nurmi. New York: Routledge Farmer.

Stolle, Dietlind, and Mark Hooghe. 2004. "The Roots of Social Capital. Attitudinal and Network Mechanisms in the Relation between Youth and Adult Indicators of Social Capital." *Acta Politica* 39, no. 4: 422–441.

Strandberg, Urban. 2006. "State, nations and democracies. A historical and conceptual introduction." *Journal of European Public Policy* 13, no. 4: 537-550.

Teorell, Jan. 2003. "Linking Social Capital to Political Participation: Voluntary Associations and Networks of Recruitment in Sweden." *Scandinavian Political Studies* 26, no. 1: 49–66.

Theiss-Morse, Elizabeth, and John R. Hibbing. 2005. "Citizenship and Civic Engagement." *Annual Review of Political Science* 8, no. 1: 227–249.

Tilton, Timothy Alan. 1991. *The Political Theory of Swedish Social Democracy: Through the Welfare State to Socialism*. Oxford: Clarendon Press.

Togeby, Lise, Jorgen Goul Andersen, Peter Munk Christiansen, Torben Beck Jörgensen, and Signild Vallgårda. 2003. *Demokratiske udfordringer. Kort udgave af Magtudredningens hovedresultater*. Århus: Magtudredningen.

Topf, Richard. 1995. "Beyond Electoral Participation." In *Citizens and the State*, ed. H.-D. Klingemann and D. Fuchs. Oxford: Oxford University Press.

Torney-Purta, Judith, Rainer Lehmann, Hans Oswald, and Wolfram Schulz. 2001. *Civic Education in Twenty-eight Countries: Civic Knowledge and Engagement at Age Fourteen*. Amsterdam: IEA.

Torpe, Lars. 2003. "Social Capital in Denmark: A Deviant Case?" *Scandinavian Political Studies* 26, no. 1: 27–48.

Torpe, Lars, and Torben K. Kjeldgaard. 2003. *Foreningssamfundets sociale kapital. Danske foreninger i et europaeisk perspektiv*. Århus: Magtudredningen.

Uslaner, Eric. 2002. *The Moral Foundation of Trust.* New York: Cambridge University Press.

Verba, Sidney, Kay Lehman Schlozman, and Henry E. Brady. 1995. *Voice and equality: civic voluntarism in American politics.* Cambridge, MA: Harvard University Press.

Vogel, Joachim, Erik Amnå, Ingrid Munck, and Lars Häll. 2003. *Associational Life in Sweden: General Welfare, Social Capital, Training in Democracy, Living Conditions.* Report no 101. Stockholm: Statistics Sweden.

Warren, Mark. 2001. *Democracy and Association.* Princeton, NJ: Princeton University Press.

Watts, Meredith W. 1999. "Are There Typical Age Curves in Political Behavior? The 'Age Invariance' Hypothesis and Political Socialization." *Political Psychology* 20, no. 3: 477–499.

Welzel, Christian, Ronald Inglehart, and Hans-Dieter Klingemann. 2003. "The Theory of Human Development: A Cross-Cultural Analysis." *European Journal of Political Research* 42, no. 2: 341–380.

Wijkström, Filip, and Tommy Lundström. 2002. *Den ideella sektorn. Organisationerna i det civila samhället.* Stockholm: Sober Förlag.

Wollebaeck, Dag, and Per Selle. 2002. "Does Participation in Voluntary Associations Contribute to Social Capital? The Impact of Intensity, Scope, and Type." *Nonprofit and Voluntary Sector Quarterly* 31, no. 1: 32–61.

Chapter 6

MORE CENTRALIZATION, LESS DEMOCRACY: THE DECLINE OF THE DEMOCRATIC INFRASTRUCTURE IN NORWAY

Tommy Tranvik and Per Selle

The relative success of the Norwegian welfare state democracy is, according to conventional wisdom, based on a simple formula: National prosperity + social equality + political freedom = strong democracy. The logic behind the formula is as simple as the formula itself: there can be no widespread political empowerment without redistribution of riches, no redistribution without substantial economic growth, and little democracy without the combined contributions of the three aforementioned factors. Or, to put it yet another way, the wealth of the nation should be divided (but not evenly) among its citizens so that ordinary people get a fair chance to influence the decisions made by public authorities.

For more than half a century, this formula has been accepted in Norway as self-evidently true by virtually all political parties and their supporters—liberals, conservatives, social democrats, agrarian centrists, Christian conservatives, and far-left socialists alike. Not that everybody agreed on everything all the time. The level of taxation, for instance, or the political regulation of the economy, subsidies to farmers, the privatization of public service production, the scope and depth of pension schemes or of social welfare rights—all these were (and still are) among the hotly contested issues that tended to pit an uneasy alliance between social democrats and far-left socialists against a motley crew of non-socialist parties. But even if the controversies over these and other issues could be bitter and acrimonious, very few seriously challenged the formula or its logic, and those who did fought an uphill battle to gain any kind of popular backing. The debate was over how to interpret and implement the formula: What types of public policies were most likely to realize the intentions that most of us agreed on?

We do not wish to second-guess the validity of the prosperity-equality-freedom formula—experience demonstrates that it has served Norway (and the other Scandinavian countries) well. What we will question, however, is the linear optimism built into the formula, that is, the sense that more of everything that is deemed good is automatically translated into increasingly healthier democratic institutions. More national prosperity, greater social equality, and ever-expanding political freedoms will not, we propose, always equal an even stronger democracy.

Optimism is warranted as long as the two most important intermediate institutions—civil society organizations and municipal government, connecting ordinary citizens and the central policy-making authorities—are able to mobilize widespread interest, support, and participation. But a weakening of these intermediary institutions' capacity to serve as a bridge between citizens and centralized authority may trigger a downward spiral, where more of all things good increasingly undermine the bridging strength of voluntary organizations and municipal institutions. In a prosperous and redistributive society, everybody tend to seem more or less the same as everybody else in social, economic and educational terms. And affluent, well-nurtured look-alikes are likely to trust that others can fend for themselves, just as they expect (and demand) to fight their own battles (though, as we shall see, not entirely alone). If this is true, as we believe it is, the successful implementation of the prosperity-equality-freedom formula has resulted in the rise of a new type of citizen, the individualized egalitarian, who thinks that "everyone should look more after themselves because very few are significantly worse off than me." What the individualized egalitarian seems to want is (among other things) the freedom to engineer his or her political participation in ways other than what the old-fashioned voluntary organizations and municipal institutions can offer.

This craving for more personal freedom does not stem from the fact that political decisions have no or little relevance for how we live our lives. It is not freedom from politics or from central authority that is sought, but freedom from being encroached upon by the collective enterprises that make democracy work (and having to share in the identities and solidarities underpinning them). If anything, we expect more from the performance of centralized authority—better quality services that are easily accessible and that duly attend to individual needs and wishes. Apathy, fatalism and indifference therefore are inherent attributes of the individualized egalitarian. What seems to be in demand is more political output with less time-consuming input: the decision-making machinery is expected to keep churning efficiently and reliably, needing only occasional and short-term guidance from informed citizens.

In nation-states where the public sector is relatively small compared to the size of the economy, and where citizens rely little on public services, occasional engagement is probably good enough. But not so in a society designed according to the prosperity-equality-freedom formula. Here, the state is big and active: thus long haul, collective undertakings aimed at influencing the state's never-resting decision-making machinery are crucial. A strong state needs vibrant intermediaries if democracy is to be reasonably representative. When intermediaries are weakened, so is the quality of democracy.

This, in essence, is our argument in the case of Norway. The quality of democracy is deteriorating because a "package" of closely connected institutional changes, brought on by the rise of the individualized egalitarian or promoted in the name of this citizen, has changed organizational structures in the voluntary sector, altered the role and autonomy of municipal institutions, and advanced new ideas about the modernization of the public sector. We will demonstrate the nature of these changes (although only briefly), how they are related, and why their effects upon a traditionally strong and robust democracy like Norway's are not benign.

New Institutional Features

The individualized egalitarians are not, as already indicated, disconnecting themselves from public life: they are not less likely to support causes that they feel strongly about, or more likely to shrug their shoulders if others stumble and fall. After all, the egalitarian instincts are still relatively strong. It is the traditional form of participation that is under pressure. Rather than being selfish, the individualized egalitarian seeks to avoid aspects of civic engagement that are seen as personally unrewarding:

- Large and bureaucratic institutions or organizations (too slow).
- Long-term commitments (too demanding).
- Administrative obligations (too boring).
- Ideology presenting encompassing analysis of what is wrong with society, and how to fix it (too political).
- Broad-ranging social solidarities (too collectivistic).

This means that an increasing number of people want to join voluntary organizations and take part in municipal decision-making only if they can do so on their own terms and with the growing expectation that others have the good sense, and ample personal resources, to do the same.

As a consequence of these preferences, the Norwegian voluntary and public sectors have undergone significant transformations over the last 20–25 years (the process of change is still gaining momentum). "New

Public Management" (NPM) is a catchphrase often used to describe what is going on. This and similar labels tend, in our opinion, to complicate things by drawing our attention to long lists of bullet-point features supposed to characterize the difference between "right now" and "back then" (and, to be sure, we have just committed the same offense). The bullet-point lists tend to include policy recommendations such as: horizontal and vertical differentiation (or specialization) of hierarchically integrated institutions, business-oriented leadership philosophies, management by objectives, outsourcing, downsizing, individual and short-term employment contracts, more differentiated salary structures, better quality of service, user/customer participation, budget discipline, cost reduction, etc. (see, for instance, Christensen and Lægreid 2001). Rather than relying on numerous bullet-points, we intend to follow Albert Einstein's dictum: everything should be made as simple as possible, but not simpler! What the transformations are all about, we propose, is the attempt to design so-called flexible forms of organization.[1]

Compared to their predecessors, these flexible organizations can be described in terms of three key features. First, they have a flatter hierarchical structure, which means fewer intermediate levels and more direct contact between the top and the bottom of hierarchies. Second, they operate with a shorter time frame. In other words, flat organizations are meant to work faster and better. The third feature is increasing centralization of power; that is, leaders are granted more authority in running the organization's activities.

The objective of flexible organization is to enable institutions to adapt more rapidly to their surroundings, which are assumed to be in a state of more or less continual flux. This rapid rate of change in organizational surroundings is closely related to the rise of the individualized egalitarian and to so-called globalization (which, in turn, is also assumed to be related to individualized egalitarianism). Because of their dislike of encompassing ideologies and of broad-ranging social solidarities, it is, for instance, taken for granted that the individualized egalitarians constitute a highly plural group of people with regard to personal tastes, political beliefs and cultural preferences. Flexible organizational structures are supposed to give the leaders a better feel of what a fragmented and volatile membership base wants, and a chance to adjust priorities accordingly. But quick adjustments to a rapidly changing environment engender greater centralization of power and authority, a trend that is augmented by the members' disdain of long-term commitments and administrative obligations.

The same reasoning is guiding public sector modernization. Here, it is argued that the nation-state's rigid and outmoded forms of government must be disassembled in order to compete globally and individualize (as far as possible) the production of public services. Thus, the idea has been to make the Norwegian welfare state more flexible and cost-effective. Favored aims are to streamline the professional welfare bureaucracy, shorten the duration of benefit schemes, tighten welfare qualification requirements, and commercialize service production. This represents, at least in part, a break with the prosperity-equality-freedom formula. Local governments, which are the most important welfare producers—responsible for the particularly heavy welfare services like basic health care, social benefit schemes and primary education[2]—are under pressure to deliver better services faster and at lower cost than before.

The institutional features of flexibility—again, flatter hierarchies (debureaucratization), shorter time frames (cost-effectiveness), and centralization of power (strong leadership)—constitute, in our view, the most fundamental problem facing Norwegian democracy today. Just as the increasing flexibility of the welfare state increases the distance between the citizen and central authorities, so will the increasing flexibility of the voluntary sector increase the distance between members and organizational elites. And just as making the welfare state more flexible tightens state control of local government, so will making voluntary organizations more flexible weaken members' political influence. In other words, more flexibility means weaker intermediaries—the democratic infrastructure is thinned out to shorten the national chain of command.

To fully appreciate how the flexible form of organization represents a break with the structural and ideological foundations of Norwegian democracy, we must turn to an issue of geography: the special relationship between the national center and the subject peripheries.

Center and Periphery

Nation-states are geographical entities that link central and peripheral areas in a common political system of governance. The center, usually the area around the capital, is where the most important political, cultural, economic, and financial institutions are located, while the periphery often consists of rural or non-urbanized areas located some distance from the center. The nation-state therefore demonstrates a more or less clear hierarchical structure, with central bodies and organizations at the top of the political/bureaucratic chain of command and regional and local peripheral bodies subject to central control. Nation-state democracy has developed in a process by which the people are integrated into the nation's governance by being included at the various levels in the hierarchical system, i.e. central, regional, and local. The democratic organization of the nation-state is thus a stable hierarchical order: popular demands and interests are communicated from the bottom up, while binding decisions are communicated from the top down. In most South and Central European countries, the justification for this hierarchical order is as follows: the center represents the modern and progressive, the periphery the more backward and primitive. The survival of the periphery must be ensured through its subjection to the political, cultural and economic leadership of the center. Only in this way can the periphery be brought up to the developmental level of the center.

Norwegians, however, have traditionally held a slightly different view of the relationship between center and periphery. True, Norwegians have also imagined that the farther one gets from the Oslo area, the further back in time one goes. But, instead of going to a primitive culture with no to-morrow, the voyage to the periphery has been interpreted as a journey back to the future: to a place where Norwegians find what is original and genuinely Norwegian (for instance, the idea of a glorious Viking past).

One has to understand that for approximately 400 years, Norway was subject to Danish rule. In 1814, Denmark, fighting on the losing side during the Napoleonic wars, ceded Norway to Sweden, and a personal union with Sweden was declared. This union lasted for almost ninety years. In 1905, Norway gained full independence as a constitutional and hereditary monarchy. But 500 years of foreign rule had left its mark: the urban merchant and administrative centers were thought to have been "contaminated" by outside influence. The proper basis for a new national identity and culture was therefore believed to be hidden in the dimly lit rural peripheries—the parts of the country where the tentacles of alien supremacy had made little impression. This means that for Norwegians, the periphery became both primitive and modern at the same time, in the sense that a reconstructed and synthesized version of periphery back-wardness was catapulted to the apex of Norwegian nationhood. Consequently, preservation of the periphery has been seen as defense of the nation. The idea that the periphery is the cultural cradle of the nation has been manifested in, among other things, Norway's regional and agricultural policy, the migration of Norwegians to mountains and fjords in their spare time and vacations, Norwegian skepticism regarding the European Union, anti-urbanism, and the acceptance of whale and seal hunting.[3]

The Norwegian hierarchical order has, as an outgrowth of this view, maintained three key features that are directly at odds with the structural characteristics of flexible organizations. First, the time frame has been one of historical continuity: that which is particularly Norwegian is found in the idea of the periphery's popular traditionalism rather than the center's avant-garde, elitist culture. Secondly, the ideological legitimacy of the periphery has lead to a relatively broad dispersion of power; in Norway, the area around the capital has not held the dominant political, cultural and economic position that it has in many other European countries.[4] And thirdly, in a mountainous country where the center is looked upon with suspicion, and where human dwellings are few and far between, the nurturing of intermediaries has been crucial for maintaining political unity. All this has had direct consequences for the structure of civil society and for the organization of state-municipal relations.

In the next section, we will first put the Norwegian voluntary sector in a European context end then take a look at the general trends in voluntary organization between 1940 and 2000. As we shall see, the rise of the individualized egalitarian and the advent of flexible forms of organization go hand-in-hand.

The Norwegian Civil Society in a European Context

In a comparative perspective the Norwegian voluntary sector of today can be described as relatively small, viewed in terms of employment and economics.[5] Including religion, the Norwegian voluntary sector had operating expenditures accounting for 3.7 percent of the country's gross domestic product. The paid workforce behind these expenditures equals 3.9 percent of all nonagricultural employees in the country. In comparison, the EU countries average 7 percent, ranging from Finland with 3.1 percent to the Netherlands with 12.7 percent.[6]

Even if the extent of paid employment is modest in a European perspective, the Norwegian voluntary sector commands considerable resources in terms of volunteer inputs. Indeed, as much as half the Norwegian population reports contributing time to voluntary organizations over one year. This translates into 6.8 percent of total nonagricultural employment in the country, compared to an average of just 4.2 percent in the EU countries.[7] Or, to put it differently, volunteering in Norway equals 26 full-time employees per 1,000 inhabitants, whereas the EU average is 20, ranging from Austria with just 5 to the UK and the Netherlands with 28 full-time employees per 1,000 inhabitants. Measured in this way, the volunteering rate of the Norwegian population is among the highest in the world.

In addition to volunteering extensively, Norwegians share an even greater propensity to join organizations as members. The total number of memberships in Norway is estimated at 8.4 million, which equals almost two per inhabitant. The field of culture and recreation attracts 36 percent of these members. Professional associations (21 percent), development and housing (13 percent), health (12 percent), civic and advocacy activities (6 percent), and religion (4 percent) comprise the bulk of the remaining memberships. According to the Survey on Giving and Volunteering (1998), 73 percent of the population were members of an organization, and 43 percent held two or more memberships (Wollebæk, Selle, and Lorentzen 2000). In comparative surveys, Norway ranks among the countries with the highest proportion of members in the population (Dekker and van den Broek 1998).

The extensive number of memberships means that the pool of resources from which organizations can draw is larger in Norway than in
most other countries. Many members drift in and out of more or less active roles and express the willingness to take part actively when needed
(Wollebæk et al. 2000: 84). Thus, extensive membership partly explains
high levels of volunteering. Moreover, the membership fees paid by passive members are very important for the organizations; in some respects
they are a functional equivalent to the private monetary donations found
in countries with a weaker membership tradition (e.g., the US).

When volunteers are added to paid workers, it is not only the size of
the sector that changes. In addition, the weight shifts dramatically to the
field of culture and recreation whose share rises from 12 to 37 percent,
making it by far the largest category. As a matter of fact, more than half
of all volunteering in the sector takes place here. This indicates the strong
position of sports and cultural organizations in the Norwegian population.
The categories development, religion, environment, and advocacy also
gain in their relative share. On the other hand, welfare services and professional organizations account for insignificant shares of volunteering.

Surprising to many, the Norwegian voluntary sector is more economically self-sustained than the EU average. As much as 56 percent of its
revenue comes from fees and charges, of which sales and membership
dues each account for around 21 percent of the total. In Sweden and Finland, the revenues from fees and charges are similarly high at 60 and 57
percent, compared to just 38 percent in the other EU countries. Furthermore, only 35 percent of the revenues of the voluntary sector in Norway
come from the public sector, compared to 55 percent in the EU countries. In Sweden and Finland, the corresponding figures are 29 and 36
percent—even lower than in the liberal UK. This is not in accordance
with the conventional image of the voluntary sectors in the social democratic Nordic countries as highly dependent on the public sector.

These numbers indicate that the Norwegian (and Scandinavian) civil
society is exceptional, compared to the EU countries. In order to fully
appreciate this execptionalism, we need to put it in an historical context.
What is the traditional structure of the Norwegian civil society, and why
do we now see profound changes in this structure? More importantly,
what may be the social and democratic ramifications of these changes?

The Traditional Structure of Civil Society
and the First Signs of Change

Organizations with origins in the labor movement, the agrarian movement, the counter-cultural movements (temperance, mission, and language), and health and social services were important players in the

grassroots mobilization that characterized the processes of democratization, nation building, and development of the welfare state in Norway (Rokkan 1970; Selle and Øymyr 1995).[8] These popular mass-movements brought together people from virtually every tiny and remote corner of the country. Of particular importance was the fact that they had ideological bases; in other words, they worked for social change and not only to promote the particular interests of their members. The organizations, hierarchically structured into local, regional and national levels, were democratically run; the members were their driving force.[9]

Moreover, they were cultural and social institutions that created a sense of security and coherence for individuals. For instance, temperance organizations influenced Norwegian alcohol policy and social policy, while laymen's organizations played an important role in the regulation of the relationship between church and state. In many rural societies ideologically influential temperance and mission associations were for a long time nearly the sole providers of culture and leisure activities. From the early twentieth century onward, the social and humanitarian organizations influenced public opinion, acted as watchdogs vis-à-vis the government, and initiated extensive welfare arrangements, which later became essential elements of the welfare state. Between 1945 and 1980, the total number of voluntary organizations almost doubled and the organizational society became much more differentiated. Later, during the 1990s there was no numerical growth, compared to an increase of 25 percent between 1980 and 1990 (Wollebæk and Selle 2002). But underneath this apparent stability, both the types of activities and the organizational structure of the associations were changing. Let us take a look at these changes.

In the period from the 1945 to 1960, public health, non-member benefit organizations with broad objectives expanded alongside the Norwegian welfare state.[10] But from the mid 1960s, the fastest-growing activities centered on recreation and culture, provided by musical groups, hobby associations, sports clubs, and associations for children and youths. Before 1960, however, such associations had been found mainly in and around the urban areas, usually as part of one of the popular mass-movements, and comprised only a modest segment of associational life. This shift in content shows that more people had more time and money on their hands, paving the way for the pursuit of recreational and private interests. Simultaneously, a shift in structure occurred. With the exception of sports clubs, most of the new leisure associations were independent of the broader popular mass-movements whose realm previously had extended to recreational activities.[11] This indicates that leisure activities were no longer primarily vehicles for promoting larger causes or ideologies, but instead were attributed intrinsic value: the individualized egalitarians were starting to influence the structure of Norwegian associationalism.

While organizations advocating group interests expanded in the health and services sector, organizations with broader and other-oriented objectives lost ground. Other popular mass-movements, in particular temperance and mission, also suffered recruitment problems and lack of innovation, the latter as part of a general secularization process running parallel with the changes in sex roles and increasing affluence. Previously outwardly directed organizations became more introverted as their support and importance diminished.

The signs of structural change from mass movements to smaller and nimbler organizations are, in short, discernible—not in Technicolor, perhaps, but clearly enough.[12] And these changes have significant ramifications for center-periphery relations.

From Mass-Movements to the New Associationalism

In spite of the formal hierarchical-bureaucratic structure of the traditional mass-movements, the local level was the most important. It was here that most of the organizational activity took place, and here that the mobilization potential was found. Also, local chapters enjoyed autonomy within the bureaucratic system of which they were part (though, of course, local-level autonomy was greater in some movements than in others). Because of this system, Norway (and partly the rest of Scandinavia), as opposed to most of the rest of Europe, developed a geographically and socially integrated organizational society. Elsewhere in Europe, the organizational society was often split in two: some organizations existed only locally, while others worked only at the national level. In Norway, such a division would have been virtually unthinkable: after all, how could there be political influence unless an organization's roots were firmly planted in the native soil from which, according to romantic notions, the nation grew: remote villages deep in the mountain valleys and fjords and along the North Sea coast?

The combination of ideological orientation and hierarchical integration that crosscut the center-periphery cleavage fostered two important characteristics: optimism and patience. For the organizations, optimism meant a belief that organizational participation and involvement could change society for the better, while patience meant a conviction that efforts toward social change would ultimately bear fruit in spite of periodic failure (which was only to be expected). Optimism and patience made it easier for members to endure the tedium of administration and to maintain the level of organizational activity. This means that the traditional mass-movements represented stable channels of communication between the political center and the peripheral local communities, and provided form and content to Norwegian democracy.

It is precisely this democratic infrastructure that is under increasing pressure from new, flexible organizational forms.[13] Starting around the mid 1960s, purely local organizations grew increasingly common, especially within the field of culture and recreation, as many of these had neither national nor political objectives. Gradually, therefore, the integrated local-national organizational society was challenged by the dual, European model. At the same time, a process of local centralization was having an impact on associational life. Small communities lost many of their previous functions and institutions (e.g., school, post office, local store), and improved communication infrastructures facilitated better and faster contact between small villages and municipal centers. Thus, organizational identity became less tied to the village community.

Despite these developments, the traditional organizational model did not disappear. In 1980, the vast majority of the local organizations were still part of bigger, democratic-hierarchical structures. But the model's hegemony was starting to erode, and this transformation gained momentum during the 1990s.

In sum, local associational life around 1990 distinguished itself in fundamental ways from associational life during the first two or three decades after the Second World War. First, the range and content of activities changed as new areas were opened up for voluntary work. The objectives became more private and individual; activity was more frequently directed toward the organizations' own members and less often toward the surrounding (local) society. Second, the gender composition changed dramatically, and acted as one of the main driving forces behind the process described above (Wollebæk and Selle 2002). Finally, organizational structures changed. The leading position once held by the democratic-hierarchical model was challenged. Of the newest organizations, i.e. those established during the 1990s, only a minority were linked up to national networks. As a result, the role of voluntary associations as identity-creating institutions was hollowed out, and participation seems to have become more random and short-term. Increasingly, volunteering takes place outside the membership institution, thus weakening the ties between the volunteer and the organization and shortening the average lifespan of organizations.

Here we have it, then: the individualized egalitarians, by opting for smaller and faster-moving associations that are not overtly political or rooted in traditional social solidarities, are producing a civil society that features as a chief attribute flexibility. But, the flattening of organizational hierarchy means, first, that the new associations are less able to integrate across the center-periphery divide. Between the local and national levels, the channels of communication and influence are either absent or extremely weak. Consequently, more and more people are less and less part of the process by which the state exercises power: the organizational society is increasingly unable to bring the needs and wishes of ordinary citizens out of the local community and into the national arena. At the same time, it becomes difficult to gain popular acceptance for decisions made centrally, because support of, or opposition to, various public policies is usually ad hoc, media-driven, and fragmented.

Second, a shorter time frame means that organizational activity must be tailored to the members' particular needs or interests. This coincides with the decline of ideology: the belief that voluntary involvement can bring about social change is losing out to the idea that the individual must feel some personal fulfillment and satisfaction from his or her participation. If participation is not sufficiently suited to individual needs, the members rapidly drop out. Ideological optimism and patience are therefore not resources that the flexible organizational society tends to foster. Membership turnover has increased, and it is difficult to recruit members to work at long-term tasks, particularly administrative ones.

Third, the shortened time frame also seems to lead to increased centralization of power and professionalization. This is particularly true for larger organizations operating at the national level, but the tendencies are also quite visible at the local level. As members avoid administrative work, outside help must be hired to keep up the level of activity, making organizations more dependent on public or private sponsors to finance the hiring of outside expertise. But since external funding often brings with it specifications and conditions regarding how the funds are to be spent, dependence on sponsors tends to leads to a less autonomous organization. This, in turn, means that a flexible civil society is less able to function as a political and ideological counterpart to the state and the market.[14] And, of course, professionalization and more external monitoring cause centralization of power: ordinary members have less say in what the organization does, while the leadership has more. Even so, leadership influence is largely a result of the weak identification of the members with their organization.

Flatter organizational hierarchies, shorter time frames for membership and participation, and greater centralization of power and professionalization tell us something about changes in the relationship between center and periphery in Norwegian politics: If the traditional organizational society assumed the form it did as a result of the special significance of the periphery in the nation-building project, then it is also likely that flexible associationalism's break with traditional structures indicates that the national significance of the periphery is declining. And when the cultural position of the periphery is in decline, organizations can be scaled back and made more flexible: after all, in this situation they do not need to build up large-scale democratic-bureaucratic structures to mobilize support and to gain popular legitimacy. In other words, the political influence and legitimacy of flexible organizations is not dependent on their presence in the periphery, but has become more dependent on the quality of full- or part-time staffers, and on their ability to stage events that pique the curiosity of the mass media.

The assertion that moving from center to periphery is to a lesser degree understood as a journey back to the future is also supported by changes in the relationship between state and local government. While municipal governments were previously considered core democratic institutions and progressive welfare pioneers, they tend now to be portrayed as obstacles to improved public services.

The State-Municipality Relation: Structure and Development

For quite some time, the Norwegian Municipality Act of 1837 held a special position in the collective Norwegian consciousness because it had established democratically elected, local institutions of self-rule in the peripheries (prior to 1837, only the cities had local political institutions. See, for instance, Pryser 1999; Bugge 1986). Even so, the political autonomy of the 430 municipalities (with an average population of less than 10,000) enjoyed no particular judicial protection—it was up to the central institutions (the parliament) to decide the scope and depth of municipal autonomy. Nevertheless, the municipalities have become powerful bodies, with responsibility for local infrastructure and the most important welfare state services.[15] Most income tax is collected locally (within limits decided by the national parliament), and the municipal authorities can take upon themselves any task that the state, through national legislation, has not explicitly defined as belonging to central or regional governments. But over the last two or three decades, local politics has increasingly become a matter of administering decisions imposed by central government—either because of the increasing number of national laws regulating the implementation of welfare schemes, or because of tighter state control of local government expenditures, or both (Fimreite, Flo, and Tranvik 2002).

The enthusiasm for the Municipality Act of 1837 highlights the fact that the political system consists of two levels that are mutually dependent: state and municipality. Mutual dependence means that if the democratic system is diminished at the local level, then introducing more democracy at the state level cannot compensate for the loss that ensues. The books cannot be balanced like this because municipal democracy is meant to advance goals that the state is unable or unsuited to cater to. A decline in municipal democracy will therefore result in an impoverished democratic system at large.[16]

Even though the authority and jurisdiction of the municipality as an institution are not even mentioned in Norway's constitution, the qualities

embedded in local government have equipped it with a strong normative suit of armor to protect against state centralization of power, control, and regulation. The legitimacy of the municipalities, like that of the
corresponding level in civil society, must be understood in light of the
particular Norwegian interpretation of the center-periphery relationship:
that, since the local communities in the periphery represented a very important economic and cultural resource for the country as a whole, it was
only natural that they were given the opportunity to govern themselves
in a meaningful way. These units, like organizations in the civil society,
were vital in linking small, and often remote, communities and social groups
more tightly to national-level entities (Tranvik and Selle 2003). Thus, the
municipal governments brought the state closer to the people and, at the
same time, the people closer to the state.

To begin with, however, municipal self-government had been neither
a bastion of local democracy nor a tool for welfare state expansion, but
rather a convenient way of dividing power between the two most powerful social groups in nineteenth century Norway: the state-building bureaucratic elites, and the peasants (farmers or smallholders) in the periphery
(Rokkan 1987). This system of power-sharing meant that the peasants controlled the level of taxation (at the time, all taxes were issued and collected locally), while the state-building elites maintained a firm grip on
the national executive institutions.[17] The period from 1837 to 1890 can
therefore be characterized in terms of modest levels of municipal activity: the peasants were mainly interested in keeping taxation low, which
implied that most local authorities lacked the necessary funding to initi-
ate welfare programs or other types of public services (Flo 2003; Næss
et al. 1987). On the other hand, local government democratization was
a significant trend during the same period, intimately linked to the expansion, and the democratic importance, of the voluntary sector: the rise
of organized activism (mass mobilization) produced competing political
elites that participated in voluntary associations and served as elected
representatives locally.[18] Suffrage was gradually extended to new groups
of citizens, and political power, which initially had been widely dispersed
among different municipal institutions, was centralized in the hands of
the democratically elected Council of Local Representatives (Hovland
1986). Especially significant was the fact that all financial decisions (taxation, budgets, etc.) had to be approved by the democratically elected
councils.

The next period, from around 1890 to the beginning of the Second
World War, proved to be a roller coaster for the local governments: great
optimism and expansion culminated in financial crises and tighter state
regulation. This period coincided with the rise of the industrial working
class and provoked a new type of political dynamics that, in part, explains municipal boom and bust: two political parties—the Liberals and

the Social-Democrats—competed for the working-class vote. Particularly in the biggest cities, this competition set off a race to introduce local welfare schemes in order to harness working-class support. The third main party, the Conservatives, tried to limit local welfare costs, but managed only to contribute to further expansion (Danielsen 1986). Like the welfare schemes, municipal investments in infrastructure (like roads, telephone and electricity networks, public transportation, and sanitation, etc.) and in local hydroelectric power plants made new demands on the public purse—to be financed either through higher taxes or, especially, by private loans. When the post-1920 economy dipped, many municipalities were unable to meet their financial obligations, resulting in local government crises. The Social Democratic Party blamed central government for this sorry state of affairs (it had obstructed, by means of tax legislation, local welfare expansion, the party claimed), while the Liberals and particularly the Conservatives blamed it on municipal recklessness. But toward the end of the interwar years, the views of the contesting parties started to converge. The financial aspects of the crises were played down, while tighter state regulation of municipal decision-making and greater economic redistribution among local governments was advanced as the solution to what was now interpreted as the real, underlying problem: socioeconomic inequalities between municipalities (Danielsen, Grønlie, and Hovland 1987).

When welfare state expansion began in earnest after the Second World War, it was time to put the hard-won prewar wisdom to the test. Despite discord over the size and scope of public welfare responsibilities, all parties agreed, to a greater or lesser extent, that local government had an important part to play in the welfare state project, not least because of the logic of the prosperity-equality-freedom formula: the special democratic qualities of local government had to be exploited if the national wealth was to benefit everyone. For this to happen, institutional reform on the municipal level was imperative. The amalgamation of municipalities—in order to facilitate greater administrative capacity, broaden the local tax-base, and strengthen bureaucratic expertise—was seen as particularly crucial if local governments were to deal effectively with new and wide-ranging responsibilities (primary education, basic health services, homes for the elderly, social benefits of various kinds, etc.). Institutional reform was especially important in the geographical peripheries, where municipalities were often small in terms of population and economic resources (consequently, periphery areas benefited handsomely from state mandated redistribution of financial resources from richer to poorer municipalities).

At the same time, it was crucial that state regulations did not encroach too much on local-level autonomy (Flo 2003). After all, it was this autonomy that had to be exploited if the welfare state project was to succeed. Municipal reform was therefore an attempt to strengthen local level autonomy by providing the necessary means to produce and deliver municipal services within the limits of discretion decided by central government. This implies that during the first few decades after the Second World War, local government still played a role as welfare pioneer. Typically, welfare schemes were introduced by a couple of vanguard municipalities, and once a "critical mass" had implemented the same schemes, the national authorities enacted legislation obliging all local governments to offer the services in question (Grønlie 1987).

But ever since the early 1970s, the seemingly never-ending expansion of public welfare services—together with the accompanying national legislation regarding the duties and responsibilities of local government, and greater dependence on central government grants—was increasingly interpreted as producing a "democratic deficit" at the municipal level: the more public services were offered locally, the less local control was exercised over municipal priorities (this may be one reason why turnout in local elections fell from 81 percent in 1963 to 57 percent in 2003). In the same vein, it was argued that the bureaucratization and professionalization of local administration led to a reduction in lay participation at the municipal level, and narrowed the opportunity to adapt welfare schemes to local conditions. Over the last 15 years or so, municipal autonomy seems to have turned into a problem because it can result in differences between the welfare systems of different municipalities, which are likely to be viewed, by citizens and politicians alike, as signs of unacceptable inequality. Consequently, the hunt is on for a national strategy to ensure the highest possible degree of egalitarian individualization.

The quest for egalitarian individualization started in the late 1980s and reached a highpoint with the new Municipality Act of 1992. The goal of this piece of legislation was to give municipal authorities more autonomy to organize administrative processes differently, to encourage municipalities to introduce clearer separation of political and administrative functions, and to promote increased service production according to local needs and wishes (a precondition for this, which still has not been met, was that the municipalities would be able to spend central government grants more freely than previously) (Bernt, Overå, and Hove 2002; Bernt 2001).[19] But, since differences in local welfare priorities were increasingly seen as a problem, new national legislation was introduced, guaranteeing individuals access to custom-made services regardless of place of habitation. Simultaneously, national standards proliferated, designed to govern the content and quality of locally produced services (spurred, to some extent, by well-organized professional interests, various trade unions, and other special interest groups).

This means that the same types of individual needs should, in principle, be treated equally in all of the 433 municipalities, which, of course, is the essence of egalitarian individualization. But it also means that nowadays local democratic processes may be bypassed: the number, quality and types of services offered stem less from local political decision-making and more from legally binding guarantees or national standards issued by central government (municipal implementation of legislation and national quality-of-service standards are carefully monitored through, for instance, central control agencies, ombudsmen, new auditing routines, and detailed local-central reporting systems; see Tranvik and Fimreite 2004). Local governments may therefore be freer to organize themselves as they see fit, but this matters little as long as the central government keeps issuing legislation that individualizes welfare claims—and, we might add, as long as sameness across municipalities is expected.[20] The point is that if people on opposite sides of the same fjord cannot do things slightly differently, then local government has lost some of its democratic significance, as it is less able to take initiatives that will make a difference in the everyday lives of ordinary people.

At the same time, the significance of earmarked grants from the central government, which are not open to municipal prioritizing but are designated for the provision of specific local welfare services, has increased over the last fifteen years. In 1998, earmarked grants constituted 17 percent of the municipal sector's total revenues, compared to 10 percent a decade earlier (Proposition to Parliament no. 150, 1999–2000). And over the same period, the number of national laws regulating various aspects of local government administration and service provision increased by 50 percent (Fimreite et al. 2004). These trends indicate that central government control is encroaching upon municipal autonomy, even as surveys conducted among local politicians and bureaucrats conclude that the reaction on the municipal level is greater distrust in central government (see Andersen, Buanes, and Aarsæther 2002; Jacobsen 2002).

Municipal Flexibility and Center-Periphery Relations

In sum, the key features of the development of the state-municipal relationship in Norway are: the introduction of individualized welfare rights, greater state regulation and financial control, and de-politicization of local democracy. These trends are intimately connected to the flexible organization form. The flattening of the hierarchical structure of the Norwegian political-administrative system is linked to the de-politicization at the local level: the municipality is weakened as a political institution as the direct link between citizen and state is shortened and strengthened. Many Norwegians regard this development with enthusiasm, believing that flatter hierarchies mean more democracy. But when the relationship between state and citizen becomes more direct, the citizens' position is more precarious than before because the intermediate level in the hierarchical pyramid, i.e. organizations in the civil sector and municipal government, no longer contributes to a spreading out of political power. Moreover, as intermediate levels are thinned out, the collective force these interconnected institutions once gave to popular demands becomes weaker, and power is concentrated at the central level.[21]

Behind the atrophy of the hierarchical chain of governance lies a shift in the time frame, namely the idea that one shouldn't have to wait for welfare. Getting state-guaranteed services today is more important than getting locally tailored services tomorrow. There seems to be little patience with the local political process, because neither the state nor the users of public services have time to wait for local governments to decide how to prioritize various welfare objectives (and they may not like the rank-order of local prioritizing). If we look ahead a bit, it is therefore likely that the activity of local governments will be pared back to areas in which there is a genuine local concern, for example, cultural affairs, planning, building and zoning, some areas of communications and transport, etc. If so, we will see the same situation emerge in the area of local government, as we saw in the organizational sector: a divided system in which what remains of local politics is separate from national politics.

As in the organizational sector, the development of a divided system signals a center-periphery relationship in transition. The periphery seems to lack the ability to, or not to believe that it actually does, represent values of importance to the nation as such—values that should be played out when national policies are implemented locally.[22] This is evident in that the citizen is redefined as a service "user," which is the role of the individualized egalitarian. The difference between citizen and individualized egalitarian is that while citizens are the bearers of interests, values, and needs that are specific to particular places, this is not the case for individualized egalitarians, who are assumed to have relatively uniform interests and needs regardless of where they live. The citizen therefore depends on opportunities for local influence to fulfill his or her specific objectives, while the needs of the individualized egalitarian can be met by anyone, anywhere—locally or centrally, privately or publicly—as long as the state provides the required legal and financial guarantees. The point is that once the cultural position of the periphery is no longer strong enough to provide a solid justification for a viable and meaningful local democracy, it is not particularly surprising that the "situated" citizen is less of a role model for public policy than the standardized and individualized egalitarian.

NPM in the Public and Voluntary Sectors

The ongoing developments in the voluntary and local government sectors must be seen in light of the neoliberal New Public Management ideology. This ideology is now providing the direction for the modernization push in the public sector. Within this program, strong hierarchical steering is combined with decentralization of executive work and a scaling back of state responsibilities, in order to achieve greater value for money (cost-effectiveness). One might have expected a heated political debate about this ideology, especially in a traditionally "state-friendly" country like Norway. But, apart from some disagreement concerning the degree of privatization and outsourcing, political parties across the spectrum seems to support NPM reforms. Meanwhile, the modernization program may further undermine the democratic foundations that underlie the organizational society and municipal government (see, for instance, Tranøy and Østerud 2001; Tranvik and Selle 2003).

The reason for this pessimistic assessment is simple. When cost-effectiveness is priority number one, the role of voluntary organizations and municipal government is redefined. In place of bridging the gap between the state and citizens, their chief role is now to implement public policies—that is, they are increasingly seen as instruments for realizing national policy aims. If the national authorities suspect that a voluntary organization or municipal government is not providing the desired value for money, it is either regulated and monitored more thoroughly by central agencies, or it is forced to compete with market actors for government contracts, or both. The idea that these intermediate levels represent democratic values that central institutions and market actors are poorly suited to cultivate cuts little ice, as long as the NPM ideology is focused on how to achieve more public service output with less input.

In conclusion, then, we can say that the successful implementation of the prosperity-equality-freedom formula has set off a chain reaction that is weakening the Norwegian democratic infrastructure: (1) the rise of the individualized egalitarian, when the national wealth is unmanageably large and well distributed among the citizens, fosters a belief that everyone has the personal resources needed to represent their own interests; (2) this leads to a turning away from large-scale ideological mass-movements and produces greater interest in smaller, flexible, non-ideological organizations that are better at catering to individual needs and wishes, but poorer at plugging members into the central decision-making institutions; (3) at the same time, flexible forms of organizing are introduced in the municipal sector, but local-level autonomy is hollowed out as individualized service schemes are imposed by the central government; (4) the New Public Management ideology, with its focus on cost-effectiveness, sees little value in the democratic role of voluntary organizations and municipal government, which are increasingly redefined as national policy implementers.

The accumulated effect of these developments may be that the center-periphery-relations, so important for understanding the structure of

Norwegian democracy, are undergoing profound changes. From being grounded in relations of popular influence and participation, they may now have come to more resemble the mechanics of centralized steering.

Notes

1. The dotcoms of the "new economy" are probably the best and purest examples of "flexibilization," but social movements like the multi-national, anti-globalization organization Attac share many of the same features. The important thing, however, is that the flexible form is now an entrenched organizational model that has spread far beyond its original core area, i.e. the "new economy" and social movements (see, for instance, Bourdieu 1998, Castells 2001 and Sennett 2003).
2. These three welfare sectors—health care, social benefits and education—represented three-quarters of local government expenditures in 2000. In 1998, 20 percent of the Norwegian work force was employed by local government (Østerud et al. 2003: 108).
3. For an extensive discussion, see Grendstad et al. (2004).
4. Level of urbanization is an indication of the traditionally strong cultural and economic position of the Norwegian periphery. In 1960, 16 percent of the Norwegian population lived in localities of 100,000 inhabitants or more, while Germany, for instance, reached this level of urbanization in 1900, Denmark in 1901, and Sweden around 1930 (Flora, Kraus, and Pfenning 1987).
5. The data in this section are taken from Sivesind et al. (2002), the main publication of the Norwegian part of the Johns Hopkins Comparative Nonprofit Sector Project (CNP), which included more than 40 countries.
6. In the following this means Austria, Finland, France, Germany, Ireland, the Netherlands, and the UK, which are the seven EU-countries in the Johns Hopkins Comparative Nonprofit Sector Project (CNP) that include religion in their figures for 1995. See Salamon et al. (1999).
7. The hours of volunteering are summed up to full time equivalent (FTE) employment to illustrate the amount of this kind of activity in relation to paid work. We do not assume that all kinds of volunteering correspond to paid employment or that volunteering would be worth a normal hourly pay in all cases. It is moreover acknowledged that a strong element of self-interest is sometimes involved. Volunteering still represents important resources for the voluntary organizations, and this may be precisely because the work is motivated by considerations other than pay.
8. The historical trends presented in the next section stem from a project entitled "Organizations in Hordaland" (POH), which consists of a survey of all organizational life in rural municipalities in the Norwegian province of Hordaland in 1980, 1990, and 2000 (Selle and Øymyr 1995; Wollebæk and Selle 2002), and a systematization of the 1940–41 Nazi registration of all voluntary organizations (Leipart and Selle 1983). Even though the data have been collected only from one of Norway's 19 provinces, we believe the developments we discern here are valid for the remainder of the country. In 1980, 4,500 organizations were registered. Each received a comprehensive questionnaire, to which approximately 2,500 responded (Leipart and Selle 1984). The next registration, in 1988 (Selle and Øymyr 1989), collected information concerning organizational structure and membership. In 1998/99, new data were gathered as part of the "Johns Hopkins Comparative Nonprofit Sector Project" (Wollebæk and Selle 2002). On this occasion, five of thirty-three local communities opted out of the project. All registered organizations received a questionnaire, to which 60 percent responded. Two other provinces, Buskerud and Finnmark, were also included for 1940 and 1990.

9. These characteristics are in many ways similar to what Skocpol (2003) finds for the United States.

10. In the Norwegian (and Scandinavian) case there is no inverse relationship between welfare state expansion and the strength of the voluntary sector. This undermines core assumptions in much of the civil society/social capital literature.

11. Many of the new local leisure organizations nevertheless chose an organizational form that linked them to national organizations, despite being independent of the popular mass-movements. This underlines the importance of generation. In the early expansion phase of the leisure sector, hierarchical structure was still predominant in organizational life, and the newly established organizations often chose this structure even if the nature of their activities suggested that it was superfluous. Today, most leisure organizations stay clear of national organizations. Alternative models are more accessible, in both a structural and cognitive sense (see Wollebæk and Selle 2002).

12. For a detailed analysis of these important changes, see Wollebæk and Selle (2002) and Tranvik and Selle (2003).

13. Associational life at the grassroots level is open and dynamic; it is easy to establish a new group and equally easy to wind it up. Thus, changes in the surroundings surface as new organizational forms and purposes at a higher pace than is the case in the public and the private sector (Dekker and van den Broek 1998; Schofer and Fourcade-Gourinchas 2001; Sivesind et al. 2002).

14. As Verba et al. (1995) and Smith (1997) have pointed out, most types of associations take political stands once their interests are involved. However, we see clear limitations to the value of the democratic involvement of purely local benefit associations. More often than not, the issues they raise concern specific interests on the part of the associations (e.g., funding for improved training facilities or getting a hole in the road fixed) and their efforts are almost always restricted to the local level. By contrast, the translocalism of the historically dominant mass-movements enabled local branches to address broader issues with much greater political impact on a larger scale.

15. The provincial (or regional) level of government was for a long time relatively weak: representatives to the regional councils were indirectly elected (appointed by the directly elected local councils), and they had no independent sources of funding. This changed in 1975, when the regional councils, for the first time, were elected by the people and gained the power to levy a special tax. Since then, however, the regional level has been systematically weakened—by lack of popular interest/support and by state policy (for instance, in 2002, the state took over the responsibility for the regional hospitals—the single most important regional government task). So, even if we do not include the regional level in our discussion, the developments here seem to confirm our message: the political system is gradually getting more centralized.

16. What democratic qualities are expressed at the local level? First, the idea that people should have an opportunity to take part in the local political-administrative processes. Second, the idea that democracy should be exercised where people live. And finally, effectiveness in setting priorities: national schemes and arrangements should be implemented and adapted to local conditions in the individual municipality (for discussion of the various roles and functions of local governments, see Wickwar 1970).

17. This arrangement worked well for about forty years. But during the 1870s, a majority of representatives in the national parliament, consisting mainly of peasants and urban liberals, started to demand that the executive branch of government (the cabinet), controlled by the state-building elites, answer to parliament. In 1884, parliamentarism was introduced: the coalition of periphery interests and urban liberals demolished the constitutionally protected power base of the state-building elites, and the cabinet subsequently had to maintain support in parliament in order to stay in power.

18. It is not for this article to decide which of the two main democratic institutions—local government or voluntary organizations—was the most important for national

integration at different periods of time, but they were definitely strongly interrelated. For instance, representatives coming from the voluntary sector have always played an important role in local government. The same mechanism has been observed in the United States (see Skocpol 2003 and 1992).

19. Case studies indicate that clearer separation of political and administrative functions has two main effects: less coordination between different service-producing entities (as they are expected to run themselves according to business management practices), and fewer opportunities for local representatives to influence the decisions made by these entities (as they are removed from the politicians' sphere of power) (Michelsen, Ramsdal, and Aarseth 2002).

20. The most significant effect of individualized and legally guaranteed welfare claims does not seem to be that citizens go to court if they feel that they do not get what they are entitled to. Rather, the main outcome is greater popular pressure on municipal and national authorities to standardize service production according to individual needs and wishes.

21. It is, however, true that some minorities (like the handicapped) are in need of special rights in order to enjoy the same benefits as the majority. This may make direct judicial links between central institutions and individual citizens desirable. But our point is that if every individual, and not only minorities, has the right to special protection from local prioritizing, the strength of municipal institutions will suffer. And such protections may not do the minorities much good either, since their rights will not be that special anymore.

22. Local government is of course not the same as periphery government. There are local governments in central areas too, but the legitimacy of municipal self-rule is closely connected to the "national ideology of the geographical periphery."

References

Andersen, Magnar, Arild Buanes, and Nils Aarsæther. 2002. *Kommunene ser staten. En sammenlikning av det kommunale lederskapets holdninger i 1976 og år 2000.* The Norwegian Study of Power and Democracy, report no. 51. Oslo: Unipub.

Bernt, Jan Fridthjof. 2001. "Kveler velferdsstaten kommunaldemokratiet?" In *Lekmannsstyret under press. Festskrift til Audun Offerdal,* ed. Anne Lise Fimreite, Helge O. Larsen and Jacob Aars. Oslo: Kommuneforlaget.

Bernt, Jan Fridthjof, Oddvar Overå, and Harald Hove. 2002. *Kommunalrett.* Oslo: Universitetsforlaget.

Bourdieu, Pierre. 1998. *Acts of Resistance. Against the New Myths of Our Time.* Cambridge: Polity Press.

Bugge, Ivar. 1986. *Kommunal forvaltning.* Oslo: Kommuneforlaget.

Castells, Manuel. 2001. *The Internet Galaxy. Reflections on the Internet, Business, and Society.* Oxford: Oxford University Press.

Christensen, Tom and Per Lægreid, eds. 2001. *New Public Management: The Transformation of Ideas and Practice.* Aldershot: Ashgate.

Danielsen, Rolf, Tore Grønlie, and Edgar Hovland. 1987. "Trengselstider. 1920–1945." In *Folkestyre i by og bygd. Norske kommuner gjennom 150 år,* ed. Hans Eyvind Næss, Edgar Hovland, Tore Grønlie, Harald Baldersheim, and Rolf Danielsen. Oslo: Universitetsforlaget.

Danielsen, Rolf. 1986. "Kommunaliseringsprosessen i norske byer, 1880–1920." In *Nordisk lokalhistoria: Lokal Praxis på det sociala området i de nordiska länderna,1800–1920,* ed. Ingrid Hammarstrøm and Lars Nilsson. Seminar report nr. 4. Stockholm: Stadshistoriska Institutet.

Dekker, Paul, and A. van den Broek. 1998. "Civil Society in Comparative Perspective: Involvement in Voluntary Associations in North America and Western Europe." *Voluntas* 9, no. 1: 11–38,

Fimreite, Anne Lise, Yngve Flo, and Tommy Tranvik. 2002. *Lokalt handlingsrom og nasjonal integrasjon. Kommuneideologiske brytninger i Norge i et historisk perspektiv.* The Norwegian Study of Power and Democracy, report no. 50. Oslo: Unipub.

Fimreite, Anne Lise, Yngve Flo, Tommy Tranvik, and Jacob Aars. 2004. *Tillitsforholdet mellom forvaltningsnivåene* (forthcoming).

Flo, Yngve. 2003. *Det lokale og det nasjonale: statlig politikk overfor det lokale og regionale styringsverket frå 1900 og til i dag.* The Norwegian Study of Power and Democracy, report no. 65. Oslo: Unipub.

Flora, Peter, Franz Kraus, and Winfried Pfenning. 1987. *State, Economy, and Society in Western Europe, 1815–1975.* Frankfurt: Campus Verlag.

Grendstad, Gunnar, Øystein Bortne, Per Selle, and Kristin Strømsnes. 2004. *Anomalous Environmentalism.* New York: Kluwer Academic/Plenum Publishers.

Grønlie, Tore. 1987. "Velferdskommune og utjevningsstat. 1945–1970." In *Folkestyre i by og bygd. Norske kommuner gjennom 150 år,* ed. Hans Eyvind Næss, Edgar Hovland, Tore Grønlie, Harald Baldersheim, and Rolf Danielsen. Oslo: Universitetsforlaget.

Hovland, Edgar. 1986. "Fra bygdekommisjon til kommunestyre. Trekk ved lokalstyret I norske bygder på 1800-tallet." In *Nordisk lokalhistoria: Lokal Praxis på det sociala området i de nordiska länderna, 1800–1920,* ed. Ingrid Hammarstrøm and Lars Nilsson. Seminar report no. 4. Stockholm: Stadshistoriska Institutet.

Jacobsen, Dag Ingvar. 2002. *Kommunepolitikere og kommunale byråkrater – hånd i hånd eller mann mot mann.* The Norwegian Study of Power and Democracy, report no. 40. Oslo: Unipub.

Leipart, Jorn, and Per Selle. 1983. *Organisasjonane i Hordaland 1941.* Bergen: Hordaland Fylkeskommune.

——— 1984. *Organisasjonane i Hordaland 1980.* Bergen: Hordaland Fylkeskommune.

Michelsen, Svein, Helge Ramsdal, and Turid Aarseth. 2002. "Kommunal organisering og posisjoneringa av profesjonane." In *Den nye kommunen. Kommunal organisering i endring,* ed. Oddbjørn Bukve and Audun Offerdal. Oslo: Det Norske Samlaget.

Næss, Hans Eyvind, Edgar Hovland, Tore Grønlie, Harald Baldersheim, and Rolf Danielsen, eds. 1987. *Folkestyre i by og bygd. Norske kommuner gjennom 150 år.* Oslo: Universitetsforlaget.

Proposition to Parliament no. 150, 1999–2000. Available at http://odin.dep.no.

Pryser, Tore. 1999. *Norsk historie 1814–1860. Frå standssamfunn mot klassesamfunn.* Oslo: Det norske samlaget.

Rokkan, Stein. 1970. *Citizens, Elections, Parties: Approaches to the Comparative Study of the Processes of Development*. Oslo: Universitetsforlaget.

—— 1987. *Stat, nasjon, klasse. Essays i politisk sosiologi*. Oslo: Universitetsforlaget.

Salamon, Lester M., Helmut K Anheiher, and Associates. 1999. *Global Civil Society: Dimensions of the Nonprofit Sector*. Baltimore, MD: The Johns Hopkins Center for Civil Society Studies.

Schofer, Evan, and Marion Fourcade-Gourinchas. 2001. "The structural contexts of civic engagement: Voluntary association membership in comparative perspective." *American Sociological Review* 66 (December): 806–828.

Selle, Per and Bjarne Øymyr. 1989. *Frivillege organisasjonar i Hordaland 1987/88*. LOS, report no. 1. Bergen: LOS-senteret.

—— 1995. *Frivillig organisering og demokrati: det frivillige organisasjonssamfunnet endrar seg, 1940–1990*. Oslo: Samlaget.

Sennett, Richard. 2003. *Respect in a World of Inequality*. New York: W.W. Norton & Company.

Sivesind, Karl Henrik, Håkon Lorentzen, Per Selle, and Dag Wollebæk. 2002. *The Voluntary Sector in Norway. Composition, Changes, and Causes*. Oslo: Institutt for samfunnsforskning.

Skocpol, Theda. 1992. *Protecting Soldiers and Mothers. The Political Origins of Social Policy in the United States*. Cambridge, MA: The Belknap Press.

—— 2003. *Diminished Democracy: From Membership to Management in American Civil Life*. Norman: University of Oklahoma Press.

Smith, David Horton. 1997. "The International History of Grassroots Associations." In *International Journal of Comparative Sociology* 38, no. 3: 189–216.

Tranvik, Tommy, and Anne Lise Fimreite. 2004. "Starkare stat, svagare lokalstyre? Demokratiska konsekvenser av kommunala reformer." In *Medborgare eller målsägare: sociala rättigheter och välfärdspolitiska dilemman*, ed. Åsa Ehinger Berling (Ansvarsprojektet): Stockholm: Svenska kommunförbundet, Landstingförbundet.

Tranvik, Tommy, and Per Selle. 2003. *Farvel til folkestyret? Staten og de nye nettverkene*. Oslo: Gyldendal Akademiske.

Tranøy, Bent Sofus, and Øyvind Østerud, eds. 2001. *Den fragmenterte staten. Reformer, makt og styring*. Oslo: Gyldendal Akademiske.

Verba, Sidney, Key L. Schlozman, and Henry E. Brady. 1995. *Voice and Equality. Civic Voluntarism in American Politics*. Cambridge, MA: Harvard University Press.

Wickwar, W. Hardy. 1970. *The Political Theory of Local Government*. Columbia, SC: University of South Carolina Press.

Wollebæk, Dag, and Per Selle. 2002. *Det nye organisasjonssamfunnet. Demokrati i endring*. Bergen: Fagbokforlaget.

Wollebæk, Dag, Per Selle, and Håkon Lorentzen. 2000. *Frivillig innsats. Sosial integrasjon, demokrati og økonomi*. Bergen: Fagbokforlaget.

Østerud, Øyvind, Fredrik Engelstad, and Per Selle. 2003. *Makten og demokratiet. En sluttbok fra Makt- og demokratiutredningen*. Oslo: Gyldendal Akademiske.

Chapter 7

THE STATE AND CIVIL SOCIETY IN A HISTORICAL PERSPECTIVE: THE SWEDISH CASE

Bo Rothstein and Lars Trägårdh

Introduction

As several chapters in this book show, the size, character, and perception of civil society differ quite substantially between Western democracies. In this chapter we will attempt to address the question of why this is the case. In particular, we will focus on the *relations between* state and civil society in Sweden. Our argument will be based on what in political science and sociology is known as the historical institutionalist approach, a way to analyze agency in a context of formal and informal "standard operating procedures" (Mahoney and Rueschmeyer 2003; Pierson 2000; Pierson 2004; Thelen 1999). We illustrate our claims through the analysis of a special empirical case, namely the relation between the Swedish state and the labor movement at the time when most western countries democratized. We argue that this relation, as it historically developed, became a template for how the state should interact with other interest groups and voluntary associations during the rest of the twentieth century and into the present (Rothstein 1992, Öberg and Svensson 2002).[1]

To put the analysis of Sweden's state-civil society relations in perspective, it is important to emphasize that the concept of civil society, such as it was launched into the international academic and political discourse of the early 1990s, was embedded in the narrative structure of Anglo-American citizenship theory (Somers 1995a; Somers 1995b). Civil society was thus understood as a sphere sharply demarcated against the state. (It was also conceived as distinct, though less so, from the market and family relations.) Adhering to classical liberal notions of the proper relationship between state and society, civil society was viewed in largely positive terms as the realm within which the "natural," "free," and "spontaneous" interplay between individuals occurred, while the state, though necessary to provide order and protection, must always be viewed with suspicion and be subject to variety of safeguards to ensure the continued liberties of the citizenry.

As this concept of civil society was imported into Sweden, the reaction was a complex and often confused one (Trägårdh 1999; Trägårdh chapter in this book). For those on the neoliberal and communitarian right, it represented a political opportunity to formulate a potent critique of the Social Democratic "cradle-to-the-grave" welfare state (Zetterberg 1995); for those on the welfare-statist left it conversely appeared as a fundamental threat to their political ambitions (Antman 1993). Academicians who became engaged in this debate reacted with some bewilderment. For some, who were well versed in the fundamental structure of the Swedish political system, the concept seemed a strange one in the Swedish context, both theoretically problematical (Dahlkvist 1995) and, at least in its Anglo-American variant, deeply at odds with the Swedish political tradition in both theory and fact (Rothstein 1995). The champions of civil society seemed to suggest that there existed a zero-sum calculus according to which a large state would lead to an atrophied civil society. While no one denied that the public sector in Sweden was large, the role played by organizations of all kinds was also celebrated. As several of the chapters in this book conclusively show, empirical research in fact suggests that the national self-understanding of Sweden as a land of many associations and a vital civil society largely was—and remains—a correct one: even if the structure and character of associational life differ in key respects between Sweden and United States (which is often viewed as the benchmark in this respect), in the aggregate the sectors are of a similar magnitude (Amnå this book; Baer this book; Jeppson Grassman and Svedberg this book; also Jeppsson Grassman and Svedberg 1999; Lundström & Wijkström 1997).

These findings have in turn prompted theoretical efforts to explain this radical discrepancy between theories generated from within the liberal Anglo-American tradition, on the one hand, and the empirical data pouring forth from researchers concerned with Scandinavia, on the other. While much of the writing on state-civil society relations has assumed a fundamental opposition between the two sectors, we will investigate why in some cases, notably the Swedish one, the relationship has been less confrontational than collaborative (Birnbaum 1988; Kuhnle and Selle 1992). Rather than trying to define the essential difference between state and civil society, or to discover the lines that separate the two spheres, we will turn our attention to the institutional ties that bind them together. By taking a closer look at the historical development of the Swedish case in a comparative perspective, we hope to provide some insight into the question of why in Sweden the boundary between state and civil society is so blurred and permeable that until very recently the Swedish word "society" *(samhälle)* was used to describe both "state" and "(civil) society." Our analysis concentrates on the historical meeting between the Swedish state and the emerging working-class organizations at the turn of the last century. We argue that the specific configuration of this meeting resulted in a historical pattern of interaction between state and civil society that had lasting impact on Swedish political culture.

States, Neocorporatism, and Collective Action

Formal democracy of the modern variant was introduced comparatively late in Sweden. Universal male suffrage was established as late as 1917, general suffrage four years later, in 1921. It came, moreover, after a long and bitter struggle that pitted the labor movement and other so-called popular movements (the free churches, the temperance movement) against the traditional elites, who stubbornly held on to power until the specter of the Russian Revolution convinced them to give in. This was, it seems, an inauspicious starting point for the development of mutual trust and close cooperation between the institutions of the state and the free associations of civil society. Yet Sweden has been considered the nearly ideal-typical case when it comes to collaborative relations between the state and the voluntary associations of civil society (Bergqvist 1999; Hermansson 1993; Öberg 1994). We will argue that the Swedish case can be explained by the specific structure of the pre-democratic Swedish state—centralized but not closed; bureaucratic and professional but not especially authoritarian; differentiated but not without central coordination of policy.

One of the most important efforts to explain variations in the collaboration between the state and the organizations on the labor market (also known as *neocorporatism*) is that by Peter Katzenstein (1985). He argues that small European nations with economies open to the world market have a greater need to be able to adapt to changes in the world market than do larger capitalist countries. The small states' need for flexible adaptation has tended to give rise to collaborative efforts and arrangements between the parties in the economy, which in turn has resulted in what Katzenstein labels *democratic neocorporatism*. His main causal factor, however, is not size, but rather the specific historical development in these small countries that made a close and nonconfrontational collaboration between the state and the organizations on the labor market possible (Katzenstein 1985: 136 f.). It is also this variation in historical circumstances before World War II that accounts for the rather great variation between these countries.

Along similar lines Seymour Martin Lipset has argued that the dominant ideological orientation of the labor movement in various countries was determined by the pattern of interaction between the labor movement and the state/bourgeois elite in the decades before World War I. The political interaction between the labor movement and its adversaries that developed then has, according to Lipset (1983), conditioned the views held ever since, by both the labor movement and its adversaries, about labor's proper role in the public policy process. More precisely, Lipset argues that two factors during this period determined the character of the labor movements. First, the more closed and rigid the class system before World War I, the stronger the radical and revolutionary tendencies in the labor movement. Second, the longer the working class's exclusion from political influence—i.e., the right to vote—and the harsher the repression of organization and strikes, the more radical the labor movement would become and the more hostile to any collaboration with the state and employers' organizations. Conversely, in a country with a relatively open class system in which the political elite was willing early on to share some of its political power with the emerging working class, reformist and moderate tendencies in the labor movement would dominate.

Katzenstein, for his part, tries to explain the Swedish case by pointing to the collaboration that took place between the Social Democrats and the Liberals until 1923 (Katzenstein 1985). We agree that this alliance, which was caused by a split on the political right, was important for strengthening the moderate wing in the labor movement. However, it is not obvious how an electoral alliance of this kind explains the development of neocorporatism. The corporatist channel of representation, by which organizations influence public policy in direct collaboration with state officials, is usually understood as an alternative to the electoral/parliamentary channel; the route from, for example, the electoral alliance of 1917 to the specific kind of neocorporatist representation so typical of modern Sweden is thus not at all clear (cf. Crouch and Dore 1990: 11). Instead of neocorporatism, one could very well argue the result should have been a strengthened parliament and a more pluralist political system. Obviously, something more is needed to explain the deviant Swedish case.

Alongside Katzenstein's mostly "society centered" argument, we wish to put forward a type of explanation for the Swedish case that has been termed "neo-institutionalist" or "state-centered" (cf. Skocpol 1985; Thelen 1999). Pierre Birnbaum has forcefully argued that, when it comes to explaining variations in neocorporatism, one very important factor is usually left out—namely, the state. In neocorporatist theory, the state is usually treated as a general entity, as if there were but a single type of capitalist state (Birnbaum 1988). Comparing primarily France, Germany, and Great Britain, Birnbaum argues that this generalized and ahistorical notion of the state is superficial, because it does not take into account that the specific character of the state varies greatly, and that "each type of state generates specific mechanisms for managing social conflicts and directs action of the working class into specific channels" (Birnbaum 1988: 109). Comparing Britain, Germany and France, Birnbaum is able to show that the differences between these states, as an independent variable, have primacy in explaining variations in corporatist arrangements (Birnbaum 1982: 497, Birnbaum 1988: 79).

The problem with Lipset's analysis of the development of reformist or revolutionary tendencies in different national labor movements is that he considers only one part of the state—the input part (suffrage). Katzenstein's analysis also leans strongly to the input side, as he stresses the question of proportional versus majoritarian electoral representation as a factor behind the development of political alliances and neocorporatism. This is not very convincing, however, as he has to make exceptions for France and Weimar Germany, neither of which, despite having proportional representation, developed any strong corporatist arrangements.

Birnbaum uses a broader notion of the state's relation to the working class. He agrees with Lipset about the importance of the historical legacy in the relation between the state and the working class, but in contrast to Katzenstein and Lipset, he points to the specific *administrative* character of different states as an explanatory factor when it comes to variations in working-class orientation and/or neocorporatism. Birnbaum argues that neocorporatism never developed in France because of the exceptional strength and administrative centralization of the French state. The French labor movement was "always excluded from the state; it had immense difficulties in having its voice heard and always had to act conflictively" (Birnbaum 1988: 123). On the other hand, no stable neocorporatism could ever develop in Britain on account of the great administrative weakness of the British state. The non-differentiated, non-autonomous, non-institutionalized character of the British state has prevented it from intervening effectively in the labor market, and has hindered the integration of unions and business organizations in the policy process (Birnbaum 1988).

Like Lipset, Birnbaum fastens on historical factors during the formative period of the labor movement, but in contrast to the former, he does not confine his analysis of the state to the question of suffrage or parliamentary representation. This broader analysis of the state is altogether in order, for particular to neocorporatism is that it increases the state's ability to intervene in society and shape its interactions with voluntary associations, and this cannot be accomplished through the electoral process, but rather through the state's *administrative* apparatuses. It is therefore the organization of the latter that should be in focus when it comes to analyzing the state as an explanation for variations in national configuration of civil society relations.

The question is this: what kind of state capacity and organization causes what kind of relations to the labor (and other) social movements? And how is this to be explained?

If Katzenstein and Lipset are correct about the pre–World War I period as the "formative moment," and if Birnbaum is right about the importance of the character of the state, then the relation of the pre–World War I Swedish state to the working-class organizations should come into focus. In the rest of this article, we will argue that what explains the Swedish case is in fact the structure and function of the Swedish state at this "formative moment." The Swedish working class was denied suffrage for a comparatively long time; reformism and close collaboration between the state and the parties on the labor market nonetheless came to dominate the major part of the Swedish society. The reason, we argue, is the early organization of a corporatist system of representation that was established by the Swedish state before World War I. Even if the Swedish working class did not receive full voting rights until 1921, this system of "early neocorporatism" gave the organized working class a channel to the Swedish state, and showed the state to be not entirely hostile to working-class demands. Moreover, this system institutionalized neocorporatism as a natural and workable political system in Sweden, with the capacity to solve conflicts between the parties to the advantage of both sides.

What follows is a description of when and where this system came about, and the reasons that were given for it, before we finally return to the question of what can be said about its long-term effects on the Swedish political system from the point of view of state–civil society relations at large. Connecting to the recent discussions among historical institutionalists about "path dependence," and to what Paul Pierson, borrowing from economists, refers to as the "increasing returns" associated with stable and enduring institutions, as well as a variety of attempts to model the varieties of "regime types," we will reflect on the peculiar configuration of state–civil society relations that characterizes Sweden, very much in contrast to not only the United States but also other Western democracies.

Background: A More Popular State

In a comparative perspective, the nineteenth-century Swedish state may be characterized as less repressive, as containing a less important feudal heritage, and as more open to popular demands than the state generally was in continental Europe. This took many forms: an (internationally unique) independent political representation of peasants in the parliament, extensive local self-government, no legal hindrance of unions or strikes, a rather low ratio of police to citizens, and local instead of central control over a part of the police force. Moreover, violent repression of the working class by the military and police was uncommon, and general public education and literacy developed earlier than in most comparable countries (Therborn et al. 1978; Therborn 1989).

The reforms of the parliament in 1866, which replaced the ancient representational system of four estates with a two-chamber parliament (with very restricted suffrage), actually increased the representation of (landowning) peasants. It is also important to note that, because of reforms in the early and mid nineteenth century, the civil service of this state was rather well paid, politically independent, tenured, professional, and uncorrupt. Moreover, it had some political influence, although it was not politically dominant. The Italian or US system of political patronage and bureaucratic clientalism did not prevail in Sweden at this time. Rather, one could speak of a classic Weberian type of nationally unified *Rechtstaat* by the turn of the century. The decisive break with aristocratic-feudal modes of state organization had been made between 1850 and 1880. From the 1860s onward several highly professional government agencies were set up to deal with the need for infrastructure (roads, energy, telecommunications). In sum, this was not a society ruled by a capricious ruling class. Through the state bureaucracies and the highly respected administrators who ran them, the Swedish state was on the contrary rather well integrated with civil society (Rothstein 1982a; Therborn 1989: 19ff.).

Contrary to the classical liberal Anglo-American model, with its emphasis on the primacy and autonomy of civil society and its clear separation between state and society, but also in contrast to a truly state-dominated society, such as France, Sweden is a case in which state and civil society, as Ronald Jepperson has put it, "are highly interpenetrated" (Jepperson 2002). He suggests that the state in Sweden, rather than acting as a powerful enforcer beholden to itself and its own interests, serves more as a number of institutional spaces in which representatives from society meet to work out policies in a spirit of consensus and compromise. Therefore, Jepperson describes Sweden as a "social-corporate system" in contrast to a "state-corporate" system, such as Germany, where the state by tradition has had a more dominant role in relation to civil society (Jepperson 2002; Schofer and Fourcade-Gourinchas 2001).

While Jepperson has created a typology of "modern polity forms" (regime types) that is both novel and illuminating, his description of Sweden as "social-corporate" polity form was foreshadowed not only in a general sense by Katzenstein and his notion of a "democratic corporatism," but also more specifically by the Swedish political scientist Hilding Johansson. Reacting to the mid-century political scientist Gunnar Heckscher, who was one of the first to describe Sweden as "corporatist," Johansson as early as 1951 critiqued this label as being too state-centered. He preferred his own term "associative democracy," which shifted the emphasis from the state to the associations, and from paternalism from above to democracy from below (Heckscher 1951, Johansson 1952). But Heckscher and Johansson were, in fact, in fundamental agreement, even if they placed their emphasis differently, one on the state, the other on the civil society organizations. From our point of view, the crucial matter is the institutionalized relationship that enabled the state and the associations of civil society to confront new challenges and work out compromise solutions in a peaceful and cooperative manner. We will now turn to those institutions and processes, taking as our point of departure the labor question as it emerged as a major social and political issue in the waning decades of nineteenth century Sweden.

The Prelude to Neocorporatism

How did this state react to the emergent "labor question?" As in all other Western countries, capitalism gave rise to the question of what was to be done about the new and problematic class of free-floating workers in society. The reaction of the Swedish state was to set up two investigatory commissions: the Workers' Insurance Commission in 1884 and the New Workers' Insurance Commission in 1891.[2] These were composed of experts and individuals representing various interests (Englund 1976; Heclo 1974: 180). In view of Sweden's late industrialization (from 1870 onward), this must be considered a rather early effort. It should be noted that it came well before the first national union organization was established in Sweden in 1898, and before the establishment of the Social Democratic Party (1889), but on the heels of the country's first major strike (1879).

The Workers' Insurance Commissions contended that the state, having witnessed the demise of the patriarchal guild system, had the responsibility of reducing the insecurity of workers who were "solely dependent on their labor" (AFK 1888, no. 1: 4). They made a rather straightforward anti-liberal, anti-market argument stating that, although compulsory insurance schemes would interfere with personal freedom, property rights, and personal responsibility, such freedom was justified only if the interests of the individual and society coincided. If this was not the case, the state had both the right and duty to intervene (AFK 1888, no. 1: 4f.).

The proposals of these commissions did not arise from any Bismarckian authoritarianism, nor were they joined to any form of legal repression against the labor movement. On the contrary, they were proposed by Liberal politicians with a humanitarian interest in social issues (Heclo 1974: 179 ff.; cf. Olsson 1990). The major argument was that a system of workers' insurance would help to contain revolutionary tendencies in the labor movement, because if would "make the great majority of the working population jointly interested in upholding the existing social organism" (quoted in Heclo 1974: 180). The commission of 1884 even included one worker, although he does not seem to have played an important role (Heclo 1974: 180f.).

What is especially interesting in this case was that the first of these government commissions argued that the insurance system they proposed should be administered by a new government agency, to which a corporatist advisory board should be attached. Disputes arising over the implementation of the insurance should, according to the commission, be settled not by the usual courts of law, but rather by a new kind of corporatively structured institution, which would consist of both experts and representatives of workers and employers, the latter two groups enjoying equal representation. The second commission argued that its proposed workers' insurance scheme should be administered by a central government agency, and by local "corporations or so-called pension boards, in which all interests would be represented" (NAFK 1893, no. 1: 105). These local, corporatively organized boards would decide all the crucial issues connected with the case-by-case implementation of the reform—fees, benefits, and so on (NAFK 1893; cf. Englund 1976: 44–84).

The Swedish parliament did not accept the proposals of either commission. This was not, however, because the commissions recommended that corporatist institutions should administer the insurance schemes; rather, the time was not yet ripe for social insurance as such in Sweden (Olsson 1990). No criticism was directed against the principle of corporatist representation. The point is that while suffrage was still very restricted and the subject of hot dispute, corporatist solutions *including labor* enjoyed legitimacy and were plainly seen as very natural forms of political representation in late nineteenth-century Swedish political culture.

The first government proposal to establish a corporatist institution came from a Conservative government, which in 1902 put forward a bill for workers' occupational accident insurance. According to the bill, a council consisting of five workers' representatives and five employers would be established to oversee the implementation of the insurance (RP 1902, no. 15). The reform as such was accepted by Parliament, becoming the first piece of modern social legislation in Sweden, but the corporatist council was rejected. The reason for this action was not any reservation about corporatist arrangements as such, but rather concerned legal technicalities about how the representatives would, according to the Bill, be chosen. In fact, several members of parliament argued that a corporatist council of the type suggested would be of great value for the successful implementation of the reform (RPFK 1902, no. 22: 23ff.; RPAK 1902, no. 31: 2ff.).

The Development of Local Neocorporatism

Corporatist institutions were first established at the local level in Sweden, not at the center. In 1902, city governments started to organize public labor exchanges, which were directly governed by corporatively organized boards. The boards' role was not merely advisory; they took full responsibility for operating the labor exchanges under the city councils. Half the representatives were from the labor movement and half were local employers, while the position of chairman was given to a neutral local official. Although this development resulted from local political initiatives, a nationally unified system quickly emerged. By 1907, all major cities had established corporative organized public labor exchanges.

The general principles were as follows: the labor exchanges were not to be restricted to specific trades or occupations, but should supply labor for all kinds of work, free of charge for both workers and employers. They were to operate on a strictly neutral basis, and were not to side with any of the parties in industrial disputes. A so-called "golden rule" was established to guide their operations, which stated that employers should get the best available workforce and the workers, in turn, the jobs best suited to them (Rothstein 1982b; Skogh 1963: 177). The most vexing issue concerned how the exchanges should behave in industrial disputes. A compromise was struck: employers hit by strikes were allowed to apply for workers at the exchanges, but at the same time the officials had the right and the duty to inform workers if the job offered was under a union blockade (Rothstein 1982b).

This peaceful development differed markedly from the general European pattern, in which control over labor exchanges usually rested either with employers' organizations or with trade unions (Schiller 1967: 9–36; cf. Pelloutier 1971). While a public and neutral public/corporatist employment exchange system rapidly became dominant in Sweden, it was usually the exception in continental Europe. In Germany, for example, the question of control over the labor exchange system had become a major source of conflict between labor and capital (Schiller 1967: 8, 31f.). The reason, of course, is that in a capitalist society, control over the supply of labor is of the greatest importance to the parties on the labor market and in the class struggle. If the unions are able to gain control of the labor exchange system, strikes and blockades can be made much more effective. Unions can also use labor exchanges in more regular bargaining with local employers, as they can discriminate between employers when supplying labor. Moreover, they can require workers to become union members if they wish to use the services of the labor exchanges—a powerful selective incentive indeed. In short, if unions control the labor exchanges, their major power resource in the class struggle—control over the supply of labor—can be greatly enhanced. Conversely, this is also why employers' organizations typically try to seize control of the labor exchange system. Strikes can be fought much more effectively, union leaders and strike activists can be forced out of the workforce, and union power generally can be minimized.

The labor exchange system is thus of pivotal importance to the parties on the labor market. In some parts of Germany, the unions had gained the upper hand, while in most areas the employers' organizations had been able to seize control. Just why events developed altogether differently in Sweden is less than plain. Neither the Swedish Employers' Federation (SAF), nor the Confederation of Trade Unions (LO), nor the Social Democratic Party propelled this development. When the establishment of a public/corporatist scheme was proposed in Parliament in 1903, the chairman of the Social Democratic Party, Hjalmar Branting, opposed the proposal. He argued that, because universal suffrage to the city councils was not yet established, the exchanges would probably side with the employers despite the corporatist principle. The main Social Democratic newspaper also warned that the exchanges might be used to recruit strikebreakers. On the other hand, Social Democrats in some city councils, while not proposing such a system, sometimes argued in favor of it (Rothstein 1982b).

As of 1903, the newly established employers' federation showed an interest in establishing an employer-controlled scheme, and sent officials to Germany to study such a system in operation. Although they came back with enthusiastic reports, and argued that such a system could be a decisive weapon against the union movement, the leadership of the SAF hesitated to put the plan into operation. The reason was probably a matter of timing, for when the SAF, after some internal turbulence, finally made up its mind in 1907 to accept the public/corporatist labor exchange system, it was already established, and employers at the local level had not hesitated to support it. Another reason, given by the chairman of the employers' federation in 1907, was that a "German" system could only be established after a major defeat of the labor movement.

In 1906, a liberal government had obtained parliamentary approval of government grants to the corporatist local labor exchange system. The condition for receiving such grants was adherence to the principles established locally in 1902, i.e., unconditional neutrality, corporatist boards, services free of charge to all occupations and trades, and the "golden rule" (Skogh 1963: 179f.). It is important to note that these principles, while established at the local level, had been confirmed at the national level since 1906 by a series of conferences on the labor exchange question organized by the National Board of Trade, to which representatives from the local public labor exchanges were invited. Although a temporary phenomenon, these conferences were the first corporative institutions established on the national level by the Swedish state.[3]

If neither the employers' federation nor the labor movement stood behind the development of public labor exchanges, who did? The answer is twofold. First, at the local level it was primarily what can be called liberal forces in the Swedish bourgeoisie that were interested in social policy and a peaceful solution to the "labor question." Some of these persons also had strong connections with the temperance movement, at this time an important force in the Swedish society (Rothstein 1982b). Second, at the central level it was the Liberal government that played the critical role. In particular, the civil servants at the Board of Trade, by initiating the series of conferences on the public labor exchange system, contributed greatly to making this system dominant in Sweden. It should be noted that the national public administration in Sweden had (and still has) a rather unusual organization. While the ministries were quite small and dealt mostly with policy issues, responsibility for actually implementing public policy rested with semi-autonomous national boards and agencies. These government organizations were not under the direct command of any minister but instead implemented policy under their own legal responsibility. This meant the top civil servants enjoyed a considerable amount of discretion and could take initiatives of their own. Whether the original initiative to arrange the conferences that from 1906 on established the corporatist principles of the labor exchanges was taken by the bureaucrats themselves, or after hints from the Liberal government, is unfortunately not known. Officially, it was the Liberal government that in 1906 requested the Board of Trade to take this initiative.[4]

It is also important to note that while the Liberal government was replaced by a Conservative one as early as 1907, the Board of Trade continued its work for the establishment of a public labor exchange. Without its semi-independent position in relation to the government, this may not have been the case (Rothstein 1982b).

The Development of Neocorporatism at the National Level

At the national level, several initiatives to establish permanent corporatist institutions were taken before 1914, as stated above. In 1909, a government commission of inquiry dealing with occupational safety also suggested a corporatist advisory board be established to counsel the work inspectorate. In 1908, the National Insurance Board (established in 1903, see above), which was led by civil servants, sent a letter to the government asking it to establish a corporatist council attached to the Board.[5]

Neocorporatism was finally established as a permanent principle of political representation in 1912 when Parliament decided to set up a new agency, the National Board for Social Affairs. In the commission planning the organization and tasks of the board, seats were given to two labor representatives, one being the chairman of the LO, the other a prominent member of the Social Democratic Party leadership. The new board was to be governed by its top civil servants according to the common rule. What was new was the presence on the board of the two outside representatives, one from the organized working class and one from the employers' federation (RP 1912, no. 108).

While it was not directly stated in the bill, the persons appointed were the chairman of the LO and the general manager of the SAF. They were not to have merely an advisory role but were to take part in all major decisions on an equal footing with the ruling civil servants. Furthermore, the new National Board for Social Affairs would be assisted by a Social Welfare Council. The council would consist mostly of representatives from the parties on the labor market, and would be divided into four different assemblies for different issues, each with about ten to fifteen members (DK 1912, no. 5:4 ff.).

Although there was opposition in Parliament to the bill establishing the National Board for Social Affairs, none of it was directed against the corporatist arrangements. Neither the Conservatives, nor the Social Democrats, nor the governing Liberals taking part in the debate even mentioned the question (RPFK 1912, no. 34: 50ff.; RPAK 1912, no. 40: 11ff.). The idea of administrative neocorporatism had obviously become generally accepted in the Swedish political culture by 1912. In a written statement to the government about the proposal to establish this new government agency, the employers' federation approved its corporatist institutions. Neither the SAF nor the LO hesitated to participate in the Board for Social Affairs (RP 1912, no. 108: 224f.).

After this breakthrough, the corporatist principle of representation developed rapidly in the pre-democratic Swedish state. When public pension reform was launched in 1913, the new National Pension Board also got a corporatist advisory board. One of its corporatist representatives was the chairman of the Social Democratic Party (Hjalmar Branting) (RP 1913, no. 298). Upon the outbreak of World War I in 1914, the newly established unemployment commission also received a corporatist board (Rothstein 1985). Before 1919, two more important corporative agencies were established in the Swedish state—the Insurance Council and the Labor Council. Neither of these corporatist institutions was limited merely to an advisory role. On the contrary, they were court-like institutions empowered to establish legally binding verdicts and precedents in two important areas. The Insurance Council was responsible for solving legal conflicts in the public occupational insurance scheme. The Labor

Council had a similar role, implementing the law on the eight-hour working day. Both included two representatives from organized labor and capital respectively, plus three neutral civil servants, mostly lawyers.

Motives for Corporatist Representation

What motives were given for establishing corporatist institutions in the Swedish state at this time? The task of the new National Board for Social Affairs was not poor-relief, as might have been expected; this matter was handled by the local authorities. Instead, it was nothing less than the "labor question." The government commission planning the work and organization of the new board argued that the reason for its existence was that "in contemporary society, human labor has become a commodity, so to speak, the supply and demand for which are subject to fluctuations and which consequently has a value that is uncertain and dependent upon shifting circumstances" (DK 1912, no. 5: 4). According to the commission, this caused the problem of this new social category's members becoming concentrated in the cities, where masses of alienated and rootless workers lived separated from any form of local community, and from the country as such. In the words of the commission:

> The more clearly the dangers of industrialism became evident even to the most capable and most irreproachable workers—and the more strongly manual laborers saw themselves as a closed class in relation to employers and other groups of citizens—the more clearly the national dangers of this situation became discernible. The rising level of public education then gave workers the means to clarify for themselves and others the source of their problems, the organizational system gave them the collective power on behalf of their own interests ... The feeling of solidarity that has emerged among the working masses, in itself praiseworthy, is limited to themselves and they do not appear to wish to extend it to the whole society in which they share responsibility and play a part. This obviously poses a national danger, which must be removed in the common interest of everyone. Everywhere the government therefore faces the difficult task of mitigating conflicts of interest and repairing the cracks that are opening in the social structure (DK 1912, no. 5: 4).

The National Board for Social Affairs was not established to implement any specific social reform. On the contrary, its task was rather vague. Yet in any case it is clear it was not established to handle the problem of widespread poverty in Swedish society. Instead, it was created to handle the "labor question" by incorporating this new and clearly threatening social class into society. Most of all it seems the new board was established to increase the state's knowledge and information about the many social problems entailed by the "labor question," thus expanding what has been called "state capacity" in this area (Skocpol 1985).

When the National Insurance Board in 1908 requested permission from the government to establish a corporatively structured council, it argued the agency would thereby "gain knowledge of different opinions among those members of the public most closely affected by the work of the Board." As shown above, the board was denied such a corporatist council when it was established in 1902, and it should be noted that it was members of the traditional corps of top civil servants in the Swedish state who asked the government for this complement.

The motive for establishing the public/corporatist labor exchanges was to find a way to decrease unemployment and improve the functioning of the labor market (Skogh 1963: 177). However, the reason for their being public and corporatist was above all to prevent a development like that in, for example, Germany, as described above. When this question was first raised publicly in Sweden in 1895, in the city council of Stockholm, the local commission of inquiry explicitly warned against allowing such a development as had taken place in Germany.[6] When the city councils of Gothenburg in 1901 and of Stockholm in 1902 decided to establish public/corporatist labor exchanges, the same argument was put forward yet more forcefully. The French "bourse du travail," which included labor exchanges under union control, was also criticized. It was argued that once either party had gained control over the labor exchange system and discovered what an excellent weapon it was in the class struggle, it would fight hard to keep that control. Such a development, it was argued, would entirely pervert the idea of labor exchanges as a way of increasing the efficiency of the labor market. Moreover—and this was the most critical argument—improving the efficiency of the labor market benefited not only employers and labor, but also society as a whole.[7]

This argument was put forward not just by the liberal political groups that stood behind the initiative to establish public/corporatist labor exchanges in Sweden. In addition, the local unions in Stockholm, which in 1901 were asked to offer their assessment of the proposal, argued that if the exchanges were to function properly, it would be imperative that these exchanges be trusted by the employers as well as by organized labor; for this a corporative organization was needed. The local commission of inquiry in Stockholm also offered its view of how the representatives should be chosen. According to the commission, it was not enough that workers and employers be equally represented on the board. Instead, it was necessary that both parties enjoy the right to choose their own representatives. No outside authority should be allowed to pick representatives because, if this occurred, these representatives would not be seen as legitimate by either unions or employers, and the impartiality of the exchanges would be doubted. This would put the whole institution at risk.[8] The need for legitimacy is emphasized time and again in the minutes from the city councils, and corporatist representation is held out as the main solution to the problem.[9]

Another important motive behind the institutionalization of neo-corporatism in the Swedish state was the need for flexibility in implementing social reforms. This is related to what nowadays is called the implementation problem—that is, the difficulties of regulating and intervening, in volatile areas such as the labor market, with precise rules and regulations. The complexity and variety of the questions to be handled make bureaucratic discretion in the implementation process a necessity. Occupational accident insurance is a good example. The Workers' Insurance Commission of 1893 had argued that "it is not possible to set these limits in such a way that all doubt as to whether or not a person is entitled to insurance is eliminated in every single case" (NAFK 1893: 103).

As in all other Western societies, the interpretation of laws in particular cases was traditionally handled by the civil court system. In opposing this solution, the commission argued that the court system, with its possibilities for appeal, would be too slow to handle occupational accident insurance cases. On other words, the time between the work injury and the final settlement of the case would be too long (RP 1916, no. 111: 95). Another, and perhaps more important argument against using the courts was that judges lacked knowledge and understanding of the "labor question." Corporatist arrangements were to be preferred, as they would provide the necessary flexibility and speed in processing insurance claims, which in turn would increase the legitimacy of the reform in the eyes of the target group (the workers) (AFK 1888, no. 1: 101). It was also argued that corporatist bodies would "give increased life and intensity to the administration (of the law) and prevent it from becoming too rigid," and that such bodies would take initiatives to change the reforms on the basis of experience in actual implementation (DK 1912, no. 5: 164).

As for the implementation of the law regulating the eight-hour working day, it was argued that the traditional juridical method of law interpretation was not suitable. Instead, a more mediatory method of law interpretation was needed. The law was written so as to give ample room for exceptions. The agency that was to authorize these exceptions could not simply interpret the law, but also had to *balance the interests* of workers and employers (DK 1912, no. 5: 166; RP 1902, no. 15: 26). According to the law this was a question not of right or wrong but of more or less. It was argued that a corporative body was more suited to this new type of law interpretation, or juridical method, than were the traditional courts. Of course, this was also related to the problem of legitimacy, because unions with representatives in, for example, the Labor Council would find it easier to accept its verdicts (RP 1919, no. 333).

Finally, the most important argument for neocorporatism during this period was the notion of the "public interest." This is clear from the arguments concerning both the labor exchanges and the National Board for Social Affairs. If the state did not intervene in the "labor question," the organized classes would simply pursue their narrow class interests, which would cause serious problems and might in the end destroy the very fabric of society. The state could not, of course, solve the class struggle, but it could transform this struggle from an unsolvable conflict into a manageable one—in game—analytical parlance, from a zero-sum to a positive sum-game. The price the established society had to pay was to accept working-class representation. It was underlined that the very implementation of laws could often give rise to misunderstanding, suspicion, and social conflicts. To avoid this, it was necessary to increase understanding and knowledge about the reforms, and the way in which they were implemented, among the target groups. It was presumed that if representatives from these groups were drawn into the state, and were granted the possibility of wielding at least some real influence over the decisions, they would change their attitudes. Or, as it was put by the commission proposing the National Board for Social Affairs, the representatives "would behave as guardians not only of special interests but also of the interests of everyone, of society as a whole ... It should certainly be expected that a representative body structured according to these principles, official and thus functioning with a sense of responsibility, should provide valuable support for the new social welfare administration" (DK 1912, no. 5: 166).

The Impact of Early Neocorporatism

The remaining question is, of course, whether this system was effective. Did it deliver the collaboration between organized labor, the employers, and the state? And did social reforms, and the state as such, enjoy enhanced legitimacy among the organized working class? The answer to both these questions is yes.

To begin with, the local employment exchanges quickly became dominant, and by 1914 almost all the important industrial cities had established this type of corporatist body. From 1906 until the exchanges came under direct state control at the outbreak of World War II, there was never any opposition in Parliament (not even from communist or left-socialist members of parliament) to the state's subsidies to the cities and municipalities for the costs of operating the public labor exchanges. Nor were the organizational principles ever questioned (Rothstein 1982b). In a 1916 report to the government regarding the operation of the exchanges, the National Board for Social Affairs declared that "no objection has appeared from any quarter against the organizational principles on which the publicly operated labor exchanges were based."[10] On the contrary, the board argued it was these very principles that had enabled the system to grow, and that had been pivotal for strengthening the confidence their operations enjoyed among both employer organizations and unions, "which in our country have fortunately abstained from utilizing the employment service as a weapon in the social struggle, which in Germany has partially distorted the whole issue of labor exchanges."[11] The board also observed that

> "despite the sharp social and political conflicts that have emerged in other areas of public life between members of the employer and worker camps, on the boards of the labor exchanges the same persons have, in the experience of the National Board for Social Affairs, continued to cooperate faithfully in the interest of objectivity."[12]

In a 1920 article, the officer at the National Board for Social Affairs responsible for overseeing the labor exchanges further argued that "it appears as if this form of organization has a number of advantages over the majority principle that rules politically elected assemblies … it is outstandingly suitable for institutions in which society needs the direct participation of the parties in the class struggle" (Järte 1920: 564). Moreover, aside from the corporatist boards, most of the officials at the labor exchanges were recruited from the labor movement. This was probably done to increase the legitimacy of the implementation process (Järte 1920).

In 1926, the National Board for Social Affairs undertook an overall evaluation of its corporative institutions. Concerning the representative system, in which the leading persons from the LO and the SAF participated in the major board decisions, the board declared the following:

> The purpose of establishing the representative system was undoubtedly to give the National Board for Social Affairs the necessary immediate contact with the main organizations in its most sensitive field of activity—the labor market and its organizations.… the Board selected persons who enjoyed a particularly high degree of confidence from employers and workers, respectively, and were suitable to represent their interests. The fact that persons in such a position became representatives with the approval of their organizations, on the other hand, imposed on them an obligation to regard themselves also as representatives of the public.[13]

The bureaucrats on the board also argued that the informal contacts that they had been able to establish with the representatives, and through them with other persons in the organizations, had been of the greatest value. Moreover, they pointed to the importance of the informal and confidential deliberations that the director general of the board often held with one or both representatives on especially sensitive and delicate issues. The value of the corporatist system of representation to the general public interest was, according to the board, that it had made it possible to sweep away prejudices and to create an understanding of the measures undertaken by the state in regard to the relationship between employers and unions. For example, conflicts could be avoided by making informal contacts at an early stage of an issues discussion, thus preventing the issue from becoming burdened with prestige and/or prejudices.[14]

The meetings between civil servants and the representatives of the Board for Social Affairs were very frequent. The records show that during the first three years of the board's operation, the two representatives met with the board almost every week and made formal decisions in about one hundred cases a year. In the following three years meetings were limited to about once a fortnight.[15] However, this was not to be seen, according to the board, as a sign of any declining interest on the part of the civil servants or the representatives in the board's operations, nor was the board to be considered any less important than before. Rather, the many meetings during the first years had been occasioned by the need to establish practices and precedents while laying the foundations of social policy in Sweden. According to the board, the decline in the number of formal meetings was compensated for by an increase in the number of informal contacts between the officials and the representatives.[16] Once again, it should be remembered that national boards and agencies in Sweden had a very strong position in both policy implementation and policy creation. The Social Welfare Council attached to the Board for Social Affairs met less often, on average six times a year between 1913 and 1919. In the statement mentioned above, the board argued that while the council had only an advisory role, it was still of great value, "because a more detailed awareness of the contents and purpose of issues could be communicated through members to circles interested in a particular issue, with the aim of eliminating prejudices, preventing misunderstandings and awakening understanding."[17]

As for the work of the Labor Council, there is nothing to indicate that it did not function to the satisfaction of both the state and the employers and trade unions. While the Conservatives in Parliament regularly questioned the law mandating the eight-hour workday until the 1930s, neither side put forward any criticism of the Labor Council. On the contrary, when the law was debated in Parliament in 1930, the general manager of the SAF, who was also a conservative member of parliament, said it had been of paramount importance for the employers that the implementation of the law was so flexible, and that not one single meeting with the Labor Council had taken place without applications for exemptions from the general eight-hour rule being granted. He argued further that many industries would not have prospered as well as they had done had not the law been made so flexible, and that the smooth workings of the Labor Council had made the law bearable for employers (RPFK 1930, no. 22: 14f.). Finally, as for the work of the Industrial Injuries Insurance

Court, it may suffice to say that this corporatist institution remained unchanged until the 1970s in the Swedish political system.

Conclusions

It is clear that, while the Swedish working class was denied universal suffrage until comparatively late, the pre-democratic Swedish state was not altogether hostile to its demands. On the contrary, in place of the parliamentary channel, this state opened up the corporatist model of political representation for the working class, seemingly without any hesitation. As indicated above, this seems to have been a very successful way of encouraging reformism and moderation in the labor movement. At the local level, the corporatist boards of the labor exchanges showed the organized working class that cooperation was possible, to the advantage of both parties and society as a whole, even in a very sensitive area. To politicians it offered proof that, if properly organized, class conflicts could be institutionalized in ways that benefit the public interest instead of rupturing the social fabric.

In regard to the central level, it is hard to overstate the importance of the regular, almost weekly, meetings between state officials and the leaders of the LO and the SAF. The effect was that both organized capital and labor loyally cooperated with the state in laying the foundations of social policy in Sweden. For the organized working class, social policy thus was not purely a device used by the ruling elite to pacify the lower orders. On the contrary, the leaders of the working class were given a say in the establishment and implementation of social policy.

Social reforms did not develop early in Sweden compared, for example, to Germany or Great Britain, which means that the timing of social reforms cannot explain the moderation and reformism of the Swedish labor movement. What was special about Sweden was that corporatist solutions for political representation found legitimacy almost two decades before democracy was established. We can thus solve the dilemma that Lipset's analysis created, by pointing to the willingness of the pre–World War I Swedish state to establish corporatist arrangements. Contrary to Katzenstein's society-centered explanations, we may observe a direct line between the particularities of the pre–World War I Swedish state and its modern neocorporatism. As Birnbaum has suggested, the main independent variable that explains variation in degrees of neocorporatism among nations seems to be the function and character of the state.

The Swedish state at this "formative moment" was not as strong and centralized as the French state, which prevented any form of incorporation of the organized working class. On the other hand, it was not so weak and decentralized (like the British state) as to prevent any form of early neocorporatism (Birnbaum 1988; cf. Crouch & Dore 1990: 11). More-over, it was not closed in the manner of the German state, which made the German working class contract into its ghetto and fed its unwilling-ness to have anything to do with the state. And while the British, French, and German states also created corporatist institutions during World War I, these arrangements were, contrary to the Swedish case, clearly excep-tional. Most important, the corporatist institutions created in these countries in wartime did not prove enduring (Maier 1984: 43).

Rather, the Swedish state was administratively strong and centralized, but not authoritarian or totally closed to new movements and organiza-tions. The civil service was indeed a professional and independent bu-reaucracy, but not to the extent that it considered any problem soluble by means of the traditional legal system. When it was forced to act in new territory (the "labor question"), it asked for and received permission from parliament and the cabinet to collaborate with the "target group," in order to increase its own knowledge, information, and most of all, le-gitimacy. The creation of neutral institutions, such as the plethora of com-mittees, commissions, and other meetings in which state representatives and leaders from the organizations of civil society could meet, were cru-cial in creating mutual trust between state and civil society actors, which in turn, we argue, made neocorporatism such a political success story in Sweden. To speak in the language of contemporary historical institution-alism, a series of relatively small and contingent events, occurring at a very early point in the process of modernization and democratization, produced large consequences. The success of early democratic neocorpo-ratism set Sweden on a particular path of institution making when it came to state–civil society relations. Subsequent successes produced, in Paul Pierson's language, "increasing returns," further strengthening these institutional arrangements (Pierson 2000).

Finally let us note that the term "neocorporatism" must be carefully qualified. Contrary to Philippe Schmitter's notion of neocorporatism, in the Swedish case it was not a strong state or political elite that created loyal interest organizations for the purpose of controlling the working class (Schmitter 1974). Nor was it the parties on the labor market, who by their very strength, were able to penetrate and capture the state at this particular time. Instead, the specific "structuration" (Cerny 1990) that took place between the state and the labor movement at the "form-ative moment" of organized capitalism was made possible by a specific type of state: centralized, but not closed; bureaucratic and professional but not especially authoritarian; differentiated, but not without central coordination of policy. Of course state institutions like the parliament and the government, as well as political processes such as elections, have played an important role in setting policies and making laws, but what is equally important is the deliberative and inclusive democratic process that has occurred outside of these ordinary contexts—that is, in the committees, commissions, and other regular meetings between leaders from state organs and civil society organizations. This pattern of trustful and close collaboration between the state and various social and organized movements became a pattern for other areas such as agriculture, the temperance questions, and the relationship between the state and the organization of small companies, to name a few (Rothstein 1992).

Notes

1. This is a substantially revised and updated version of an article that previously was published in *Scandinavian Political Studies* (Rothstein 1991).
2. The system of commissions is itself of great significance. As is argued in another chapter in this book (Trägårdh), the commissions can be viewed as the linchpin of the Swedish political system, the institutionalized space in which representatives of the state can meet with members of civil society organizations to work out new policy proposals and drafts of new laws.
3. Socialstyrelsens arkiv, Arbetsmarknadsbyrån: Arbetsförmedlingens historia. *Riksarkivet*. Stockholm [Archives of the National Board for Social Affairs, the Labor Market Bureau: History of the Labor Exchanges. National Archives. Stockholm.]
4. Socialstyrelsens arkiv, Arbetsmarknadsbyrån: Arbetsförmedlingens historia. *Riksarkivet*. Stockholm [Archives of the National Board for Social Affairs, the Labor Market Bureau: History of the Labor Exchanges. National Archives. Stockholm.]
5. Riksförsäkringsanstaltens arkiv: Utlåtande med förslag rörande ändring av vissa delar av lagen angående ersättning för skada till följd av olycksfall i arbetet, 10 jan 1908. *Riksarkivet*. Stockholm. [Archives of the National Insurance Board, Statement ... 10 January 1908. National Archives. Stockholm.]
6. Stockholms stadsfullmäktiges handlingar 1895 bihang 27: 158. [Records from The City Council of Stockholm 1895 number 27: 158].
7. Göteborgs stadsfullmäktiges handlingar 1901 no. 132; Stockholms stadsfullmäktiges handlingar 1902 bihang no. 10. [Records from the City Council of Gothenburg 1901 no. 132; Records from the City Council of Stockholm city 1902 no. 10].
8. Stockholms stadsfullmäktiges handlingar 1902 bihang no. 10:5. [Records from the City Council of Stockholm 1902 no. 10:5].
9. See Stockholms stadsfullmäktiges handlingar 1895 bihang 27: 158. [Records from The City Council of Stockholm 1895 number 27: 158]; Göteborgs stadsfullmäktiges handlingar 1901 no. 132; Stockholms stadsfullmäktiges handlingar 1902 bihang no. 10. [Records from the City Council of Gothenburg 1901 no. 132; Records from the City Council of Stockholm city 1902 no. 10]; and Stockholms stadsfullmäktiges handlingar 1902 bihang no. 10:5. [Records from the City Council of Stockholm 1902 no. 10:5].
10. Socialstyrelsens arkiv, underdånigt yttrande angående statens medverkan för befrämjande av den offentliga arbetsförmedlingen m.m. den 17 april 1916. *Riksarkivet*. Stockholm. [Archives of the National Board for Social Affairs, statement ... 17 April 1916. National Archives. Stockholm].
11. Socialstyrelsens arkiv, underdånigt yttrande angående statens medverkan för befrämjande av den offentliga arbetsförmedlingen m.m. den 17 april 1916. *Riksarkivet*. Stockholm. [Archives of the National Board for Social Affairs, statement ... 17 April 1916. National Archives. Stockholm].

12. Socialstyrelsens arkiv, underdånigt yttrande angående statens medverkan för befrämjande av den offentliga arbetsförmedlingen m.m. den 17 april 1916. *Riksarkivet.* Stockholm. [Archives of the National Board for Social Affairs, statement ... 17 April 1916. National Archives. Stockholm].
13. Socialstyrelsens arkiv. Yttrande 30 sept 1926 till sakkunniga för verkställande av utredning angående fullmäktigesystemet inom statsförvaltningen. *Riksarkivet.* Stockholm. [Archives of the National Board for Social Affairs, statement ... 30 September 1926. National Archives. Stockholm.]
14. Socialstyrelsens arkiv. Yttrande 30 sept 1926 till sakkunniga för verkställande av utredning angående fullmäktigesystemet inom statsförvaltningen. *Riksarkivet.* Stockholm. [Archives of the National Board for Social Affairs, statement ... 30 September 1926. National Archives. Stockholm.]
15. Socialstyrelsens arkiv. Yttrande 30 sept 1926 till sakkunniga för verkställande av utredning angående fullmäktigesystemet inom statsförvaltningen. *Riksarkivet.* Stockholm. [Archives of the National Board for Social Affairs, statement ... 30 September 1926. National Archives. Stockholm.]
16. Socialstyrelsens arkiv. Yttrande 30 sept 1926 till sakkunniga för verkställande av utredning angående fullmäktigesystemet inom statsförvaltningen. *Riksarkivet.* Stockholm. [Archives of the National Board for Social Affairs, statement ... 30 September 1926. National Archives. Stockholm.]
17. Socialstyrelsens handlingar, Sociala Rådets protokoll 1913–1926, *Riksarkivet.* Stockholm. [Archives of the National Board for Social Affairs, Records from the Social Welfare Council 1913–1926. National Archives. Stockholm].

References

AFK. 1888. *Arbetareförsäkringskomitens betänkande.* Stockholm.

Antman, Peter, ed. 1993. *Systemskifte.* Stockholm: Carlssons.

Bergqvist, Christina, ed. 1999. *Likestilte demokratier? Kjønn og politik i Norden.* Oslo: Universitetsforlaget.

Birnbaum, Pierre. 1982. "The State versus Neo-corporatism: France and England." *Politics& Society* 11: 477–501.

——— 1988. *States and Collective Action. The European Experience.* Cambridge: Cambridge University Press.

Cerny, Philip. 1990. *The Changing Architecture of Politics.* London: Sage.

Crouch, Colin, and Richard Dore. 1990. "Whatever happened to Neo-corporatism?" In *Neo-corporatism and Accountability,* ed. C. Crouch and R. Dore. Oxford: Oxford University Press.

Dahlkvist, Mats. 1995. "'Det civila samhället' i samhällsteori och samhällssdebatt. En kritisk analys." In *Civilt samhälle kontra offentlig sektor,* ed. Lars Trägårdh. Stockholm: SNS.

DK. 1912. Departementalkomiterades betänkande. Stockholm.

Englund, Karl. 1976. *Arbetarförsäkringsfrågen i svensk politik 1884–1901.* Uppsala: Acta Universitatis Upsaliensis.

Heckscher, Gunnar. 1951. *Staten och organisationerna.* Stockholm: KF:s bokförlag.

Heclo, Hugh. 1974. *Modern Social Politics in Britain and Sweden.* London: Yale University Press.

Hermansson, Jörgen. 1993. *Politik som intressekamp.* Stockholm: Norstedts.
Jepperson, Ronald. 2002. "Political Modernities: Disentangling Two Underlying Dimensions of Institutional Differentiation." *Sociological Theory* 20, no.1: 61–85.
Jeppsson Grassman, Eva, and Lars Svedberg. 1999. "Medborgarskapets gestaltningar. Insatser i och utanför föreningslivet." In *Civilsamhället*, ed. Erik Amnå. SOU 1999: 84.
Johansson, Hilding. 1952. *Folkrörelserna och det demokratiska statskicket i Sverige.* Karlstad: Gleerups.
Järte, O. 1920. "Ett steg mot arbetsmarknadens centralisering." *Sociala Meddelanden* 17: 562–571.
Katzenstein, Peter. 1985. *Small States in World Markets.* Ithaca, NY: Cornell University Press.
Kuhnle, Stein, and Per Selle. 1992. *Government and Voluntary Associations.* Aldershot: Avebury.
Lipset, Seymor L. 1983. "Radicalism or Reformism: The Sources of Working-Class Politics." *American Political Science Review* 77: 1–23.
Lundström, Tommy, and Filip Wijkström. 1997. *The Nonprofit Sector in Sweden.* Johns Hopkins Nonprofit Series 11. Manchester and New York: Manchester University Press.
Mahoney, James, and Dietrich Rueschemeyer. 2003. *Comparative Historical Analysis in the Social Sciences.* Cambridge: Cambridge University Press.
Maier, Charles. 1984. "Preconditions for Neo-corporatism." In *Order and Conflict in Contemporary Capitalism*, ed. J. Goldthorpe. Oxford: Oxford University Press.
NAFK. 1893. *Nya arbetareförsäkringskomitens betänkande.* Stockholm.
Pelloutier, Ferdinand. 1971. *Histoire de bourses du trauail.* Paris.
Pierson, Paul. 2000. "Increasing Returns, Path Dependence, and the Study of Politics." *American Political Science Review* 94: 251–267.
——— 2004. *Politics in Time: History, Institutions, and Social Analysis.* Princeton, N.J.: Princeton University Press.
Olsson, Sven. 1990. *Social Policy and Welfare State in Sweden.* Lund: Arkiv förlag.
RP. 1902. 1912. 1916. 1919. *Regeringens proposition.* [Proceedings of the Swedish Parliament, Government Bill].
RPAK. 1902 *Riksdagens protokoll. Andra Kammaren.* [Proceedings of the Swedish Parliament. Second Chamber].
RPFK. 1902. *Riksdagens protokoll. Första Kammaren.* [Proceedings of the Swedish Parliament. First Chamber].
Rothstein, Bo. 1982a. "Den svenska byråkratins uppgång . . . och fall." *Häften för Kritiska Studier* 15: 27–46.
——— 1982b. "Från det svenska systemet till den svenska modellen." *Arkiv för Studier i Arbetarrörelsens Historia* 23: 1–24.
——— 1985. "The Success of the Swedish Labour Market Policy: The Organizational Connection to Policy." *European Journal of Political Research* 13: 153–165.
——— 1987. "Neo-corporatism and Reformism. The Social Democratic Institutionalization of Class Conflict." *Acta Sociologica* 30: 295–311.

————— 1990. "Marxism, Institutional Analysis and Working-Class Power: The Swedish Case." *Politics & Society* 18: 317–345.

————— 1991. "State Structure and Variation in Corporatism: The Swedish Case." *Scandinavian Political Studies* 14, no. 2: 149–170.

————— 1992. *Den korporativa staten. Intresseorganisationer och statsförvaltning i svensk politik.* Stockholm: Norstedts.

————— 1995. "Svensk välfärdspolitk och det civila samhället." In *Civilt samhälle kontra offentlig sektor,* ed. Lars Trägårdh. Stockholm: SNS.

Schiller Bernt. 1967. *Storstrejken 1909. Förhistoria och orsaker.* Göteborg: Akademiförlaget.

Schmitter, Philippe. 1974. "Still the Century of Neo-corporatism?" *Review of Politics* 36: 85–131.

Schofer, Evan and Marion Fourcade-Gourinchas. 2001. "The Structural Contexts of Civil Engagement: Voluntary Association Membership in Comparative Perspective." *American Sociological Review* 66 (December): 806–828.

Skocpol, Theda. 1985. "Bringing the State Back In." In *Bringing the State Back In,* ed. P. Evans, D. Rueschemeyer and T. Skocpol. New York: Cambridge University Press.

Skogh, Sven. 1963. *Arbetets marknad.* Stockholm: Almqvist & Wiksell.

Somers, Margaret. 1995a. "What's Political or Cultural about Political Culture and the Public Sphere? Toward a Historical Sociology of Concept Formation." *Sociological Theory* 13, no. 2: 113–144.

————— 1995b. "Narrating and Naturalizing Civil Society and Citizenship Theory: The Place of Political Culture and the Public Sphere." *Sociological Theory* 13, no. 3: 229–274.

Thelen, Kathleen. 1999. "Historical Institutionalism in Comparative Perspective." *Annual Review of Political Science* 2: 369–404.

Therborn, Göran. 1985. *Why Are Some People More Unemployed than Others?* London: Verso.

————— 1989. *Borgarklass och byråkrati i Sverige.* Lund: Arkiv förlag.

Therborn, Göran, Anders Kjellberg, Staffan Marklund, and Ulf Ölund. 1978. "Sweden Before and After Social Democracy: A First Overview." *Acta Sociologica* 21, Supplement: 37–58.

Trägårdh, Lars, ed. 1995. *Civilt samhälle kontra offentlig sektor.* Stockholm: SNS Förlag.

————— 1999. "Det civila samhället som analytiskt begrepp och politisk slogan." In *Civilsamhället,* ed. Erik Amnå. SOU 1999:84.

Zetterberg, Hans. 1995. "Civila samhället, demokratin och välfärdsstaten." In *Civilt samhälle kontra offentlig sektor,* ed. Lars Trägårdh. Stockholm: SNS.

Öberg, Per-Ola. 1994. *Särintresse och allmänintresse: Korporatismens ansikten.* Stockholm: Norstedts.

Öberg, Per-Ola, and Torsten Svensson. 2002. "Power, Trust and Deliberation in Swedish Labour Market Politics." *Economic and Industrial Democracy* 23: 451–490.

Östberg, Kjell. 1990. *Byråkrati och reformism.* Lund: Arkiv Förlag.

Chapter 8

DEMOCRATIC GOVERNANCE AND THE CREATION OF SOCIAL CAPITAL IN SWEDEN: THE DISCREET CHARM OF GOVERNMENTAL COMMISSIONS

Lars Trägårdh

Introduction: From Government to Governance

As many chapters in this book attest, Sweden stands out as a society characterized by not only a high degree of social capital at large but also by a special combination of social capital in society and trust in the institutions of the state. In this chapter I will look more closely at a particular institutional arrangement—the Swedish governmental commissions—which, I argue, serve as the institutional linchpin in a system of democratic governance whose hallmark is deliberative political practices that involve a mix of civil servants, politicians, academics, experts, and representatives of relevant civil society organizations. As an institution and a process, the ideal-typical commission is to be understood neither as a voluntary organization, nor simply as a government agency, but as precisely the arena where representatives of both the state and civil society organizations meet and engage in the art and practice of deliberative democracy. The commissions are thus sociopolitical spaces with potential to promote the creation of trust between the participating parties to the extent that all parties feel recognized and heard. When this occurs, the commissions become sites for the production of social capital, both at the organizational and individual levels.

In this sense the commissions exemplify what in recent years has come to be known as a move from "government" to "governance." As Marilyn Taylor has pointed out, while there is some agreement on the general description of what this means—a more complex system in which states seek, or are forced, to cooperate with other actors in new spaces—there is less agreement on whether this is a "good thing" from the point of view of deepening and widening democracy (Taylor 2005). For some, governance embodies the hope of erecting new political opportunity structures that will allow for more points of entry for community and civil society organizations. For others, governance is a rhetoric that tends to "dissolve notions of power and agency," suggesting that it may in fact become "the burial ground of accountability" (Parry and Moran 1994; Rhodes 1997; Taylor 2005). As Jean Cohen argues in her chapter in this book, this is not least true in the global contexts, where the absence of a state poses a fundamental problem for the very idea of governance as a democratic process as opposed to a form of management with very weak democratic controls.

Ultimately the question of whether a particular political structure and process should be held to entail cooptation and insidious abuse of power or the opening up of the political system to more actors from civil society must be answered on the basis of empirical evidence. This also applies for the Swedish governmental commissions, which have, in fact, been seen both as the epitome of deliberative democracy and, more cynically, as a quasi-corrupt and secretive system whereby a cabal of insiders representing privileged organizations have been able to strike favorable deals with agents of the state. In this chapter I will not be in a position to fully address this question. My aim is limited to prepare the ground for more empirical research by bringing attention to a particular example of institutionalized democratic governance that has a long history in Sweden.

The Creation and Decline of Social Capital: The Governance Perspective

The question of how social capital actually is created is a notoriously difficult one to answer.[1] The reality is that while we now have a body of worldwide comparative data that measures the existence of trust and the prevalence of corruption, we still know very little about why trust varies and how it is created in the first place. To be sure, studies have juxtaposed different sets of data, suggesting a link of some sort between social capital and participation of voluntary associations. But these findings finally amount to little more than statistically verifiable correlations: the causal links have yet to be proven. Indeed, it may well be that those individuals who choose to become members of voluntary associations are those who already score high when it comes to trust, and that high rates of membership in voluntary associations thus is an effect rather than a cause of generalized high rates of trust in a society.

As Bo Rothstein has pointed out, "the social capital literature is clearly divided on the question of the causes and origin of social capital." In analyzing the theories that attempt to account for variation when it comes to creating and sustaining social capital, Rothstein contrasts what he calls "society-centered accounts" with those that look to the role played by state institutions ("institution-centered") (Rothstein 2002; Rothstein and Stolle 2003).

According to the society-centered accounts (among which one would count Putnam's analysis of democracy, social capital, and trust), the capacity for generating trust and social capital is a function of deep-rooted and culturally embedded institutions, with special emphasis placed on the importance of the voluntary associations. However, as Rothstein tries to show, when one actually tests the hypothesis that individual membership in associations produces values that translate in generalized trust in a society, it appears that it is hard to discern such effects. Rather, Rothstein argues, the data indicate that "people with higher levels of trust indeed self-select into associations" (Rothstein and Stolle 2003).

Putnam and others who give preference to society-centered theories of social capital creation betray what we may call the communitarian prejudice: they tend to favor civil society over the institutions of the state as the "natural" site for the creation of bonds of community and relations of trust. At the same time, as Jean Cohen has noted, Putnam's work is interesting in that one can see a shift from his early work on Italy to his later work on the US. In his book on Italy the emphasis lies, as the title of the book suggested, on the question of what it is that "makes democracy work." That is, the focus was on the institutions of the state as well as on the associations of civil society. Putnam indeed emphasized the role played by the independent courts and impartial and reliable administrative state structures of the Communes on Northern Italy for maintaining social trust. In his later work on the US, however, Putnam "turns away from state structures to 'soft' socio-cultural solutions"—the concern is first and foremost on the apparent decline in social capital as measured by participation in bowling clubs, singing choirs, and the like (Cohen 1999: 219). As Cohen argues, the great success of *Bowling Alone* notwithstanding, from a theoretical standpoint the book represents a step backward. Largely gone is the engagement with political theory that made *Making Democracy Work* such a stimulating work. Instead we are left with a rather conservatively tinged, even nostalgic, lament over a golden age of caring communities losing out to a colder, television-watching, individualistic, narcissistic modernity (Cohen 1999).

From this point of view it is fruitful to read Putnam against Theda Skocpol. Analyzing the history of civil society organizations in the US, Skocpol recently argued in her book *Diminished Democracy* that civic-minded civil society organizations have historically both mimicked the democratic constitutions and practices of the state, and worked together with the state institutions to promote the political agenda of the organizations. "At once luxuriant and contentious, American civic voluntarism always flourished as a vital part of muscular representative democratic governance—and never was in any sense a substitute for it" (Skocpol 2003).

According to Skocpol, since the 1960s this intimate linkage between civil society and the state has begun to break apart for complex reasons. To be sure, latter-day theories posing an intrinsic antagonism between the state and civil society are to some extent part and parcel of a politically motivated attempt to delegitimize politics and government via a right-wing Republican attack on the legacy of Democratic New Deal liberalism. But the diminishment of democracy that Skocpol claims to discern is not simply a political and rhetorical fiction; it is in fact all too real. Furthermore, the causes of this increasing alienation of "the people" from their government, which is feeding antistatist populism in the United States, are rooted in changes in American civic life itself.

Skocpol's point here differs significantly from the thesis that Putnam and his followers have been promoting, though Putnam and Skocpol agree that negative changes are afoot. But rather than focusing simply on the number of people that are active in voluntary associations in some way or another (and thus are thought to be producers of social capital), Skocpol looks at changes in how the organizations are structured internally and how they relate to government institutions. The key shift, as Skocpol describes it, is a move from membership organizations that are steeped in internal democratic practices and set up as federations with active local chapters electing a national leadership, to new social movements and philanthropic foundations that are characterized by top-down management, the rule of experts, a highly centralized structure, and relatively passive members who are more likely to mail in checks than to vote for local representatives (Skocpol 2003).

However, while Skocpol is clearly out to re-legitimize the democratic state as a key partner and even a model for civic-minded civil society organizations, she still tends to focus on the organizations themselves rather than on the state. Thus her concern is with the internal practices of the organizations, the extent to which they can be viewed as schools of democracy or not. What is less developed in her analysis is attention to the way in which the institutions of the state promote trust-building relations among the state, the organizations of civil society, and the citizens themselves.

For a more radical shift in perspective, we may turn back to Bo Rothstein. Rothstein has argued for some time that, far from posing a threat to civil society, the state is in fact what creates the institutional conditions necessary for a civil society to emerge (Rothstein 1994, 1995, 2002; Rothstein and Stolle 2003). Indeed, Rothstein proposes a very strong version of the thesis that trust is less a function of face-to-face interaction in voluntary associations and more the result of determined attempts by the state to create trust-building institutions. Noting, as we have done above, that empirical evidence shows "that social capital is most developed in strong welfare states," Rothstein fastens upon an analysis of the difference between universalism and means-testing that distinguishes welfare regimes from one another, concluding with the claim that "means-tested welfare states are more prone to corruption, abuse of power, arbitrary decisions from civil servants and bureaucrats, and most importantly systematic discrimination than universal welfare states" (Rothstein and Stolle 2003; Kumlin and Rothstein 2003).

Without denying the importance of universal vs. means-tested welfare, it may well be that Rothstein here is placing too much emphasis on the top-down relationship between the benevolent welfare state and the grateful and thus trusting subject. It is a negative argument that perhaps helps us understand the lack of trust that may exist in the relations typical of a means-tested welfare regime—i.e., between a client who seeks to extract resources from the state, and a social worker whose job is partly is to be suspicious of clients who may attempt to cheat the state. However, it is less clear how one moves from this negative argument to a positive one that explains the creation of trust.

Furthermore, explicitly contrasting Sweden (the universalist welfare state par excellence) with the United States (characterized by means-tested welfare) is deeply problematic. Although it is true that Sweden scores high when it comes to trust and social capital, the US can hardly be dismissed as a low scorer. Indeed, while the exact structures of the American and Swedish civil societies differ in crucial ways, and while the patterns also vary in a significant manner when it comes to social capital, the bottom line is that the US, like Sweden, counts among the high scorers when it comes to social capital.[2]

A more nuanced model that combines a long-term "society-centered" perspective with close attention to political institutions, and also takes into account not just differences but similarities between the Nordic and the Anglo-American polities, has been proposed by Ronald Jepperson and his followers. Jepperson's model is based on constitutive dimensions along two axes, producing four ideal-typical polity models (Jepperson 2002). Along one axis he contrasts two modes of collective agency, which he terms societal and statist. The former is characterized by a larger role for public opinion, a self-organizing civil society, and a weaker state, while the latter involves a much more dominating role of a state bureaucracy that is conceived as a universalizing intelligence promoting national and state interest, whereas society is the realm of self-interest and conflict.

Along the other axis, Jepperson posits contrasting ways in which society is organized, formulated in terms relative to "corporateness." At the one end stand the more corporate societies, which are organized as communal orders with subsidiary elements that often are collectivities themselves. At the other we have societies organized according to what Jepperson calls the "associational" model, less rooted in the old feudal tradition and instead organized on the principle of fellowship and "based more on a unified market, legal and associational system (Jepperson 2002)."

This schema then yields four predominant polity models, the "state-corporate" form of which Germany is an example, the "state-nation" form, exemplified by France, the "liberal" form (Anglo-American), and the "social-corporate" form, which Jepperson associates with the Nordic polities. While the first three polity models appear rather familiar, echoing many other accounts of an Anglo-American liberal model, a French statist model, and a German corporatist model, the fourth one—the Nordic one—is far more innovative and at first even startling. Given that most accounts of the Nordic welfare states tend to emphasize the statist aspect, is it noteworthy that Jepperson classifies the Nordic polities as "societal." Indeed, quoting Joseph Nettle, he even suggests that the Nordic system reflects an "absence of state" when analyzed from a comparative point of view (Nettl cited in Jepperson 2003: 75). What does Jepperson have in mind with this rather astonishing pronouncement?

What leads Jepperson to talk of an absence of a state is a perceived lack of a clear state/society divide. In contrast to Germany or France, there is less centralist arrogation of collective agency; rather, the government is envisioned as an intermediary between the organized interests of society. Noting that in Swedish and Norwegian discourse the words for state and society are used interchangeably, and that many social scientists often refer to the Nordic model as a welfare society (rather than as a welfare state), Jepperson thus highlights the fluid boundaries and the high degree of interpenetration of state and society in Scandinavia. He also notes the "absence of inherent distrust" between the public and the state authorities, and the image of the government as benefactor rather than oppressor. This, he argues, is also linked to a pronounced lack of deference to traditional hierarchy and a deep commitment to an egalitarianism in which the chief avenue to social respect is functional competence.

These observations lead Jepperson to emphasize the multiple and highly institutionalized ways in which the state and the organized corporate blocs in society interact and co-govern, invoking the concept of self-governance and underlining the crucial roles played by civil society organization, viewed as having special functional competences. In other words, Jepperson turns on its head the traditional conception of the Nordic states, and of Sweden in particular, as a corporatist state in which the organizations of civil society are junior parties and even supplicants, to instead present a vision of a polity in which the state is a facilitating and mediating institution that serves as the institutional arena in which the self-governing organizations of civil society play first fiddle.

Building on Jepperson's model, Evan Schofer and Marion Fourcade-Gourinchas have used the World Values Study to analyze civic engagement and trust in terms of Jepperson's polity forms. Consistent with the analysis above, they conclude that (a) statism tends to constrain associational activity and that (b) corporateness positively affects membership. Accordingly, their data show that in the World Values Survey of 1991, of the top seven countries in terms of percentage of individuals reporting membership in associations, five were Nordic. The other two were the United States (ranked sixth) and Netherlands (third), both of which are societal polity structures though the US scores much lower in terms of corporateness (Schofer and Fourcade-Gourinchas 2001).

Developing this perspective, I would like to suggest that a fruitful way to conceive of this relationship is to employ the notion of *governance* as opposed to *government*. What I refer to by governance are the institutions and practices whereby society, as it were, governs itself, through a mode of democracy in which the boundaries between the government and the governed, between citizen and subject, are highly fluid and permeable on a continuing basis. Government, on the other hand, connotes a more top-down conception in which the role of the citizenry is limited to that of electing representatives that then do the job of day-to-day governing (Schofer and Fourcade-Gourinchas 2001).

Returning to the claim made by Rothstein, that the key to understanding the relative strength of social capital and trust in Sweden lies in the universal—as opposed to means-tested—provision of welfare, I would thus like to posit that equally important for creating trust and social capital is the sense of participation and having a stake that is promoted by involving the institutions of civil society, and thus the citizens, in the making of law and policy. My thesis is, simply put, that the legitimacy of law and public policy is increased if such laws and policies are viewed as being not simply imposed from above by elected but remote politicians but in fact at least partly designed and deliberated upon with input from "below," i.e., from society itself.

Concretely, one key institutional form that such societal self-governance has traditionally taken in Sweden is the practice of appointing governmental commissions *(statliga utredningar)* to aid in preparing new laws and creating new policies and public programs. Depending on the particular issue at hand, representatives from the political parties and the organizations deemed to have a special interest and/or a special functional competence are appointed to the commission. Furthermore, drafts of reports and proposed new laws and policies are sent out at various stages for review, comments, and counter proposals to large numbers of organizations that are viewed as having a stake in the process, what in Swedish is called *remiss*. Effectively, this allows for open-ended co-governance, linking the state and the institutions of civil society in a mutually beneficial and trust-building political process.

We will return below to an analysis of the commissions, but first let us contextualize them by placing them in their proper polito-legal context, namely the making of law. If the key to understanding the high degree of trust and social capital lies not simply in high rates of membership in voluntary organizations but in the institutionalized interpenetration of state and society, how do we in turn best understand this fusion of state and society? It is my argument that the underlying determinant here is centrality of rule of law.

"Land skall med lag byggas"
("The land shall be built through law-making")

Among sociologists and political theorists it is customary to conceive of the state as defined by it having established a monopoly on violence. This is what we can think of as the Hobbesian state. However, I would like to posit that this conception, however valuable in many contexts, fails to capture the essential character of the Nordic and Anglo-American societies. These should rather be viewed as communities of law, where in fact law-bound social orders were created prior to the creation of the modern state. What sets the Nordic countries apart, along with the Netherlands and the Anglo-American countries, is the extent to which rule of law and lawful behavior has been accepted, naturalized, and internalized in those societies. In fact, if lawful behavior actually depended solely on continual enforcement by the state, the resources of the state would soon be depleted and life itself would become a miserable matter of constant surveillance and control. Only if members of society willingly follow the law of their own accord can society simultaneously be free and lawful. The key statistics for understanding trust and social capital are therefore not the rates of participation in voluntary organizations, or even measures of trust, but those that track corruption. The persistent lack of corruption in the Nordic states is an indication of the extent to which lawfulness has become naturalized. Of course, this is also why citizens of other countries sometimes view Swedes and other Nordics as somewhat naïve and credulous, both in their trust in other fellow citizens and in their faith in the fundamental goodness of their state.

This devotion to law depends on the members of society understanding themselves to be not merely subjects to law made by their rulers but also makers of law as citizens partaking of the sovereignty of the community of law. To grasp this point it is helpful to consider the Scandinavian word for a court, namely *ting*. The ting was not only the court in the sense of a place where justice was carried out; it was also the democratic forum in which law was made. Even today, the Danish, Norwegian, and Icelandic languages include "ting" in their words for parliament: *Folketing, Storting, Allting*. From this point of view the first democratic institutions in the modern world were the old courts of the medieval Scandinavian societies and England. These marked a shift from traditional societies of honor, in which conflicts led to costly blood feuds, to proto-modern societies in which the logic of blood honor gave way to submission to law and the decisions made by courts. This new rationality was in turn predicated on trust, or more precisely, confidence from a game-theoretical perspective that others would play by the same rules.

Precisely how this shift occurred, is less certain. Given the dramatic change in rationality—one that appears to have happened very rarely in history and today seems so hard to export to countries outside of the West—we may posit a magical moment and call for a more focused study of this transition in Scandinavia. The link between lawmaking and adjudication that is captured in the double meaning of the word ting, also suggests the fusion of the figures of the citizen and the subject, so central to the sense that state and society, rulers and the ruled, are in fact the one and the same and that thus the government and the state are legitimate from a democratic governance perspective. Unfortunately, the study of law in this societally embedded sense has been relatively neglected by historians, legal scholars, political theorists, and sociologists alike. To be sure, legal historians have produced histories of legal doctrines, but histories of comparative political culture that focus on law are largely absent (for early modern Sweden, see Hildebrand 1896; Österberg 1989, 1992, 1993).

This relative lack of attention to law is also observable among the theoreticians of social capital today. Ironically, even though Putnam and his followers love to invoke and cite Tocqueville as the grand-daddy of social capital theory, they by and large ignore his insistence that the key to understanding "democracy in America" is to study what he calls the "infusion of the legal spirit." For Tocqueville, America was first and foremost a country of rule of law (Whittington 1998). The jury was the very epitome of the democratic spirit, and the judiciary the most important and most thoroughly "American" branch of government. What Tocqueville understood was precisely that it was not simply associational life that mattered, but the links between civil society, the republic, the market, and the citizens that all rested on not just the written constitution and the body of law, but on the naturalized devotion to the rule of law itself. To be a man of honor was to be a law-abiding citizen, in other words. This is what set the United States apart from the Latin American countries that came into being at much the same time (and with constitutions virtually identical to that of the United States). This is also what connects the Anglo-American societies to the Nordic ones.

Governance and Government Commissions in Sweden

Were one to suggest to an average Swede that governmental commissions *(statliga utredningar)* should be a matter of great and urgent interest, even a key to understanding the very essence of Swedish political culture, one would be less likely to meet with protest than with a yawn and a shrug. What topic could be more boring than *det statliga utredningsväsendet?* This attitude seems to be largely shared by the academic community in Sweden and those abroad who study Swedish political institutions and practices. In the former case, one suspects, the commissions are taken for granted, almost too ordinary and natural to warrant special emphasis. In the latter case, they are often overlooked because they are so peculiarly Swedish that they do not easily register with someone not already familiar with them. This does not mean that they have not been studied,[3] nor does it nullify the longstanding debate about Swedish political culture that partly centers on the commissions and how they should be viewed analytically. We shall get back to this, but first a few words are warranted to give a sense of the commissions' prevalence and character.

The commissions are appointed by the government, usually at the request of a particular minister. One reason this happens so often is the size of the ministries, which by international standards are extremely small, a peculiar aspect of the Swedish political system. The appointment of a commission is a way to temporarily expand the staff of a ministry outside of the regular budget in order to formulate new policy and prepare new legislation. Furthermore, each commission is appointed to deal with a particular issue. They are, in other words, ad-hoc commissions rather than standing committees. As the Swedish political scientist Rune Premfors has observed, "virtually every important piece of legislation is prepared through the work of specially appointed government commissions" (Premfors 1983). The commissions also enjoy considerable autonomy, once constituted. As Premfors notes, since both interest organizations and opposition parties are routinely represented and able to affect the outcome, "the Swedish commissions make up an important arena for political negotiation" (Premfors 1983: 628).

The commissions are also very common. Exact numbers have fluctuated greatly over the past two hundred years, increasing dramatically since the beginning of the twentieth century, but in recent decades between 200 and 300 commissions have been at work at any given moment. As these numbers suggest, we are not talking about commissions set up just to handle extraordinary and pressing matters, such as is usually the case with Royal Commissions in the UK or similar commissions and hearings in the US. Rather, the range of topics is very broad, ranging from the most narrowly technical matters to the most basic constitutional issues.

Another hallmark of the commissions is that they engage in both politicking and fact-finding. This once led the American political scientist Thomas Anton to describe Swedish political culture as particularly deliberative, rationalistic, and consensual (Anton 1969, 1980). The word *utredning* itself suggest not political debate or compromise but rather rational *(saklig)* investigation of a particular problem or question through the medium of scientific knowledge accumulation and analysis in order to arrive at factual truth and rational solution. And indeed, many commissions do in fact engage natural and social scientists as well as other experts to assist in the work of the commission (Foyer 1969; Premfors 1983; Ruin 1981). At the same time, however, the commissions are profoundly political, and while facts unearthed by social scientists are not exactly ignored, nor do they trump politically motivated compromises.

A particularly celebrated yet strangely understudied aspect of the commissions is the so-called *remiss* system, often described as both the most uniquely Swedish and the most democratic aspect of the commission process (Erickson, Lemne, and Pålsson 1999; Nilsson-Stjernquist 1947; Pestoff 1984). This is the procedure whereby the reports produced by the commission are sent out to a large number of affected government agencies and interest organizations. The *remiss* system is not formally inscribed in law, but it is a long-established praxis. Anyone, even an individual citizen, is free to send a written comment, which then will be included in the final report that becomes part of the record, the basis on which the government will write a bill for the parliament to consider. This process, with its open feedback cycle, not only serves to alert the commissions to ideas, information, and political opinions they might otherwise have missed or neglected; it also legitimizes the final policy or law by giving a hearing to a maximum number of views.

Finally, it should be noted that besides being very common, involving many state as well as civil society actors, and covering a very broad range of policy areas, the commissions often work over very long periods of time. While efforts have been made both in the past and more recently to limit both the number and size of commissions as well as the duration of its work, it has not been uncommon for the lawmaking process to last some six to eight years or even longer, starting with appointment of the commission, study and deliberation, report, *remiss*, then the writing of draft legislation, debate in parliament, and finally voting it into law. While this slow progress often is criticized as ineffective from a purely instrumental point of view, it on the other hand allows a more measured and deliberative democratic process to play itself out.

As we noted above, the system of commissions is relatively poorly studied in spite of the fact that it is routinely described as "unique" and as "playing a central role in the Swedish democracy," as it was put in a commission on the commissions (Ds SB 1984: 1). Three dissertations have been written on the subject, in 1927 (Gunnar Hesslén), 1956 (Hans Meijer), and 1992 (Jan Johansson), each covering a different period of time, with the two later ones taking up from where the previous scholar left off. Additionally a dozen articles and government reports have been published dealing with some aspect of the commission system, often summarizing the findings and conclusions of the three dissertations cited above (Brantgärde 1979; Johansson 1979; Zetterberg 1990; Gunnarsson and Lemne 1998; Nyman 1999; Immergut 1992; Enzell 2002). However, none of the dissertations or the articles contain a systematic analysis of the *remiss* procedure.

The Commissions: Cooptation by the State or Democratic Governance

In her book on state-civil society relations in Sweden, the political scientist Michele Micheletti, concludes that: "The system of commissions is an important pillar of Swedish political culture, corporatism, and strong society. It symbolizes the Swedish model" (Micheletti 1994: 76). By invoking both the notions of "corporatism" and "strong society," Micheletti captures a crucial ambivalence or tension that runs through much of the academic debate as it has unfolded during the past eighty years or so about the character of the Swedish political culture. Her own work is suffused by this ambivalence: one moment she worries about the state dominating civil society ("corporatism"); next she emphasizes the open political opportunity structures that allow for a "strong society" to share and balance power with the state.

In this she is not alone. If we go back to two influential books on the Swedish political system written within a few years of each other around 1950, *Staten och organisationerna* by Gunnar Heckscher (1946) and *Folkrörelserna och det demokratiska statskicket i Sverige* by Hilding Johansson (1952), we see this tension reflected in both their key concepts and their analyses. Thus Heckscher, in writing about civil society organizations, uses the neutral word "organizations," whereas in describing the political system as a whole he chooses the rather more controversial term "corporatism," although he crucially adds the qualifier "free" to set this Swedish variant of corporatism apart from what he calls "the corporative experiments of the dictatorships" (writing in 1946). Johansson, on the other hand, prefers the positively charged term *folkrörelserna* meaning "popular or people's movements," to designate civil society organizations. Turning to the Swedish social and political order, he argues that the position of the popular movements constitutes "the very peculiarity of the present Swedish social order," which he goes on to describe as "a democracy of popular movements, or *associative* democracy" (his emphasis in the English summary of the book; in Swedish he uses the term *folkrörelsebaserad demokrati* or *folkrörelsesamhälle*, Johansson 1952: 296).

Johansson rejects Heckscher's use of the term "free corporatism," a concept that other, later scholars have alternately used or rejected but nearly always taken as a point of departure. Nils Elvander, for example, in his influential book *Intresseorganisationerna i dagens Sverige* from 1969, finds the expression inadvisable even as he also avoids the quasi-romantic term *folkrörelse* and instead describes the civil society organizations as "interest organizations" (Elvander 1969). Victor Pestoff, on the other hand, relates to Heckscher's terminology via Schmitter's distinction between state corporatism and societal corporatism (Pestoff 1984). Bo Rothstein, finally, largely echoes Heckscher by using the term corporatism in his book *Den korporativa staten*, where just like Heckscher he carefully draws a line separating the democratic Swedish variant from the odious, fascist one (Rothstein 1992).

While the difference in conceptual usage and analytical emphasis between Heckscher and Johansson, and those who follow in their respective tracks, is a real one, it should also be noted that the gulf that separates them is not particularly wide. Heckscher is careful to extol the role played by the organizations in safeguarding the Swedish democratic form of government. His notion of a "free" corporatism is, he writes, meant to suggest a fundamental equality between state and society: "In a democratic society one might say that the state, the organizations, and the individuals are all equal rather than there existing an unambiguous relation of subordination with the state on top" (Heckscher 1946: 227). He even appears to foreshadow Putnam in emphasizing that if they are to sustain their position, the organizations must protect and develop the "trust capital" they hold (Heckscher 1946: 258). Johansson, on the other hand, while predominantly confident in celebrating the virtues of Swedish "associative democracy," also warns that once the organizations themselves cease to be internally democratic, then great dangers lie ahead: "Should the members no longer have real influence on their organizations, then not only would the organizations loose their democratic character, but there is also the risk that the national democracy too would become in fact a dictatorship ruled by the bosses who run the parties and organizations" (Johansson 1952: 258). This sounds very much like a form of elite dominated—if not outright fascist—corporatism.

So where should one come down on this matter? It would appear that we need more empirical research, both to challenge the "statist" interpretation of the so-called Swedish model and to test Johansson's notion of "associative democracy," a concept that rather closely echoes Ronald Jepperson's description of the Nordic model, a societal corporate mode of governance that places the civil society organizations in a position of co-governance.

The linchpin of this system are the governmental commissions and the procedure of *remiss*, which routinely bring together the agents of the state and the representatives of the organizations in the fundamental yet humdrum tasks of law- and policymaking. Every such encounter that ends in some measure of success, be it even in the form of compromise at the end of a long and unglamorous negotiation, will also add to the social capital and trust that is essential for the next round of negotiations as well as for the broad and deep acceptance of the newly made laws and policies as the law of the land, not merely the imposition of state or party interest.

Contemporary Trends

If this diagnosis of what makes the Nordic countries unique from a social capital perspective is correct, then it is also possible to view with some clarity what are ominous tendencies in contemporary Sweden. The fact that democratic self-governance is conducted through organizations, rather than through an unmediated relationship between atomized individuals and the state, suggests the importance of a linked network of democratically constituted institutions, including the national state, local government, and civil society organizations. From this perspective we may want to ask if Skocpol's worrisome analysis of American organizations, characterized by what she calls "diminished democracy," or the decline of democratic governance, is also relevant for Sweden. To what extent, we may ask, is the institutional nexus that enables the fluid interpenetration between state and society still intact? What about the system of government commissions—including the *remiss* procedure—that involve the civil society organizations? And to what extent do the organizations themselves still embody the practice of democratic governance? Are we moving away from organizations based on grassroots membership toward those based on management by elites and experts?

The chapter by Per Selle and Tommy Tranvik in this book tends to confirm that Skocpol's analysis is applicable to the Norwegian experience as well. And at least some of the data presented by Amnå in his chapter on recent changes in the character of Swedish organizational life indicate that Sweden too is prey to a similar secular trend. These findings suggest that a slow erosion is evident in the older organizations with active members engaged in internal democratic practices. The aggregate numbers continue to look good, but this is largely owing to new organizations whose members are more likely to simply pay for services or donate money than to engage in civic activism (Petersson et al. 1989, Petersson et al. 1998; Vogel et al. 2003).

In conclusion, we have neither enough data on the actual performance of Swedish style "associative democracy" in the past, nor sufficient evidence regarding current trends to be able to justify with any degree of confidence either an alarmist or an optimistic view of what the future holds. But a continued and deepened analysis of the Swedish experience would seem to hold the potential to offer important insights for the students of democratic governance and its enemies, past, present, and future.

Notes

1. In this chapter I will use "social capital" and "trust" interchangeably. The focus will be on social capital in the sense of both horizontal social trust between actors in civil society and vertical political trust between the institutions of the state and the actors in civil society. Furthermore, I will be concerned with trust at the individual level but also at the organizational level, that is, with what Rothstein has called "organized social capital" (Rothstein 2002).
2. According to World Values Survey data. Also see Baer this book.
3. The most important works on the commissions are those by Gunnar Hesslén, Hans Meijer, and Jan Johansson. For more complete references, see the bibliography.

References

Anton, Thomas J. 1969. "Policy-Making and Political Culture in Sweden." *Scandinavian Political Studies* 4: 88–102.

———. 1980. *Administered Politics: Elite Political Culture in Sweden*. Boston: Martinus Nijhoff,.

Brantgärde, Lennart. 1979. *Utredningsväsendet och svensk efterkrigslagstiftning.* Rapportserien 1979: 1. Göteborg: Göteborgs universitet.

Cohen, Jean. 1999. "Trust, Voluntary Association and Workable Democracy: the Contemporary American Discourse of Civil Society." In *Democracy and Trust*, ed. Mark Warren. Cambridge: Cambridge University Press.

Ds Ju 1975: 14. Rapport om utredningsväsendet.

Ds SB 1984: 1. Promemoria om det svenska utredningsväsendet.

Elvander, Nils. 1969. *Intresseorganisationerna i dagens Sverige*. Lund: Gleerup.

Enzell, Magnus. 2002. *Requiem for a Constitution: Constitutionalism and Political Culture in Early 20th Century Sweden*. Edsbruk: Akademitryck AB.

Erickson, Lars-Erik, Marja Lemne, and Inger Pålsson. 1999. *Demokrati på remiss*. SOU 1999: 144.

Foyer, Lars. 1969. "The Social Sciences in Royal Commission Studies in Sweden." *Scandinavian Political Studies* 4: 183–204.

Gunnarsson, Viviann, and Marja Lemne. *Kommittéerna och bofinken: kan en kommitté se ut hur som helst?* Ds 1998: 57. Stockholm: Nordstedts Tryckeri AB.

Heckscher, Gunnar. 1946. *Staten och organisationerna.* Stockholm: KFs bokförlag.

Herlitz, Nils. 1964 [1928]. *Grunddragen av det svenska statsskickets historia.* Stockholm: Nordstedts.

Hermansson, Jörgen. 1993. *Politik som intressekamp.* Stockholm: Nordstedts.

Hesslén, Gunnar. 1927. *Det svenska kommittéväsendet intill år 1905, dess uppkomst, ställning och betydelse.* Uppsala: Berlings.

Hildebrand, Emil. 1896. *Svenska statsförvaltningens historia.* Stockholm: Nordstedt & Söner.

Immergut, Ellen M. 1992. *Health Politics: Interests and Institutions in Western Europe.* Cambridge: Cambridge University Press.

Jepperson, Ronald. 2002. "Political Modernities: Disentangling Two Underlying Dimensions of Institutional Differentiation," *Sociological Theory* 20, no. 1: 61–85.

Johansson, Folke. 1979. *Offentliga utredningars genomslag i politiska beslut.* Rapportserien 1979: 2. Göteborg: Göteborgs universitet.

Johansson, Hilding. 1952. *Folkrörelserna och det demokratiska statskicket i Sverige.* Karlstad: Gleerups.

———. 1980. *Folkrörelserna i Sverige.* Stockholm: Sober.

Johansson, Jan. 1992. *Det statliga kommittéväsendet: kunskap, kontroll, konsensus.* Edsbruk: Akademitryck AB.

Kumlin, Staffan, and Bo Rothstein. 2003. "Staten och det sociala kapitalet." In *Välfärdstat i otakt,* ed. Jon Pierre and Bo Rothstein. Malmö: Liber.

Laginder, Ann-Marie. 1989. *Framtidsbilder i offentligt utredande.* Linköping: Tema Teknik, Linköpings universitet.

Meijer, Hans. 1956. *Kommittépolitik och kommittéarbete.* Lund: Gleerups.

———. 1969. "Bureaucracy and Policy Formulation in Sweden," *Scandinavian Political Studies* 4: 103–116.

Michelletti, Michele. 1994. *Det civila samhället och staten.* Stockholm: Fritzes.

Nilsson-Stjernquist, Nils. 1947. "Organisationerna och det statliga remissväsendet," *Förvaltningsrättslig tidskrift.*

Nyman, Torkel. 1999. *Kommittépolitik och parlamentarism.* Uppsala.

Parry, G., and Moran, M. 1994. *Democracy and Democratization.* London: Routledge

Pestoff, Victor (with U. Swahn). 1984. "The Swedish Organizational Community and Its Participation in Public Policy-making: An Introductory Overview." Research Report No. 6, University of Stockholm, Department of Political Science.

Petersson, Olof, Anders Westholm, and Göran Blomberg. 1989. *Medborgarnas Makt.* Stockholm: Carlssons.

Petersson, Olof, Jörgen Hermansson, Michele Micheletti, Jan Teorell and Anders Westholm. 1998. *Demokrati och medborgarskap.* Stockholm: SNS.

Premfors, Rune. 1982. "Social Research and Governmental Commissions in Sweden." Research Report No. 22. University of Stockholm, Department of Political Science.

————. 1983. "Governmental Commissions in Sweden." *American Behavioral Scientist* 26, no. 5: 623–642.

————. 2000. *Den starka demokratin*. Stockholm: Atlas.

Rhodes, R. 1997. *Understanding governance policy networks, governance, reflexivity and accountability.* Maidenhead: Open University Press

Rothstein, Bo. 1992. *Den korporativa staten.* Stockholm: Nordstedts.

————. 1994. *Vad bör staten göra?* Stockholm: SNS.

———— 1995. "Svensk välfärdspolitik och det civila samhället." In *Civilt samhälle kontra offentlig sekton*, ed. Lars Trägårdh. Stockholm: SNS.

————. 2002. "Sweden: Social Capital in the Social Democratic State." In *Democracies in Flux? The Evolution of Social Capital in Contemporary Society*, ed. Robert Putnam. Oxford: Oxford University Press.

Rothstein, Bo, and Dietlind Stolle. 2003. "Introduction: Social Capital in Scandinavia." *Scandinavian Political Studies* 26, no 1: 1–26.

Ruin, Olof. 1981. "Att komma överens och tänka efter före. Politisk stil och 1970-talets svenska samhällssutveckling." Research Report No. 1981: 1. University of Stockholm, Department of Political Science.

Schofer, Evan, and Marion Fourcade-Gourinchas. 2001. "The Structural Contexts of Civil Engagement: Voluntary Association Membership in Comparative Perspective." *American Sociological Review* 66: 806–828.

Skocpol, Theda. 2003. *Diminished Democracy: From Membership to Management in American Civic Life.* Norman: Oklahoma University Press.

Taylor, Marilyn. 2005. "Community Participation in the Real World: The Opportunities and Pitfalls in New Governance Spaces." Presentation to the Kick-Off Conference for CINEFOGO Network of Excellence 17–19 October 2005.

Thörnberg, E.H.. 1943. *Folkrörelser och samhällsliv i Sverige.* Stockholm: Bonniers.

Vogel, Joachim, Erik Amnå, Ingrid Munck, and Lars Häll. 2003. *Associational Life in Sweden: General Welfare, Social Capital, Training in Democracy, Living Conditions.* Report no 101. Stockholm: Statistics Sweden.

Whittington, Keith. 1998. "Revisiting Tocqueville's America: Society, Politics, and Association in the Nineteenth Century." *American Behavioral Scientist* 40, no. 5.

Zetterberg, Kent. 1990. "Det statliga kommittéväsendet." In Departementshistoriekommittén, *Att styra riket: regeringskansliet 1840–1990*. Stockholm: Allmänna förlaget.

Österberg, Eva. 1989. "Bönder och centralmakt i det tidigmoderna Sverige: konflikt - kompromiss - politisk kultur." *Scandia* 55.

Österberg, Eva. 1992. "Folklig mentalitet och statlig makt." *Scandia* 58.

Österberg, Eva. 1993. "Vardagens sköra samförstånd. Bondepolitik i den svenska modellen från Vasatid till Frihetstid." In *Tänka, tycka, tro*, ed. Gunnar Broberg, Ulla Wikander and Klas Åmark. Stockholm: Ordfront.

INDEX

www.ingramcontent.com/pod-product-compliance
Lightning Source LLC
Chambersburg PA
CBHW060029030426
42334CB00019B/2242